Teach
Yourself
CORBA

in 14 days

D1361562

Teach Yourself
CORBA
in 14 days

Jeremy L. Rosenberger

SAMS
PUBLISHING

201 West 103rd Street
Indianapolis, Indiana 46290

To Camilla: For your limitless patience and support while I turned your entire life upside down.

To my parents: Without you, it is improbable that I would ever have had the opportunity to write this book.

Copyright©1998 by Sams Publishing

FIRST EDITION

International Standard Book Number: 0-672-31208-5

Library of Congress Catalog Card Number: 97-68736

01   00   99   98   4   3   2   1

Interpretation of the printing code: The rightmost double-digit number is the year of the book's printing; the rightmost single-digit, the number of the book's printing. For example, a printing code of 98-1 shows that the first printing of the book occurred in 1998.

Composed in AGaramond and MCPdigital by Macmillan Computer Publishing

Printed in the United States of America

Trademarks

President   Richard K. Swadley
Publisher   Joseph B. Wikert
Managing Editor   Jodi Jensen
Indexing Manager   Johnna L. VanHoose
Director of Software and User Services   Cheryl Willoughby
Brand Director   Alan Bower

Acquisitions Editor
Steve Straiger

Development Editor
Tony Amico

Production Editor
Susan Ross Moore

Copy Editor
Kate Talbot

Indexer
Bruce Clingaman

Technical Reviewer
Andrew Watson

Editorial Coordinators
Mandie Rowell
Katie Wise

Team Coordinator
Carol Ackerman

Editorial Assistants
Carol Ackerman
Andi Richter
Rhonda Tinch-Mize
Karen Williams

Cover Designer
Karen Ruggles

Cover Illustration
Eric Lindley

Book Designer
Gary Adair

Copy Writer
David Reichwein

Production Team Supervisor
Andrew Stone

Production Team
Chris Livengood
Shawn Ring

Overview

Contents

Acknowledgments

First and foremost, the good people at Sams Publishing deserve many thanks for making this book possible. In particular, acquisitions editor Steve Straiger is especially deserving of gratitude for his generous flexibility with the development schedule.

I would also like to acknowledge my personal friend and colleague, Michael Jones, who encouraged me to rise to the challenge of writing this book. Also worthy of recognition are my other colleagues at Hughes Information Technology Systems, who were gracious enough to tolerate my highly nontraditional work schedule (especially around deadline time).

Additionally, the folks at Visigenic Software deserve credit for making excellent software and for making this software available for usable evaluation periods.

Finally, an honorable mention goes to Stonehenge Internet and to GTE Internet for their faithful, reliable delivery of Internet service—which is indispensable for writing a book in this Information Age.

About the Author

Born and raised in Toledo, Ohio, **Jeremy Rosenberger** received his Bachelor's degree in computer science and engineering from Cornell University in Ithaca, New York. Since then, Jeremy has lived in Boston and St. Louis, and at present resides in Denver with his wife, Camilla.

Jeremy currently works as a software engineer for Hughes Information Systems in Aurora, Colorado, where he develops applications by using a variety of tools such as C++, CORBA, Java, and software agent technologies. He is a contributing author to *Javology* (http://www.javology.com/) and has written two chapters of *Special Edition Using JavaBeans* (Que/Ziff-Davis Press, 1997), covering the use of Java with CORBA, as well as a preview of the Java Platform for the Enterprise. He also aspires to form a consulting firm catering to clients in the Denver area.

When he isn't working at developing software or writing his latest and greatest book, Jeremy can usually be found spending time with his wife, building scale model cars, composing and playing music, or playing volleyball. Occasionally, he can be found engaging in outdoor activities in the high altitudes of the Rocky Mountains.

Although Jeremy is a man of many email addresses, he can always be reached at jlr4@cornell.edu.

Tell Us What You Think!

As a reader, you are the most important critic of and commentator on our books. We value your opinion and want to know what we're doing right, what we could do better, what areas you'd like to see us publish in, and any other words of wisdom you're willing to pass our way. You can help us make strong books that meet your needs and give you the computer guidance you require.

Do you have access to the World Wide Web? Then check out our site at http://www.mcp.com.

 NOTE

> If you have a technical question about this book, call the technical support line at 317-581-3833 or send email to support@mcp.com.

As the team leader of the group that created this book, I welcome your comments. You can fax, email, or write me directly to let me know what you did or didn't like about this book—as well as what we can do to make our books stronger. Here's the information:

Fax: 317-581-4669

Email: programming_mgr@sams.mcp.com

Mail: Joe Wikert
          Comments Department
          Sams Publishing
          201 W. 103rd Street
          Indianapolis, IN 46290

Introduction

Welcome to *Teach Yourself CORBA in 14 Days*! This book explores the development of distributed applications using the Common Object Request Broker Architecture (CORBA). In two weeks, it introduces you to the fundamental concepts of CORBA, walks you through the development of a simple CORBA application, and then starts you developing a more complex application. You'll learn about CORBA's Interface Definition Language (IDL) and how to use it to describe interfaces between application components. You'll also be introduced to the Object Management Group, the organization responsible for developing the Object Management Architecture, a specification in which CORBA plays one part. Additionally, you'll learn about the CORBA architecture and related components of the Object Management Architecture—such as CORBAservices and CORBAfacilities—and see how these building blocks are used to develop distributed enterprise applications. You'll gain familiarity with writing CORBA applications in both C++ and Java, the two preeminent languages for CORBA development.

In addition to the 14 Lessons, two Appendixes introduce you to many of the CORBA development tools available, and give you an overview of what the future holds for CORBA. Although CORBA can sometimes move at the speed of a standard defined by a committee (not surprising, given the process used by the OMG to adopt new standards), CORBA continues to make strides that ensure its place at the forefront of distributed application development.

Assumptions

You'll get the most out of this book if you have the following:

- ☐ Some knowledge of C++ or Java, although experience with any programming language will help you to understand the concepts presented in this book.
- ☐ Familiarity with the development tools, such as Visual C++, Java Development Kit (JDK), or other development environments, on your platform(s) of choice.
- ☐ Understanding of object-oriented analysis and design concepts. Such knowledge isn't absolutely necessary because this book introduces you to these concepts, but because CORBA is an object-oriented architecture, you'll benefit most from reading this if you're already familiar with object-oriented analysis and design.

The best way to learn any new subject is to practice and experiment. To follow the examples presented in each chapter, as well as each quiz and exercise, you need access to the following:

- ☐ A computer of some kind. Because CORBA is cross-platform, almost any kind of computer will do—from a Macintosh, to a PC running Windows, to a UNIX workstation. Any machine supported by a CORBA development product (see the next bullet point) will do.

- ☐ A CORBA development product for your machine. Two of the more popular products include IONA Technologies' Orbix and Visigenic Software's VisiBroker. Many vendors offer an evaluation period for their products that provides more than enough time to complete this book. The C++ examples were developed using VisiBroker for C++; the Java examples use Sun's Java IDL package. However, the examples work with other products, with few or no changes.

- ☐ The appropriate compiler and/or other software development tools necessary to support your chosen CORBA development product. For instance, VisiBroker for C++ on Windows 95 or Windows NT requires Visual C++ 4.2 or higher (although compilers from other vendors work as well). For Java-based CORBA products, usually you only need a recent version of the Java Development Kit (JDK).

Week
1

1

2

3

4

5

6

7

At a Glance

You begin this book by first covering the groundwork of CORBA development. Days 1–4 walk you through the basics of the CORBA architecture, the Interface Definition Language (IDL), and finish with a basic sample application to demonstrate what you've learned. On Days 5–7 you walk through several iterations of developing a sample CORBA application that you continue in the following week.

Getting Started

Day 1 introduces you to the Common Object Request Broker Architecture, otherwise known as CORBA. You learn where CORBA fits into the various models of software development, followed by some history of CORBA itself and finally an overview of the CORBA architecture. On Day 2 you explore the CORBA architecture in detail, learning about the Object Request Broker (ORB), the Interface Definition Language

(IDL), and other architectural features. Day 3 further familiarizes you with IDL, as you spend some time learning about the various constructs made available to you. On Day 4 you apply this knowledge by building a simple CORBA application.

Developing a CORBA Application, Part 1

In the second part of the first week you begin building a more complex CORBA application, starting in the analysis and design stage on Day 5. Here you receive a crash course in object-oriented analysis and design, learn a little bit about the Unified Modeling Language (UML), and begin designing the application (a simulated banking system). On Day 6 you implement the initial, basic capabilities of this system, and you'll no doubt see a few weaknesses in the initial design. You finish up the week, on Day 7, by modifying the sample application to use exception handling, enhancing the robustness of the application.

Day 1

Getting Familiar with CORBA

The Purpose of This Book

Certainly, this isn't the first book to be written on the subject of the Common Object Request Broker Architecture (CORBA)—not by a long shot. However, among CORBA books currently on shelves, it might be unique in its approach. At the time this book was written, few, if any, texts were available that covered CORBA at an introductory level. This book attempts to fill that gap.

CORBA is not a subject for the fainthearted, to be sure. Although development tools that hide some of the complexity of CORBA exist, if you embark on a project to develop a reasonably sophisticated CORBA application, chances are that you will experience some of CORBA's complexities firsthand. However, though there might be a steep learning curve associated with CORBA, a working knowledge of CORBA fundamentals is well within the grasp of any competent programmer.

For the purposes of this book, it is assumed that you already have a good deal of programming experience. CORBA is a language-independent architecture, but because C++ and Java are the principal languages used to develop CORBA applications, it would be preferable if you had experience with one of these languages. (Most of the examples are written in C++, with a healthy dose of Java thrown in for good measure.) It wouldn't hurt if you were familiar with object-oriented analysis and design concepts either, but just in case you need a refresher, this book will help you review these concepts.

Operating under the assumption that learning CORBA is a surmountable (if daunting) goal for most programmers, this book begins teaching the fundamentals of CORBA, starting with an overview of the architecture. You'll then move on to a primer on the Interface Definition Language (IDL), a cornerstone on which most CORBA applications are based. After that, you'll start building CORBA applications, and before you know it, you'll be exposed to advanced concepts and design issues, along with other useful things such as CORBAservices, CORBAfacilities, and the Dynamic Invocation Interface, or DII (don't worry—you'll learn what all this means, in due time). All this—and more—in a mere 14 days.

What this book does not do—indeed, cannot do—is make you a CORBA expert overnight (or even in 14 days, for that matter). It does put you well on your way to mastering CORBA. Keep in mind that CORBA is a complex architecture, full of design issues and tradeoffs as well as implementation nuances. As such, it can only be mastered through experience—something you will gain only by designing and developing CORBA applications. Perhaps this book does not make you an expert in all things CORBA, but it does put you on the right track toward achieving that goal.

Background: History of Distributed Systems

If you're interested enough in CORBA to be reading this book, you probably know a thing or two already about distributed systems. Distributed systems have been around, in one form or another, for some time, although they haven't always been called that and they certainly haven't always had the flexibility that they do now. To discover where CORBA fits in, let's briefly review the history of distributed systems, starting with the venerable mainframe.

The Beginning: Monolithic Systems and Mainframes

In the beginning (or close to it), there was the mainframe. Along with it came hierarchical database systems and dumb terminals, also known as green screens. Mainframes usually cost a great deal to maintain but were capable of serving large numbers of users and had the advantage (or disadvantage, depending on one's point of view) of being centrally managed.

Software systems written for mainframes were often monolithic—that is, the user interface, business logic, and data access functionality were all contained in one large application. Because the dumb terminals used to access mainframes didn't do any of their own processing, the entire application ran in the mainframe itself, thus making the monolithic architecture reasonable. A typical monolithic application architecture is illustrated in Figure 1.1.

Figure 1.1.

Typical monolithic application architecture.

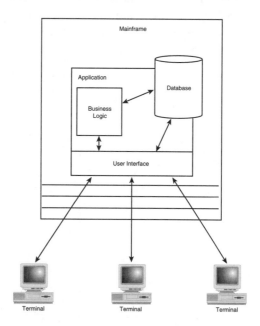

The Revolution: Client/Server Architecture

The advent of the PC made possible a dramatic paradigm shift from the monolithic architecture of mainframe-based applications. Whereas these applications required the mainframe itself to perform all the processing, applications based on the client/server architecture allowed some of that processing to be offloaded to PCs on the users' desktops.

Along with the client/server revolution came the proliferation of UNIX-based servers. Many applications simply did not require the massive power of mainframes, and because the client/server architecture was capable of moving much of the processing load to the desktop PC, these smaller UNIX-based server machines were often more cost-effective than mainframes. Also, these machines were much more affordable to small businesses than mainframes, which were often simply out of reach for companies with relatively small bank account balances. Still another benefit was the empowerment of individual departments within an organization to deploy and manage their own servers. The result was that these departments could be more responsive to their specific needs when developing their own applications, rather than having to jump through proverbial hoops to get the department controlling the mainframes to develop applications, as was often the case. Finally, whereas terminals were typically restricted to running only applications on the mainframe, a PC was capable of performing many other tasks independently of the mainframe, further enhancing its usefulness as a desktop machine.

Client/server applications typically distributed the components of the application so that the database would reside on the server (whether a UNIX box or mainframe), the user interface would reside on the client, and the business logic would reside in either, or both, components. When changes were made to parts of the client component, new copies of the client component (usually executables or a set of executables) had to be distributed to each user.

With the advent of multitier client/server architecture (discussed in the next section), the "original" client/server architecture is now referred to as "two-tier" client/server. The two-tier client/server architecture is illustrated in Figure 1.2.

Figure 1.2.

Two-tier client/server architecture.

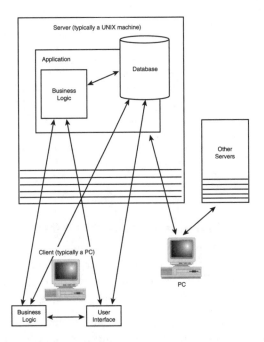

The Evolution: Multitier Client/Server

The client/server architecture was in many ways a revolution from the old way of doing things. Despite solving the problems with mainframe-based applications, however, client/server was not without faults of its own. For example, because database access functionality (such as embedded database queries) and business logic were often contained in the client component, any changes to the business logic, database access, or even the database itself, often required the deployment of a new client component to all the users of the application.

Usually, such changes would break earlier versions of the client component, resulting in a fragile application.

The problems with the traditional client/server (now often called "two-tier" client/server) were addressed by the multitier client/server architecture. Conceptually, an application can have any number of tiers, but the most popular multitier architecture is three-tier, which partitions the system into three logical tiers: the user interface layer, the business rules layer, and the database access layer. A three-tier client/server architecture is illustrated in Figure 1.3.

Figure 1.3.

Three-tier client/server architecture.

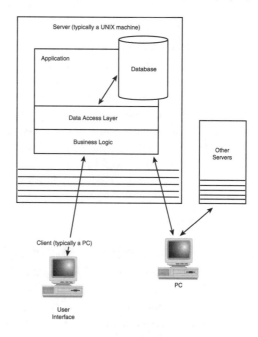

Multitier client/server architecture enhances the two-tier client/server architecture in two ways: First, and perhaps most importantly, it makes the application less fragile by further insulating the client from changes in the rest of the application. Also, because the executable components are more fine-grained, it allows more flexibility in the deployment of an application.

Multitier client/server reduces application fragility by providing more insulation and separation between layers. The user interface layer communicates only with the business rules layer, never directly with the database access layer. The business rules layer, in turn, communicates with the user interface layer on one side and the database access layer on the other. Thus, changes in the database access layer will not affect the user interface layer because they are insulated from each other. This architecture enables changes to be made in the application with less likelihood of affecting the client component (which, remember, has to be redistributed when there are any changes to it).

Because the multitier client/server architecture partitions the application into more compo-nents than traditional two-tier client/server, it also allows more flexibility in deployment of the application. For example, Figure 1.3 depicts a system in which the business rules layer and database access layer, although they are separate logical entities, are on the same server machine. It is also possible to put each server component on a separate machine. Indeed, multiple business logic components (and multiple database access components, if multiple databases are being used) can be created for a single application, distributing the processing load and thus resulting in a more robust, scalable application.

NOTE

It is interesting to note that the multitier client/server architecture might actually have had its roots in mainframe applications. COBOL applications on IBM mainframes could define the user interface by using a tool called Message Format Service (MFS). MFS abstracted the terminal type (terminals could, for instance, have varying numbers of rows and columns) from the rest of the application. Similarly, applica-tions could specify the database interfaces as well. Although the application would still run in one monolithic chunk, the available tools enabled the design of applications using a logical three-tier architecture.

The Next Generation: Distributed Systems

The next logical step in the evolution of application architectures is the distributed system model. This architecture takes the concept of multitier client/server to its natural conclusion. Rather than differentiate between business logic and data access, the distributed system model simply exposes all functionality of the application as objects, each of which can use any of the services provided by other objects in the system, or even objects in other systems. The architecture can also blur the distinction between "client" and "server" because the client components can also create objects that behave in server-like roles. The distributed system architecture provides the ultimate in flexibility.

The distributed system architecture achieves its flexibility by encouraging (or enforcing) the definition of specific component interfaces. The interface of a component specifies to other components what services are offered by that component and how they are used. As long as the interface of a component remains constant, that component's implementation can change dramatically without affecting other components. For example, a component that provides customer information for a company can store that information in a relational database. Later, the application designers might decide that an object-oriented database would be more appropriate. The designers can make any number of changes to the component's implementation—even sweeping changes such as using a different type of database—provided that they leave the component's interface intact. Again, as long as the interface of that component remains the same, the underlying implementation is free to change.

NEW TERM An *interface* defines the protocol of communication between two separate components of a system. (These components can be separate processes, separate objects, a user and an application—any separate entities that need to communicate with each other.) The interface describes what services are provided by a component and the protocol for using those services. In the case of an object, the interface can be thought of as the set of methods defined by that object, including the input and output parameters. An interface can be thought of as a contract; in a sense, the component providing an interface promises to honor requests for services as outlined in the interface.

Distributed systems are really multitier client/server systems in which the number of distinct clients and servers is potentially large. One important difference is that distributed systems generally provide additional services, such as directory services, which allow various components of the application to be located by others. Other services might include a transaction monitor service, which allows components to engage in transactions with each other.

NEW TERM *Directory services* refers to a set of services that enable objects—which can be servers, businesses, or even people—to be located by other objects. Not only can the objects being looked up differ in type, but the directory information itself can vary as well. For example, a telephone book would be used to locate telephone numbers and postal addresses; an email directory would be used to locate email addresses. Directory services encompass all such information, usually grouping together related information (for example, there are separate volumes of the yellow pages for different cities; contents of each volume are further divided into types of businesses).

NEW TERM A *transaction monitor* service oversees transactions on behalf of other objects. A transaction, in turn, is an operation or set of operations that must be performed *atomically*; that is, either all objects involved in the transaction must *commit* the transaction (update their own records) or all objects involved must *abort* the transaction (return to their original state before the transaction was initiated). The result is that whether a transaction commits or aborts, all involved objects will be in a consistent state. It is the job of a transaction monitor to provide transaction-related services to other objects.

To sum up, business applications have evolved over a period of time from a relatively rigid monolithic architecture to an extremely flexible, distributed one. Along the way, application architectures have offered increasing robustness because of the definitions of interfaces between components and the scalability of applications (furnished in part by the capability to replicate server components on different machines). Additionally, services have been introduced that enable the end user of an application to wade through the myriad of available services. Those who have been designing and developing business applications since the days of mainframes have certainly had an interesting ride.

Why CORBA?

So far, in this evolution of business applications from the monolithic mainframe architecture to the highly decentralized distributed architecture, no mention has been made of CORBA. Therefore, you might be asking yourself at this point where CORBA fits in to all this. The answer, as you will see, is emphasized throughout the rest of this book. Recall that distributed systems rely on the definition of interfaces between components and on the existence of various services (such as directory registration and lookup) available to an application. CORBA provides a standard mechanism for defining the interfaces between components as well as some tools to facilitate the implementation of those interfaces using the developer's choice of languages. In addition, the Object Management Group (the organization responsible for standardizing and promoting CORBA) specifies a wealth of standard services, such as directory and naming services, persistent object services, and transaction services. Each of these services is defined in a CORBA-compliant manner, so they are available to all CORBA applications. Finally, CORBA provides all the "plumbing" that allows various components of an application—or of separate applications—to communicate with each other.

NEW TERM The capabilities of CORBA don't stop there. Two features that CORBA provides—features that are a rarity in the computer software realm—are *platform independence* and *language independence*. Platform independence means that CORBA objects can be used on any platform for which there is a CORBA ORB implementation (this includes virtually all modern operating systems as well as some not-so-modern ones). Language independence means that CORBA objects and clients can be implemented in just about any programming language. Furthermore, CORBA objects need not know which language was used to implement other CORBA objects that they talk to. Soon you will see the components of the CORBA architecture that make platform independence and language independence possible.

Exploring CORBA Alternatives

When designing and implementing distributed applications, CORBA certainly isn't a developer's only choice. Other mechanisms exist by which such applications can be built. Depending on the nature of the application—ranging from its complexity to the platform(s) it runs on to the language(s) used to implement it—there are a number of alternatives for a developer to consider. In this section you'll briefly explore some of the alternatives and see how they compare to CORBA.

Socket Programming

NEW TERM In most modern systems, communication between machines, and sometimes between processes in the same machine, is done through the use of *sockets*. Simply put, a socket is a channel through which applications can connect with each other and communicate. The most straightforward way to communicate between application components, then, is to use sockets directly (this is known as *socket programming*), meaning that the developer writes data to and/or reads data from a socket.

The Application Programming Interface (API) for socket programming is rather low-level. As a result, the overhead associated with an application that communicates in this fashion is very low. However, because the API is low-level, socket programming is not well-suited to handling complex data types, especially when application components reside on different types of machines or are implemented in different programming languages. Whereas direct socket programming can result in very efficient applications, the approach is usually unsuitable for developing complex applications.

Remote Procedure Call (RPC)

NEW TERM One rung on the ladder above socket programming is *Remote Procedure Call (RPC)*. RPC provides a function-oriented interface to socket-level communications. Using RPC, rather than directly manipulating the data that flows to and from a socket, the developer defines a function—much like those in a functional language such as C—and generates code that makes that function look like a normal function to the caller. Under the hood, the function actually uses sockets to communicate with a remote server, which executes the function and returns the result, again using sockets.

Because RPC provides a function-oriented interface, it is often much easier to use than raw socket programming. RPC is also powerful enough to be the basis for many client/server applications. Although there are varying incompatible implementations of RPC protocol, a standard RPC protocol exists that is readily available for most platforms.

OSF Distributed Computing Environment (DCE)

The Distributed Computing Environment (DCE), a set of standards pioneered by the Open Software Foundation (OSF), includes a standard for RPC. Although the DCE standard has been around for some time, and was probably a good idea, it has never gained wide acceptance and exists today as little more than an historical curiosity.

Microsoft Distributed Component Object Model (DCOM)

The Distributed Component Object Model (DCOM), Microsoft's entry into the distributed computing foray, offers capabilities similar to CORBA. DCOM is a relatively robust object model that enjoys particularly good support on Microsoft operating systems because it is integrated with Windows 95 and Windows NT. However, being a Microsoft technology, the availability of DCOM is sparse outside the realm of Windows operating systems. Microsoft is working to correct this disparity, however, in partnering with Software AG to provide DCOM on platforms other than Windows. At the time this was written, DCOM was available for the Sun Solaris operating system, with support promised for Digital UNIX, IBM MVS, and other operating systems by the end of the year. By the time you read this, some or all of these ports will be available. (More information on the ports of DCOM to other platforms is available at http://www.softwareag.com/corporat/dcom/default.htm.)

Microsoft has, on numerous occasions, made it clear that DCOM is best supported on Windows operating systems, so developers with cross-platform interests in mind would be well-advised to evaluate the capabilities of DCOM on their platform(s) of interest before committing to the use of this technology. However, for the development of Windows-only applications, it is difficult to imagine a distributed computing framework that better integrates with the Windows operating systems.

One interesting development concerning CORBA and DCOM is the availability of CORBA-DCOM bridges, which enable CORBA objects to communicate with DCOM objects and vice versa. Because of the "impedance mismatch" between CORBA and DCOM objects (meaning that there are inherent incompatibilities between the two that are difficult to reconcile), the CORBA-DCOM bridge is not a perfect solution, but it can prove useful in situations where both DCOM and CORBA objects might be used.

Java Remote Method Invocation (RMI)

The tour of exploring CORBA alternatives stops with Java Remote Method Invocation (RMI), a very CORBA-like architecture with a few twists. One advantage of RMI is that it supports the passing of objects by value, a feature not (currently) supported by CORBA. A disadvantage, however, is that RMI is a Java-only solution; that is, RMI clients and servers must be written in Java. For all-Java applications—particularly those that benefit from the capability to pass objects by value—RMI might be a good choice, but if there is a chance that the application will later need to interoperate with applications written in other languages, CORBA is a better choice. Fortunately, full CORBA implementations already exist for Java, ensuring that Java applications interoperate with the rest of the CORBA world.

CORBA History

Now that you know a little bit of CORBA's background and its reason for existence, it seems appropriate to briefly explore some of the history of CORBA to understand how it came into being.

Introducing the Object Management Group (OMG)

The Object Management Group (OMG), established in 1989 with eight original members, is a 760-plus–member organization whose charter is to "provide a common architectural framework for object-oriented applications based on widely available interface specifications." That's a rather tall order, but the OMG achieves its goals with the establishment of the Object Management Architecture (OMA), of which CORBA is a part. This set of standards delivers the common architectural framework on which applications are built. Very briefly, the OMA consists of the Object Request Broker (ORB) function, object services (known as CORBAservices), common facilities (known as CORBAfacilities), domain interfaces, and application objects. CORBA's role in the OMA is to implement the Object Request Broker function. For the majority of this book, you will be concentrating on CORBA itself, occasionally dabbling into CORBAservices and CORBAfacilities.

CORBA 1.0

Following the OMG's formation in 1989, CORBA 1.0 was introduced and adopted in December 1990. It was followed in early 1991 by CORBA 1.1, which defined the Interface Definition Language (IDL) as well as the API for applications to communicate with an Object Request Broker (ORB). (These are concepts that you'll explore in much greater detail on Day 2.) A 1.2 revision appeared shortly before CORBA 2.0, which with its added features quickly eclipsed the 1.x revisions. The CORBA 1.x versions made an important first step toward object interoperability, allowing objects on different machines, on different architectures, and written in different languages to communicate with each other.

CORBA 2.0 and IIOP

CORBA 1.x was an important first step in providing distributed object interoperability, but it wasn't a complete specification. Although it provided standards for IDL and for accessing an ORB through an application, its chief limitation was that it did not specify a standard protocol through which ORBs could communicate with each other. As a result, a CORBA ORB from one vendor could not communicate with an ORB from another vendor, a restriction that severely limited interoperability among distributed objects.

Enter CORBA 2.0. Adopted in December 1994, CORBA 2.0's primary accomplishment was to define a standard protocol by which ORBs from various CORBA vendors could communicate. This protocol, known as the Internet Inter-ORB Protocol (IIOP, pronounced "eye-op"), is required to be implemented by all vendors who want to call their products CORBA 2.0 compliant. Essentially, IIOP ensures true interoperability among products from numerous vendors, thus enabling CORBA applications to be more vendor-independent. IIOP, being the *Internet* Inter-ORB Protocol, applies only to networks based on TCP/IP, which includes the Internet and most intranets.

The CORBA standard continues to evolve beyond 2.0; in September 1997, the 2.1 version became available, followed shortly by 2.2; 2.3 is expected in early 1998. (The OMG certainly is keeping itself busy!) These revisions introduce evolutionary (not revolutionary) advancements in the CORBA architecture.

CORBA Architecture Overview

Finally, having learned the history and reasons for the existence of CORBA, you're ready to examine the CORBA architecture. You'll cover the architecture in greater detail on Day 2, but Day 1 provides you with a very general overview—an executive summary, if you will—of what composes the CORBA architecture.

First of all, CORBA is an object-oriented architecture. CORBA objects exhibit many features and traits of other object-oriented systems, including interface inheritance and polymorphism. What makes CORBA even more interesting is that it provides this capability even when used with nonobject-oriented languages such as C and COBOL, although CORBA maps particularly well to object-oriented languages like C++ and Java.

| NEW TERM | *Interface inheritance* is a concept that should be familiar to Objective C and Java developers. In the contrasting *implementation inheritance,* an implementation unit (usually a class) can be derived from another. By comparison, interface inheritance allows an interface to be derived from another. Even though interfaces can be related through inheritance, the implementations for those interfaces need not be.

The Object Request Broker (ORB)

Fundamental to the Common Object Request Broker Architecture is the Object Request Broker, or ORB. (That the ORB acronym appears within the CORBA acronym was just too much to be coincidental.) An ORB is a software component whose purpose is to facilitate communication between objects. It does so by providing a number of capabilities, one of which is to locate a remote object, given an object reference. Another service provided by the ORB is the marshaling of parameters and return values to and from remote method invocations. (Don't worry if this explanation doesn't make sense; the ORB is explained in much greater detail on Day 2.) Recall that the Object Management Architecture (OMA) includes a provision for ORB functionality; CORBA is the standard that implements this ORB capability. You will soon see that the use of ORBs provides platform independence to distributed CORBA objects.

Interface Definition Language (IDL)

Another fundamental piece of the CORBA architecture is the use of the Interface Definition Language (IDL). IDL, which specifies interfaces between CORBA objects, is instrumental in ensuring CORBA's language independence. Because interfaces described in IDL can be mapped to any programming language, CORBA applications and components are thus independent of the language(s) used to implement them. In other words, a client written in C++ can communicate with a server written in Java, which in turn can communicate with another server written in COBOL, and so forth.

One important thing to remember about IDL is that it is not an implementation language. That is, you can't write applications in IDL. The sole purpose of IDL is to define interfaces; providing implementations for these interfaces is performed using some other language. When you study IDL more closely on Day 3, you'll learn more about this and other assorted facts about IDL.

The CORBA Communications Model

| NEW TERM | CORBA uses the notion of *object references* (which in CORBA/IIOP lingo are referred to as Interoperable Object References, or IORs) to facilitate the communication between objects. When a component of an application wants to access a CORBA object, it first obtains an IOR for that object. Using the IOR, the component (called a *client* of that object) can then invoke methods on the object (called the *server* in this instance).

In CORBA, a *client* is simply any application that uses the services of a CORBA object; that is, an application that invokes a method or methods on other objects. Likewise, a *server* is an application that creates CORBA objects and makes the services provided by those objects available to other applications. A much more detailed discussion of CORBA clients and servers is presented on Day 2.

As mentioned previously, CORBA ORBs usually communicate using the Internet Inter-ORB Protocol (IIOP). Other protocols for inter-ORB communication exist, but IIOP is fast becoming the most popular, first of all because it is the standard, and second because of the popularity of TCP/IP (the networking protocols used by the Internet), a layer that IIOP sits on top of. CORBA is independent of networking protocols, however, and could (at least theoretically) run over any type of network protocols. For example, there are also implementations of CORBA that run over DCE rather than over TCP/IP, and there is also interest in running CORBA over ATM and SS7.

The CORBA Object Model

In CORBA, all communication between objects is done through object references (again, these are known as Interoperable Object References, or IORs, if you're using IIOP). Furthermore, visibility to objects is provided *only* through passing references to those objects; objects cannot be passed by value (at least in the current specification of CORBA). In other words, remote objects in CORBA *remain* remote; there is currently no way for an object to move or copy itself to another location. (You'll explore this and other CORBA limitations and design issues on Day 10.)

Another aspect of the CORBA object model is the Basic Object Adapter (BOA), a concept that you'll also explore on Day 2. A BOA basically provides the common services available to all CORBA objects.

CORBA Clients and Servers

Like the client/server architectures, CORBA maintains the notions of *clients* and *servers*. In CORBA, a component can act as both a client and as a server. Essentially, a component is considered a server if it contains CORBA objects whose services are accessible to other objects. Likewise, a component is considered a client if it accesses services from some other CORBA object. Of course, a component can simultaneously provide and use various services, and so a component can be considered a client or a server, depending on the scenario in question.

Stubs and Skeletons

When implementing CORBA application components, you will encounter what are known as *client stubs* and *server skeletons*. A client stub is a small piece of code that allows a client component to access a server component. This piece of code is compiled along with the client portion of the application. Similarly, server skeletons are pieces of code that you "fill in" when you implement a server. You don't need to write the client stubs and server skeletons themselves; these pieces of code are generated when you compile IDL interface definitions. Again, you'll soon see all this firsthand.

Beyond the Basics: CORBAservices and CORBAfacilities

In addition to the CORBA basics of allowing objects to communicate with each other, recall that the OMA—of which CORBA is a part—also provides additional capabilities in the form of CORBAservices and CORBAfacilities. As you'll find out, CORBAservices and CORBAfacilities provide both horizontal (generally useful to all industries) and vertical (designed for specific industries) services and facilities. You'll look at the capabilities provided in greater detail on Day 12, after which you'll get the opportunity to use some of this functionality in a CORBA application.

Summary

Today you had a very brief overview of the CORBA architecture, along with a history of business application development and where CORBA fits in. You now know what you can expect to get out of this book—you won't become a CORBA expert overnight, but you will gain valuable exposure to the process of designing and developing CORBA-based applications.

In the next few days, you'll explore the CORBA architecture in much greater detail, learn more than you ever wanted to know about IDL, and you'll be well on your way to developing CORBA applications.

Q&A

Q I'm still not very clear on why I would want to use CORBA as opposed to some other method of interprocess communication.

A There are a few areas where CORBA really shines. For applications that have various components written in different languages and/or need to run on different platforms, CORBA can make a lot of sense. CORBA takes care of some potentially messy details for you, such as automatically converting (through the marshaling process) number formats between different machines. In addition, CORBA provides an easily understood abstraction of distributed applications, consisting of object-oriented design, an exception model, and other useful concepts. But where CORBA is truly valuable is in applications used throughout an enterprise. CORBA's many robust features—as well as those provided by the OMA CORBAservices and CORBAfacilities—and especially CORBA's scalability, make it well suited for enterprise applications.

Q **What is IDL and why is it useful?**

A IDL, or Interface Definition Language, will be covered in greater detail over the next two Days. For now, it is useful to understand that the value in IDL comes from its abstraction of various language, hardware, and operating system architectures. For example, the IDL long type will automatically be translated to the numeric type appropriate for whatever architecture the application is run on. In addition, because IDL is language-independent, it can be used to define interfaces for objects that are implemented in any language.

Workshop

The following section will help you test your comprehension of the material presented today and put what you've learned into practice. You'll find the answers to the quiz in Appendix A. On most days, a few exercises will accompany the quiz; today, because no real "working knowledge" material was presented, there are no exercises.

Quiz

1. What does IIOP stand for and what is its significance?
2. What is the relationship between CORBA, OMA, and OMG?
3. What is a client stub?
4. What is an object reference? An IOR?

Day **2**

Understanding the CORBA Architecture

Overview

On the first day, you learned about CORBA's history and saw how the CORBA architecture fits into the world of client/server application development. You were also presented with a brief overview of the CORBA architecture. By the end of this Day, you will have a deeper understanding of the CORBA architecture and its components. These are the major aspects covered in this chapter:

- ☐ The Object Request Broker (ORB), one of the cornerstones of the CORBA architecture

- ☐ The Interface Definition Language (IDL), the other CORBA architectural cornerstone

- ☐ The CORBA communications model, how CORBA objects fit within the network architecture

- ☐ The CORBA object model, including object references and Basic Object Adapters (BOAs)

☐ The definition and roles of clients and servers in the CORBA architecture

☐ The use of client stubs and server skeletons to build CORBA applications

☐ An overview of CORBAservices and CORBAfacilities, which provide additional functionality to CORBA applications

The Object Request Broker (ORB)

As one might guess, a fundamental part of the Common Object Request Broker architecture is the *Object Request Broker (ORB)*. The concept of an ORB is this: When an application component wants to use a service provided by another component, it first must obtain an object reference for the object providing that service. (How this object reference is obtained is an issue in its own right—and will be discussed later—but for the purposes of studying the ORB mechanism, assume for the time being that the object reference is already available.) After an object reference is obtained, the component can call methods on that object, thus accessing the desired services provided by that object. (The developer of the client component knows at compile time which methods are available from a particular server object.) The primary responsibility of the ORB is to resolve requests for object references, enabling application components to establish connectivity with each other. (See Figure 2.1 for an illustration of these ORB concepts.) As you will see, the ORB has other responsibilities as well.

Figure 2.1.

ORB resolution of object requests.

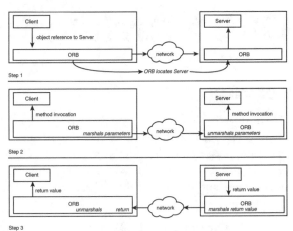

Marshaling

After an application component has obtained a reference to an object whose services the component wants to use, that component can invoke methods of that object. Generally, these methods take parameters as input and return other parameters as output. Another responsibility of the ORB is to receive the input parameters from the component that is calling the method and to *marshal* these parameters. What this means is that the ORB translates the parameters into a format that can be transmitted across the network to the remote object. (This is sometimes referred to as an *on-the-wire* format.) The ORB also *unmarshals* the returned parameters, converting them from the on-the-wire format into a format that the calling component understands. The marshaling process can be seen in Figure 2.2.

Figure 2.2.

Marshaling parameters and return values.

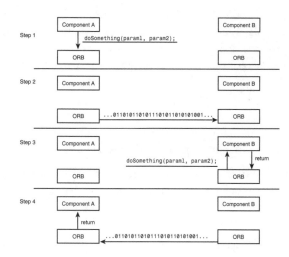

Step 1	Component A			Component B
	doSomething(param1, param2);			
	ORB			ORB
Step 2	Component A			Component B
	ORB	...0110101101011101011010101001...		ORB
Step 3	Component A			Component B
	doSomething(param1, param2);		return	
	ORB			ORB
Step 4	Component A			Component B
	return			
	ORB	...0110101101011101011010101001...		ORB

NEW TERM   *Marhsaling* refers to the process of translating input parameters to a format that can be transmitted across a network.

Unmarshaling is the reverse of marshaling; this process converts data from the network to output parameters.

An *On-the-wire format* specifies the format in which data is transmitted across the network for the marshaling and unmarshaling processes.

The entire marshaling process takes place without any programmer intervention whatsoever. A client application simply invokes the desired remote method—which has the appearance of being a local method, as far as the client is concerned—and a result is returned (or an exception is raised), again, just as would happen with a local method. The entire process of marshaling input parameters, initiating the method invocation on the server, and unmarshaling the return parameters is performed automatically and transparently by the ORB.

Platform Independence

A product of the marshaling/unmarshaling process is that, because parameters are converted upon transmission into a platform-independent format (the on-the-wire format is provided as part of the CORBA specification) and converted into a platform-specific format upon reception, the communication between components is platform-independent. This means that a client running on, for instance, a Macintosh system can invoke methods on a server running on a UNIX system. In addition to independence of operating system used, differences in hardware (such as processor byte ordering, or endianness) are also rendered irrelevant because the ORB automatically makes these conversions as necessary. In essence, any differences in platforms—be it operating system, endianness, word size, and so on—are accounted for by the ORB.

Note again that the process of marshaling and unmarshaling parameters is handled completely by the ORB, entirely transparent to both the client and server. Because the entire process is handled by the ORB, the developer need not concern himself with the details of the mechanism by which the parameters are marshaled and unmarshaled.

ORB Summary

Because the concept of the ORB is central to an understanding of the CORBA architecture, it is important to make sure that you grasp the ORB concepts. To summarize the purpose of the ORB, its responsibilities are as follows:

☐ Given an object reference from a client, the ORB locates the corresponding object implementation (the server) on behalf of the client. (Note that it is the responsibility of the client to obtain an object reference in the first place, through a process you'll learn later.)

☐ When the server is located, the ORB ensures that the server is ready to receive the request.

☐ The ORB on the client side accepts the parameters of the method being invoked and marshals (see the next section) the parameters to the network.

☐ The ORB on the server side unmarshals (again, see the next section) the parameters from the network and delivers them to the server.

☐ Return parameters, if any, are marshaled/unmarshaled in the same way.

The major benefit offered by the ORB is its platform-independent treatment of data; parameters can be converted on-the-fly between varying machine formats as they are marshaled and unmarshaled.

Interface Definition Language (IDL)

If the concept of the Object Request Broker is one cornerstone of the CORBA architecture, the *Interface Definition Language* (IDL) is the other. IDL, as its name suggests, is the language used to define interfaces between application components. Note that IDL is not a procedural language; it can define only interfaces, not implementations. C++ programmers can think of IDL definitions as analogous to header files for classes; a header file typically does not contain any implementation of a class but rather describes that class's interface. Java programmers might liken IDL definitions to definitions of Java interfaces; again, only the interface is described—no implementation is provided.

NEW TERM   The *Interface Definition Language (IDL)* is a standard language used to define the interfaces used by CORBA objects. It is covered in great detail on Day 3.

The IDL specification is responsible for ensuring that data is properly exchanged between dissimilar languages. For example, the IDL `long` type is a 32-bit signed integer quantity, which can map to a C++ `long` (depending on the platform) or to a Java `int`. It is the responsibility of the IDL specification—and the IDL compilers that implement it—to define such data types in a language-independent way.

IDL will be covered in great detail in the next chapter. After that, you will use IDL to—what else?—define interfaces for the examples used throughout this book.

Language Independence

The IDL language is part of the standard CORBA specification and is independent of any programming language. It achieves this language independence through the concept of a *language mapping*. The OMG has defined a number of standard language mappings for many popular languages, including C, C++, COBOL, Java, and Smalltalk. Mappings for other languages exist as well; these mappings are either nonstandard or are in the process of being standardized by the OMG.

NEW TERM   A *language mapping* is a specification that maps IDL language constructs to the constructs of a particular programming language. For example, in the C++ language mapping, the IDL `interface` maps to a C++ `class`.

Language independence is a very important feature of the CORBA architecture. Because CORBA does not dictate a particular language to use, it gives application developers the freedom to choose the language that best suits the needs of their applications. Taking this freedom one step further, developers can also choose multiple languages for various components of an application. For instance, the client components of an application might be implemented in Java, which ensures that the clients can run on virtually any type of machine. The server components of that application might be implemented in C++ for high performance. CORBA makes possible the communication between these various components.

The CORBA Communications Model

In order to understand CORBA, you must first understand its role in a network of computing systems. Typically, a computer network consists of systems that are physically connected (although the advent of wireless network technology might force us to revise our understanding of what "physically connected" means). This physical layer provides the medium through which communication can take place, whether that medium is a telephone line, a fiber-optic cable, a satellite uplink, or any combination of networking technologies.

Somewhere above the physical layer lies the transport layer, which involves protocols responsible for moving packets of data from one point to another. In this age of the Internet, perhaps the most common transport protocol in use is TCP/IP (Transmission Control Protocol/Internet Protocol). Most Internet-based applications use TCP/IP to communicate with each other, including applications based on FTP (File Transfer Protocol), Telnet (a host communication protocol), and HTTP (Hypertext Transport Protocol, the basis for the World Wide Web).

Inter-ORB Protocols

So how does CORBA fit into this networking model? It turns out that the CORBA specification is neutral with respect to network protocols; the CORBA standard specifies what is known as the General Inter-ORB Protocol (GIOP), which specifies, on a high level, a standard for communication between various CORBA ORBs and components. GIOP, as its name suggests, is only a general protocol; the CORBA standard also specifies additional protocols that specialize GIOP to use a particular transport protocol. For instance, GIOP-based protocols exist for TCP/IP and DCE (the Open Software Foundation's Distributed Computing Environment protocol). Additionally, vendors can (and do) define and use proprietary protocols for communication between CORBA components.

NEW TERM   The *General Inter-ORB Protocol (GIOP)* is a high-level standard protocol for communication between ORBs. Because GIOP is a generalized protocol, it is not used directly; instead, it is specialized by a particular protocol that would then be used directly.

For discussion and use of CORBA in this book, your main interest will be the GIOP-based protocol for TCP/IP networks, known as the Internet Inter-ORB Protocol (IIOP). As of the 2.0 version of the CORBA specification, vendors are required to implement the IIOP protocol in order to be considered CORBA-compliant (although they might offer their proprietary protocols in addition to IIOP). This requirement helps to ensure interoperability between CORBA products from different vendors because each CORBA 2.0-compliant product must be able to speak the same language. Some vendors have gone so far as to adopt IIOP as their products' native protocol (the protocol used by default) rather than use a proprietary protocol; however, an ORB is allowed to support any number of protocols, as long as IIOP is supported (when communicating with each other, ORBs can negotiate which protocol to use). Additionally, a number of vendors are including IIOP-compliant ORBs with products ranging from database servers to application development tools to Web browsers. IIOP, as you can see, is an important key to CORBA interoperability.

NEW TERM   The *Internet Inter-ORB Protocol (IIOP)* is a specialization of the GIOP. IIOP is the standard protocol for communication between ORBs on TCP/IP based networks. An ORB must support IIOP (but can support other additional protocols) in order to be considered CORBA 2.0-compliant.

2

CORBA and the Networking Model

With all this discussion of inter-ORB protocols, you have yet to see where CORBA fits in with the rest of the networking model. Figure 2.3 illustrates the network architecture of a typical CORBA application. Essentially, CORBA applications are built on top of GIOP-derived protocols such as IIOP. These protocols, in turn, rest on top of TCP/IP, DCE, or whatever underlying transport protocol the network uses. CORBA applications aren't limited to using only one of these protocols; an application architecture can be designed to use a bridge that would interconnect, for instance, DCE-based application components with IIOP-based ones. You can see, then, that rather than supplant network transport protocols, the CORBA architecture creates another layer—the inter-ORB protocol layer—which uses the underlying transport layer as its foundation. This, too, is a key to interoperability between CORBA applications, as CORBA does not dictate the use of a particular network transport protocol.

Figure 2.3.

Architecture of a distributed CORBA application.

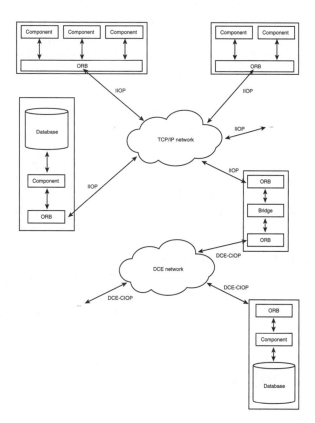

The CORBA Object Model

Every object-oriented architecture features an object model, which describes how objects are represented in the system. Of course, CORBA, being an object-oriented architecture, has an object model as well. Because CORBA is a distributed architecture, however, its object model probably differs somewhat from the traditional object models with which most readers are familiar (such as C++'s or Java's object model). Three of the major differences between the CORBA object model and traditional models lie in CORBA's "semi-transparent" support for object distribution, its treatment of object references, and its use of what are called object adapters—particularly the Basic Object Adapter (BOA). You will now explore these concepts in greater depth.

Object Distribution

To a CORBA client, a remote method call looks exactly like a local method call, thanks to the use of client stubs (a concept you'll explore later in this chapter). Thus, the distributed nature of CORBA objects is transparent to the users of those objects; the clients are unaware that they are actually dealing with objects which are distributed on a network.

Actually, the preceding statement is almost true. Because object distribution brings with it more potential for failure (due to a network outage, server crash, and so on), CORBA must offer a contingency to handle such possibilities. It does so by offering a set of system exceptions, which can be raised by any remote method. You'll learn about exceptions more in later chapters—on Day 3, you'll see how exceptions are declared in IDL; on Day 7, you'll add exception handling to a sample application. For the time being, though, all you need to know is that all operations in all CORBA objects implicitly can raise a CORBA system exception, which signals a network error, server unavailability, or other such situation. Thus, with the exception—pun intended—of this additional exception raised by CORBA object methods, a remote method is otherwise identical to its local counterpart.

Object References

In a distributed application, there are two possible methods for one application component to obtain access to an object in another process. One method is known as *passing by reference,* illustrated in Figure 2.4. In this method, the first process, Process A, passes an object reference to the second process, Process B. When Process B invokes a method on that object, the method is executed by Process A because that process owns the object. (The object exists in the memory and process space of Process A.) Process B only has visibility to the object (through the object reference), and thus can only request that Process A execute methods on Process B's behalf. Passing an object by reference means that a process grants visibility of one of its objects to another process while retaining ownership of that object.

2

When an object is *passed by reference,* the object itself remains "in place" while an object reference for that object is passed. Operations on the object through the object reference are actually processed by the object itself.

Figure 2.4.

Passing an object by reference.

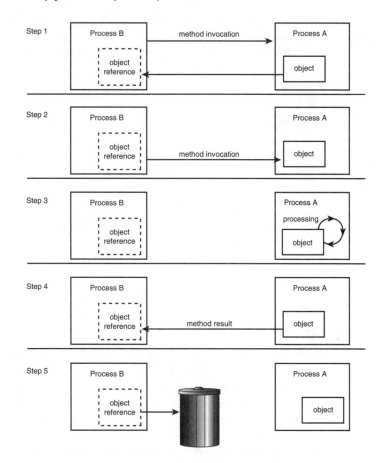

The second method of passing an object between application components is known as *passing by value* and is depicted in Figure 2.5. In this method, the actual state of the object (such as the values of its member variables) is passed to the requesting component (typically through a process known as serialization). When methods of the object are invoked by Process B, they are executed by Process B instead of Process A, where the original object resides. Furthermore, because the object is passed by value, the state of the original object is not changed; only the copy (now owned by Process B) is modified. Generally, it is the responsibility of the developer to write the code that serializes and deserializes objects (although this capability is built into some languages, such as Java).

NEW TERM When an object is *passed by value,* the object's state is copied and passed to its destination, where a new copy of the object is instantiated. Operations on that object's copy are processed by the copy, not by the original object.

Serialization refers to the encoding of an object's state into a stream, such as a disk file or network connection. When an object is serialized, it can be written to such a stream and subsequently read and *deserialized,* a process that converts the serialized data containing the object's state back into an instance of the object.

Figure 2.5.

Passing an object by value.

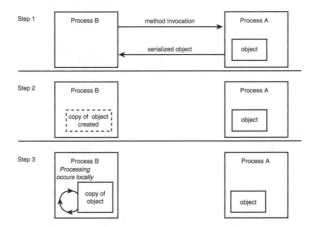

One important aspect of the CORBA object model is that *all* objects are passed by reference. (Actually, at the time of this writing, the OMG has issued an RFP (Request for Proposals) for adding to CORBA the capability to pass objects by value, so it is likely that this capability will be added to the CORBA standard in the near future.) In order to facilitate passing objects by value in a distributed application, in addition to passing the state of the object across the network, it is also necessary to ensure that the component receiving the object has implementations for the methods supported by that object. (This is not necessary when objects are passed by reference; recall that method invocations are executed by the component that owns the actual object.) When the CORBA pass-by-value capability is specified, it will need to address these issues; readers should stay tuned to OMG announcements for updates on this development. (The OMG Web site, which makes available a great deal of CORBA-related information and specifications, is located at `http://www.omg.org/`.)

There are a few issues associated with passing objects by reference only. Remember that when passing by reference is the only option, methods invoked on an object are always executed by the component that owns that object (in other words, the component that has created that object); an object cannot migrate from one application component to another. (However, you can devise methods that simulate this behavior; it simply is not provided by the CORBA architecture itself at this time.) This also means that all method calls are remote method calls (unless both the calling object and called object are owned by the same application component). Obviously, if a component invokes a lengthy series of method calls on a remote object, a great deal of overhead can be consumed by the communication between the two components. For this reason, it might be more efficient to pass an object by value so the component using that object can manipulate it locally. On Day 10 you'll explore this issue in greater detail, but in the meantime, readers should be aware that CORBA's current lack of pass-by-value semantics does raise this issue.

Basic Object Adapters (BOAs)

The CORBA standard describes a number of what are called *object adapters,* whose primary purpose is to interface an object's implementation with its ORB. The OMG recommends that new object adapter types be created only when necessary and provides three sample object adapters: the Basic Object Adapter (BOA), which you will concentrate on, and the Library Object Adapter and Object-Oriented Database Adapter, both of which are useful for accessing objects in persistent storage. (The CORBA specification describes these object adapters in greater detail.) Again, you will concern yourself only with the Basic Object Adapter, by far the most commonly used object adapter.

The BOA provides CORBA objects with a common set of methods for accessing ORB functions. These functions range from user authentication to object activation to object persistence. The BOA is, in effect, the CORBA object's interface to the ORB. According to the CORBA specification, the BOA should be available in every ORB implementation, and this seems to be the case with most (if not all) CORBA products available.

Server Activation Policies

One particularly important (and useful) feature of the BOA is its object activation and deactivation capability. The BOA supports four types of *activation policies,* which indicate how application components are to be initialized. These activation policies include the following:

- [ ] The *shared server* policy, in which a single server (which in this context usually means a process running on a machine) is shared between multiple objects

- [ ] The *unshared server* policy, in which a server contains only one object

- [ ] The *server-per-method* policy, which automatically starts a server when an object method is invoked and exits the server when the method returns

- [ ] The *persistent server* policy, in which the server is started manually (by a user, batch job, system daemon, or some other external agent)

A server *activation policy* indicates how that particular server is intended to be accessed; for example, if there is a single server used by all clients, or a new instance of the server should be started for each client, and so on.

This variety of activation policies allows an application architect to choose the type of behavior that makes the most sense for a particular type of server. For instance, a server requiring a length of time to initialize itself might work best as a persistent server, because the necessary initialization time would adversely affect the response time for that server. On the other hand, a server that starts up quickly upon demand might work well with the server-per-method policy.

NOTE

It is worth noting here that the term *persistent server* has nothing to do with the common use of the term *persistent,* which refers to the capability of an object to store its state in some sort of nonvolatile storage facility such as a database of disk files. A persistent server does not necessarily store its state in persistent storage (although it could); in this case, the term merely implies that the server runs persistently or, in other words, continuously.

CORBA Clients and Servers

Traditionally, in a client/server application, the server is the component, or components, that provides services to other components of the application. A client is a component that consumes services provided by a server or servers. The architecture of a CORBA application is no different; generally, certain components of an application provide services that are used by other components of the application. Not surprisingly, the general terms *client* and *server* refer to these components of a CORBA application. When considering a single remote method invocation, however, the roles of client and server can be temporarily reversed because a CORBA object can participate in multiple interactions simultaneously.

In a CORBA application, any component that provides an implementation for an object is considered a server, at least where that object is concerned. If a component creates an object and provides other components with visibility to that object (in other words, allows other components to obtain references to that object), that component acts as a server for that object; any requests made on that object by other components will be processed by the component that created the object. Being a CORBA server means that the component (the server) executes methods for a particular object on behalf of other components (the clients).

Multiple Personalities? Being Both a Client and a Server

Frequently, an application component can provide services to other application components while accessing services from other components. In this case, the component is acting as a client of one component and as a server to the other components (see Figure 2.6). In fact, two components can simultaneously act as clients and servers to each other. To understand this situation, consider the following scenario (illustrated in Figure 2.7): The first component, Component A, receives a reference to an object created by a second component, Component B, and calls a method on that object. Here, Component A acts as a client and Component B acts as a server. Now assume that as a parameter of the method called, Component A passes a reference to an object that it has created (and thus provides an implementation for the object). Assume further that Component B now calls some method on that object. For this particular method invocation, Component A acts as a server, whereas Component B acts as a client. The two components have not changed their overall roles in the application, but they have temporarily reversed their roles as client and server. Therefore, from this example you see that in a CORBA application, the terms *client* and *server* might depend on the context of the method being called and in which component that method's object resides.

Figure 2.6.

Acting as a client and a server.

One last point to consider in the terminology of clients and servers: Although an application component can function as both a client and a server, it is nevertheless typical to label such a component as one or the other (not both). In the preceding example, assume that for the most part, Component A calls methods on objects owned by Component B. As illustrated in the example, some (or even all) of these method calls can pass object references to Component B, which can then make calls through those object references back to Component A. Although Component A is acting as a server for these method calls, because the overall function of the component is to use services provided by Component B, and only provides objects as arguments to methods in Component B, you might very well refer to Component A as the client and to Component B as the server. Methods called in this way are generally referred to as *client callback methods,* or simply *callbacks.* Callbacks are especially important given CORBA's current lack of pass-by-value capability; the capability to pass objects by value, when it becomes available, will eliminate the need for many callbacks.

NEW TERM | *Client callback method,* or simply *callback,* is a generic term given to a method that is implemented by a client and called by a server. Callbacks essentially make a client into a type of a limited server.

Figure 2.7.
A client callback method.

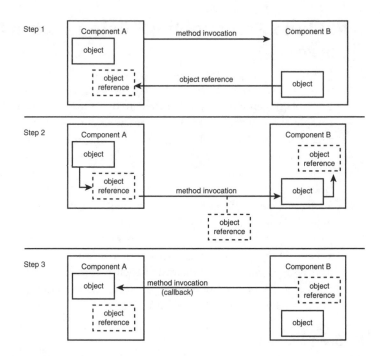

Stubs and Skeletons

After a developer creates component interface definitions using IDL, he or she processes the resulting IDL files with an IDL compiler. The IDL compiler generates what are known as *client stubs* and *server skeletons*. Client stubs and server skeletons serve as a sort of "glue" that connects language-independent IDL interface specifications to language-specific implementation code. Client stubs for each interface are provided for inclusion with clients that use those interfaces. The client stub for a particular interface provides a dummy implementation for each of the methods in that interface. Rather than execute the server functionality, however, the client stub methods simply communicate with the ORB to marshal and unmarshal parameters.

 A *client stub,* which is generated by the IDL compiler, is a small piece of code that makes a particular CORBA server interface available to a client.

A *server skeleton,* also generated by the IDL compiler, is a piece of code that provides the "framework" on which the server implementation code for a particular interface is built.

On the other side, you have server skeletons, providing the framework upon which the server is built. For each method of an interface, the IDL compiler generates an empty method in the server skeleton. The developer then provides an implementation for each of these methods. Figure 2.8 illustrates how client stubs and server skeletons fit into a CORBA application.

Figure 2.8.

Client stubs and server skeletons.

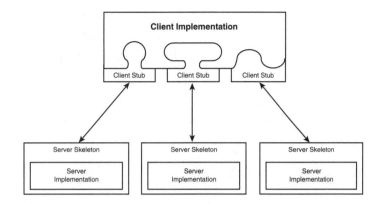

You will study the process of building a CORBA client and server in detail on Day 4. There you will find how to use the IDL compiler, how to build a CORBA client using the client stubs generated by the IDL compiler, and how to build a CORBA server, starting from the server skeletons also generated by the IDL compiler. Eventually, you will see that you can build CORBA clients without using client stubs at all, using what is known as the Dynamic Invocation Interface (DII). Rather than being statically linked to server interfaces, such clients can discover server interfaces dynamically and use services not even conceived of at the time the clients were built. (However, using the DII significantly increases the complexity of a client application and is probably best left for a certain niche of applications.) Because the Dynamic Invocation Interface is considered an advanced topic, you won't be seeing any more of it until Day 11.

Beyond the Basics: CORBAservices and CORBAfacilities

Certainly, much can be accomplished using just the basics of CORBA: using IDL to create component interfaces, then implementing those interfaces and developing clients to exploit the services provided. However, the Object Management Architecture (which you'll recall is the Object Management group's overall architecture which includes CORBA) provides much more than the basic ORB capabilities in the form of *CORBAservices* and *CORBAfacilities*. These capabilities include event management, licensing, object persistence, naming, security, transactions, user interface management, data interchange, and much more. The interfaces for using these capabilities are standardized by the OMG, meaning that their usage is (or will be) consistent across platforms and products. What's more, the interfaces for CORBAservices and CORBAfacilities are specified in IDL, meaning that applications can use these services just as they use any other CORBA objects.

You will examine the CORBAservices and CORBAfacilities, both present and future, on Day 12. For the time being, you should be aware that there is a difference between what services and facilities are specified by the OMG and what services and facilities are available in various CORBA products. Before deciding to use a particular service or facility in an application design, you should first ensure that a product actually exists that implements that functionality. Also note that in order to be considered CORBA 2.0-compliant, a product need not implement any of the CORBAservices or CORBAfacilities; only the CORBA core functionality is required.

Summary

In this chapter, you first discovered the two cornerstones of the CORBA architecture: the Object Request Broker (ORB), which manages the communication of CORBA objects with each other, and the Interface Definition Language (IDL), which defines application component interfaces upon which CORBA applications are built. You explored the CORBA object model, where you learned about inter-ORB protocols (particularly IIOP), CORBA's use of object references, and the concept of the Basic Object Adapter. You defined the terms *client* and *server* in the context of CORBA and saw that a single application component can simultaneously act as both a client and a server. You also saw how IDL definitions create client stubs and server skeletons, which in turn implement CORBA clients and servers. Finally, you were introduced to CORBAservices and CORBAfacilities, which provide additional functionality for CORBA applications.

Now that you have developed an understanding of the overall CORBA architecture, you will move on to the basics of IDL, starting with simple data types and working up to more complex IDL constructs. You will find this knowledge of IDL necessary to design and implement CORBA applications.

Q&A

Q Why would the capability to pass objects by value eliminate the need for many callbacks?

A In many cases, a client might only need to pass a simple object to a server method. Because objects cannot be passed by value, the server must use callbacks to the client to manipulate the object (even if it only wants to read the object's state). If the object can be passed by value, the server can operate on a local copy of the object, eliminating the need for client callbacks. (Of course, in some cases the client will want to retain ownership of the object and will want the server to make callbacks; in such cases, the callback paradigm would be retained.)

2

Q **Client stubs seem too restrictive for my application; do I need to use DII?**

A For an overwhelming majority of applications, if you think DII is necessary, you might want to reconsider. Due to the complexity and overhead of using DII, it is almost always best to avoid it. (See Chapter 11 for more information on when the use of DII might be appropriate.)

Q **Why are language mappings a necessary part of CORBA?**

A Because CORBA object interfaces are specified in IDL, which is independent of any implementation language, it is necessary to specify a methodology for converting IDL data types to data types of the implementation language(s) chosen. The language mapping for a particular implementation language describes this methodology. Furthermore, language mappings for many common languages are standardized, meaning that an application written to use one CORBA product can be made to work with a different product with little or no modification (as long as the application uses only features of the standard language mapping).

Workshop

The following section will help you test your comprehension of the material presented today and put what you've learned into practice. You'll find the answers to the quiz in Appendix A. On most days, a few exercises will accompany the quiz; today, because no real "working knowledge" material was presented, there are no exercises.

Quiz

1. Earlier in the chapter, you claimed that the capability to pass objects by value, when it becomes available, will eliminate the need for many callbacks. Why is this true?

2. An architect of a CORBA application wants to include two server components in the application. The first component has a single method that simply returns the time of day. The second component, when initialized, performs a lengthy calculation on a large database table; it features a single method that returns the precalculated result. Which server activation policies will the architect want to use for these two components, and why?

3. Can you think of a drawback to the use of client stubs in a CORBA client application? (Hint: What potentially useful capability does the Dynamic Invocation Interface (DII) provide?)

4. Why are language mappings a necessary part of CORBA?

Day 3

Mastering the Interface Definition Language (IDL)

Overview

On Day 2 you learned about the details of the CORBA architecture and attained an understanding of the various CORBA application components and their purposes. One chief component of the CORBA architecture, as you saw, is the use of the Interface Definition Language (IDL). IDL is used to describe the interfaces between CORBA objects. You also learned that IDL is neutral with respect to implementation language; in other words, IDL interfaces can be implemented in any language for which a language mapping exists, such as Java, C, C++, and a number of others.

Today you'll explore the various constructs of IDL and learn their uses. You'll start with the primitive data types, such as Booleans, floating point types, integer types, and characters and character strings, which you will find similar to data types found in most programming languages. You'll then move on to constructed types—the enumerated type, the structure type, the union type, and the interface type—which are simply types constructed from other types. Finally, you'll learn about advanced types, such as container types (sequences and arrays), exceptions, and others. By the end of the chapter you'll have covered virtually all there is to know about IDL.

IDL Ground Rules

Before you begin with IDL data types and other constructs, you'll want to cover a few ground rules of IDL syntax and other aspects of the IDL language. In particular, IDL has rules regarding case sensitivity, definition syntax, comment syntax, and C preprocessor usage.

Case Sensitivity

In IDL, identifiers (such as names of interfaces and operations) are case sensitive. In other words, an interface called myObject cannot be referred to later as myOBJECT. Besides these identifiers being case sensitive, IDL imposes another restriction: The names of identifiers in the same scope (for instance, two interfaces in the same module or two operations in the same interface) cannot differ in case only. For example, in the myObject interface, IDL would not allow an operation named anOperation and another operation named anOPERATION to be defined simultaneously. Obviously, you haven't yet been exposed to modules, interfaces, and operations; stay tuned to this chapter for more details on these constructs.

NOTE

What the OMG refers to as *operations,* you might know as *methods, member functions,* or even *messages.* Whatever name you know it by, an operation defines a particular behavior of an interface, including the input and output parameters of that particular behavior. Throughout this book, the terms *operation* and *method* will be used interchangeably, because they refer to exactly the same concept.

IDL Definition Syntax

All definitions in IDL are terminated by a semicolon (;), much as they are in C, C++, and Java. Definitions that enclose other definitions (such as modules and interfaces) do so with braces ({}), again like C, C++, and Java. When a closing brace also appears at the end of a definition, it is also followed by a semicolon. An example of this syntax appears in Listing 3.2 in the section, "The Module."

IDL Comments

Comments in IDL follow the same conventions as Java and C++. Both C-style and C++-style comments are allowed, as illustrated in Listing 3.1. (Note that the second comment in the listing contains embedded comment characters; these are for description purposes only and are not actually allowed by IDL.)

Listing 3.1. IDL comments.

```
1: // This is a C++-style comment. Anything following the "//"
2: // characters, to the end of the line, is treated as part of the
3: // comment.
4: /* This is a C-style comment. Anything between the beginning
5:    "/*" characters and the trailing "*/" characters is treated
6:    as part of the comment. */
```

Use of the C Preprocessor

IDL assumes the existence of a C preprocessor to process constructs such as macro definitions and conditional compilation. If the IDL you write does not make use of these features, you can do without a C preprocessor, but you should recognize that IDL can make use of C preprocessor features.

> **NOTE**
>
> The C preprocessor, included with C and C++ compilers and with some operating systems, is a tool that is essential to the use of those languages. (The Java language does not use a preprocessor.) Before a C or C++ compiler compiles code, it runs the preprocessor on that code. The preprocessor, among other things, resolves macros, processes directives such as #ifdef...#endif and #include, and performs substitutions of #defined symbols. For more information on the C preprocessor, consult a C or C++ text, or if you have access to a UNIX system, try man cpp.

The `Module`

The first IDL language construct to examine is the `module`. The `module` construct is used to group together IDL definitions that share a common purpose. The use of the `module` construct is simple: A `module` declaration specifies the `module` name and encloses its members in braces, as illustrated in Listing 3.2.

 The grouping together of similar interfaces, constant values, and the like is commonly referred to as *partitioning* and is a typical step in the system design process (particularly in more complex systems). Partitions are also often referred to as modules (which should be no surprise) or as packages (in fact, the IDL module concept closely resembles the Java package concept—or the other way around, because IDL came first).

Listing 3.2. `Module` **example.**

```
1: module Bank {
2:     interface Customer {
3:         ...
4:     };
5:     interface Account {
6:         ...
7:     };
8:     ...
9: };
```

The example in Listing 3.2 defines a `module` called `Bank`, which contains two `interfaces` called `Customer` and `Account` (ellipses are used to indicate that the actual definitions are omitted). The examples get ahead of themselves somewhat by using the `interface` construct here; interfaces are described later in this chapter.

Coupling and Cohesion

NEW TERM So, now that you have the ability to group interfaces together, how do you decide which interfaces to group together? This is really a question of system design and would be best answered in a text dedicated to that subject. (There are plenty of excellent books available on the subject of object-oriented analysis and design.) However, an overall guideline is that a good design generally exhibits two attributes: *loose coupling* and *tight cohesion*. The first means that components in separate `modules` are not tightly integrated with each other; an application using components in one `module` generally need not know about components in another module. (Of course, there is often some overlap between `modules` for various reasons, such as the need to share data between `modules` or to facilitate common functionality between modules.) When there is little or no dependency between components, they are said to be loosely coupled.

On the other hand, within a single `module` it is advantageous for a design to achieve tight cohesion. This means that interfaces within the `module` are tightly integrated with each other. For example, a `module` called InternalCombustionEngine might contain interfaces such as CylinderHead, TimingChain, Crankshaft, Piston, and many others. It is difficult to describe the purpose of one of these components without referring to the others; hence, one might say that the components are tightly cohesive. By way of comparison, you would probably find very little in common between the components of InternalCombustionEngine and, for instance, AudioSystem; InternalCombustionEngine components such as OilFilter and SparkPlug are loosely coupled to AudioSystem components such as CompactDiscPlayer and Subwoofer.

Figure 3.1 illustrates the concepts of coupling and cohesion; note that there are many relationships between components within the same module, whereas there are few relationships between components within separate modules. The figure also illustrates the advantage of loose coupling between modules: Imagine if, when you installed a new CD player in your car, you had to change the spark plugs and replace your timing chain! Loose coupling of components reduces the possibility that changes to one component will require changes to another.

Figure 3.1.

Coupling and cohesion.

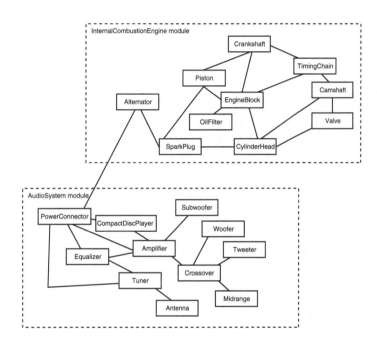

Primitive Types

Like most programming languages, IDL features a variety of primitive types (which can then be combined into aggregate types). These types store simple values such as integral numbers, floating point numbers, character strings, and so on.

void

The IDL void type is analogous to the void type of C, C++, and Java. It is pointless to have a variable of type void, but the type is useful for methods that don't return any value.

boolean

The IDL boolean type, as its name suggests, stores a Boolean value. IDL defines two boolean constants, true and false, which have obvious meanings. Depending on the programming language used, the IDL boolean type can map to an integral type (such as C/C++'s short) or to the language's native Boolean type (as is the case with Java).

```
boolean aBoolean;
```

char and wchar

The char type in IDL, analogous to the char type in C, C++, and Java, stores a single character value. As expected, it maps directly to the char type in these languages. The char data type is an 8-bit quantity.

```
char aChar;
```

In version 2.1, CORBA added the wchar, or wide character type, which has an implementation-dependent width (which is likely to be 16 bits, but you might want to consult with your ORB documentation).

Floating Point Types

IDL defines a number of types to represent floating point values; these are already familiar to most developers.

float

The IDL float type represents an IEEE single-precision floating point value. Again, it is analogous to the C, C++, and Java type of the same name.

```
float aFloat;
```

double and long double

The double type represents an IEEE double-precision floating point value. Not surprisingly, it corresponds to the familiar double type of a number of languages.

```
double aDouble;
```

The long double type, introduced in CORBA 2.1, represents an IEEE double-extended floating point value, having an exponent of at least 15 bits and a signed fraction of at least 64 bits.

Integer Types

IDL also defines a number of integral numeric types. Again, most developers will recognize these. Unlike most familiar programming languages, though, IDL doesn't define a plain int type, only short and long integer types.

3

long and long long

The IDL long type represents a 32-bit signed quantity (with a range of $-2^{31}..2^{31}-1$), like C/C++'s int (on most platforms) and Java's int (on all platforms, because Java, unlike C/C++, explicitly specifies the size of int).

```
long aLong;
```

In CORBA 2.1, the long long type was added, which is a 64-bit signed quantity (with a range of $-2^{63}..2^{63}-1$).

unsigned long and unsigned long long

The unsigned long type in IDL is an unsigned version of the long type; its range is $0..2^{32}-1$.

```
unsigned long anUnsignedLong;
```

CORBA 2.1 added the unsigned long long type, which is a 64-bit unsigned quantity with a range of $0..2^{64}-1$.

short

The short type represents a 16-bit signed quantity, like C/C++'s short or short int (again, on most platforms) and Java's short. Its range is $-2^{15}..2^{15}-1$.

```
short aShort;
```

unsigned short

The unsigned short type, as expected, is the unsigned version of short, with a range of $0..216-1$.

```
unsigned short anUnsignedShort;
```

octet

The octet type is an 8-bit quantity that is not translated in any way during transmission. This type has no direct counterpart in C and C++, although the char or unsigned char types are often used to represent this type of value. Java, of course, has the byte type, which is similar.

```
octet anOctet;
```

string

The string type represents a string of characters, similar to C++'s Cstring and Java's String class. C has no direct counterpart (because there is no "true" string type in C); character arrays are used instead. IDL supports both fixed- and variable-length strings.

```
string aFixedLengthString[20];
string aVariableLengthString;
```

The const **Modifier**

In addition to these standard types, IDL, like C and C++, also allows constant values to be specified by using the const modifier. const values are useful for values that should not change, such as physical constants such as *pi* or *c*. The scope of a const value, like any value, is that of its enclosing interface or module.

```
const float aFloatConstant = 3.1415926535897932384;
const long aLongConstant = 12345;
const string aStringConstant = "Ain't IDL great?";
```

Constructed Types

Constructed types, which combine other types, enable the creation of user-defined types. Perhaps the most useful of these constructs is the interface, which defines the services provided by your application objects. Because IDL is, after all, the Interface Definition Language, it seems fitting that interfaces should comprise the bulk of IDL source code.

The Enumerated Type

The enumerated type, enum, allows the creation of types that can hold one of a set of predefined values specified by the enum. Although the identifiers in the enumeration comprise an ordered list, IDL does not specify the ordinal numbering for the identifiers. Therefore, comparing enum values to integral values might not be safe, and would almost certainly not be portable across languages. C and C++ also have an enumerated type that works similarly. An example of the enum type appears in Listing 3.3.

Listing 3.3. enum example.

```
1: enum DaysOfWeek {
2:      Sunday,
3:      Monday,
4:      Tuesday,
5:      Wednesday,
6:      Thursday,
7:      Friday,
8:      Saturday
9: };
```

The Structure Type

IDL provides a structure type—struct—that contains, as in C and C++, any number of member values of disparate types (even other structs). structs are especially useful in IDL because, unlike CORBA objects (which are represented by interfaces), structs are passed by value rather than by reference. In other words, when a struct is passed to a remote object, a copy of that `struct`'s values is created and marshaled to the remote object. An example of the `struct` type appears in Listing 3.4.

Listing 3.4. `struct` **example.**

```
1: struct DateStruct {
2:     short year,
3:     short month,
4:     short day,
5:     short hour,
6:     short minute,
7:     short second,
8:     long microsecond
9: };
```

The `union` Type

The IDL union type, like a `struct`, represents values of different types. The IDL union type will appear somewhat odd to C and C++ programmers, resembling something of a cross between a C/C++ union and a `case` statement, but Pascal programmers should recognize the format. An example of a union definition appears in Listing 3.5.

Listing 3.5. `union` **example.**

```
1: union MultiplePersonalities switch(long) {
2:     case 1:
3:         short myShortPersonality;
4:     case 2:
5:         double myDoublePersonality;
6:     case 3:
7:     default:
8:         string myStringPersonality;
9: };
```

In the example in Listing 3.5, a variable of type `MultiplePersonalities` might have either a `short` value, a `double` value, or a `string` value, depending on the value of the parameter when the union is used in a method call. (The parameter is known as a *discriminator.*)

NEW TERM   A *discriminator,* as used in an IDL union, is a parameter that determines the value used by the union. In the example in Listing 3.5, a `long` was used for the discriminator; other types can be used also, including `long`, `long long`, `short`, `unsigned long`, `unsigned long long`, `unsigned short`, `char`, `boolean`, or `enum`. The constant values in the `case` statements must match the discriminator's type.

NOTE

In practice, IDL unions are rarely useful. Whereas the traditional C union might find a use in optimization of native C code, unions almost never appear in distributed applications. Behavior of objects is usually better abstracted through the use of interfaces. However, should the need for a union arise, IDL provides this type, just in case.

The interface Type

The interface type is by far the most versatile of IDL data types. The interface describes the services provided by a CORBA object. These services appear in the form of operations (or methods), resembling methods in object-oriented languages like C++ and Java. The difference, again, is that IDL is used only to specify the interfaces of these methods, whereas languages like Java and C++ are used to specify interfaces and (usually) provide implementations for those interfaces' methods.

The IDL interface type is very much like the Java interface type because neither provides an implementation for the methods defined. (However, a major difference is that IDL interfaces can contain attributes, whereas Java interfaces don't.) C++, on the other hand, has no direct counterpart to IDL's interface, although it is common for C++ applications to use a header file to define the interface of a class. An IDL interface definition can thus be compared to a C++ header file containing a class definition. Also, a C++ class whose methods are all pure virtual can be considered analogous to the IDL interface.

Like a Java or C++ class, an IDL interface can contain attributes (also commonly known as member variables) and operations (which, again, you may know as methods or member functions). Like Java's interface, all methods defined within an IDL interface are public—they can be called by any other object having a reference to the interface's implementation object. Finally, because IDL interfaces usually describe remote objects, IDL also provides some additional modifiers to further describe the interface and its members. For example, methods can be declared as oneway; arguments to methods can be declared as in, out, or inout; and attributes can be declared as readonly. In a few moments, you'll explore what each of these modifiers means, how it is used, and why.

Methods and Parameters

Methods of an interface are, in essence, what define an object's functionality. Although the object's implementation determines how the object behaves, the interface's method definitions determine what behavior the object implementing that interface provides. These method definitions are often called *method signatures*, or just *signatures*. IDL methods can use any IDL data types as input and output parameters—primitive types, structs, sequences, and even interfaces. The general syntax for a method declaration is as follows:

```
[oneway] return_type methodName(param1_dir param1_type param1_name,
        param2_dir param2_type param2_name, ...);
```

The oneway modifier is optional; return_type specifies the type of data returned by the method, the param*n*dir modifier specifies the direction of each parameter (one of in, out, or inout), and param*n*type specifies the type of each parameter. Modifiers such as these are not commonly found in programming languages and thus merit some attention.

NEW TERM   A *method signature,* often simply called a *signature,* describes what a method does (ideally, the method name should specify, at least in general terms, what the method does), what parameters (and their types) the method takes as input, and what parameters (and their types) it returns as output.

in, out, **and** inout **Parameters**

As already mentioned, parameters in a method can be declared as in, out, or inout. These names are fairly self-explanatory: An in parameter serves as input to the method; an out parameter is an output from the method; and an inout parameter serves as an input to and an output from the method.

In remote method terms, this means that before the method is invoked, any in and inout parameters are marshaled across the network to the remote object. After the method executes, any out and inout parameters—along with the method's return value, if any—are marshaled back to the calling object. Note particularly that inout parameters are marshaled twice—once as an input value and once as an output value.

oneway **Methods**

The typical paradigm for calling a remote method is as follows: When an object calls a method on a remote object, that calling object waits (this is called *blocking*) for the method to execute and return. When the remote object finishes processing the method invocation (often called a *request*), it returns to the calling object, which then continues its processing. Figure 3.2 illustrates this process.

NEW TERM   In general, the term *blocking* refers to any point at which a process or thread is waiting for a particular resource or another process/thread. Within the context of CORBA, if a client invokes a remote method and must wait for the result to be returned, the client is said to *block.*

A *request* is simply another name for a remote method invocation. The term is commonly used when referring to the operation of a distributed system. In fact, when you study CORBA's Dynamic Invocation Interface (DII), you'll see that remote methods can be invoked through a Request object.

3

Figure 3.2.

Blocking on a remote method call.

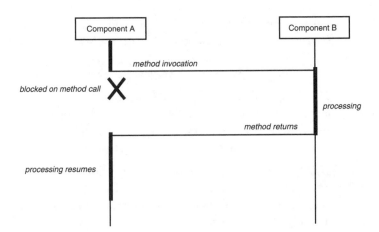

When a method is declared oneway, it means that the object calling that method will not block. Rather, that object will call the remote method and then immediately continue processing, while the remote object executes the remote method. The advantage to this approach is that the calling object can continue working rather than wait for the remote object to complete the request. Figure 3.3 illustrates the operation of a oneway method.

Figure 3.3.

The oneway *(nonblocking) remote method call.*

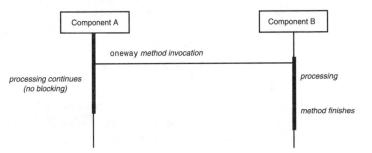

The flexibility of the oneway calling paradigm comes at a price, however. Because the method invocation returns before the method execution is completed, the method cannot return a value. Therefore, for a oneway method, the return value must be declared void, and all parameters must be declared as in (out and inout parameters are not allowed). In addition, a oneway method cannot raise any exceptions. Also, the calling object has no way of knowing whether the method executed successfully; the CORBA infrastructure makes a best-effort attempt to execute the method, but success is not guaranteed. (Readers familiar with the User Datagram Protocol will recognize the similarity.) Therefore, oneway methods are most useful for situations in which one object wants to inform another object of a particular status but (1) does not consider the message to be essential and (2) does not expect (or desire) a response.

NOTE

A method that has only in parameters, returns a void, and does not raise any exceptions is not automatically a oneway method. The difference between such a method and a oneway method is that, whereas the latter is not guaranteed to execute successfully (and the client will have no way of determining whether it did), the former will result in the client blocking until a result is returned from the remote method (even though the result will be null). The important difference here is that the success of the non-oneway method can be determined, because a CORBA system exception would be raised if this were not the case.

There are ways of overcoming the issues associated with blocking. Most commonly, the use of multithreading can circumvent the blocking "problem" by creating a separate thread to invoke the remote method. While that thread is blocked waiting for the result to be returned, other threads can continue working. On Day 10 you'll study issues such as this in greater detail and learn about some possible resolutions to these issues.

Attributes

An attribute of an IDL interface is analogous to an attribute of a Java or C++ class, with the exception that IDL attributes always have public visibility. (Indeed, everything in an IDL interface has public visibility.) The general syntax for defining an attribute is this:

```
[readonly] attribute attribute_type attributeName;
```

In Java and C++, it is generally considered good programming practice to provide accessor and mutator methods for attributes of a class, and to make the attribute itself protected or private. IDL advances this concept one step further: IDL attributes map to accessor and mutator methods when the IDL is compiled. For instance, the following definition:

```
attribute short myChannel;
```

maps to the following two methods:

```
short myChannel();
void myChannel(short value);
```

readonly **Attributes**

The preceding example indicates the optional use of the readonly modifier. As the name suggests, this modifier is used to specify that a particular attribute is for reading only; its value cannot be modified directly by an external object. (The object implementing the interface is, of course, free to modify values of its own attributes as it sees fit.) Although a non-readonly attribute maps to a pair of accessor/mutator methods, for a readonly attribute the IDL compiler will generate only an accessor method.

Inheritance of `interfaces`

IDL `interfaces`, like the Java and C++ constructs they resemble, support the notion of inheritance. That is, an `interface` can inherit the methods and attributes of another (one can also say that the former `interface` derives from or is derived from the latter). In addition to inheriting its superclass' methods and attributes, a subclass can define additional methods and attributes of its own. The subclass can also be substituted anywhere that its superclass is expected; for example, if a method takes a parameter of type `Fish` and the `Halibut interface` is a subclass of the `Fish interface`, then that method can be called with a parameter of type `Halibut` instead of `Fish`.

> **NEW TERM** A *subclass*, or *derived class*, is a class that inherits methods and attributes from another class. The class from which these methods and attributes are inherited is known as the *superclass*, or *parent class*. Although IDL uses `interfaces` and not classes, these general terms can still be applied.

> **NEW TERM** In object speak, *polymorphism* refers to the ability to substitute a derived class into a parameter that expects that class's superclass. Because in a sense the subclass *is* an instance of the superclass (as a Beagle *is* a Dog), any operation that acts on the superclass can also act on the subclass. Polymorphism is a fundamental property of object-oriented architecture.

The syntax for specifying `interface` inheritance resembles the syntax used by C++ and Java. The exception in IDL is that no visibility for the superclass is specified (recall that all methods and attributes are implicitly public). The inheritance syntax is illustrated in Listing 3.6.

Listing 3.6. Inheritance syntax example.

```
1: interface Fish {
2:     ...
3: };
4: interface Halibut : Fish {
5:     ...
6: };
```

In Listing 3.6, the `Halibut interface` inherits from the `Fish interface`, as indicated by the colon (:) operator. Attributes and methods have, of course, been omitted.

One last word with respect to inheritance of IDL `interfaces`: IDL `interfaces`, like C++ classes, can inherit from more than one superclass. This capability, known as *multiple inheritance,* is not available in Java, although Java allows a single class to implement multiple interfaces, a feature that often achieves the same result as multiple inheritance. The syntax for multiple inheritance in IDL is illustrated in Listing 3.7.

3

Listing 3.7. Multiple inheritance syntax example.

```
1: interface LandVehicle {
2:     ...
3: };
4: interface WaterVehicle {
5:     ...
6: };
7: interface AmphibiousVehicle : LandVehicle, WaterVehicle {
8:     ...
9: };
```

In Listing 3.7, the AmphibiousVehicle interface, being both a LandVehicle and a WaterVehicle, inherits both those interfaces. Note that due to the polymorphic behavior of derived classes, an AmphibiousVehicle can be substituted for either a LandVechile or a WaterVehicle.

interface Definition Syntax

The syntax for an interface definition is not unlike the syntax used in C++ or Java. The body of the interface contains method signatures and attribute declarations, in no particular order. A few sample interface definitions appear in Listing 3.8.

Listing 3.8. Sample IDL interfaces.

```
1: // This module defines some useful household appliances.
2: module Appliances {
3:     // Television interface definition.
4:     interface Television {
5:         // My serial number.
6:         readonly attribute string mySerialNumber;
7:         // My current volume level.
8:         attribute short myVolume;
9:         // My current channel.
10:        attribute short myChannel;
11:        // Turn this Television on.
12:        void turnOn();
13:        // Turn this Television off.
14:        void turnOff();
15:        // Set this Television's sleep timer.
16:        void setSleepTimer(in short minutes);
17:    };
18:    interface WWWTelevision : Television {
19:        // Surf to the given URL.
20:        void surfTo(in Internet::URL url);
21:    };
22: };
```

Close inspection reveals that IDL interfaces don't specify constructors or destructors. Java developers should not be surprised at this because Java interfaces don't include constructors or destructors either (but then again, there are also no destructors in Java). C++ developers, however, might be wondering what happened to the constructors and destructors. As it turns out, constructors and destructors are still a part of CORBA objects; they just aren't included as part of the object's `interface`. You'll see the reason for this when you begin building a CORBA application in the next chapter.

Other IDL Constructs

IDL supports several other useful constructs. Among these are the capability to refer to any IDL type by a user-specified type name and the capability to declare a type name without defining it, which is helpful for handling circular references.

typedef

Like C and C++, IDL supports a `typedef` statement to create a user-defined type name. `typedef` can make any IDL type accessible by a type name of the user's choosing, a capability that adds convenience to the language. For example, in Listing 3.8, the `Television interface` contains the member `mySerialNumber`, which is of type `string`. Because the use of the `string` type isn't very telling, it might be preferable to define a `SerialNumber` type that can then be used by any `interfaces` and methods requiring a serial number. Assuming that the `string` type is adequate for storing serial numbers, it would be convenient to use a `string` type but refer to it as a `SerialNumber`. The `typedef` statement allows you to do just this. The statement

```
typedef string SerialNumber;
```

means that anywhere the `SerialNumber` type is found, it should be treated as a `string`.

Forward Declarations

Occasionally, you will create `interfaces` that reference each other—that is, within the first `interface` you'll have an `attribute` of the second `interface`'s type, or a method that uses the second `interface`'s type as a parameter or return value. The second `interface`, similarly, will reference the first `interface` in the same way. Listing 3.9 illustrates this concept, known as a *circular reference*.

 A *circular reference* occurs when two classes (or `interfaces`, in the context of IDL) each have attributes or methods that refer to the other class.

Listing 3.9. Circular reference example.

```
1: module Circular {
2:     interface A {
3:         void useB(in B aB);
4:     }
5:     interface B {
```

```
6:          void useA(in A anA);
7:     }
8: };
```

In Listing 3.9, the A interface references the B interface, which in turn references the A interface. If you were to attempt to compile this code as it is listed, the IDL compiler would report an error in the useB() method definition because the B interface is unknown. If you were to reverse the order of definition of the A and B interfaces, the IDL compiler would signal an error in the useA() method because the A interface is unknown. As you can see, the circular reference problem is a bit of a Catch 22.

C and C++ programmers might already know the answer to the circular reference problem: the *forward declaration.* A forward declaration allows you to inform the IDL compiler that you intend to define the declared type later, without defining the type at that point. (You will have to define the type at some point, however.) The syntax of a forward declaration, which closely resembles the C/C++ syntax, is simple:

```
interface B;
```

This tells the IDL compiler that a definition for the Bar interface will appear at some point in the future but that for now it should accept references to the as-yet-undefined Bar. Listing 3.10 illustrates how the forward declaration would fit into the previous example.

Listing 3.10. Circular reference example.

```
 1: module Circular {
 2:     // Forward declaration of the B interface.
 3:     interface B;
 4:     interface A {
 5:         void useB(in B aB);
 6:     }
 7:     interface B {
 8:         void useA(in A anA);
 9:     }
10: };
```

In Listing 3.10, when the IDL compiler reaches the definition for useB(), it sees that the B interface has already been declared (by the forward declaration) and thus will not report an error.

NOTE

You could just as well have defined the B interface first and made a forward declaration to the A interface; the IDL compiler does not impose a particular order in which interfaces must be defined.

Container Types

Most programming languages include constructs for dealing with multiple values of similar types. Arrays are common throughout programming languages: Java includes java.util.Vector, C++ features its Standard Template Library (STL), and, of course, various libraries of container classes abound. IDL is no exception, featuring two such constructs: the sequence, which is a dynamically sizable array, and the array, which mirrors the array constructs found in many languages.

The sequence Type

An IDL sequence is simply a dynamically sizable array of values. These values can be dynamically inserted in or removed from the sequence; the sequence manages its size accordingly. All values of a sequence must be of the same type or derived from the same type (with the exception of the any type. For example:

```
sequence<float> temperatureSequence;
```

defines a sequence of float values and assigns this type to the variable temperatureSequence. Values of type float can subsequently be added to temperatureSequence, or values can be removed. Recalling the Appliances example (refer to Listing 3.8), you can also create a sequence of Television objects:

```
sequence<Television> televisionInventory;
```

In this case, televisionInventory can be populated with objects of type Television, or any objects derived from Television, in this case WWWTelevision. If you had created a third interface derived from Television—for instance, PortableTelevision—the televisionInventory sequence could contain Televisions, WWWTelevisions, and PortableTelevisions.

The Array

An IDL array corresponds directly to the array constructs in C, C++, and Java. An array stores a known-length series of similar data types. For example:

```
string DayNames[7];
```

defines an array, with the name DayNames, of seven string values. Arrays can hold elements of any IDL data type; as in the Appliances example (refer to Listing 3.8), you can define the following array:

```
Television TVArray[10];
```

to define an array of ten Televisions. Remember that, due to polymorphism, each array element can hold either a plain Television or the derived WWWTelevision.

The exception Type

One concept embraced recently by developers is the use of exceptions to perform error handling. Exceptions, featured in object-oriented languages such as Java and C++, are constructs which are created to signify some error condition. When a method raises an exception, the method stops what it is doing and returns immediately. When the calling method catches the exception, it can either handle the exception or throw it up to that method's caller. This process might continue all the way up to the top level (typically, `main()`); if the top-level method does not handle the exception, the application usually exits (although allowing this to happen is generally considered poor programming practice).

NEW TERM When a method passes an exception back to its caller, it is said that the method *throws* an exception, or in CORBA-speak, *raises* an exception.

CORBA and IDL fully support exception handling through predefined standard exceptions and user-defined exceptions. IDL allows developers to define exceptions and specify which exceptions are raised by what methods. When an exception is raised, the ORB passes that exception back to the calling object's ORB, which then passes the exception back to the calling object. In this way, CORBA extends the familiar exception-passing mechanism to a distributed architecture.

In addition to their distributed nature, IDL exceptions differ from their counterparts in C++ and Java in other ways. C++ exceptions can be virtually any type; C++ does not even require that exception objects be derived from a certain type (for instance, a method could throw a `const char*`, if it so desired). Java exceptions can be any type that implements the `java.lang.Throwable` interface. IDL, however, is somewhat more restrictive than these languages; exception objects must be declared explicitly as such. Furthermore, whereas C++ and Java allow exception types to be derived from other types, IDL does not support inheritance of exception types.

exception

The IDL `exception` type itself is similar to a `struct` type; it can contain various data members (but no methods). The definition for an `exception` type also resembles the `struct` definition, as the example in Listing 3.11 shows. The example demonstrates that an `exception` need not have any members at all; sometimes the mere act of raising an exception provides enough error-handling information.

Listing 3.11. exception **definition example.**

```
1: // This exception might be used where a file to be opened
2: // couldn't be located. Since it might be useful for the caller
3: // to know the invalid filename, the exception provides that
```

continues

Listing 3.11. continued

```
 4: // information.
 5: exception FileNotFoundException {
 6:     string fileName;
 7: };
 8: // This exception might be used where a particuar operation,
 9: // which was supposed to have completed within a given amount
10: // of time, failed to do so. The exception provides the
11: // operation name and the time length given for the operation.
12: exception OperationTimedOutException {
13:     string operationName;
14:     long timeoutLength;
15: };
16: // This exception might be used where an attempt to log into a
17: // system failed. No other information is necessary, so none is
18: // provided.
19: exception InvalidLoginException {
20: };
```

Standard Exceptions

In addition to allowing developers to create user-defined exceptions, CORBA also provides a number of standard exceptions, or system exceptions. Exceptions in this set might be raised by any remote method invocation. IDL method definitions don't explicitly declare that they raise a system exception; rather, these exceptions are raised implicitly. (Actually, when the IDL code is compiled, the generated method definitions do declare that CORBA system exceptions are raised, as well as any user-defined exceptions raised by those methods.) In addition to regular methods, even the accessor/mutator methods—corresponding to the attributes of interfaces—can raise standard exceptions, even though they cannot raise user-defined exceptions.

The standard exceptions provided by CORBA are listed in Table 3.1.

Table 3.1. CORBA standard exceptions.

Exception Name	Description
UNKNOWN	The unknown exception.
BAD_PARAM	An invalid parameter was passed.
NO_MEMORY	Dynamic memory allocation failure.
IMP_LIMIT	Violated implementation limit.
COMM_FAILURE	Communication failure.
INV_OBJREF	Invalid object reference.

3

Exception Name	Description
NO_PERMISSION	No permission for attempted operation.
INTERNAL	ORB internal error.
MARSHAL	Error marshaling parameter or result.
INITIALIZE	ORB initialization failure.
NO_IMPLEMENT	Operation implementation unavailable.
BAD_TYPECODE	Bad TypeCode.
BAD_OPERATION	Invalid operation.
NO_RESOURCES	Insufficient resources for request.
NO_RESPONSE	Response to request not yet available.
PERSIST_STORE	Persistent storage failure.
BAD_INV_ORDER	Routine invocations out of order.
TRANSIENT	Transient failure—re-issue request.
FREE_MEM	Cannot free memory.
INV_IDENT	Invalid identifier syntax.
INV_FLAG	Invalid flag was specified.
INTF_REPOS	Error accessing interface repository.
BAD_CONTEXT	Error processing context object.
OBJ_ADAPTER	Failure detected by object adapter.
DATA_CONVERSION	Data conversion error.
OBJECT_NOT_EXIST	Nonexistent object—delete reference.

3

The any Type

For those occasional methods that need to accept any sort of CORBA object as a parameter or take a parameter that could potentially be one of several unrelated data types (in other words, none of the data types are inherited from any of the others), IDL provides the any type. When any is used as the type of a parameter or return value, that value can literally be any IDL type. A method that accepts an any as an input parameter will usually need to determine precisely what type of object is being passed before it can manipulate the object; you will see how this is done when you begin implementing CORBA clients and servers.

NOTE

For a method that must accept one of various types of CORBA objects as a parameter, the any is not always the only choice. If the type of the parameter can be one of only a few types, and the type of the parameter is known, then the union type might be a better choice. However, with the union type, all of the types must be known in advance; this is not true for an any type. An any parameter can literally hold any type of object, even one that is unknown to the server receiving the any parameter.

For an example of the any type, see Listing 3.12. In this example, the browseObject() method accepts a single parameter, called object, of type any. A client calling this method can use an object of any IDL type to fill this parameter. Internally to browseObject(), the method will attempt to determine what the actual type of object is. If it determines that object is a type of object it can interact with, it will do so. Otherwise, it will raise the UnknownObjectType exception, which is returned to the caller.

Listing 3.12. any example.

```
1: interface ObjectBrowser {
2:     exception UnknownObjectType {
3:         string message;
4:     };
5:     void browseObject(in any object) raises (UnknownObjectType);
6: };
```

The TypeCode **Pseudotype**

Along with the any type comes the TypeCode pseudotype. TypeCode is not actually an IDL type; instead, it provides type information to a CORBA application. In most method calls, the types of the parameters passed to the method are known because they are specified by the IDL method signatures. However, when a method accepts an any type as an argument, the actual type of that object is unknown. This is where TypeCode comes in. Because every CORBA type—both standard types such as long and string and user-defined types such as Television—has a unique TypeCode associated with it, a method implementation can determine which type of object was sent through its any parameter. When the object's type is determined, the method can act on that object. Think of TypeCodes as a sort of runtime-type information for CORBA applications.

Summary

This chapter presented the basic data types provided by CORBA's Interface Definition Language (IDL), including integer and floating point numeric types, Boolean values, and characters and character strings. Because many of these data types closely resemble data types of programming languages like C, C++, or Java, readers who are already familiar with one of these languages will have little difficulty assimilating the IDL types.

You have expanded your knowledge of IDL to now include higher-level data types—particularly the user-defined types—and their uses. Most importantly, you are familiar with the `interface` construct and how it defines the behavior of CORBA objects. Because the `interface` is one of the fundamental IDL data types, a clear understanding of this construct is essential to the design of CORBA applications. Indeed, you cannot design or implement a CORBA application without `interfaces`.

Today you have seen some very useful IDL data types and constructs, in particular, the `sequence` and array types for storing multiple values of similar types. You learned about the `exceptions` in IDL, including the predefined CORBA standard exceptions. Finally, you looked at the `any` type, which can contain a value of any IDL type, and its counterpart, the `TypeCode` pseudotype, for determining unknown data types passed to a method. These constructs—particularly the `sequences` and `exceptions`—are essential for building robust CORBA applications.

You've covered just about everything there is to know about IDL; now it's time to apply it. In the next chapter—Day 4, "Building a CORBA Application"—you'll do just that, translating IDL definitions into working CORBA server and client applications.

Q&A

Q What's the point of having both sequence and array types?

A Array types are useful when the number of elements in an array is fixed and known in advance. In many instances, though, this is not the case; arrays often vary in size as members are dynamically added and removed. Consequently, a dynamically sizable array, such as the IDL sequence, is often much more convenient. For maximum flexibility, IDL offers both.

Q What are all those exceptions and when (or how) are they raised?

A First of all, nondistributed methods have little need for many of the CORBA standard exceptions, but they make a lot more sense in a distributed environment. As mentioned previously, the standard exceptions are generally not raised by any code that you will write; rather, the exceptions in this set are raised automatically by the ORB when an error condition occurs. Remember that all IDL methods implicitly raise these exceptions, even the accessor/mutator methods generated by the IDL compiler for each attribute.

Q **Why isn't (insert your favorite primitive data type here) supported?**

A Because one primary goal of IDL is to be language-neutral, it isn't practical to support all primitive data types contained in all languages. Rather than attempt to provide this level of support (nearly impossible to achieve), IDL provides the most common and useful primitive data types.

Q **How does an object modify one of its `attributes` when that `attribute` is declared to be `readonly`?**

A If you're asking questions like this, you're definitely thinking ahead. When you learn about implementation of IDL interfaces on Day 4, it will become clear how this is accomplished. For the time being, though, remember that the object implementing an `interface` has full access to its own state. A `readonly attribute` is mapped to a method of that object, and that method can return any value the object wants. Typically, the implementing object will define actual attributes of its own that correspond to `attributes` in the IDL `interface`, although this isn't strictly necessary.

Q **Because Java does not support multiple inheritance, how is multiple inheritance of IDL interfaces achieved in Java?**

A You'll see when you begin implementing IDL `interfaces` in Java that the IDL language mapping for Java maps IDL `interfaces` to Java `interfaces`. Although multiple inheritance of classes is not supported in Java, multiple inheritance of `interfaces` is.

Workshop

The following section will help you test your comprehension of the material presented in this chapter and put what you've learned into practice. You'll find the answers to the quiz in Appendix A.

Quiz

1. Define a type (using `typedef`) called `temperatureSequence` that is a sequence of sequences of `float`s (yes, this is legal).
2. Why might a type as described in the preceding question be useful?
3. Why are exceptions useful?
4. Why is the `module` construct useful?
5. Name some practical uses for the `octet` data type.
6. Define an enumerated type containing the months of the year.

7. Why might a nonblocking remote method call be advantageous, compared to a blocking method call?

8. Imagine a compound data type with a large number of data members. This data type will frequently be used by a client application, which will generally need to access each of the data members. Would it be more efficient to encapsulate this data type into a `struct` or an `interface`? Why?

9. Because an IDL method can return a value, what is the purpose of `out` and `inout` parameter types?

10. Why is a oneway method unable to return any value to the caller? Can you think of a mechanism, using `oneway` calls, to return a result to the caller?

Exercises

1. Consider the following classes: `Conduit`, `Faucet`, `FuseBox`, `Outlet`, `Pipe`, `WaterHeater`, `WaterPump`, and `Wire`. How would you partition these classes? What relationships, if any, are there between the partitions you have created?

2. Create an `interface` that describes a clock/radio (which can set the hours, set the minutes, set the alarm time, and so on).

3

Day 4

Building a CORBA Application

Up to this point, you've spent most of your time learning about CORBA's Interface Definition Language (IDL). You saw that IDL is used to define the interfaces of CORBA objects; you've even created some IDL interfaces of your own. Now it's time to put your IDL knowledge to use by not only defining object interfaces, but also by implementing those interfaces to build a CORBA server. This chapter will walk you through that process, from defining object interfaces to running the server. The outline of the process is this:

1. Define the server's interfaces using IDL.

2. Choose an implementation approach for the server's interfaces. (You'll see that CORBA provides two such approaches: inheritance and delegation.)

3. Use the IDL compiler to generate client stubs and server skeletons for the server interfaces. (For now, you'll only be concerned with the server skeletons.)

4. Implement the server interfaces.

5. Compile the server application.

6. Run the server application. (With any luck, everything will fall into place!)

Your next task will be to build a client that uses the services you implemented in the first part of this chapter. Conceptually speaking, the process of building the client is much simpler; you only need to decide what you want the client to do, include the appropriate client stubs for the types of server objects you want to use, and implement the client functionality. Then you'll be ready to compile and run the client.

Building a CORBA Server

The first step in building a CORBA application is usually to implement the server functionality. The reason for this is that while a server can be tested (at least in a limited way) without a client, it is generally much more difficult to test a client without a working server. There are exceptions to this, of course, but typically you'll need to at least define the server interfaces before implementing the client; server and client functionality can then be developed in parallel. For the sake of simplicity, in this book you'll implement server functionality first, followed by client functionality.

On a high level, to build the server you'll need to first define the server interfaces (which define the capabilities that will be made available by the server and how those capabilities are accessed), implement those interfaces, and finally compile and run the server. There are a few issues you'll encounter along the way, which will be discussed in this section.

Defining the Server Interfaces

This is where you begin to apply the knowledge you assimilated on Day 3, "Mastering the Interface Definition Language (IDL)." There you learned much about IDL but had no real chance to apply that knowledge. Now you can use that knowledge to transform a clean slate into a system design.

A Few Words About System Design

Obviously, in order to build a system, one must first have an idea of what that system is supposed to accomplish. Before you're ready to write a single line of IDL, you must first have a notion of what you're trying to achieve. Although the subject of system design is far beyond the scope of this book, on Day 5, "Designing the System: A Crash Course in Object-Oriented Analysis and Design," you'll be exposed to some of the basic concepts of designing a system and mapping a system design into IDL. In this chapter, the work will be done for you; in the real world, this is seldom the case.

The Stock Market Server Example

At this point, it's preferable to examine a simple example to help you focus on the process of implementing a CORBA server. A complex example would likely bog you down in various implementation details and is best avoided until later.

Consider a stock market-related example: A service is desired that, when given a stock symbol, will return the value of that stock at that particular time. As an added convenience, the service will also return a list of all known stock symbols upon request.

A cursory analysis of this scenario suggests that a StockServer interface could be defined that provides two services (methods): getStockValue() and getStockSymbols(). getStockValue() should take a StockSymbol as a parameter and return a floating-point result (float will probably do). getStockSymbols() need not take any arguments and should return a list of StockSymbol objects.

NOTE

During the process of determining StockServer system capability, the StockSymbol class was inadvertently produced. This spontaneous generation of classes, often a by-product of object-oriented analysis, can lead to a better understanding of how a particular system works.

4

Listing 4.1. StockMarket.idl.

```
 1: // StockMarket.idl
 2:
 3: // The StockMarket module consists of definitions useful
 4: // for building stock market-related applications.
 5: module StockMarket {
 6:
 7:     // The StockSymbol type is used for symbols (names)
 8:     // representing stocks.
 9:     typedef string StockSymbol;
10:
11:     // A StockSymbolList is simply a sequence of
12:     // StockSymbols.
13:     typedef sequence<StockSymbol> StockSymbolList;
14:
15:     // The StockServer interface is the interface for a
16:     // server which provides stock market information.
17:     // (See the comments on the individual methods for
18:     // more information.)
19:     interface StockServer {
20:
21:         // getStockValue() returns the current value for
22:         // the given StockSymbol. If the given StockSymbol
```

continues

Listing 4.1. continued

```
23:            // is unknown, the results are undefined (this
24:            // would be a good place to raise an exception).
25:            float getStockValue(in StockSymbol symbol);
26:
27:            // getStockSymbols() returns a sequence of all
28:            // StockSymbols known by this StockServer.
29:            StockSymbolList getStockSymbols();
30:      };
31: };
```

Mapping this particular design to IDL is a clear-cut process; the final result, StockMaret.idl, appears in Listing 4.1. First, because it's good practice to group together related interfaces and types into IDL modules, start by including all the definitions in a module called StockMarket:

```
module StockMarket {
```

Next, consider the use of the StockSymbol class. For the purposes of this example, it really doesn't require any functionality over and above the string type. Thus, you can either substitute the string type anywhere that the StockSymbol type would have been used, or you can use typedef to define StockSymbol as a string. In a complex system, using specific data types such as StockSymbol makes the system design easier to comprehend. To reinforce this practice, use typedef to define StockSymbol as a string:

```
typedef string StockSymbol;
```

You're now ready to define the interface for the StockServer object:

```
interface StockServer {
```

The first method in StockServer is a method that takes a StockSymbol as input and returns a float. Expressing this in IDL is uncomplicated:

```
float getStockValue(in StockSymbol symbol);
```

NOTE

It's conceivable that a client could call getStockValue() with an invalid StockSymbol name. To handle this, getStockValue() could (and probably should) raise an exception when an invalid name is passed to it. For the sake of simplicity, though, this example does not make use of exceptions.

The other StockServer method takes no arguments and returns a list of StockSymbols. Recall that IDL offers two constructs to represent lists: the sequence and the array. Because the size of the list is unknown in this case, it might be advantageous to use a sequence. However, a method cannot return a sequence directly; you'll first need to typedef a sequence of StockSymbols to use with this method. For the sake of convenience, add the typedef immediately following the typedef of the StockSymbol type:

```
typedef sequence<StockSymbol> StockSymbolList;
```

You're now ready to add the getStockSymbols() method to the StockServer interface. This method is described in IDL as follows:

```
StockSymbolList getStockSymbols();
```

That's all the IDL you need for this example. Armed with the StockMarket.idl file, you're now ready for the next step: deciding how you'd like to implement these IDL definitions.

Choosing an Implementation Approach

Before actually implementing the server functionality, you'll first need to decide on an implementation approach to use. CORBA supports two mechanisms for implementation of IDL interfaces. Developers familiar with object-oriented concepts might recognize these mechanisms, or at least their names. These include the *inheritance* mechanism, in which a class implements an interface by inheriting from that interface class, and the *delegation* mechanism, in which the methods of the interface class call the methods of the implementing class (delegating to those methods). These concepts are illustrated in Figures 4.1 and 4.2. Figure 4.2 also illustrates that a tie class can inherit from any class—or from no class—in contrast to the inheritance approach, in which the implementation class must inherit from the interface class that it implements.

NEW TERM   Implementation by *inheritance* consists of a base class that defines the interfaces of a particular object and a separate class, inheriting from this base class, which provides the actual implementations of these interfaces.

Implementation by *delegation* consists of a class that defines the interfaces for an object and then delegates their implementations to another class or classes. The primary difference between the inheritance and delegation approaches is that in delegation, the implementation classes need not derive from any class in particular.

A *tie class,* or simply a *tie,* is the class to which implementations are delegated in the delegation approach. Thus, the approach is often referred to as the *tie* mechanism or *tying*.

Most IDL compilers accept command-line arguments to determine which implementation approach to generate code for. Therefore, before you use the IDL compiler to generate code from your IDL definitions, you'll want to determine the approach you want to use. Consult your IDL compiler's documentation to determine which command-line arguments, if any, the IDL compiler expects.

Figure 4.1.
*Implementation
by inheritance.*

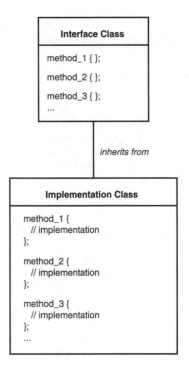

Figure 4.2.
*Implementation
by delegation.*

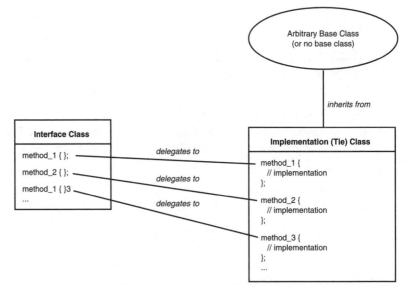

4

How to Choose an Implmentation Approach

One question you might be asking by now is how to choose an implementation approach. In many cases, this is probably a matter of taste. However, there are certain cases that work well with a particular approach. For example, recall that in the inheritance approach, the implementation class derives from a class provided by the IDL compiler. If an application makes use of legacy code to implement an interface, it might not be practical to change the classes in that legacy code to inherit from a class generated by the IDL compiler. Therefore, for such an application it would make more sense to use the delegation approach; existing classes can readily be transformed into tie classes.

WARNING

After you've chosen an implementation approach and have written a great deal of code, be prepared to stick with that approach for that server. Although it's possible to change from one implementation approach to another, this is a very tedious process if a lot of code has already been written. This issue doesn't present itself very often, but you should be aware of it.

For the purposes of this example, either implementation approach will do. The example will use the delegation approach; implementing the server using inheritance will be left as an exercise.

Note that you can usually mix and match the implementation and delegation approaches within a single server application. Although you'll use only one approach per interface, you could choose different approaches for different interfaces in the system. For example, if you had decided that the inheritance approach was the best match for your needs, but you had a few legacy classes that mandated the use of the tie approach, you could use that approach for those classes while using the inheritance approach for the remainder.

Using the IDL Compiler

Now that you have defined your system's object interfaces in IDL and have decided on an implementation approach, you're ready to compile the IDL file (or files, in a more complex system).

NOTE

The method and command-line arguments for invoking the IDL compiler vary across platforms and products. Consult your product documentation for specific instructions on using your IDL compiler.

Recall that this example will use the delegation approach—also called the tie mechanism—so be sure to consult your IDL compiler documentation for the appropriate command-line arguments (if any are required) to generate the proper files and source code. For example, the command to invoke the IDL compiler included with Sun's Java IDL product is this:

```
idltojava -fno-cpp -fclient -fserver StockMarket.idl
```

In this case, the IDL compiler is named `idltojava`. The `-fno-cpp` switch instructs the IDL compiler to not invoke the C preprocessor before compiling the file. The `-fclient` and `-fserver` switches instruct the IDL compiler to generate client stubs and server skeletons, respectively. For now, you could get by without the `-fclient` switch because you'll only be implementing the server, but because you'll want the client stubs later, it will save time to generate them now.

The command to invoke the IDL compiler included in Visigenic's VisiBroker/C++ for Windows 95 is as follows:

```
orbeline -h h StockMarket.idl
```

Here, the IDL compiler, named `orbeline`, generates client stubs and server skeletons for the `StockMarket.idl` file. The `-c cpp` switch instructs the compiler to use the `.cpp` filename extension for C++ source files; similarly, `-h h` tells the compiler to use the `.h` extension for header files. You can, of course, substitute your favorite filename extensions in place of these.

TIP

> As with any utility run from the command line, before you can run the IDL compiler, you might have to set the PATH variable in your system's environment to include the directory where the IDL compiler resides. Generally, your CORBA product's documentation will tell you how to set the PATH variable to include the proper directories.

Client Stubs and Server Skeletons

When the IDL compiler is invoked, it generates code that conforms to the language mapping used by that particular product. The IDL compiler will generate a number of files—some of them helper classes, some of them client stub classes, and some of them server skeleton classes.

NOTE

> Recall from Day 2 that *client stubs* for an interface are pieces of code compiled with client applications that use that interface. These stubs do nothing more than tell the client's ORB to marshal and unmarshal outgoing and incoming parameters. Similarly, *server skeletons* are

> snippets of code that create the server framework. These skeletons pass
> incoming parameters to the implementation code—written by you, the
> developer—and pass outgoing parameters back to the client.

The names of the files generated by the IDL compiler are dependent on the language mapping used and sometimes on command-line arguments passed to the IDL compiler. (For example, some IDL compilers accept switches that specify prefixes and suffixes to be added to the class names.) The contents of these files will remain the same, for the most part, regardless of the IDL compiler used (assuming the products conform to the standard language mappings). For example, the output of the IDL compiler in IONA's Orbix/C++ will be roughly the same as the output of Visigenic's VisiBroker/C++ IDL compiler. Similarly, the corresponding Java products will output nearly the same source code.

NOTE

> Strictly speaking, the term "IDL compiler" is a misnomer. Whereas a
> compiler generally converts source code to object code, the IDL
> compiler is more of a translator: It converts IDL source code to C++
> source code, or Java source code, and so on. The generated code, along
> with the implementations that you provide, are then compiled by the
> C++ compiler, or Java compiler, and so on.

4

Implementing the Server Interfaces

After you have successfully used the IDL compiler to generate server skeletons and client stubs for your application, you are ready to implement the server interfaces. The IDL compiler generates a number of files; for each IDL `interface`, the compiler will generate a source file and header file for the client stub and a source file and header file for the server skeleton, resulting in four files per `interface`. (This is for an IDL compiler targeting C++; an IDL compiler targeting Java will, of course, not generate header files.) Additionally, the IDL compiler can create separate directories for IDL `modules`; it can also create additional files for helper classes. Also, most IDL compilers allow you to specify the suffix to use for client stubs and server skeletons. For example, the client stub files can be named `StockMarket_c.h` and `StockMarket_c.cpp`, or `StockMarket_st.h` and `StockMarket_st.cpp`. Refer to your IDL compiler's documentation to determine what files it produces, what filenames it uses, and how to change the default filename suffixes.

To keep the example as simple as possible, Java is used as the implementation language. Java was chosen for this example because of its relative simplicity, particularly when developing CORBA applications. Of all the languages commonly used for CORBA application development, Java probably gets in the way of the developer the least, making it the best suited for an introductory example. Most of the remainder of this book will use C++ for example code, with the exception of the Java-specific Chapters 13 and 14.

Using Server Skeletons

The server skeleton, as you have learned, provides a framework upon which to build the server implementation. In the case of C++, a server skeleton is a set of classes that provides pure virtual methods (methods with no implementations) or methods that delegate to methods in another class (the tie class discussed previously). You, the developer, provide the implementation for these methods. In the case of Java, a server skeleton combines a set of helper classes with an interface, for which you, again, provide the implementation.

Assuming you use Sun's Java IDL compiler to produce the server skeletons for your application, you will see that the compiler produced a directory called StockMarket (corresponding to the name of the IDL module defined in StockMarket.idl). Within this directory are a number of files containing client stub and server skeleton definitions:

```
StockSymbolHelper.java
StockSymbolListHolder.java
StockSymbolListHelper.java
StockServer.java
StockServerHolder.java
StockServerHelper.java
_StockServerStub.java
_StockServerImplBase.java
```

At this point, your only concern is with the server skeleton portion of these files. In particular, note that the Java interface describing the StockServer services is contained in the StockServer.java file. Its contents appear in Listing 4.2. The StockServerImplBase.java file contains a helper class from which you'll derive your server implementation class; you need not concern yourself with its contents because it provides functionality that works under the hood.

Listing 4.2. StockServer.java.

```
 1: /*
 2:  * File: ./StockMarket/StockServer.java
 3:  * From: StockMarket.idl
 4:  * Date: Mon Jul 21 16:12:26 1997
 5:  *   By: D:\BIN\DEVEL\JAVA\JAVAIDL\BIN\IDLTOJ~1.EXE JavaIDL
 6:  *   Thu Feb 27 11:22:49 1997
 7:  */
 8:
 9: package StockMarket;
10: public interface StockServer
11:     extends org.omg.CORBA.Object {
12:     float getStockValue(String symbol)
13: ;
14:     String[] getStockSymbols()
15: ;
16: }
```

Examining Listing 4.2, you see that the StockServer interface is placed in the StockMarket package. Furthermore, you can see that this interface extends the org.omg.CORBA.Object interface. All CORBA object interfaces extend this interface, but you need not concern yourself with this interface's contents either. Finally, you can see that the StockServer interface contains two methods that correspond to the IDL methods in StockServer.idl. Note, however, that the IDL types have been mapped to their Java counterparts: StockSymbol, which was typedef'ed as an IDL string, maps to a Java String; StockSymbolList, which was a sequence of StockSymbols, is mapped to a Java array of Strings. The IDL float, not surprisingly, is mapped to a Java float.

Writing the Implementation

The implementation for the StockServer is straightforward. This section walks you through the implementation (the example uses the class name StockServerImpl, but you can name the implementation class anything you want) line by line and explains what is happening at every step of the way.

Listing 4.3. StockServerImpl.java.

```
 1: // StockServerImpl.java
 2:
 3: package StockMarket;
 4:
 5: import java.util.Vector;
 6:
 7: import org.omg.CORBA.ORB;
 8: import org.omg.CosNaming.NameComponent;
 9: import org.omg.CosNaming.NamingContext;
10: import org.omg.CosNaming.NamingContextHelper;
11:
12: // StockServerImpl implements the StockServer IDL interface.
13: public class StockServerImpl extends _StockServerImplBase implements
14:         StockServer {
15:
16:     // Stock symbols and their respective values.
17:     private Vector myStockSymbols;
18:     private Vector myStockValues;
19:
20:     // Characters from which StockSymbol names are built.
21:     private static char ourCharacters[] = { 'A', 'B', 'C', 'D', 'E', 'F',
22:             'G', 'H', 'I', 'J', 'K', 'L', 'M', 'N', 'O', 'P', 'Q', 'R',
23:             'S', 'T', 'U', 'V', 'W', 'X', 'Y', 'Z' };
24:
25:     // Path name for StockServer objects.
26:     private static String ourPathName = "StockServer";
27:
28:     // Create a new StockServerImpl.
29:     public StockServerImpl() {
30:
31:         myStockSymbols = new Vector();
```

continues

4

Listing 4.3. continued

```
32:              myStockValues = new Vector();
33:
34:              // Initialize the symbols and values with some random values.
35:              for (int i = 0; i < 10; i++) {
36:
37:                  // Generate a string of four random characters.
38:                  StringBuffer stockSymbol = new StringBuffer("    ");
39:                  for (int j = 0; j < 4; j++) {
40:
41:                      stockSymbol.setCharAt(j, ourCharacters[(int)(Math.random()
42:                              * 26f)]);
43:                  }
44:
45:                  myStockSymbols.addElement(stockSymbol.toString());
46:
47:                  // Give the stock a value between 0 and 100. In this example,
48:                  // the stock will retain this value for the duration of the
49:                  // application.
50:                  myStockValues.addElement(new Float(Math.random() * 100f));
51:              }
52:
53:              // Print out the stock symbols generated above.
54:              System.out.println("Generated stock symbols:");
55:              for (int i = 0; i < 10; i++) {
56:                  System.out.println("  " + myStockSymbols.elementAt(i) + " " +
57:                          myStockValues.elementAt(i));
58:              }
59:              System.out.println();
60:          }
61:
62:          // Return the current value for the given StockSymbol.
63:          public float getStockValue(String symbol) {
64:
65:              // Try to find the given symbol.
66:              int stockIndex = myStockSymbols.indexOf(symbol);
67:              if (stockIndex != -1) {
68:
69:                  // Symbol found; return its value.
70:                  return ((Float)myStockValues.elementAt(stockIndex)).
71:                          floatValue();
72:              } else {
73:
74:                  // Symbol was not found.
75:                  return 0f;
76:              }
77:          }
78:
79:          // Return a sequence of all StockSymbols known by this StockServer.
80:          public String[] getStockSymbols() {
81:
82:              String[] symbols = new String[myStockSymbols.size()];
83:              myStockSymbols.copyInto(symbols);
84:
85:              return symbols;
```

```
 86:     }
 87:
 88:     // Create and initialize a StockServer object.
 89:     public static void main(String args[]) {
 90:
 91:         try {
 92:
 93:             // Initialize the ORB.
 94:             ORB orb = ORB.init(args, null);
 95:
 96:             // Create a StockServerImpl object and register it with the
 97:             // ORB.
 98:             StockServerImpl stockServer = new StockServerImpl();
 99:             orb.connect(stockServer);
100:
101:             // Get the root naming context.
102:             org.omg.CORBA.Object obj = orb.
103:                     resolve_initial_references("NameService");
104:             NamingContext namingContext = NamingContextHelper.narrow(obj);
105:
106:             // Bind the StockServer object reference in the naming
107:             // context.
108:             NameComponent nameComponent = new NameComponent(ourPathName,
109:                     "");
110:             NameComponent path[] = { nameComponent };
111:             namingContext.rebind(path, stockServer);
112:
113:             // Wait for invocations from clients.
114:             java.lang.Object waitOnMe = new java.lang.Object();
115:             synchronized (waitOnMe) {
116:                 waitOnMe.wait();
117:             }
118:         } catch (Exception ex) {
119:             System.err.println("Couldn't bind StockServer: " + ex.
120:                     getMessage());
121:         }
122:     }
123: }
```

The entire listing for StockServerImpl.java appears in Listing 4.3; the remainder of this section will walk you through the file step by step, so that you can see the details of what's going on.

```
package StockMarket;
```

Because the StockServer interface is part of the StockMarket module, the IDL compiler places the Java class and interface definitions into the StockMarket package. For convenience, StockServerImpl is placed into this package as well. (If you're not familiar with Java or with packages, you can safely ignore this bit of code for now.)

```
import java.util.Vector;
```

StockServerImpl will make use of the Vector class. This import should look familiar to Java developers already. If you're not familiar with Java, the import statement behaves much like the #include preprocessor directive in C++; the java.util.Vector class is a container class that behaves as a growable array of elements.

```
import org.omg.CORBA.ORB;
import org.omg.CosNaming.NameComponent;
import org.omg.CosNaming.NamingContext;
import org.omg.CosNaming.NamingContextHelper;
```

The classes being imported here are commonly used in CORBA applications. The first, of course, is the class that provides the ORB functionality; the other classes are related to the CORBA Naming Service, which you'll explore further on Day 12.

```
// StockServerImpl implements the StockServer IDL interface.
public class StockServerImpl extends _StockServerImplBase implements
        StockServer {
```

Given the StockServer IDL interface, the IDL compiler generates a class called StockServerImplBase and an interface called StockServer. To implement the StockServer IDL interface, your StockServerImpl class must extend _StockServerImplBase and implement StockServer, which is exactly what is declared here:

```
// Stock symbols and their respective values.
private Vector myStockSymbols;
private Vector myStockValues;
```

StockServerImpl uses Vectors to store the stock symbols and their values.

```
// Characters from which StockSymbol names are built.
private static char ourCharacters[] = { 'A', 'B', 'C', 'D', 'E', 'F',
'G', 'H', 'I', 'J', 'K', 'L', 'M', 'N', 'O', 'P', 'Q', 'R',
'S', 'T', 'U', 'V', 'W', 'X', 'Y', 'Z' };
```

The ourCharacters array contains the set of characters from which stock symbols are built.

```
// Path name for StockServer objects.
private static String ourPathName = "StockServer";
```

The ourPathName variable stores the pathname by which this StockServer object can be located in the Naming Service. This can be any name, but for the purposes of this example, StockServer works well.

```
// Create a new StockServerImpl.
public StockServerImpl() {
myStockSymbols = new Vector();
myStockValues = new Vector();
```

Although constructors aren't a part of an IDL interface, the class implementing that interface will still have constructors so that the server can create the implementation objects. StockServerImpl has only a default constructor, but like any other class, a class that implements an IDL interface can have any number of constructors.

This part of the constructor creates Vectors to hold the stock symbols and their respective values.

```
// Initialize the symbols and values with some random values.
for (int i = 0; i < 10; i++) {
```

Rather arbitrarily, the StockServerImpl creates ten stock symbols.

```
// Generate a string of four random characters.
StringBuffer stockSymbol = new StringBuffer("    ");
for (int j = 0; j < 4; j++) {
    stockSymbol.setCharAt(j, ourCharacters[(int)(Math.random()
            * 26f)]);
}
myStockSymbols.addElement(stockSymbol.toString());
```

For each stock symbol, the StockServerImpl creates a string of four random characters (chosen from the preceding ourCharacters array). The four-character length, like the number of symbols, was chosen arbitrarily. For the sake of simplicity, no checks are made for duplicate strings.

```
// Give the stock a value between 0 and 100. In this example,
// the stock will retain this value for the duration of the
/ application.
myStockValues.addElement(new Float(Math.random() * 100f));
}
```

Here, a random value between 0 and 100 is given to each stock symbol. In this example, the stock will retain the assigned value for as long as the StockServerImpl runs.

```
// Print out the stock symbols generated above.
System.out.println("Generated stock symbols:");
for (int i = 0; i < 10; i++) {
    System.out.println("   " + myStockSymbols.elementAt(i) + " " +
            myStockValues.elementAt(i));
}
 System.out.println();
}
```

Finally, the constructor prints out the stock symbols and their values.

```
// Return the current value for the given StockSymbol.
public float getStockValue(String symbol) {

    // Try to find the given symbol.
    int stockIndex = myStockSymbols.indexOf(symbol);
    if (stockIndex != -1) {

        // Symbol found; return its value.
        return ((Float)myStockValues.elementAt(stockIndex)).
                floatValue();
    } else {

        // Symbol was not found.
        return 0f;
    }
}
```

The getStockValue() method takes a String, attempts to find a match in the myStockSymbols data member, and returns the value for the stock symbol (if found). If the stock symbol is not found, a zero value is returned.

> **NOTE**
>
> Naturally, the getStockValue() method is an excellent candidate to raise an exception—if an invalid stock symbol were passed to the method, it could raise (for example) an InvalidStockSymbolException rather than return zero, as it currently does. This is an exercise at the end of the chapter.

```
// Return a sequence of all StockSymbols known by this StockServer.
public String[] getStockSymbols() {

    String[] symbols = new String[myStockSymbols.size()];
    myStockSymbols.copyInto(symbols);

    return symbols;
}
```

The getStockSymbols() method simply creates an array of Strings, copies the stock symbols (contained in myStockSymbols) into the array, and returns the array.

```
// Create and initialize a StockServer object.
public static void main(String args[]) {
```

The main() method in StockServerImpl creates a StockServerImpl object, binds that object to a naming context, and then waits for clients to call methods on that object.

```
try {
```

Because the methods that main() will later call might throw exceptions, those calls are wrapped in a try ... catch block.

```
// Initialize the ORB.
ORB orb = ORB.init(args, null);
```

Before doing anything with the ORB, the server application must first initialize the ORB.

```
// Create a StockServerImpl object and register it with the
// ORB.
StockServerImpl stockServer = new StockServerImpl();
orb.connect(stockServer);
```

Here a new StockServerImpl object is created and registered with the ORB.

```
// Get the root naming context.
org.omg.CORBA.Object obj = orb.
        resolve_initial_references("NameService");
NamingContext namingContext = NamingContextHelper.narrow(obj);
```

Now for a little black magic. The CORBA Naming Service is a service that allows CORBA objects to register by name and subsequently be located, using that name, by other CORBA objects. As mentioned before, use of the Naming Service will be described in detail on Day 12, but the sample client application in this chapter will still need to be able to locate a server; therefore the Naming Service is introduced here, though somewhat prematurely. Consequently, in this chapter, don't worry if you don't understand all the details of the Naming Service or how it is used.

In order for clients to connect to the StockServerImpl, they must have some way of locating the service on the network. One way to accomplish this is through the CORBA Naming Service. Here, a NamingContext object is located by resolving a reference to an object named NameService.

```
// Bind the StockServer object reference in the naming
// context.
NameComponent nameComponent = new NameComponent(ourPathName,
        "");
NameComponent path[] = { nameComponent };
namingContext.rebind(path, stockServer);
```

Now the NamingContext object is asked to bind the StockServerImpl object to the pathname defined earlier (StockServer). Clients can now query the Naming Service for an object by this name; the Naming Service will return a reference to this StockServerImpl object.

```
// Wait for invocations from clients.
java.lang.Object waitOnMe = new java.lang.Object();
synchronized (waitOnMe) {
    waitOnMe.wait();
}
```

Because the StockServerImpl object is now registered with the Naming Service, the only thing left to do is to wait for clients to invoke methods on the object. Because the actual handling of these method invocations occurs in a separate thread, the main() thread simply needs to wait indefinitely.

```
    } catch (Exception ex) {
        System.err.println("Couldn't bind StockServer: " + ex.
            getMessage());
    }
  }
}
```

If any exceptions are thrown by any of the methods called, they are caught and handled here.

Compiling and Running the Server

Now you're ready to compile and run the server. Compiling the server application is simple. If you're using an integrated development environment, use that tool's "build" command (or equivalent) to build the application. If you're using the JDK from the command line, change directories to the directory where `StockMarket.idl` is located (there should also be a directory called `StockMarket` contained in this directory). Then issue the command

```
javac StockMarket\StockServerImpl.java
```

(You might have to substitute the appropriate directory separator for your platform in the preceding command.) This will compile the server implementation and all the source files it depends on.

TIP

> Before compiling the server, make sure that your `CLASSPATH` contains the appropriate directory or file for the CORBA classes. For Sun's `JavaIDL` package, the file (directory where `JavaIDL` is installed) `/lib/classes.zip` will appear in the `CLASSPATH`. Consult your CORBA product's documentation to determine your `CLASSPATH` setting.

Assuming that the server application compiled correctly, you're about ready to run the server. Before you do that, though, you need to run the Name Server. (Recall that the client application uses the CORBA Naming Service to locate the server application; the Name Server provides the mechanism that makes this possible.)

The exact method for running the Name Server varies from product to product, but the end result is the same. For Sun's `JavaIDL`, simply running `nameserv` will bring up the Name Server.

When the Name Server is running, you're ready to run the server. You can invoke the server with the command

```
java StockMarket.StockServerImpl
```

For the sake of simplicity, you'll want to run the Name Server and your server application on the same machine for now. If everything works correctly, you will see output similar to Listing 4.4. The stock symbols and their values will, of course, vary, but you will see output resembling Listing 4.4 without any exception messages following the output.

Listing 4.4. Sample `StockServer` output.

```
 1: Generated stock symbols:
 2:    PTLF 72.00064
 3:    SWPK 37.671585
 4:    CHHL 78.37782
 5:    JTUX 75.715645
 6:    HUPB 41.85024
 7:    OHQR 14.932466
 8:    YOEX 64.3376
 9:    UIBP 75.80115
10:    SIPR 91.13683
11:    XSTD 16.010124
```

If you got this far, congratulations! You have successfully designed, implemented, and deployed a CORBA server application. After reveling in your success, feel free to terminate the application because you won't have a client to connect to it until the end of this chapter. Alternatively, you can leave the server running to save yourself the trouble of restarting it later (or just to impress and amaze your friends).

Building a CORBA Client

In the first half of this chapter, you were left hanging with a server that couldn't do much because there were no clients to connect to it. Now you'll remedy that unfortunate situation by implementing a client that will utilize the services provided by the server you built. Because you've already written and compiled the IDL interfaces (and implemented them, for that matter), implementing the client will be a much simpler process. Additionally, clients are often (though not always) simpler than servers by nature, so they are easier to implement in that regard as well.

Implementing the Client

As mentioned already, implementing the client is a straightforward process. There are only a handful of concepts involved: how to use client stubs in the client implementation, how to locate a server object, and how to use the interfaces of a server object after it has been located.

Using Client Stubs

When you compiled StockServer.idl, the IDL compiler generated client stubs as well as server skeletons. Because client stubs aren't used for server implementations, you ignored the stubs for the time being. Now, it's time to use them. If you're curious, open the _StockServerStub.java file and have a look at it. You'll see a fair amount of cryptic code along with two familiar methods:

```
public float getStockValue(String symbol) {
    ...
}
public String[] getStockSymbols() {
    ...
}
```

The implementations for these methods, as discussed before, marshal the parameters through the ORB to the remote object and then marshal the return value back to the client. (This is what all that cryptic-looking code is doing.)

You really needn't concern yourself with the contents of _StockServerStub.java; all you need to know is that this file contains the client stub for the StockServer interface. The Java compiler is smart enough to compile this file automatically, but if you were implementing a client in C++, you'd have to be sure to link the client stub object with the rest of the client application.

The other thing to know about the client stub is that it specifies the actual interfaces for the server object. In other words, you can see in the preceding example that the getStockValue() method takes a Java String as a parameter and returns a Java float. Similarly, getStockSymbols() takes no parameters and returns a Java array of Strings.

Locating a Server Object

Just as a server application is practically useless if it cannot make its location known, a client application cannot do useful work if it cannot locate services to use. This is where the CORBA Naming Service steps in again. After a server registers itself with the Name Server, clients can locate that server object through the Name Server, bind to that server object, and subsequently call methods on the server object. Again, do not be concerned if there are details of the Naming Service which escape you, as it will be discussed in greater detail on Day 12.

In the StockMarketClient, binding to the server object takes place in the connect() method, as shown in Listing 4.5. This method first binds to the Name Server by looking for an object with the name NameService. Upon successfully locating a Name Server, the client proceeds to bind to an object with the name StockServer, which incidentally is the same name you registered the StockServerImpl under (actually, the names must be the same if the example is to work successfully). After this object is bound, the client is ready to do some work.

Listing 4.5. Binding to the StockServer server.

```
 1: // Connect to the StockServer.
 2: protected void connect() {
 3:
 4:     try {
 5:
 6:         // Get the root naming context.
 7:         org.omg.CORBA.Object obj = ourORB.
 8:                 resolve_initial_references("NameService");
 9:         NamingContext namingContext = NamingContextHelper.narrow(obj);
10:
11:         // Attempt to locate a StockServer object in the naming context.
12:         NameComponent nameComponent = new NameComponent("StockServer",
13:                 "");
14:         NameComponent path[] = { nameComponent };
15:         myStockServer = StockServerHelper.narrow(namingContext.
16:                 resolve(path));
17:     } catch (Exception ex) {
18:         System.err.println("Couldn't resolve StockServer: " + ex);
19:         myStockServer = null;
20:         return;
21:     }
22:
23:     System.out.println("Succesfully bound to a StockServer.");
24: }
```

4

Using Server Object Interfaces

Listing 4.6 shows an example of how the server object interfaces are used, after the client has bound the server object. As you might expect, the client simply calls the server methods as it sees fit. Again, you can refer to the client stub (_StockServerStub.java) or better yet, to the StockServer interface in StockServer.idl to see the method signatures for the StockServer. The usage of these methods is clear-cut, as illustrated in Listing 4.6.

Listing 4.6. Using the StockServer services.

```
 1: // Do some cool things with the StockServer.
 2: protected void doSomething() {
 3:
 4:     try {
 5:
 6:         // Get the valid stock symbols from the StockServer.
 7:         String[] stockSymbols = myStockServer.getStockSymbols();
 8:
 9:         // Display the stock symbols and their values.
10:         for (int i = 0; i < stockSymbols.length; i++) {
11:             System.out.println(stockSymbols[i] + " " +
12:                     myStockServer.getStockValue(stockSymbols[i]));
13:         }
14:     } catch (org.omg.CORBA.SystemException ex) {
15:         System.err.println("Fatal error: " + ex);
16:     }
17: }
```

In Listing 4.6, the StockServer is first asked, through a call to getStockSymbols(), for a list of all stock symbols recognized by the server. The client then iterates through the list of stock symbols and queries the server, using getStockValue(), for the value of each stock. Each stock symbol and its respective value are printed to standard output.

Compiling and Running the Client

The entire listing for StockMarketClient.java appears in Listing 4.7. Note that most of the work for the client is done in the connect() and doSomething() methods, which you've already looked at.

Listing 4.7. StockMarketClient.java.

```
 1: // StockMarketClient.java
 2:
 3: package StockMarket;
 4:
 5: import org.omg.CORBA.ORB;
 6: import org.omg.CosNaming.NameComponent;
```

continues

Listing 4.7. continued

```
 7: import org.omg.CosNaming.NamingContext;
 8: import org.omg.CosNaming.NamingContextHelper;
 9:
10: // StockMarketClient is a simple client of a StockServer.
11: public class StockMarketClient {
12:
13:     // Create a new StockMarketClient.
14:     StockMarketClient() {
15:
16:     }
17:
18:     // Run the StockMarketClient.
19:     public void run() {
20:
21:         connect();
22:
23:         if (myStockServer != null) {
24:             doSomething();
25:         }
26:     }
27:
28:     // Connect to the StockServer.
29:     protected void connect() {
30:
31:         try {
32:
33:             // Get the root naming context.
34:             org.omg.CORBA.Object obj = ourORB.
35:                     resolve_initial_references("NameService");
36:             NamingContext namingContext = NamingContextHelper.narrow(obj);
37:
38:             // Attempt to locate a StockServer object in the naming
39:             // context.
40:             NameComponent nameComponent = new NameComponent("StockServer",
41:                     "");
42:             NameComponent path[] = { nameComponent };
43:             myStockServer = StockServerHelper.narrow(namingContext.
44:                     resolve(path));
45:         } catch (Exception ex) {
46:             System.err.println("Couldn't resolve StockServer: " + ex);
47:             myStockServer = null;
48:             return;
49:         }
50:
51:         System.out.println("Succesfully bound to a StockServer.");
52:     }
53:
54:     // Do some cool things with the StockServer.
55:     protected void doSomething() {
56:
57:         try {
58:
59:             // Get the valid stock symbols from the StockServer.
60:             String[] stockSymbols = myStockServer.getStockSymbols();
```

```
61:
62:                    // Display the stock symbols and their values.
63:                    for (int i = 0; i < stockSymbols.length; i++) {
64:                        System.out.println(stockSymbols[i] + " " +
65:                                myStockServer.getStockValue(stockSymbols[i]));
66:                    }
67:                } catch (org.omg.CORBA.SystemException ex) {
68:                    System.err.println("Fatal error: " + ex);
69:                }
70:        }
71:
72:        // Start up a StockMarketClient.
73:        public static void main(String args[]) {
74:
75:            // Initialize the ORB.
76:            ourORB = ORB.init(args, null);
77:
78:            StockMarketClient stockClient = new StockMarketClient();
79:
80:            stockClient.run();
81:
82:            // This simply waits forever so that the DOS window doesn't
83:            // disappear (for developers using Windows IDEs).
84:            while (true)
85:                ;
86:        }
87:
88:        // My ORB.
89:        public static ORB ourORB;
90:
91:        // My StockServer.
92:        private StockServer myStockServer;
93: }
```

4

Compiling the client application is an uncomplicated process. Like the server, the client can be compiled simply with the command

```
javac StockMarket\StockMarketClient.java
```

Again, ensure you are in the proper directory when compiling the client. You should be in the same directory as the one in which you compiled the server.

Assuming the client application compiled successfully, you're just about ready to run the application. First, start the Name Service and the StockServer application (as you did previously), if they aren't running already. Then to execute the client application, type the command

```
java StockMarket.StockMarketClient
```

If the client runs successfully, you will see output similar to Listing 4.8.

Listing 4.8. `StockMarketClient` **output.**

```
 1: Succesfully bound to a StockServer.
 2: PTLF 72.00064
 3: SWPK 37.671585
 4: CHHL 78.37782
 5: JTUX 75.715645
 6: HUPB 41.85024
 7: OHQR 14.932466
 8: YOEX 64.3376
 9: UIBP 75.80115
10: SIPR 91.13683
11: XSTD 16.010124
```

The stock symbols and their values will appear exactly as they appear in the server output.

Summary

In this chapter you started out by defining the interfaces for a CORBA server, using IDL. You then implemented the server using the inheritance approach (as opposed to the delegation approach) and learned a little bit about using the CORBA Naming Service along the way. You then created a simple client application that used the services provided by the StockServer application. In the process, you learned how to use the Naming Service to locate the StockServer object and how the client stubs fit into the client application. Finally, you ran the CORBA server and client together, creating what might be your very first distributed CORBA application. Congratulations! This is no small feat.

What Comes Next?

This chapter concludes the first section of this book, which has dealt with basic CORBA architecture and methodology. In the next section of the book, spanning Days 5 through 9, you'll design and build a larger, more complex CORBA application, starting with some basic functionality and adding more capabilities to the application in subsequent chapters. You'll apply the same techniques you've already learned; the only difference will be that you'll deal with more complex IDL and thus more complex servers and clients. You currently have the basic knowledge required to build an entire CORBA application; the next days will give you the opportunity to practice applying that knowledge to a more sophisticated system.

Q&A

Q I'm a C++ programmer, and I'm not sure I understand all the Java syntax.

A For the most part, Java syntax is very similar to C++, but Java introduces some constructs of its own. Don't be overly concerned if you don't understand certain aspects of the language, as long as you can grasp the concepts of what the code is doing.

Q If I implement my server interfaces using the inheritance approach and later rewrite the server to use the delegation approach, will I have to rewrite my client(s) as well?

A Regardless of the approach used to implement the server, the client code remains the same. Therefore, should you ever need to rewrite a server to use a different approach, rest assured that no changes will have to be made to the clients.

Q How can the classes that implement IDL interfaces have constructors when IDL doesn't specify any?

A IDL only specifies *public* interfaces—that is, methods that can be used by other objects anywhere else on the network. However, the class that implements an IDL interface can also provide additional methods, although such methods won't be visible anywhere outside the object's process space. Such methods can be useful *within* the server application, though; constructors are an example of this. (Server objects need to be created somehow.) So feel free to include additional methods (public, protected, and private) in your server implementations if it makes sense to do so.

Workshop

The following section will help you test your comprehension of the material presented in this chapter and put what you've learned into practice. You'll find the answers to the quiz and exercises in Appendix A.

Quiz

1. What is the purpose of server skeletons and client stubs?
2. Why does the server need to register the implementation object with the CORBA Naming Service?
3. Why do the client and server need to catch exceptions, especially when none are raised by the IDL operations you defined?

Exercises

1. It was pointed out in the StockMarket example that it would be a good idea to raise an exception in the getStockValue() method if an invalid StockSymbol was passed in. Modify StockMarket.idl so that the method can raise an InvalidStockSymbolException. (You'll also need to add a definition for this exception.)

2. In the StockMarket example, an implementation was provided that used the delegation approach. Implement the StockServer to use the inheritance approach. (Extra credit: Also include the exception-raising mechanism from the first exercise.)

Day 5

Designing the System: A Crash Course in Object-Oriented Analysis and Design

With a knowledge of CORBA basics—such as the concept of the Object Request Broker (ORB) and the Interface Definition Language (IDL)—along with an understanding of the IDL language, you are ready to develop and deploy CORBA-based applications. You've already gained firsthand experience implementing a simple CORBA server and client. Now you'll design, implement, and enhance a more sophisticated CORBA application. To help you see what's ahead, the following road map is provided:

☐ Today you'll design the sample system, a scaled-down banking application. Because CORBA is an object-oriented architecture, this chapter will introduce you to object-oriented analysis and design concepts while working through the design of the system.

☐ On Day 6, you'll map the system design into an IDL specification. You'll see how system objects map to IDL classes, how partitions map to IDL modules, and other aspects of the interface definition process. You'll also consider various CORBAservices and CORBAfacilities to see how they might fit into your system design. You'll then implement the basic capabilities of the banking application. You'll use the IDL definitions you created as a starting point, from which you'll write separate implementations for the server and client.

☐ On Day 7, you'll extend the basic capabilities of the application to include exception handling. Exception handling provides error-checking capability, making the application implementation more robust. Changes to the application begin in the IDL code and then propagate through the implementation code.

☐ On Day 8, the application will gain complexity as you add another CORBA client to the mix: the Automated Teller Machine (ATM) client. CORBA applications usually include more than one client component, so this chapter gives you some exposure to managing multiple clients in a CORBA application.

☐ On Day 9, you'll wrap up the banking application example with one final enhancement: the capability to "push" update information from the server to the client(s), using client callbacks.

What Is Object-Oriented Analysis and Design?

Although object-oriented technologies have existed for quite some time, the phrase "object-oriented" has gained much popularity (along with buzzword status) in recent years. Indeed, the phrase is often bandied about with reckless abandon, which serves to obscure its real meaning. To further confuse matters, it is used to describe everything from development environments to programming languages to databases.

So what does the term *object-oriented* really mean? The term seems to be thrown about indiscriminately; anything from programming languages to drawing tools might be labeled as "object-oriented." For the purposes of this book, you will be interested primarily in three uses of object-oriented methodology: object-oriented analysis (OOA), which deals with the design requirements and overall architecture of a system; object-oriented design (OOD), which translates a system architecture into programming constructs (such as interfaces, classes, and method descriptions); and object-oriented programming (OOP), which implements these programming constructs. So, for your purposes, *object-oriented* can be taken to mean the various methodologies, described briefly herein, used to design and implement software. This chapter deals primarily with object-oriented analysis. On Day 6 you'll work with object-oriented design; when implementing system functionality, you'll be using object-oriented programming techniques.

Although this book introduces you to object-oriented analysis, design, and programming concepts, it does not attempt to cover these topics in detail. A number of books already written on these subjects provide a definitive introduction to and explanation of these concepts. Time spent familiarizing yourself with these concepts would be time well spent.

Introducing the Unified Modeling Language (UML)

The Unified Modeling Language (UML) is a powerful tool for expressing object-oriented designs. Developed by Rational Software Corporation, UML is an evolution of previous modeling languages and techniques. A description of UML, along with a set of links to UML-related resources, appears on Rational's Web site at `http://www.rational.com/uml/index.html`.

History

UML is an evolution of previous modeling languages and techniques. Prior to UML, many object-oriented methodologies existed. Of these, the three major methodologies included Grady Booch's Booch 1993 method, Jim Rumbaugh's Object Modeling Technique (OMT) method, and Ivar Jacobson's Object-Oriented Software Engineering (OOSE) method. In October 1994, Booch and Rumbaugh joined forces to unify their methods, resulting in what was called the Unified Method 0.8 in October 1995. Around that time they were joined by Jacobson, merging the OOSE method with Booch and Rumbaugh's work to form UML 0.9 in June 1996. The UML Partners consortium—consisting of companies such as Digital, Hewlett-Packard, IBM, Microsoft, Oracle, Rational, and Unisys—was then formed to refine UML even further, resulting in UML 1.0 in January 1997. The UML 1.0 documents were submitted for standardization to the Object Management Group (OMG)—the organization responsible for the specification of CORBA standards.

Terminology and Symbols

The Unified Modeling Language is a highly visual language; in addition to words and text, it also consists (and in fact primarily consists) of graphs and symbols. Perhaps one of the most important diagrams you will encounter in object-oriented analysis and design is the class diagram, which in turn consists of notations for classes, associations, and inheritance (among other things, but these are the three aspects you'll study here).

The Class Diagram

One important element of the Unified Modeling Language (or any modeling language, for that matter) is the *class diagram*. The class diagram, sometimes called (incorrectly) an object diagram or object model, describes classes and their relationships to other classes in the system. The class diagram specifies only static relationships—how classes are related to each other—and not dynamic relationships, such as when objects are created or invoke services of other objects.

5

A *class diagram* graphically depicts the relationships between classes in a system. Depending on the level of the diagram's scope, it may also describe the attributes and operations provided by each class.

The class diagram is one of the most important elements of an object-oriented methodology. It is essential to the understanding of a complex system architecture and provides a great deal of insight into a system design.

Classes

Naturally, the existence of the class diagram implies the existence of the class. As you might expect, the class in UML is analogous to a class in an object-oriented programming language such as Java or C++. A class has a name, zero or more attributes, and zero or more operations. Think of attributes as member data and operations as member functions or methods. In a class diagram, a class description can take on one of the forms shown in Figure 5.1.

Figure 5.1.

UML class descriptions.

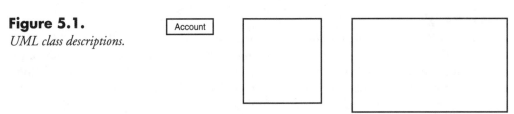

Figure 5.1 depicts three examples for the representation of a class. In the first example, only the class name is visible. This form is suitable for a class diagram that focuses primarily on the relationships between classes. For example, an extremely complex class diagram benefits from this type of simplification, especially if the diagram is only to be used to provide an overview of an entire system. The second example shows the class name, its attributes, and its operations, but attributes and operations are listed by name only—types and parameters are omitted. The third example shows a fully embellished class description, with class name, attributes and their types, and operations with their parameters and return types. These types of class descriptions are useful when detailed information about a system and its classes is required.

A class description can also provide visibility modifiers for its attributes and operations. The visibility modifier, which is optional, immediately precedes the attribute or operation that it describes. (When no visibility modifier is given, the attribute or method is usually assumed to be public.) A description of each of these modifiers appears in Table 5.1.

Table 5.1   UML Visibility Modifiers.

Symbol	Description	Meaning
+	Public attribute/operation	Public attributes and operations of a class are available to that class and to any other class.
#	Protected attribute/operation	Protected attributes and operations of a class are available only to that class and its subclasses.
-	Private attribute/operation	Private attributes and operations of a class are available only to that class, excluding even subclasses.
/	Derived attribute	A derived attribute is an attribute that is dependent on another attribute. For example, although a person's age can be considered an attribute, it is dependent on the current date and the person's birth date. Derived attributes can also be public, protected, or private.
$	Class attribute/operation	A class attribute or operation can be accessed without an instance of the class. Class attributes and operations are analogous to static class members in C++ or Java. Class attributes and operations can also be public, protected, or private.

Associations

A class typically does not exist and act within a vacuum; generally it will interact with other classes as well. Thus, it can be said that a class has relationships to other classes. UML refers to these relationships as associations. A class has an *association* with another class if it uses services of that class in some way. Optionally, the association can be given a name; additionally, the roles that each class plays in an association can be given names as well. Figure 5.2 illustrates the notation for an association, which is indicated by a line drawn between two classes.

 NEW TERM An *association* between two classes means that the classes are somehow related. Typically this means that one of the classes uses services of the other or has a member which is an instance of the other class.

An association can also have *multiplicity,* meaning that a certain number of one class can be associated to a certain number of the other class. For example, Figure 5.2 indicates that a Customer can hold more than one Account. Furthermore, an Account can be held by more than one Customer (as is the case with joint Accounts). Finally, an Account can be owned by only one Bank. Essentially, there are three types of multiplicities in relationships:

☐ A *one-to-one* association is an association between exactly one of each type of object.

☐ A *one-to-many* (or, conversely, *many-to-one*) association is an association between exactly one of one type of object and zero or more of the other type.

☐ A *many-to-many* association is an association between zero or more of each type of object.

Figure 5.2.
UML class associations.

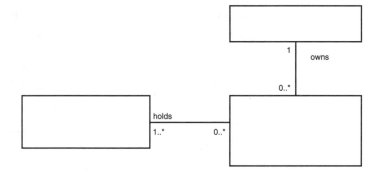

| NEW TERM | *Multiplicity* refers to the number of classes involved in an association. Examples of multiplicity are *one-to-one, one-to-many,* and *many-to-many.* |

Specifying multiplicity is optional; this information is sometimes omitted for the sake of clarity in high-level class diagrams. However, you need to specify multiplicities of associations before implementing your design, as the details of the implementation depend on this multiplicity information.

Inheritance

Inheritance is actually a special case of an association. It has the same meaning as you would expect in an object-oriented language; a class that inherits from (or derives from) another class (recall from Day 3 that this is referred to as the *superclass*) inherits the nonprivate attributes and methods of that superclass. Again recalling from Day 3, remember that the *derived class* can be substituted wherever its base class is required (as a parameter to a method call, for instance); this behavior is known as *polymorphism.*

In UML, inheritance is represented as an arrow drawn from the derived class to its base class. UML supports the notion of multiple inheritance as well; in this case, arrows are drawn from the derived class to each of its base classes. Examples of UML expressions of inheritance associations are illustrated in Figure 5.3.

Basic Methodology

Again, it is far beyond the scope of this book to discuss object-oriented analysis and design methodologies in depth. However, a good first step in the analysis phase is to identify the objects, or classes, that compose the system. Many objects in the system are easy to identify; one method is to first write a description of the system and its function. When the description is complete, review it and look for nouns. When you encounter a noun, chances are that it will represent an object in the system. For example, in the sentence "Customers hold accounts in a bank," potential object candidates are Customer, Account, and Bank. This process, sometimes called object discovery, is very useful in understanding the scope of a particular system.

Figure 5.3.

UML inheritance associations.

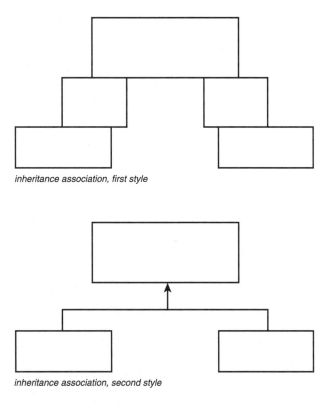

inheritance association, first style

inheritance association, second style

After the candidate objects have been identified, you determine the relationships between the classes. These relationships are often expressed in the form of verbs in the system description. In the preceding example, for instance, you see that Customers hold Accounts, suggesting a relationship between these two classes. Furthermore, you can see that Accounts are part of a Bank, although it is not clear precisely what the relationship is between an Account and a Bank. Associations between classes don't have to be named, although named associations often provide additional insight into the design of a system.

NOTE

> If you infer from this process that classes ought to be named with nouns and associations ought to be named with verbs, you are correct. This naming scheme is a generally accepted convention of object-oriented analysis. Another convention is to give singular names to classes, for example, Account rather than Accounts.

After the classes and their associations have been identified, you'll want to spend some time determining the attributes and operations within classes. This requires more thought than the first two steps, and chances are you won't get it right the first time. In fact, the entire process is an iterative one. While identifying relationships between classes, you might discover new classes, or while determining operations on objects, you might discover new associations or new classes. In fact, your design might change drastically from start to finish; this is a normal aspect of software design. Multiple iterations of this process help you create a robust design, and creating a solid design early on will help you avoid headaches later on in the development phase. (It is often observed that the later in the development process a change needs to be made, the more costly that change will be. Therefore, it is to your advantage to spend a good amount of time refining your design.)

UML Summary

UML is a very broad-reaching tool that encompasses not only the static design of a system (such as the class diagram) but also the dynamic design (including use cases, state transition diagrams, and other tools). Because this book can barely scratch the surface of UML and its functionality as a design tool, you should explore either the Rational Software Corporation Web site (provided at the beginning of this section) or one of several other sources for more information on UML.

The Bank Example

The next several chapters center around a single example—an electronic banking system. In this chapter, you'll use object-oriented analysis to define the objects in the system and create an application object model. In subsequent chapters, you'll implement the system's basic functionality and then implement additional capabilities and robustness. In the end, you'll have built a complex (although still trivial by enterprise application standards) CORBA application. Along the way, you'll discover some of the issues involved in building such a system.

The Bank application supports electronic banking. It allows for multiple banks, multiple accounts (checking and savings), multiple customers, opening and closing accounts, and the withdrawal, deposit, and transfer of funds between accounts. (More capabilities are added in later chapters, but the basic Bank application begins with this functionality.)

Defining System Requirements and Capabilities

The first step in designing any system is to determine what the system needs to do. Depending on the nature of the application, this process can involve meeting with customers and/or potential users of the system, conducting market research, or just providing a solution to a particular problem. Requirements often have to be refined or clarified later, so don't be surprised if you find yourself revisiting this step again.

For the Bank example, the capabilities of the basic system are defined as follows:

☐ Supports multiple banks

☐ Supports multiple accounts within banks

☐ Supports multiple customers holding accounts

☐ Supports customers holding multiple accounts

☐ Supports the capability to open (create) new accounts

☐ Supports the capability to close (delete) existing accounts

☐ Supports the capability to enumerate a bank's accounts

☐ Supports the capability to determine an account's owner(s)

☐ Supports the capability to withdraw funds from an account

☐ Supports the capability to deposit funds into an account

☐ Supports the capability to transfer funds between accounts within a single bank

☐ Supports the capability to transfer funds between accounts in different banks

☐ Supports checking accounts (which don't gain interest)

☐ Supports savings accounts (which do gain interest)

Notice that each line item describes one capability; for instance, the capabilities to create and delete accounts compose separate line items. This convention facilitates the development of testing requirements because the functionality described in each line item is individually testable. Note also that when analyzing system requirements, it is generally good practice to ensure that each capability is indeed testable. For example, a requirement such as "Must be easy to use" is subjective and so probably not testable. Avoid vague requirements like this; a more useful set of requirements would list specific user-interface features that one might consider "easy to use."

Defining System Objects

Now that you have arrived at a set of system requirements, you are ready to determine what objects exist in the system. As suggested previously, you do this by scanning the application description and requirements for nouns. Nouns that you'll encounter are *bank*, *account* (specifically, *checking account* and *savings account*), *customer*, and *funds*. All these are candidates for inclusion in the object model (or class diagram). One way to determine

5

whether a class should be created for a candidate is to ask yourself this question: Is there an identity or behavior associated with this object? If the answer is yes, then the candidate should be an object. Try this test on your list of candidate objects:

☐ *Bank:* A bank does indeed have identity; the Eighth National Bank is distinguishable from the CORBA Developers Credit Union. Furthermore, a bank has associated behavior; it can open and close accounts on behalf of customers, among other things. Therefore, you might conclude that Bank is indeed an object in your system.

☐ *Account:* Accounts, like banks, have identity as well; they can be distinguished from each other. Also, accounts have associated behavior; funds can be deposited in, withdrawn from, and transferred between accounts. Therefore, Account will be an object in the system as well.

☐ *Customer:* Customers certainly have identity—John Doe can be distinguished from Joe Blow, the person holding Social Security number 123-45-6789 can be distinguished from the person holding Social Security number 234-56-7890, and so on. Customers don't have any associated behavior, at least for the purposes of this application, but their identity alone suggests that Customer ought to be an object in the system.

☐ *Funds:* Funds don't really have identity—one $150.00 amount is, practically speaking, indistinguishable from another $150.00 amount. There is no behavior directly associated with funds either; they can be deposited in, withdrawn from, and transferred between accounts, but this is a behavior of the account rather than the funds themselves. Finally, funds can be easily represented by a simple floating-point value rather than by a class. For these reasons, you probably do not want to include funds in the application's object model.

From this analysis, you can see that the system will include at least three major classes: Bank, Account, and Customer. Now you need to focus your attention on the attributes and behaviors of such objects.

Bank

Several of the system requirements suggest behaviors that should be included in the Bank class:

☐ Supports multiple banks.

Although not actually a behavior of a Bank, this capability requires that more than one Bank object can exist. Furthermore, in a CORBA application, this requirement suggests that a mechanism exist that can provide clients with visibility to Bank objects. One approach is to require Banks to register with the Naming Service so they can be located by clients; another approach is to create a separate object—BankServer, for instance—that provides visibility to Bank objects. This application uses the latter approach.

NOTE

In a C++ or Java application that does not use CORBA, you can very well provide a static method of Bank that would return a list of Bank objects, which is a reasonable approach. However, because CORBA objects don't support static methods, an alternative approach—such as those mentioned previously—is required.

☐ Supports multiple accounts within banks.

This requirement suggests that a Bank maintain a list of its Accounts, although this list might not necessarily be accessible to objects outside the Bank.

☐ Supports the capability to open (create) new accounts.

This requirement suggests that a Bank support an operation such as createAccount(), which presumably will take as input a Customer (or group of Customers) and perhaps an opening balance and will return a new Account object. In other words, Bank will provide the following operation:

```
createAccount(customer : Customer, openingBalance : float) : Account
```

☐ Supports the capability to close (delete) existing accounts.

Because an Account must first exist in order to be deleted, this behavior could actually belong either to the Bank class or to the Account class. For the sake of consistency with createAccount(), it is included in the Bank class.

deleteAccount(), as this operation might be called, doesn't require any information other than the Account to be deleted, so its signature might look like this:

```
deleteAccount(account : Account) : void
```

NOTE

You will often encounter situations like the preceding one, where there is no clear answer as to where certain behavior should be placed. Use your best judgment, or sometimes even make an arbitrary decision.

☐ Supports the capability to enumerate a bank's accounts.

It was suggested previously that a Bank would maintain a list of its Accounts; this requirement suggests that the Bank's Accounts be made accessible to other objects. In a real-world system, access to Account information should probably be restricted, but because there is no such requirement in this system (yet), this operation is straightforward:

```
getAccounts() : Account[]
```

The [] notation indicates that listAccounts() returns an array of Account objects.

5

Additional attributes of a `Bank` might prove useful; for instance, the `Bank` should probably have a name and perhaps an address. For this application, these attributes will be kept simple:

```
name : string
address : string
```

BankServer

`BankServer` is a class that was unanticipated in the preliminary analysis but popped up during your analysis of the `Bank` class. The `BankServer` class is very simple, its only job being to provide visibility to `Bank` objects. In order to provide this capability, the following operations are required: Register a `Bank` with the `BankServer`, unregister a `Bank` from the `BankServer`, and list all `Banks` currently registered with the `BankServer`. More formally, these operations are defined as follows:

```
registerBank(bank : Bank) : void
unregisterBank(bank : Bank) : void
getBanks() : Bank[]
```

For the purposes of this application, no other capabilities are required of the `BankServer` class.

Account

The next class you will consider is the `Account`. This class implements a great deal of the `Bank` application's initial functionality. Here is how the `Account` class meets the requirements of the system design:

☐ Supports multiple customers holding accounts.

This capability is supported by a many-to-one relationship between `Customers` and `Accounts`, but it also implies that an `Account` object will support an operation that shows which `Customers` are associated with that `Account`:

```
getCustomers() : Customer[]
```

☐ Supports customers holding multiple accounts.

This capability, coupled with the requirement to support multiple customers holding accounts, implies a many-to-many relationship between `Customers` and `Accounts` (rather than the many-to-one relationship mentioned previously). However, the actual functionality related to this requirement belongs in the `Customer` class.

☐ Supports the capability to determine an account's owner(s).

This capability implies an operation that returns the `Customers` associated with a given `Account`. Incidentally, this operation was already provided previously.

☐ Supports the capability to withdraw funds from an account.

The capability to withdraw funds from an `Account` would most likely come in the form of a `withdraw()` operation, which takes the amount to be withdrawn as an argument. For the sake of convenience, this operation will return the new balance of the Account:

```
withdraw(amount : float) : float
```

☐ Supports the capability to deposit funds into an account.

Depositing funds has the same semantics as withdrawing funds; the amount to be deposited is an argument, and the return value is the new balance of the Account:

```
deposit(amount : float) : float
```

☐ Supports the capability to transfer funds between accounts within a single bank.

Transferring funds between Accounts is slightly more complicated than simply depositing or withdrawing funds. In this case, the second Account must also be specified. The amount of the transaction must be specified as well, of course. As with the deposit() and withdraw() operations, the transfer() operation will return the new balance of the Account (meaning the Account from which the funds are transferred):

```
transfer(other : Account, amount : float) : float
```

☐ Supports the capability to transfer funds between accounts in different banks.

This capability is already supported by the transfer() operation because the Account passed to that operation can belong to any Bank. Therefore, it is unnecessary to provide a separate operation for transferring funds between Accounts in different Banks.

☐ Supports checking accounts (which don't gain interest).

☐ Supports savings accounts (which do gain interest).

These requirements suggest that specializations of the Account class will exist. In particular, you will use CheckingAccount and SavingsAccount. Although one could argue that the account type is actually an attribute of the Account class, for the purposes of this application, the CheckingAccount and SavingsAccount will be subclasses of Account. This approach makes sense because a SavingsAccount has attributes and behaviors not applicable to a CheckingAccount, and vice versa. Because these classes exhibit different behaviors, it is probably better to create separate classes for each of them.

Finally, the Account should probably contain some additional attributes to make it interesting. First, it should have an account number so that it can be identified by a human customer (and also to identify the account on printed checks); it would also be nice to retain the creation date of the account. Note that these capabilities were not spelled out in the requirements, so you could technically do without them. However, they are likely to become useful sooner or later, hence their inclusion here:

```
accountNumber : string
creationDate : date
getAccountNumber() : string
getCreationDate() : date
```

5

Notice that the operations listed here are redundant with the attributes. This is in keeping with the typical practice of making attributes private and allowing access to those attributes through accessor methods. Although you can choose not to follow this convention for non-CORBA applications, access to attributes of CORBA objects always takes place through accessor methods. Remember, though, that one advantage to this convention is that it allows you, if you so desire, to restrict external access to object attributes to reading only. Such is the case in this example, as only accessors—no mutators—are provided. This ensures that attributes that should be immutable—such as creation date and account number—cannot be altered.

CheckingAccount

`CheckingAccount`, which derives from `Account`, provides additional attributes and behaviors. However, at this point in the application design, `CheckingAccount` adds nothing new to `Account`.

SavingsAccount

`SavingsAccount`, which also derives from `Account`, provides additional attributes and behaviors as well. In particular, a `SavingsAccount` has an associated interest rate, along with an accessor and mutator for this attribute:

```
interestRate : float
getInterestRate() : float
setInterestRate(newRate : float) : float
```

`setInterestRate()` returns the old interest rate as a convenience to the user.

Customer

The `Customer` in this application is a relatively simple class because it is mostly a consumer of services offered by other classes. Only one of the system requirements falls to the `Customer` class's responsibility.

☐ Supports customers holding multiple accounts.

Because a customer can hold multiple accounts, it makes sense that the `Customer` class would support an operation that enumerates `Accounts` held by that `Customer`:

```
getAccounts() : Account[]
```

Additionally, to make the `Customer` interesting, a few attributes will be added to provide the `Customer`'s name, Social Security number (as a means of identification), address, and mother's maiden name (for security reasons and just plain old tradition):

```
name : string
socialSecurityNumber : string
address : string
mothersMaidenName : string
```

To keep things simple, the address attribute is simplified into a string rather than street address, city, state, ZIP code, and so on. However, providing a separate `Address` class (which could possibly have derived classes as well) might not be a bad idea for a more robust system.

A Word About Object Identity

Notice that nowhere in the previously described classes is there any mention of attributes whose purpose is to uniquely identify the object. (The possible exceptions are the Customer's Social Security number and the Account's account number, which will be discussed in a moment.) This is because object-oriented analysis makes the assumption that objects implicitly have unique identity, making an identity attribute redundant. Therefore, at the analysis level, classes should not contain attributes that exist solely to identify the object.

There are exceptions to this rule. Most notably, a Customer has a socialSecurityNumber—an attribute that exists primarily to uniquely identify the Customer. However, this type of identity attribute is often used because it corresponds to a real-world concept. A person, for example, has a unique identity simply by virtue of the fact that he or she exists. The Social Security number, because it is a ubiquitous method of identifying people (at least in the U.S.A.), is often convenient to use in software applications.

Other identification attributes exist as well and are perfectly legitimate for use in an application design. Another example is the account number in the Account class. Account numbers are often used to identify an account on a printed check or on a statement sent to the customer.

The key to understanding when identity attributes are appropriate is this: An artificial identity attribute has no place in a class description, whereas an identity attribute that exists in the real world—such as a socialSecurityNumber—is acceptable and even useful.

Creating an Application Class Diagram

Now that you've identified the components (classes) of the system and described their attributes and behaviors, you're ready to put them together into a cohesive class diagram. The class diagram shows not only the classes themselves (including, if desired, their attributes or operations) but also the relationships between classes.

Figure 5.4 shows the initial class diagram for the Bank application. (You'll be making changes to the class diagram from time to time as the system design evolves throughout the next few chapters.) Notice that this diagram introduces the UML notation for class inheritance; the SavingsAccount and CheckingAccount classes both inherit from the Account class.

Again, it is stressed that the analysis and design phase is an iterative process. You will often find yourself going back and tweaking various aspects of the design as you discover features that were left out or as you learn (stumble across) a more elegant way of doing things. Revisiting and making changes to work you've already completed is quite normal in this stage of the game. Strive for the highest possible quality system design; when you begin implementing the system, sweeping changes to the design become much more costly. Better to spend more time on it now, during the design phase, when making changes is much cheaper.

5

Figure 5.4.

The Bank *application class diagram.*

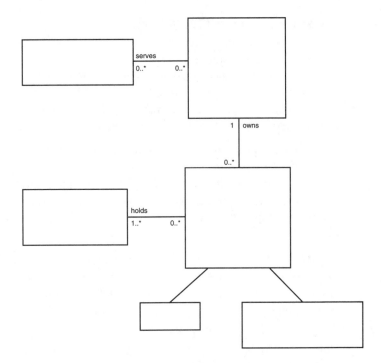

For Further Study...

Of course, there is much, much more to object-oriented analysis and design than is covered here. Also, a very important part of object-oriented methodology is the development of *use cases,* which describe scenarios in which various parts of the system interact. These scenarios contain *actors,* such as a user or another object, that act on other objects. Use cases describe how an actor interacts with the system, what the results are, and the order in which these events occur. There are many possible use cases for a single scenario; for example, for a given dialog box, there might be a use case for when the user enters valid data and a separate use case for when the user enters invalid data.

Another powerful tool of object-oriented analysis and design is the *design pattern.* Design patterns can be thought of as building blocks for more complex object-oriented constructs. For instance, one common design pattern—one with which you might already be familiar— is the *model-view* pattern. In this pattern, one object, called a *model,* represents a piece of data or concept. Another object, called a *view,* tells a model that it wants to receive updates whenever the model's state changes. An example of a model class is a TemperatureSensor, which monitors the outdoor temperature. A view class, such as TemperatureDisplay, might be a view of the TemperatureSensor class, meaning that when the TemperatureSensor detects a change in the outdoor temperature, it notifies the TemperatureDisplay of the change. The TemperatureDisplay obtains and displays the new temperature information. A model might have multiple views, as well; in this case, the TemperatureSensor notifies multiple TemperatureDisplays when the outdoor temperature changes.

A number of excellent books have long been available on subjects such as use cases, design patterns, and other important object-oriented concepts. Again, you are encouraged to explore these topics in depth; knowledge of such concepts pay off in designing any type of system—not just CORBA applications.

Summary

In this chapter, you took what was essentially a crash course in object-oriented analysis and design. You learned a bit about the Unified Modeling Language, its notation, and the basic methodologies involved. You applied these concepts to the design of a basic Bank application. In the analysis and design phase, not much attention is given to the details of implementation; in fact, it is recommended that you avoid implementation details at this stage of application development. A system design that does not depend on such details enjoys greater flexibility than a design that is dependent on the details of a particular implementation.

In the analysis and design phase, you performed three major steps:

- [ ] Investigated and defined the requirements for the system.
- [ ] Identified the potential classes that compose the system.
- [ ] Mapped the system requirements to class attributes and operations.
- [ ] Created a class diagram that integrated the classes in the system into a coherent model.

What Comes Next?

In the final part of the design phase—on Day 6, "Implementing Basic Application Capabilities"—you'll translate the system design into an IDL specification. The IDL will be used as—you guessed it—a baseline for the system implementation. You'll then proceed to do exactly this—implement the system's basic capabilities. Future days will be spent enhancing the basic functionality.

Q&A

Q In the Bank application, what's to prevent someone from transferring funds between accounts without authorization?

A The short answer is this: absolutely nothing. This application, being an oversimplification of a real-world bank system, makes no attempts at providing security of any kind. Obviously, in a production system, there would have to be security measures in place to prevent this sort of thing. (If you're truly ambitious, design such a mechanism as an exercise.)

Q What use are use cases?

A Use cases are a powerful tool in system design; in addition to helping the system architects/designers/developers better understand how the system works, the practice of building use cases can often uncover scenarios that may not have been anticipated. Murphy's Law being what it is, a user will likely uncover all unanticipated scenarios—usually with undesirable results—so it is always better for the application designers to find them first.

Workshop

The following section will help you test your comprehension of the material presented in this chapter and put what you've learned into practice. You'll find the answers to the quiz and exercise in Appendix A.

Quiz

1. Identify the potential objects in the system described here: An ordering system allows customers to order products from a particular company. Each order consists of one or more line items, each of which identifies a quantity and a particular product. Each product, in turn, has an associated price.

2. What is UML and what is it good for?

3. For an order processing system design, one requirement given is "must be fast." Is this a reasonable expression of this requirement, or could it be made better? If so, how?

Exercise

Modify the system design so that a Bank consists of Branches, each of which owns some of the Customer Accounts. Draw the class diagram for the modified design.

Day 6

Implementing Basic Application Capabilities

On Day 5, "Designing the System: A Crash Course in Object-Oriented Analysis and Design," you mapped an application design to a set of IDL interfaces that defined the structure on which that design would be realized. Today you'll implement those interfaces, thus creating an operational set of servers and clients that implement the basic capabilities of the Bank application. You'll enhance the application with additional functionality in future chapters, but in this chapter you'll concentrate on implementing the core set of features of the application.

NOTE

The examples in this chapter have been developed using Visigenic Software's (http://www.visigenic.com/) VisiBroker/C++ product. Despite the existence of a standard IDL language mapping for C++, various inconsistencies still exist between CORBA products. If you are using a different product, such as IONA Technologies' Orbix, you might need to modify the sample code slightly, although these changes will be minimal. Consult your product documentation for language mapping information if you experience difficulty compiling the examples.

Implementing Basic Bank Server Capabilities

The server functionality of the Bank application is encapsulated in three main interfaces: the BankServer, the Bank, and the Account. The Account interface is subdivided into two derived interfaces, CheckingAccount and SavingsAccount. This set of interfaces defines the core functionality of the Bank application. After you provide implementations for these interfaces, you move on to implement the client capabilities as well. The sole interface implemented by the client is the Customer interface, used by the client to access various bank services.

Implementing the BankServer Interface

The first server interface to implement is the BankServer. Recall that the purpose of the BankServer is to enable clients to locate Bank objects. BankServer objects, in turn, are located by clients and Bank objects through the CORBA Naming Service or another similar mechanism. When a Bank object is created, it locates and registers with a BankServer; in the same fashion, when the Bank object is ready to shut down, it unregisters with the BankServer.

The IDL for the BankServer interface (from Day 5) is defined in Listing 6.1.

Listing 6.1. BankServer.idl.

```
1: // BankServer.idl
2:
3: #ifndef BankServer_idl
4: #define BankServer_idl
5:
6: #include "Bank.idl"
7:
8: // A BankServer provides clients with visibility to Bank objects.
9: interface BankServer {
```

```
10:
11:     // Register the given Bank with this BankServer. The Bank will
12:     // be listed by getBanks() until unregisterBank() is called with
13:     // that Bank.
14:     void registerBank(in Bank bank);
15:
16:     // Unregister the given Bank from this BankServer. If the Bank
17:     // was not previously registered, this operation does nothing.
18:     void unregisterBank(in Bank bank);
19:
20:     // Return a list of all Banks currently registered with this
21:     // BankServer.
22:     BankList getBanks();
23: };
24:
25: #endif
```

It is up to you to provide implementations for the registerBank(), unregisterBank(), and getBanks() methods, as well as the constructor (or constructors) and destructor for this class.

Examining BankServerImpl.h in Listing 6.2, notice first (in line 10) that the BankServerImpl class extends the _sk_BankServer class. _sk_BankServer is the server skeleton for the BankServer interface. If you were to examine the source file for this class, you would see that it provides pure virtual methods corresponding to the IDL methods you defined earlier. Because it is a skeleton, though, it doesn't provide any implementations for these methods; that is the job of the BankServerImpl class. Also, note that the name BankServerImpl was chosen arbitrarily; you can name the class whatever you want, but it is recommended that you devise and follow a naming convention for your implementation classes.

Listing 6.2. BankServerImpl.h.

```
 1: // BankServerImpl.h
 2:
 3: #ifndef BankServerImpl_h
 4: #define BankServerImpl_h
 5:
 6: #include <vector>
 7:
 8: #include "../BankServer_s.h"
 9:
10: class BankServerImpl : public _sk_BankServer {
11:
12: public:
13:
14:     // Constructor.
15:     BankServerImpl();
16:
17:     // Destructor.
18:     ~BankServerImpl();
19:
```

6

continues

Listing 6.2. continued

```
20:      // These methods are described in BankServer.idl.
21:      virtual void registerBank(Bank_ptr bank);
22:      virtual void unregisterBank(Bank_ptr bank);
23:      virtual BankList* getBanks();
24:
25: private:
26:
27:      // This BankServer's list of Banks.
28:      std::vector<Bank_ptr> myBanks;
29: };
30:
31: #endif
```

Also, notice the following:

```
#include <vector>
```

and

```
// This BankServer's list of Banks.
std::vector<Bank_ptr> myBanks;
```

If you guessed that the implementation utilizes C++'s Standard Template Library (STL), you are correct. Most modern C++ compilers include STL; if yours doesn't, you can either obtain an implementation of STL or modify the sample code to avoid STL. One source for STL implementations is ObjectSpace (at http://www.objectspace.com/), which provides an STL implementation for many platforms and compilers free of charge.

Further examining BankServerImpl.h, you'll see that the IDL methods defined previously map to the following C++ methods:

```
virtual void registerBank(Bank_ptr bank);
virtual void unregisterBank(Bank_ptr bank);
virtual BankList* getBanks();
```

Notice in particular that the Bank references are mapped to the Bank_ptr type, and the BankList to BankList*. Other than these changes and the appearance of the virtual keyword (which is unnecessary for CORBA implementation classes but usually preferable), the C++ method definitions strongly resemble their IDL counterparts.

Listing 6.3 contains the implementation class BankServerImpl.cpp, which provides the implementation for the _sk_BankServer interface.

Listing 6.3. BankServerImpl.cpp.

```
1: // BankServerImpl.cpp
2:
3: #include "BankServerImpl.h"
```

```
 4:
 5: #include <algorithm>
 6: #include <functional>
 7:
 8: // STL-derived unary function which returns TRUE if Banks are equal.
 9: class IsBankEqual : public std::unary_function<Bank_ptr, bool> {
10: public:
11:     IsBankEqual(argument_type bank) { myBank = bank; }
12:     result_type operator()(argument_type bank) { return bank->
13:             _is_equivalent(myBank) != 0; }
14: private:
15:     argument_type myBank;
16: };
17:
18: // Constructor.
19: BankServerImpl::BankServerImpl() : myBanks() {
20:
21: }
22:
23: // Destructor.
24: BankServerImpl::~BankServerImpl() {
25:
26: }
27:
28: void BankServerImpl::registerBank(Bank_ptr bank) {
29:
30:     // Add the given Bank at the end of the list.
31:     cout << "BankServerImpl: Registering Bank \"" << bank->name() <<
32:             "\"." << endl;
33:     myBanks.push_back(Bank::_duplicate(bank));
34: }
35:
36: void BankServerImpl::unregisterBank(Bank_ptr bank) {
37:
38:     std::vector<Bank_ptr>::iterator first = myBanks.begin();
39:     std::vector<Bank_ptr>::iterator last = myBanks.end();
40:     IsBankEqual predicate(bank);
41:
42:     std::vector<Bank_ptr>::iterator matchedBank = std::
43:             find_if(first, last, predicate);
44:     if (matchedBank == last) {
45:
46:         // Invalid Bank; do nothing.
47:         cout << "BankServerImpl: Ignored attempt to unregister "
48:                 "invalid Bank." << endl;
49:         return;
50:     }
51:     cout << "BankServerImpl: Unregistering Bank \"" << bank->name()
52:             << "\"." << endl;
53:
54:     // Delete the given Bank.
55:     myBanks.erase(matchedBank);
56:     bank->_release();
57: }
58:
```

continues

Listing 6.3. continued

```
59: BankList* BankServerImpl::getBanks() {
60:
61:     BankList* list = new BankList(myBanks.size());
62:     CORBA::Long i;
63:
64:     for (i = 0; i < myBanks.size(); i++) {
65:         (*list)[i] = Bank::_duplicate(myBanks[i]);
66:     }
67:
68:     return list;
69: }
```

Of particular interest in this class are the following highlights:

BankServerImpl.cpp makes use of STL-provided algorithms and functions, as evidenced by the #include directives in lines 5 and 6.

The IsBankEqual class, occupying lines 8 through 16, is an encapsulation of a function that compares two Bank references for equality (that is, they both refer to the same Bank object). The equality test is performed through the _is_equivalent() method, which returns a TRUE (nonzero) result if its object and the argument object indeed refer to the same object.

NOTE

According to the CORBA specification, _is_equivalent() might actually return FALSE even if two object references are equivalent. The only guarantee made by the CORBA specification is that if _is_equivalent() returns TRUE, then the object references are equivalent; otherwise, they may or may not be equivalent. (See the CORBA specification document for more information.)

The registerBank() method (lines 28-34) simply adds the given Bank to the BankServerImpl's internal list of Banks (in the myBanks member). Note the use of the Bank class's _duplicate() method, which increments the *reference count* of the given Bank object by one. This indicates to the Bank object that the BankServerImpl intends to retain a reference to that object. The reference count for an object, in turn, simply maintains a count of outstanding references to that object. (You'll see later how the BankServerImpl releases its reference to the Bank object.)

Now you'll examine the unregisterBank() method in several parts.

The first part of unregisterBank(), in lines 36-52, iterates through the BankServerImpl's internal list of Banks (again, stored in the myBanks member). The isBankEqual class discussed earlier is used to determine equality of Bank references; in this example, the std::find_if()

method uses an isBankEqual object to compare object references. This step is necessary so that when a Bank is unregistered, the BankServerImpl can remove it from its internal list of Banks.

In the last part of unregisterBank(), lines 54-56, the given Bank is first removed from myBanks, via the erase() method. Then BankServerImpl indicates to the Bank that it is no longer keeping a reference to that Bank by calling the _release() method. _release() is the counterpart to the _duplicate() method mentioned previously; _release() decrements the reference count of an object. When that object's reference count reaches zero, the object can be (but not necessarily) destroyed. Because the BankServerImpl increments a Bank's reference count when it registers and decrements the Bank's reference count when it unregisters, the net change of the Bank's reference count after it has registered and later unregistered is zero.

On its own, the BankServerImpl class doesn't do anything useful. To realize its capability, you must provide code that creates a BankServerImpl and makes it available to other objects on the network. This is done in BankServerMain.cpp, which appears in Listing 6.4.

Listing 6.4. BankServerMain.cpp.

```
1: // BankServerMain.cpp
2:
3: #include "BankServerImpl.h"
4: #include <iostream.h>
5:
6: int main(int argc, char *const *argv) {
7:
8:     // Initialize the ORB and BOA.
9:     CORBA::ORB_var orb = CORBA::ORB_init(argc, argv);
10:     CORBA::BOA_var boa = orb->BOA_init(argc, argv);
11:
12:     // Create a BankServerImpl object.
13:     BankServerImpl bankServer;
14:
15:     // Notify the BOA that the BankServerImpl object is ready.
16:     boa->obj_is_ready(&bankServer);
17:
18:     // Wait for CORBA events.
19:     cout << "BankServer ready." << endl;
20:     boa->impl_is_ready();
21:
22:     // When this point is reached, the application is finished.
23:     return 0;
24: }
```

The first thing a CORBA application must do is initialize its environment, that is, its Object Request Broker (ORB) and Basic Object Adapter (BOA). This is accomplished through the ORB_init() and BOA_init() methods in lines 8-10.

6

After the ORB and BOA are initialized, other CORBA objects can be created and made available to the network. This is done on a per-object basis using the obj_is_ready() method (in lines 15-16).

The preceding code notifies the BOA that the BankServerImpl object is ready to be used by other objects on the network. The BOA also provides the impl_is_ready() method, which you see used in lines 18-20.

The impl_is_ready() method notifies the BOA that the application is ready to receive events. Typically, impl_is_ready() will wait for events for an implementation-dependent period of time; usually, this is configurable by the application developer. For instance, impl_is_ready() can process events until the application is interrupted, or it can terminate the application after a predetermined amount of time has elapsed—an hour, for instance—without any events being received.

Now that the BankServer interface has been implemented, you can turn your attention to the interface that interacts with the BankServer: the Bank interface.

Implementing the Bank Interface

The Bank interface, as you recall from Day 5, describes the services provided by a Bank— generally, the manipulation of Accounts within that Bank. The IDL for the Bank interface is defined as shown in Listing 6.5.

Listing 6.5. Bank.idl.

```
 1: // Bank.idl
 2:
 3: // Forward declaration of Bank interface.
 4: interface Bank;
 5:
 6: #ifndef Bank_idl
 7: #define Bank_idl
 8:
 9: // sequence of Banks
10: typedef sequence<Bank> BankList;
11:
12: #include "Customer.idl"
13: #include "Account.idl"
14:
15: // A Bank provides access to Accounts. It can create an Account
16: // on behalf of a Customer, delete an Account, or list the current
17: // Accounts with the Bank.
18: interface Bank {
19:
20:     // This Bank's name.
21:     attribute string name;
22:
23:     // This Bank's address.
```

```
24:     attribute string address;
25:
26:     // Create an Account on behalf of the given Customer, with the
27:     // given account type ("savings" or "checking", where case is
28:     // significant), and the given opening balance.
29:     Account createAccount(in Customer customer, in string
30:            accountType, in float openingBalance);
31:
32:     // Delete the given Account. If the Account is not with this
33:     // Bank, this operation does nothing.
34:     void deleteAccount(in Account account);
35:
36:     // List all Accounts with this Bank.
37:     AccountList getAccounts();
38: };
39:
40: #endif
```

Here, you'll need to provide implementations for name() and address()—which have both accessor and mutator forms for the name and address attributes—along with createAccount(), deleteAccount(), and getAccounts(), as well as the constructor (or constructors) and destructor for this class.

After looking at BankServerImpl.h (back in Listing 6.2), nothing in BankImpl.h should be too surprising (see Listing 6.6). Again, the mapping of IDL methods to C++ methods is straightforward (although you'll notice the use of the CORBA::Float type that the IDL float type mapped to), and the BankImpl makes use of STL in much the same way as BankServerImpl.

Listing 6.6. BankImpl.h.

```
1: // BankImpl.h
2:
3: #ifndef BankImpl_h
4: #define BankImpl_h
5:
6: #include <vector>
7:
8: #include "../Bank_s.h"
9:
10: class BankImpl : public _sk_Bank {
11:
12: public:
13:
14:     // Constructor.
15:     //
16:     // name - This Bank's name.
17:     BankImpl(const char* name);
18:
19:     // Destructor.
20:     ~BankImpl();
```

continues

Listing 6.6. continued

```
21:
22:      // These methods are described in Bank.idl.
23:      virtual char* name();
24:      virtual void name(const char* val);
25:      virtual char* address();
26:      virtual void address(const char* val);
27:      virtual Account_ptr createAccount(Customer_ptr customer,
28:              const char* accountType, CORBA::Float openingBalance);
29:      virtual void deleteAccount(Account_ptr account);
30:      virtual AccountList* getAccounts();
31:
32: protected:
33:
34:      // Return the next available account number. The result is
35:      // returned in a static buffer.
36:      char* getNextAccountNumber();
37:
38:      // Return the current date in the form "Mmm DD YYYY". The result
39:      // is returned in a static buffer.
40:      char* getCurrentDate();
41:
42: private:
43:
44:      // Default constructor.
45:      BankImpl();
46:
47:      // This Bank's name.
48:      char* myName;
49:
50:      // This Bank's address.
51:      char* myAddress;
52:
53:      // This Bank's Accounts.
54:      std::vector<Account_ptr> myAccounts;
55:
56:      // The next available account number.
57:      unsigned int myNextAccountNumber;
58: };
59:
60: #endif
```

You haven't seen it yet, but BankMain.cpp defines a global variable called boa (see line 14 of Listing 6.7), which is a reference to the Basic Object Adapter used by the application. Although the simplicity of a global boa variable makes it appropriate for a sample application, in a production application you want a cleaner mechanism for sharing the reference to the BOA. For example, you can provide a class that makes the BOA available through a static member, or you can write class constructors to take a BOA as an argument. Regardless of how you accomplish this, there will sometimes be a need for various objects in an application to access the BOA. (In this example, a BankImpl needs to call obj_is_ready() on Account objects that it creates.)

6

Listing 6.7. `BankImpl.cpp.`

```
 1: // BankImpl.cpp
 2:
 3: #include "BankImpl.h"
 4:
 5: #include <time.h>
 6: #include <string.h>
 7: #include <iostream.h>
 8: #include <algorithm>
 9: #include <functional>
10:
11: #include "SavingsAccountImpl.h"
12: #include "CheckingAccountImpl.h"
13:
14: extern CORBA::BOA_var boa;
15:
16: // STL-derived unary function which returns TRUE if Accounts are
17: // equal.
18: class IsAccountEqual : public std::unary_function<Account_ptr,
19:         bool> {
20: public:
21:     IsAccountEqual(argument_type account) { myAccount = account; }
22:     result_type operator()(argument_type account) { return account->
23:             _is_equivalent(myAccount) != 0; }
24: private:
25:     argument_type myAccount;
26: };
27:
28: // Constructor.
29: //
30: // name - This Bank's name.
31: BankImpl::BankImpl(const char* name) : myAccounts(),
32:         myName(strdup(name)), myAddress(strdup("123 Elm Street, "
33:         "Anyware USA 12345")), myNextAccountNumber(0) {
34:
35: }
36:
37: // Default constructor.
38: BankImpl::BankImpl() : myAccounts(), myName(NULL), myAddress(NULL),
39:         myNextAccountNumber(0) {
40:
41: }
42:
43: // Destructor.
44: BankImpl::~BankImpl() {
45:
46:     cout << "Bank \"" << name() << "\" being destroyed." << endl;
47:     free(myName);
48:     free(myAddress);
49: }
50:
51: char* BankImpl::name() {
52:
```

continues

Listing 6.7. continued

```
53:      return CORBA::strdup(myName);
54: }
55:
56: void BankImpl::name(const char* val) {
57:
58:      free(myName);
59:      myName = strdup(val);
60: }
61:
62: char* BankImpl::address() {
63:
64:      return CORBA::strdup(myAddress);
65: }
66:
67: void BankImpl::address(const char* val) {
68:
69:      free(myAddress);
70:      myAddress = strdup(val);
71: }
72:
73: Account_ptr BankImpl::createAccount(Customer_ptr customer,
74:         const char* accountType, CORBA::Float openingBalance) {
75:
76:      Account_ptr newAccount;
77:
78:      if (strcmp(accountType, "savings") == 0) {
79:
80:          // Create a new SavingsAccountImpl object for the Account.
81:          cout << "BankImpl: Creating new SavingsAccount for "
82:                  "Customer " << customer->name() << "." << endl;
83:          newAccount = new SavingsAccountImpl(getNextAccountNumber(),
84:                  getCurrentDate(), openingBalance, customer, 10.0);
85:      } else if (strcmp(accountType, "checking") == 0) {
86:
87:          // Create a new CheckingAccountImpl object for the Account.
88:          cout << "BankImpl: Creating new CheckingAccount for "
89:                  "Customer " << customer->name() << "." << endl;
90:          newAccount = new CheckingAccountImpl(getNextAccountNumber(),
91:                  getCurrentDate(), openingBalance, customer);
92:      } else {
93:
94:          // Invalid Account type; do nothing.
95:          cout << "BankImpl: Customer " << customer->name() <<
96:                  " requested invalid Account type \"" << accountType
97:                  << "\"." << endl;
98:          return Account::_nil();
99:      }
100:
101:      // Add the created Account at the end of the list and return it.
102:      ::boa->obj_is_ready(newAccount);
103:      myAccounts.push_back(Account::_duplicate(newAccount));
104:      return newAccount;
105: }
106:
```

6

```
107: void BankImpl::deleteAccount(Account_ptr account) {
108:
109:     std::vector<Account_ptr>::iterator first = myAccounts.begin();
110:     std::vector<Account_ptr>::iterator last = myAccounts.end();
111:     IsAccountEqual predicate(account);
112:
113:     std::vector<Account_ptr>::iterator matchedAccount = std::
114:             find_if(first, last, predicate);
115:     if (matchedAccount == last) {
116:
117:         // Invalid Account; do nothing.
118:         cout << "BankImpl: Ignored attempt to delete invalid " <<
119:                 "Account." << endl;
120:         return;
121:     }
122:     cout << "BankImpl: Deleting Account \"" << account->
123:             accountNumber() << "\"." << endl;
124:
125:     // Delete the given Account.
126:     myAccounts.erase(matchedAccount);
127:     account->_release();
128: }
129:
130: AccountList* BankImpl::getAccounts() {
131:
132:     AccountList* list = new AccountList(myAccounts.size());
133:     CORBA::Long i;
134:
135:     for (i = 0; i < myAccounts.size(); i++) {
136:         (*list)[i] = Account::_duplicate(myAccounts[i]);
137:     }
138:
139:     return list;
140: }
141:
142: // Return the next available account number. The result is returned
143: // in a static buffer.
144: char* BankImpl::getNextAccountNumber() {
145:
146:     static char accountNumber[16] = "Account        ";
147:
148:     sprintf(accountNumber + 7, "%08u", myNextAccountNumber++);
149:
150:     return accountNumber;
151: }
152:
153: // Return the current date in the form "Mmm DD YYYY". The result is
154: // returned in a static buffer.
155: char* BankImpl::getCurrentDate() {
156:
157:     static char currentDate[12] = "           ";
158:
159:     time_t ltime;
160:     time(&ltime);
161:     char* ctimeResult = ctime(&ltime);
```

continues

Listing 6.7. continued

```
162:
163:        memcpy(currentDate, ctimeResult + 4, 3);
164:        memcpy(currentDate + 4, ctimeResult + 8, 2);
165:        memcpy(currentDate + 7, ctimeResult + 20, 4);
166:
167:        return currentDate;
168: }
```

Here are the highlights from BankImpl.cpp (refer to Listing 6.7).

Notice that when a string is returned by a CORBA method, as in the first form of the name() method (see lines 51-54), it must be done in the proper manner. When a CORBA method returns a string, it must use the CORBA::strdup() method (note that this is not the same as the standard library strdup() method) on that string. Using CORBA::strdup() allows the application to free the memory used by the string after it has been marshaled back to the caller. The preceding example demonstrates this for the name() accessor method; you will notice that the address() accessor method is similar.

Also, examine the last few lines of the createAccount() method (see lines 101-104).

Notice that when a new Account object is created, you must inform the BOA that the object is ready, again using the obj_is_ready() method. (This is why the BankImpl object needs visibility to the BOA.) Note also that before the newly created Account object is passed back to the caller, its reference count is incremented by the _duplicate() method. This is important because when an object reference is passed back to a caller (either as a return value or as an out or inout parameter), the reference count is decremented. Therefore, when returning a CORBA object reference in this manner, you must always _duplicate() the object reference before returning it.

The remainder of BankImpl.cpp will be recognized by C++ programmers or remembered from BankServerImpl.cpp. Like BankServerImpl, the BankImpl must also be accompanied by a bit of extra code to start up the BankImpl and make it available to the rest of the network. This code can be seen in Listing 6.8.

Listing 6.8. BankMain.cpp.

```
1: // BankMain.cpp
2:
3: #include "BankImpl.h"
4:
5: #include <iostream.h>
6:
7: #include "../BankServer_c.h"
8:
```

```
 9: CORBA::BOA_var boa;
10:
11: int main(int argc, char *const *argv) {
12:
13:     // Check the number of arguments; there should be exactly one
14:     // (two counting the executable name itself).
15:     if (argc != 2) {
16:         cout << "Usage: Bank <bankname>" << endl;
17:         return 1;
18:     }
19:
20:     // Assign the bank name to the first argument.
21:     const char* bankName = argv[1];
22:
23:     // Initialize the ORB and BOA.
24:     CORBA::ORB_var orb = CORBA::ORB_init(argc, argv);
25:     ::boa = orb->BOA_init(argc, argv);
26:
27:     // Create a Bank object.
28:     BankImpl bank(bankName);
29:
30:     // Notify the BOA that the BankImpl object is ready.
31:     ::boa->obj_is_ready(&bank);
32:
33:     // Locate a BankServer object and register with it.
34:     BankServer_var bankServer;
35:     try {
36:         bankServer = BankServer::_bind();
37:     } catch (const CORBA::Exception& ex) {
38:
39:         // The bind attempt failed...
40:         cout << "BankImpl: Unable to bind to a BankServer." << endl;
41:         cout << ex << endl;
42:         return 1;
43:     }
44:     try {
45:         bankServer->registerBank(&bank);
46:     } catch (const CORBA::Exception& ex) {
47:
48:         // The registerBank() attempt failed...
49:         cout << "BankImpl: Unable to register Bank." << endl;
50:         cout << ex << endl;
51:         return 1;
52:     }
53:
54:     // Wait for CORBA events.
55:     cout << "Bank \"" << bankName << "\" ready." << endl;
56:     ::boa->impl_is_ready();
57:
58:     // When this point is reached, the application is finished.
59:     return 0;
60: }
```

6

A key difference between BankServerMain.cpp and BankMain.cpp is that, whereas a BankServer doesn't need to locate and connect to other objects, a Bank needs to locate a BankServer and register with it. This is accomplished by the code in lines 33-43.

The BankServer::_bind() call attempts to bind, or connect, to a BankServer object. Optionally, _bind() can specify a name of an object to connect to, but when the name is omitted, _bind() will attempt to connect to any available object of the requested type. If the _bind() attempt fails, a CORBA::Exception is thrown, then caught, and its contents printed to the console.

NOTE

> Although the _bind() functionality is available in several ORB products (including IONA Technologies' Orbix and Visigenic's VisiBroker products), it is not included in the CORBA standard. In any case, the _bind() mechanism is probably unsuitable for large-scale production systems anyway; you'll most likely want to use the CORBA Naming Service or Trader Service to locate objects on the network. (See Day 12 for a more in-depth discussion of the CORBAservices.)

If the application successfully binds to a BankServer object, it will register the Bank with it, as in lines 44-52.

Here, registerBank() is the remote method of the BankServer interface. As with all remote methods, registerBank() can throw a CORBA::Exception, and thus this exception should be caught by the application. In this case, the exception is caught and an error message printed.

A Bank object is essentially a factory for Account objects, and the implementations of the Account and its derived interfaces are what you will study next.

Implementing the Account Interface

The Account interface defines the capabilities of a generic bank account, such as the withdrawal and deposit of funds. The IDL for the Account interface is defined as shown in Listing 6.9.

Listing 6.9. Account.idl.

```
1: // Account.idl
2:
3: // Forward declaration of Account interface.
4: interface Account;
5:
6: #ifndef Account_idl
```

```
 7: #define Account_idl
 8:
 9: // sequence of Accounts
10: typedef sequence<Account> AccountList;
11:
12: #include "Customer.idl"
13:
14: // An Account is an entity owned by a Bank and held by a Customer
15: // (or multiple Customers). An Account has a balance which can be
16: // affected by deposits and withdrawals.
17: interface Account {
18:
19:     // This Account's account number.
20:     readonly attribute string accountNumber;
21:
22:     // This Account's creation date.
23:     readonly attribute string creationDate;
24:
25:     // This Account's current balance.
26:     readonly attribute float balance;
27:
28:     // Return a list of Customers who hold this Account.
29:     CustomerList getCustomers();
30:
31:     // Withdraw the given amount from this Account. Returns the new
32:     // account balance.
33:     float withdraw(in float amount);
34:
35:     // Deposit the given amount into this Account. Returns the new
36:     // account balance.
37:     float deposit(in float amount);
38: };
39:
40: #endif
```

Thus, you'll need to provide implementations for the following methods: accountNumber(), creationDate(), and balance(), which are accessors for the accountNumber, creationDate, and balance attributes, respectively, as well as getCustomers(), withdraw(), and deposit(), along with the constructor (or constructors) and destructor for this class. The header file for the implementation (AccountImpl.h) appears in Listing 6.10, followed by the implementation itself (AccountImpl.cpp) in Listing 6.11.

Listing 6.10. AccountImpl.h.

```
1: // AccountImpl.h
2:
3: #ifndef AccountImpl_h
4: #define AccountImpl_h
5:
6: #include "../Account_s.h"
```

continues

Listing 6.10. continued

```
 7:
 8: class AccountImpl : public _sk_Account {
 9:
10: // Allow CheckingAccountImpl and SavingsAccountImpl access to the
11: // protected constructor.
12: friend class CheckingAccountImpl;
13: friend class SavingsAccountImpl;
14:
15: public:
16:
17:     // Destructor.
18:     ~AccountImpl();
19:
20:     // These methods are described in Account.idl.
21:     virtual char* accountNumber();
22:     virtual char* creationDate();
23:     virtual CORBA::Float balance();
24:     virtual CustomerList* getCustomers();
25:     virtual CORBA::Float withdraw(CORBA::Float amount);
26:     virtual CORBA::Float deposit(CORBA::Float amount);
27:
28: protected:
29:
30:     // Constructor.
31:     //
32:     // accountNumber - Account number.
33:     // creationDate - Account creation date.
34:     // initialBalance - Initial Account balance.
35:     // customer - Initial Account owner.
36:     AccountImpl(const char* accountNumber, const char* creationDate,
37:             CORBA::Float initialBalance, Customer_ptr customer);
38:
39: private:
40:
41:     // Default constructor.
42:     AccountImpl();
43:
44:     // This Account's account number.
45:     char* myAccountNumber;
46:
47:     // This Account's creation date.
48:     char* myCreationDate;
49:
50:     // This Account's current balance.
51:     CORBA::Float myBalance;
52:
53:     // This Account's owners.
54:     CustomerList myOwners;
55: };
56:
57: #endif
```

6

Listing 6.11. `AccountImpl.cpp.`

```
 1: // AccountImpl.cpp
 2:
 3: #include "AccountImpl.h"
 4:
 5: #include <string.h>
 6:
 7: // Constructor.
 8: //
 9: // accountNumber - Account number.
10: // creationDate - Account creation date.
11: // initialBalance - Initial Account balance.
12: // customer - Initial Account owner.
13: AccountImpl::AccountImpl(const char* accountNumber, const char*
14:         creationDate, CORBA::Float initialBalance, Customer_ptr
15:         customer) : myAccountNumber(strdup(accountNumber)),
16:         myCreationDate(strdup(creationDate)),
17:         myBalance(initialBalance), myOwners() {
18:
19:     // Add the Customer to the owner list.
20:     myOwners.length(1);
21:     myOwners[0] = Customer::_duplicate(customer);
22: }
23:
24: // Default constructor.
25: AccountImpl::AccountImpl() : myAccountNumber(NULL),
26:         myCreationDate(NULL), myBalance(0.0), myOwners() {
27:
28: }
29:
30: // Destructor.
31: AccountImpl::~AccountImpl() {
32:
33:     free(myAccountNumber);
34:     free(myCreationDate);
35: }
36:
37: char* AccountImpl::accountNumber() {
38:
39:     return CORBA::strdup(myAccountNumber);
40: }
41:
42: char* AccountImpl::creationDate() {
43:
44:     return CORBA::strdup(myCreationDate);
45: }
46:
47: CORBA::Float AccountImpl::balance() {
48:
49:     return myBalance;
50: }
51:
52: CustomerList* AccountImpl::getCustomers() {
```

continues

Listing 6.11. continued

```
53:
54:     return &myOwners;
55: }
56:
57: CORBA::Float AccountImpl::withdraw(CORBA::Float amount) {
58:
59:     myBalance -= amount;
60:
61:     return myBalance;
62: }
63:
64: CORBA::Float AccountImpl::deposit(CORBA::Float amount) {
65:
66:     myBalance += amount;
67:
68:     return myBalance;
69: }
```

Implementing the CheckingAccount Interface

The CheckingAccount interface is the easiest interface to implement because it doesn't define any additional methods. The IDL definition for the CheckingAccount interface is shown in Listing 6.12.

Listing 6.12. CheckingAccount.idl.

```
 1: // CheckingAccount.idl
 2:
 3: #ifndef CheckingAccount_idl
 4: #define CheckingAccount_idl
 5:
 6: #include "Account.idl"
 7:
 8: // A CheckingAccount is an Account which supports checking. It
 9: // does not gain any interest, as its sibling, the SavingsAccount,
10: // does.
11: interface CheckingAccount : Account {
12:
13: };
14:
15: #endif
```

Again, because there are no attributes or methods defined as part of the CheckingAccount interface, there is little to do for the implementation class. Simply providing an empty constructor and destructor is sufficient. The implementation for the CheckingAccount interface can be seen in Listings 6.13 and 6.14.

Listing 6.13. `CheckingAccountImpl.h`.

```
1: // CheckingAccountImpl.h
2:
3: #ifndef CheckingAccountImpl_h
4: #define CheckingAccountImpl_h
5:
6: #include "../CheckingAccount_s.h"
7: #include "AccountImpl.h"
8:
9: class CheckingAccountImpl : public _sk_CheckingAccount {
10:
11: public:
12:
13:     // Constructor.
14:     //
15:     // accountNumber - Account number.
16:     // creationDate - Account creation date.
17:     // initialBalance - Initial Account balance.
18:     // customer - Initial Account owner.
19:     CheckingAccountImpl(const char* accountNumber, const char*
20:             creationDate, CORBA::Float initialBalance, Customer_ptr
21:             customer);
22:
23:     // Destructor.
24:     ~CheckingAccountImpl();
25:
26:     // These methods are described in Account.idl.
27:     virtual char* accountNumber();
28:     virtual char* creationDate();
29:     virtual CORBA::Float balance();
30:     virtual CustomerList* getCustomers();
31:     virtual CORBA::Float withdraw(CORBA::Float amount);
32:     virtual CORBA::Float deposit(CORBA::Float amount);
33:
34: private:
35:
36:     // Default constructor.
37:     CheckingAccountImpl();
38:
39:     // My associated AccountImpl object.
40:     AccountImpl myAccount;
41: };
42:
43: #endif
```

Listing 6.14. `CheckingAccountImpl.cpp`.

```
1: // CheckingAccountImpl.cpp
2:
3: #include "CheckingAccountImpl.h"
4:
```

continues

Listing 6.14. continued

```
 5: // Constructor.
 6: //
 7: // accountNumber - Account number.
 8: // creationDate - Account creation date.
 9: // initialBalance - Initial Account balance.
10: // customer - Initial Account owner.
11: CheckingAccountImpl::CheckingAccountImpl(const char* accountNumber,
12:         const char* creationDate, CORBA::Float initialBalance,
13:         Customer_ptr customer) : myAccount(accountNumber,
14:         creationDate, initialBalance, customer) {
15:
16: }
17:
18: // Default constructor.
19: CheckingAccountImpl::CheckingAccountImpl() : myAccount(NULL, NULL,
20:         0.0, Customer::_nil()) {
21:
22: }
23:
24: // Destructor.
25: CheckingAccountImpl::~CheckingAccountImpl() {
26:
27: }
28:
29: char* CheckingAccountImpl::accountNumber() {
30:
31:     return myAccount.accountNumber();
32: }
33:
34: char* CheckingAccountImpl::creationDate() {
35:
36:     return myAccount.creationDate();
37: }
38:
39: CORBA::Float CheckingAccountImpl::balance() {
40:
41:     return myAccount.balance();
42: }
43:
44: CustomerList* CheckingAccountImpl::getCustomers() {
45:
46:     return myAccount.getCustomers();
47: }
48:
49: CORBA::Float CheckingAccountImpl::withdraw(CORBA::Float amount) {
50:
51:     return myAccount.withdraw(amount);
52: }
53:
54: CORBA::Float CheckingAccountImpl::deposit(CORBA::Float amount) {
55:
56:     return myAccount.deposit(amount);
57: }
```

Implementing the SavingsAccount Interface

The SavingsAccount interface is more complicated than the CheckingAccount interface and so requires a bit more effort to implement. The SavingsAccount IDL definition is shown in Listing 6.15.

Listing 6.15. SavingsAccount.idl.

```
 1: // SavingsAccount.idl
 2:
 3: #ifndef SavingsAccount_idl
 4: #define SavingsAccount_idl
 5:
 6: #include "Account.idl"
 7:
 8: // A SavingsAccount is an Account which supports savings
 9: // account semantics, such as gaining interest.
10: interface SavingsAccount : Account {
11:
12:     // This Account's interest rate.
13:     readonly attribute float interestRate;
14:
15:     // Set this Account's interest rate to the given rate.
16:     // Returns the previous rate.
17:     float setInterestRate(in float rate);
18: };
19:
20: #endif
```

For the SavingsAccount implementation class, you need to define getinterestRate() (an accessor for the interestRate attribute), setInterestRate(), and the class constructor (or constructors) and destructor. The implementation class appears in Listings 6.16 and 6.17.

Listing 6.16. SavingsAccountImpl.h.

```
 1: // SavingsAccountImpl.h
 2:
 3: #ifndef SavingsAccountImpl_h
 4: #define SavingsAccountImpl_h
 5:
 6: #include "../SavingsAccount_s.h"
 7: #include "AccountImpl.h"
 8:
 9: class SavingsAccountImpl : public AccountImpl {
10:
11: public:
12:
13:     // Constructor.
14:     //
```

continues

Listing 6.16. continued

```
15:      // accountNumber - Account number.
16:      // creationDate - Account creation date.
17:      // initialBalance - Initial Account balance.
18:      // customer - Initial Account owner.
19:      // interestRate - Initial Account interest rate.
20:      SavingsAccountImpl(const char* accountNumber, const char*
21:              creationDate, CORBA::Float initialBalance, Customer_ptr
22:              customer, CORBA::Float interestRate);
23:
24:      // Destructor.
25:      ~SavingsAccountImpl();
26:
27:      // These methods are described in Account.idl.
28:      virtual char* accountNumber();
29:      virtual char* creationDate();
30:      virtual CORBA::Float balance();
31:      virtual CustomerList* getCustomers();
32:      virtual CORBA::Float withdraw(CORBA::Float amount);
33:      virtual CORBA::Float deposit(CORBA::Float amount);
34:
35:      // These methods are described in SavingsAccount.idl.
36:      virtual CORBA::Float interestRate();
37:      virtual CORBA::Float setInterestRate(CORBA::Float rate);
38:
39: private:
40:
41:      // Default constructor.
42:      SavingsAccountImpl();
43:
44:      // This Account's interest rate.
45:      CORBA::Float myInterestRate;
46:
47:      // My associated AccountImpl object.
48:      AccountImpl myAccount;
49: };
50:
51: #endif
```

Listing 6.17. SavingsAccountImpl.cpp.

```
1: // SavingsAccountImpl.cpp
2:
3: #include "SavingsAccountImpl.h"
4:
5: // Constructor.
6: //
7: // accountNumber - Account number.
8: // creationDate - Account creation date.
9: // initialBalance - Initial Account balance.
10: // customer - Initial Account owner.
```

```
11: // interestRate - Initial Account interest rate.
12: SavingsAccountImpl::SavingsAccountImpl(const char* accountNumber,
13:         const char* creationDate, CORBA::Float initialBalance,
14:         Customer_ptr customer, CORBA::Float interestRate) :
15:         myAccount(accountNumber, creationDate, initialBalance,
16:         customer), myInterestRate(interestRate) {
17:
18: }
19:
20: // Default constructor.
21: SavingsAccountImpl::SavingsAccountImpl() : myAccount(NULL, NULL,
22:         0.0, Customer::_nil()), myInterestRate(0.0) {
23:
24: }
25:
26: // Destructor.
27: SavingsAccountImpl::~SavingsAccountImpl() {
28:
29: }
30:
31: char* SavingsAccountImpl::accountNumber() {
32:
33:     return myAccount.accountNumber();
34: }
35:
36: char* SavingsAccountImpl::creationDate() {
37:
38:     return myAccount.creationDate();
39: }
40:
41: CORBA::Float SavingsAccountImpl::balance() {
42:
43:     return myAccount.balance();
44: }
45:
46: CustomerList* SavingsAccountImpl::getCustomers() {
47:
48:     return myAccount.getCustomers();
49: }
50:
51: CORBA::Float SavingsAccountImpl::withdraw(CORBA::Float amount) {
52:
53:     return myAccount.withdraw(amount);
54: }
55:
56: CORBA::Float SavingsAccountImpl::deposit(CORBA::Float amount) {
57:
58:     return myAccount.deposit(amount);
59: }
60:
61: CORBA::Float SavingsAccountImpl::interestRate() {
62:
63:     return myInterestRate;
64: }
65:
```

6

continues

Listing 6.17. continued

```
66: CORBA::Float SavingsAccountImpl::setInterestRate(CORBA::Float rate) {
67:
68:     CORBA::Float oldInterestRate = myInterestRate;
69:
70:     myInterestRate = rate;
71:
72:     return oldInterestRate;
73: }
```

Implementing Basic Client Capabilities

Now that you have implemented the basic capabilities of the CORBA server for the Bank application, you're ready to begin working on the basic client capabilities. Since most of the work is done by the server in this application, you'll find the client to be fairly simple by comparison.

Implementing the Customer Interface

The Customer interface encapsulates the attributes and behaviors of a Customer of a Bank. For the most part, this interface serves as a container for Account objects. The IDL definition for the Customer interface is shown in Listing 6.18.

Listing 6.18. Customer.idl.

```
1: // Customer.idl
2:
3: // Forward declaration of Customer interface.
4: interface Customer;
5:
6: #ifndef Customer_idl
7: #define Customer_idl
8:
9: // sequence of Customers
10: typedef sequence<Customer> CustomerList;
11:
12: #include "Account.idl"
13:
14: // A Customer can hold one or more Accounts. Presumably, the
15: // Customer is what drives the rest of this application.
16: interface Customer {
17:
18:     // This Customer's name.
19:     attribute string name;
20:
21:     // This Customer's Social Security number.
22:     readonly attribute string socialSecurityNumber;
23:
```

```
24:     // This Customer's address.
25:     attribute string address;
26:
27:     // This Customer's mother's maiden name.
28:     readonly attribute string mothersMaidenName;
29:
30:     // Return a list of Accounts held (or co-held) by this
31:     // Customer.
32:     AccountList getAccounts();
33: };
34:
35: #endif
```

You need to implement getname(), setname(), getsocialSecurityNumber(), getaddress(), setAddress(), and getmothersMaidenName(), which are the accessors and mutators for various attributes of Account, along with getAccounts() and the class constructor (or constructors) and destructor. The implementation for CustomerImpl appears in Listings 6.19 and 6.20.

Listing 6.19. CustomerImpl.h.

```
1: // CustomerImpl.h
2:
3: #ifndef CustomerImpl_h
4: #define CustomerImpl_h
5:
6: #include "../Customer_s.h"
7:
8: class CustomerImpl : public _sk_Customer {
9:
10: public:
11:
12:     // Constructor.
13:     //
14:     // name - Customer's name.
15:     // socialSecurityNumber - Customer's Social Security number.
16:     // address - Customer's address.
17:     // mothersMaidenName - Customer's mother's maiden name.
18:     CustomerImpl(const char* name, const char* socialSecurityNumber,
19:             const char* address, const char* mothersMaidenName);
20:
21:     // Destructor.
22:     ~CustomerImpl();
23:
24:     // These methods are described in Customer.idl.
25:     virtual char* name();
26:     virtual void name(const char* val);
27:     virtual char* socialSecurityNumber();
28:     virtual char* address();
29:     virtual void address(const char* val);
```

continues

Listing 6.19. continued

```
30:     virtual char* mothersMaidenName();
31:     virtual AccountList* getAccounts();
32:
33: private:
34:
35:     // Default constructor.
36:     CustomerImpl();
37:
38:     // This Customer's name.
39:     char* myName;
40:
41:     // This Customer's Social Security number.
42:     char* mySocialSecurityNumber;
43:
44:     // This Customer's address.
45:     char* myAddress;
46:
47:     // This Customer's mother's maiden name.
48:     char* myMothersMaidenName;
49:
50:     // This Customer's Accounts.
51:     AccountList myAccounts;
52: };
53:
54: #endif
```

Listing 6.20. CustomerImpl.cpp.

```
1: // CustomerImpl.cpp
2:
3: #include "CustomerImpl.h"
4:
5: #include <string.h>
6:
7: // Constructor.
8: //
9: // name - Customer's name.
10: // socialSecurityNumber - Customer's Social Security number.
11: // address - Customer's address.
12: // mothersMaidenName - Customer's mother's maiden name.
13: CustomerImpl::CustomerImpl(const char* name, const char*
14:         socialSecurityNumber, const char* address, const char*
15:         mothersMaidenName) : myName(strdup(name)),
16:         mySocialSecurityNumber(strdup(socialSecurityNumber)),
17:         myAddress(strdup(address)),
18:         myMothersMaidenName(strdup(mothersMaidenName)),
19:         myAccounts() {
20:
21: }
22:
```

```
23: // Default constructor.
24: CustomerImpl::CustomerImpl() : myName(NULL),
25:         mySocialSecurityNumber(NULL), myAddress(NULL),
26:         myMothersMaidenName(NULL), myAccounts() {
27:
28: }
29:
30: // Destructor.
31: CustomerImpl::~CustomerImpl() {
32:
33:     free(myName);
34:     free(mySocialSecurityNumber);
35:     free(myAddress);
36:     free(myMothersMaidenName);
37: }
38:
39: char* CustomerImpl::name() {
40:
41:     return CORBA::strdup(myName);
42: }
43:
44: void CustomerImpl::name(const char* val) {
45:
46:     free(myName);
47:     myName = strdup(val);
48: }
49:
50: char* CustomerImpl::socialSecurityNumber() {
51:
52:     return CORBA::strdup(mySocialSecurityNumber);
53: }
54:
55: char* CustomerImpl::address() {
56:
57:     return CORBA::strdup(myAddress);
58: }
59:
60: void CustomerImpl::address(const char* val) {
61:
62:     free(myAddress);
63:     myAddress = strdup(val);
64: }
65:
66: char* CustomerImpl::mothersMaidenName() {
67:
68:     return CORBA::strdup(myMothersMaidenName);
69: }
70:
71: AccountList* CustomerImpl::getAccounts() {
72:
73:     return &myAccounts;
74: }
```

6

Implementing Additional Client Functionality

In addition to the Customer interface, any useful client needs to implement additional functionality. An examination of the Customer implementation will suggest to you why this is so: Although the implementation allows a Customer to interact with various other components of the Bank application (such as Bank and Account objects), there is no functionality in the Customer implementation that directs the client application to actually do something. Therefore, any client application will not consist solely of the Customer interface implementation but will add extra functionality that performs useful work.

Listing 6.21 contains a sample client application that creates a new Customer object, opens a new Account with a Bank, and then performs some operations on that Account (a deposit and a withdrawal). This application is very simple and not very interactive (it obtains all of its parameters from the command line), but it demonstrates how operations on CORBA objects are invoked.

Listing 6.21. NewCustomerMain.cpp.

```
 1: // NewCustomerMain.cpp
 2:
 3: #include <iostream.h>
 4:
 5: #include "../Customer/CustomerImpl.h"
 6:
 7: #include "../Bank_c.h"
 8:
 9: int main(int argc, char *const *argv) {
10:
11:     // Check the number of arguments; there should be exactly four
12:     // (five counting the executable name itself).
13:     if (argc != 5) {
14:         cout << "Usage: NewCustomer <name> <social security number>"
15:                 " <address> <mother's maiden name>" << endl;
16:         return 1;
17:     }
18:
19:     // Assign the command line arguments to the Customer attributes.
20:     const char* name = argv[1];
21:     const char* socialSecurityNumber = argv[2];
22:     const char* address = argv[3];
23:     const char* mothersMaidenName = argv[4];
24:
25:     // Initialize the ORB and BOA.
26:     CORBA::ORB_var orb = CORBA::ORB_init(argc, argv);
27:     CORBA::BOA_var boa = orb->BOA_init(argc, argv);
28:
29:     // Create a Customer object.
30:     cout << "NewCustomer: Creating new Customer:" << endl;
31:     cout << "  name: " << name << endl;
32:     cout << "  Social Security number: " << socialSecurityNumber <<
```

6

```
33:            endl;
34:        cout << "   address: " << address << endl;
35:        cout << "   mother's maiden name: " << mothersMaidenName << endl;
36:        CustomerImpl customer(name, socialSecurityNumber, address,
37:                mothersMaidenName);
38:
39:        // Notify the BOA that the CustomerImpl object is ready.
40:        boa->obj_is_ready(&customer);
41:
42:        // Locate a Bank object and register with it.
43:        Bank_var bank;
44:        try {
45:            bank = Bank::_bind();
46:        } catch (const CORBA::Exception& ex) {
47:
48:            // The bind attempt failed...
49:            cout << "NewCustomer: Unable to bind to a Bank." << endl;
50:            cout << ex << endl;
51:            return 1;
52:        }
53:
54:        // Do some cool stuff.
55:
56:        cout << "NewCustomer: Connected to Bank \"" << bank->name() <<
57:                "\"." << endl;
58:        Account_var account;
59:
60:        try {
61:            account = bank->createAccount(&customer, "checking", 0.0);
62:        } catch (const CORBA::Exception& ex) {
63:
64:            // The createAccount() attempt failed...
65:            cout << "NewCustomer: Unable to create Account." << endl;
66:            cout << ex << endl;
67:            return 1;
68:        }
69:
70:        try {
71:
72:            // Print out some Account statistics.
73:            cout << "NewCustomer: Opened new Account:" << endl;
74:            cout << "   account number: " << account->accountNumber() <<
75:                    endl;
76:            cout << "   creation date: " << account->creationDate() <<
77:                    endl;
78:            cout << "   account balance: " << account->balance() << endl;
79:
80:            // Perform some transactions on the Account.
81:            cout << "NewCustomer: Performing transactions." << endl;
82:            cout << "   Depositing $250.00; new balance is $" <<
83:                    account->deposit(250.00) << endl;
84:            cout << "   Withdrawing $500.00; new balance is $" <<
85:                    account->withdraw(500.00) << " (Whoops!)" << endl;
86:
```

continues

Listing 6.21. continued

```
87:        // Get rid of the Account.
88:        bank->deleteAccount(account);
89:    } catch (const CORBA::Exception& ex) {
90:
91:        // Some operation on the Account failed...
92:        cout << "NewCustomer: Error accessing Account." << endl;
93:        cout << ex << endl;
94:        return 1;
95:    }
96:
97:    // When this point is reached, the application is finished.
98:    return 0;
99: }
```

Running the Examples

Now that you've implemented all the server and client components of the Bank application, you're ready to try it out. Running the application consists of the following steps:

1. Start the CORBA Naming Service—or a similar type of service—which will be required by the BankServer when it starts up.

2. Start the BankServer server. The BankServer will register itself with the Naming Service.

3. Start one or more Bank servers. Upon startup, each Bank server will locate a BankServer through the Naming Service and register itself with the BankServer.

4. Run the NewCustomer client application. The NewCustomer application will create a new Customer and Account, verifying that the Bank and BankServer objects are working correctly.

Starting the CORBA Naming Service

Generally, before starting any CORBA applications, you first need to invoke the mechanism by which the application components can find each other. Sometimes this is a CORBA Naming Service (which you'll use later); other times it's a simple executable included with the CORBA product you are using. Because the method by which these executables are invoked varies from one product to the next, you'll want to consult your product's documentation to determine how this is done.

For Visigenic's VisiBroker, you'll want to run the provided osagent utility. Running the utility is simple; at the command line, simply type the following:

osagent

The osagent utility produces no output, but it begins a new process (which appears as an icon on the taskbar if you're using Windows 95 or Windows NT 4.0). The process—often referred to as a *daemon* in UNIX-speak—is called the ORBeline Smart Agent and allows CORBA applications using VisiBroker to locate each other.

NOTE

> As directed in the VisiBroker documentation, you'll want to ensure that the VisiBroker bin directory is in your system's PATH environment variable. (The method for adding directories to the PATH varies between systems; consult the VisiBroker or system documentation to determine how this is accomplished.) Other products work similarly; it's often convenient to place the software's bin directory into your system's PATH.

Starting the BankServer Component

After you start the Naming Service (or ORBeline Smart Agent, in the case of VisiBroker), begin the BankServer application component. The BankServer must be run before any other components of the application because Customers need to connect to Banks, which in turn need to connect to BankServers.

To start the BankServer, first change to the directory where the BankServer executable resides. (If you're using Microsoft's Visual C++, the compiler by default places the executable in a directory under the project directory called Debug or Release, depending on the version of the executable you compiled.) Type the following at the command prompt:

```
BankServer
```

You will see this output:

```
BankServer ready.
```

The BankServer is now running and listening for incoming requests; you can now advance to starting a Bank server component.

Starting the Bank Component

To start the Bank component, open a separate command window. (UNIX users can "background" the BankServer application and use the same window, but for the sake of clarity, application components should be run in separate windows, at least for now).

To start the Bank component, change to the directory where the Bank executable is located, as you did with the BankServer component. Then choose a name for the Bank (any name will do), for example, "First Bank." The name of the Bank can contain spaces, but if it does, you

6

have to quote the name so the application perceives it as a single parameter. Using the name "First Bank," type the following at the command prompt:

```
Bank "First Bank"
```

Like the `BankServer` component, the `Bank` component does not produce much output at this time—simply the following:

```
Bank "First Bank" ready.
```

The `Bank` component is now ready for client components to connect to it, so you're ready for the next step.

Running the Client Application

Again, open a new command window and change to the directory containing the executable to start the client application component. For the `NewCustomer` component, you need the following `Customer` information for parameters: name, Social Security number, address, and mother's maiden name. Again, parameters can contain spaces, as long as you surround each parameter with quotations. For example:

```
NewCustomer "Jeremy Rosenberger" 123456789 "123 Main Street,
Denver, CO 12345" Stroustrup
```

The output of the client component will be the following:

```
NewCustomer: Creating new Customer:
  name: Jeremy Rosenberger
  Social Security number: 123456789
  address: 123 Main Street, Denver, CO 12345
  mother's maiden name: Stroustrup
NewCustomer: Connected to Bank "First Bank".
NewCustomer: Opened new Account:
  account number: Account00000000
  creation date: Sep 28 1997
  account balance: 0
NewCustomer: Performing transactions.
  Depositing $250.00; new balance is $250
  Withdrawing $500.00; new balance is $-250 (Whoops!)
```

When you get this far, congratulations! You have successfully developed and run a fully functional CORBA application.

Summary

In this chapter you started with an IDL specification, implemented the interfaces described in that specification, and created server and client executables that communicated by using those interfaces. Along the way you learned about some other aspects of CORBA applications:

☐ CORBA provides the _duplicate() and _release() methods to track usage of CORBA objects. Although CORBA doesn't specify it, reference counting is a typical mechanism which is realized by the use of these methods.

☐ CORBA servers indicate that their objects are ready (or the server itself is ready) by calling the obj_is_ready() and impl_is_ready() methods in the Basic Object Adapter (BOA).

☐ CORBA clients connect to server objects by binding to them, using the _bind() method (a nonstandard method used in the examples in this chapter) or via an appropriate CORBAservice (which you'll explore later on Day 12). After an object is bound, the client can call methods on that object just as if the object were local.

Next you'll concentrate on enhancing the Bank example by adding new functionality and robustness to the application components. On Day 7, you'll add exception handling code to the application. Exceptions allow the application more flexibility in handling error conditions—a concept familiar to C++ and Java programmers. For this application, it would be useful if an attempt to withdraw funds from an Account that did not have such funds available signalled an error. (Recall from the example output that in the current application, withdrawing from an Account with insufficient funds simply makes the Account balance go negative.) One task you'll take on in the next chapter is to add an exception which traps this condition.

Q&A

Q Why do CORBA objects need to be reference counted?

A In a non-distributed application, it is a simple matter to determine when an object is no longer required (in other words, no longer referenced by any other object) and thus destroy it, removing it from memory. In fact, some languages, such as Java, provide this functionality—known as *garbage collection*—as a feature built into the language. Distributed applications, however, make the issue of destroying unused objects more complicated because it is difficult to determine which objects are in use by other (potentially remote) objects. CORBA thus provides the reference counting mechanism to facilitate the tracking of object usage. Another method of achieving this is for each object to occasionally "ping" the objects it references, updating reference counts as necessary. However, this approach can be problematic, depending on the number of objects in the system.

Q Okay, I understand reference counting now, but what if a client application crashes and thus _release() is never called? Is the object never destroyed?

6

A Indeed, the reference counting system employed by CORBA is not without its flaws, and this is one of them. If a client application that references a remote object crashes, _release() will not be called enough times on that object, and thus the object's reference count will never reach zero. There are design patterns (which you'll learn about on Day 10) that deal with issues such as this; the basic approach is for servers to evict objects into a database or persistent store after they have been unused for a preset period of time. If the object is required again, it can be retrieved from the persistent store or re-created in some other fashion.

Workshop

The following section will help you test your comprehension of the material presented in this chapter and put what you've learned into practice. You'll find the answers to the quiz and exercise in Appendix A.

Quiz

1. It was noted earlier that _is_equivalent() is not guaranteed to return TRUE when two object references refer to the same object. Can you think of a mechanism that would more reliably determine whether two references refer to the same object? (For simplicity, assume the objects are of the same type.)

2. What would happen if _release() were not called on an object which had earlier been _duplicate()d?

3. Why does NewCustomerMain.cpp have a try ... catch (const CORBA::Exception& ex) block?

Exercise

Modify the client application so that it prints the names of the Customers who are associated with the Account that was created. (The single Customer printed should be the same Customer whose information was entered on the command line.)

Day 7

Using Exceptions to Perform Error Checking

On Day 6, you created a basic CORBA application from a set of IDL specifications. The application implemented some basic functionality but lacked robustness; for example, the client component of the application demonstrated that it was possible to withdraw from an Account an amount greater than the Account's balance (without any sort of overdraft capability). In this chapter, you'll enhance the application to better handle error conditions (such as attempting to withdraw too many funds from an Account).

Defining Exceptions for the Application

To intelligently add error-checking capability to the application, you need to go back through the design, look at each method, determine what error conditions can occur in each method, and determine whether the error condition should be handled by the method itself or thrown (*raised* in CORBA lingo) back to the client to be handled. In this section, you'll analyze each IDL interface again, determining what exceptions can be thrown and from where.

NOTE

> When a method throws an exception back to its caller, CORBA refers to this action as *raising* an exception. However, many languages—particularly Java and C++—refer to this as *throwing* an exception. Because both terms have identical meaning and are commonly used, you will see them used interchangeably throughout this chapter.

Exceptions in `BankServer`

You'll start by adding exception-handling capability to the `BankServer` interface. For your review (and convenience), Listing 7.1 contains the original `BankServer.idl` from Day 6, which you'll then modify with the exception-handling definitions.

Listing 7.1. Original `BankServer.idl`.

```
 1: // BankServer.idl
 2:
 3: #ifndef BankServer_idl
 4: #define BankServer_idl
 5:
 6: #include "Bank.idl"
 7:
 8: // A BankServer provides clients with visibility to Bank objects.
 9: interface BankServer {
10:
11:     // Register the given Bank with this BankServer. The Bank will
12:     // be listed by getBanks() until unregisterBank() is called with
13:     // that Bank.
14:     void registerBank(in Bank bank);
15:
16:     // Unregister the given Bank from this BankServer. If the Bank
17:     // was not previously registered, this operation does nothing.
18:     void unregisterBank(in Bank bank);
19:
20:     // Return a list of all Banks currently registered with this
21:     // BankServer.
22:     BankList getBanks();
23: };
24:
25: #endif
```

Starting your analysis with the BankServer interface, you can see that three methods can potentially throw exceptions. The first method, registerBank() (lines 11-14), can conceivably throw an exception if an attempt is made to register a Bank that is already registered. Make a note of this exception; you can call it InvalidBankException (it is a good practice to make exception names as self-explanatory as possible). Moving on to the next method, unregisterBank() (lines 16-18), you can see that it is possible that a Bank that was never registered with the BankServer can attempt to unregister. Similarly, this method might throw an InvalidBankException. Finally, getBanks() (lines 20-22) need not throw any exception; if no Banks are registered with the BankServer, it can simply return an empty BankList.

Your analysis of the BankServer interface has turned up two methods that raise exceptions. The new signatures for these methods, modified to raise the exceptions described previously, are as follows:

```
void registerBank(in Bank bank)
        raises (InvalidBankException);

void unregisterBank(in Bank bank)
        raises (InvalidBankException);
```

Exceptions in Bank

You can now move on to the Bank interface, the next interface to which you'll be adding exception-handling capability. Again, the original Bank.idl listing from Day 6 reappears in Listing 7.2.

Listing 7.2. Original Bank.idl.

```
 1: // Bank.idl
 2:
 3: // Forward declaration of Bank interface.
 4: interface Bank;
 5:
 6: #ifndef Bank_idl
 7: #define Bank_idl
 8:
 9: // sequence of Banks
10: typedef sequence<Bank> BankList;
11:
12: #include "Customer.idl"
13: #include "Account.idl"
14:
15: // A Bank provides access to Accounts. It can create an Account
16: // on behalf of a Customer, delete an Account, or list the current
17: // Accounts with the Bank.
18: interface Bank {
19:
20:     // This Bank's name.
21:     attribute string name;
22:
```

continues

Listing 7.2. continued

```
23:      // This Bank's address.
24:      attribute string address;
25:
26:      // Create an Account on behalf of the given Customer, with the
27:      // given account type ("savings" or "checking", where case is
28:      // significant), and the given opening balance.
29:      Account createAccount(in Customer customer, in string
30:              accountType, in float openingBalance);
31:
32:      // Delete the given Account. If the Account is not with this
33:      // Bank, this operation does nothing.
34:      void deleteAccount(in Account account);
35:
36:      // List all Accounts with this Bank.
37:      AccountList getAccounts();
38: };
39:
40: #endif
```

The Bank interface contains three methods: createAccount() (lines 26-30), which need not throw any exceptions; deleteAccount() (lines 32-34), which throws an exception if the specified Account object does not exist in the Bank; and getAccounts() (lines 36-37), which also need not throw any exceptions.

Again using a self-explanatory exception name, the modified deleteAccount() signature looks like this:

```
void deleteAccount(in Account account)
        raises (InvalidAccountException);
```

Exceptions in Account

Listing 7.3 contains the Account interface (again making a reappearance from Day 6), the next candidate for adding exception raising.

Listing 7.3. Original Account.idl.

```
 1: // Account.idl
 2:
 3: // Forward declaration of Account interface.
 4: interface Account;
 5:
 6: #ifndef Account_idl
 7: #define Account_idl
 8:
 9: // sequence of Accounts
10: typedef sequence<Account> AccountList;
11:
12: #include "Customer.idl"
```

```
13:
14: // An Account is an entity owned by a Bank and held by a Customer
15: // (or multiple Customers). An Account has a balance which can be
16: // affected by deposits and withdrawals.
17: interface Account {
18:
19:     // This Account's account number.
20:     readonly attribute string accountNumber;
21:
22:     // This Account's creation date.
23:     readonly attribute string creationDate;
24:
25:     // This Account's current balance.
26:     readonly attribute float balance;
27:
28:     // Return a list of Customers who hold this Account.
29:     CustomerList getCustomers();
30:
31:     // Withdraw the given amount from this Account. Returns the new
32:     // account balance.
33:     float withdraw(in float amount);
34:
35:     // Deposit the given amount into this Account. Returns the new
36:     // account balance.
37:     float deposit(in float amount);
38: };
39:
40: #endif
```

Analyzing the Account interface's methods, in lines 28-29 you encounter getCustomers(), which need not throw any exceptions (again, an empty list can be returned if there are no Customers, even though this should never happen). Lines 31-33 contain the withdraw() method, which throws an exception if insufficient funds are available in the specified account. Finally, deposit() (lines 35-37) throws an exception if an invalid amount is specified (for instance, a negative amount). Actually, withdraw() throws an exception when given an invalid amount, as well.

This analysis leads to the following method signatures:

```
float withdraw(in float amount)
       raises (InvalidAmountException,
       InsufficientFundsException);

float deposit(in float amount)
       raises (InvalidAmountException);
```

Exceptions in CheckingAccount

Because the CheckingAccount interface adds no new methods to the Account interface, no additional analysis is necessary to determine exception raising for this interface. For your review, the listing for CheckingAccount.idl reappears in Listing 7.4.

7

Listing 7.4. Original `CheckingAccount.idl`.

```
// CheckingAccount.idl

#ifndef CheckingAccount_idl
#define CheckingAccount_idl

#include "Account.idl"

// A CheckingAccount is an Account which supports checking. It
// does not gain any interest, as its sibling, the SavingsAccount,
// does.
interface CheckingAccount : Account {

};

#endif
```

Exceptions in `SavingsAccount`

Listing 7.5 reproduces the `SavingsAccount.idl` listing from Day 6.

Listing 7.5. Original `SavingsAccount.idl`.

```
 1: // SavingsAccount.idl
 2:
 3: #ifndef SavingsAccount_idl
 4: #define SavingsAccount_idl
 5:
 6: #include "Account.idl"
 7:
 8: // A SavingsAccount is an Account which supports savings
 9: // account semantics, such as gaining interest.
10: interface SavingsAccount : Account {
11:
12:     // This Account's interest rate.
13:     readonly attribute float interestRate;
14:
15:     // Set this Account's interest rate to the given rate.
16:     // Returns the previous rate.
17:     float setInterestRate(in float rate);
18: };
19:
20: #endif
```

The `SavingsAccount` interface defines one additional method, `setInterestRate()` (lines 15-17), which can throw an exception if an invalid rate (for example, a negative one) is specified. In the interest of not using too many different exception names, you can reuse the `InvalidAmountException` from the preceding `Account` interfaces:

```
float setInterestRate(in float rate)
        raises (InvalidAmountException);
```

Exceptions in `Customer`

The `Customer` interface defines only one method, `getAccounts()`, which need not raise any exceptions. For your review, the original `Customer.idl` appears in Listing 7.6.

Listing 7.6. Original `Customer.idl`.

```
 1: // Customer.idl
 2:
 3: // Forward declaration of Customer interface.
 4: interface Customer;
 5:
 6: #ifndef Customer_idl
 7: #define Customer_idl
 8:
 9: // sequence of Customers
10: typedef sequence<Customer> CustomerList;
11:
12: #include "Account.idl"
13:
14: // A Customer can hold one or more Accounts. Presumably, the
15: // Customer is what drives the rest of this application.
16: interface Customer {
17:
18:     // This Customer's name.
19:     attribute string name;
20:
21:     // This Customer's Social Security number.
22:     readonly attribute string socialSecurityNumber;
23:
24:     // This Customer's address.
25:     attribute string address;
26:
27:     // This Customer's mother's maiden name.
28:     readonly attribute string mothersMaidenName;
29:
30:     // Return a list of Accounts held (or co-held) by this
31:     // Customer.
32:     AccountList getAccounts();
33: };
34:
35: #endif
```

Modifying Server IDL to Use Exceptions

Much of the work of adding exceptions has already been done (adding the `raises` clauses to the methods that throw exceptions). However, you did not yet define the exceptions themselves. For the sake of simplicity, define all exceptions in a single file—`Exceptions.idl`, which can be `#included` from other IDL files. `Exceptions.idl` appears in Listing 7.7.

7

Listing 7.7. `Exceptions.idl`.

```
 1: // Exceptions.idl
 2:
 3: #ifndef Exceptions_idl
 4: #define Exceptions_idl
 5:
 6: // This exception is thrown when an invalid amount is passed to a
 7: // method; for instance, if an account is asked to deposit a
 8: // negative amount of funds.
 9: exception InvalidAmountException {
10:
11: };
12:
13: // This exception is thrown when an invalid Account is passed to a
14: // method expecting an Account object.
15: exception InvalidAccountException {
16:
17: };
18:
19: // This exception is thrown when an invalid Bank is passed to a
20: // method expecting a Bank object.
21: exception InvalidBankException {
22:
23: };
24:
25: // This exception is thrown when there are insufficient funds to
26: // cover a transaction; for instance, if a withdrawal attempts to
27: // remove more funds than are available in an account.
28: exception InsufficientFundsException {
29:
30: };
31:
32: #endif
```

Modifying each IDL file to reflect the changes is a simple matter. Listings 7.8–7.13 show the modified IDL files for each interface, with the changes from the original versions highlighted in **bold.**

Listing 7.8. Modified `BankServer.idl`.

```
 1: // BankServer.idl
 2:
 3: #ifndef BankServer_idl
 4: #define BankServer_idl
 5:
 6: #include "Bank.idl"
 7: #include "Exceptions.idl"
 8:
 9: // A BankServer provides clients with visibility to Bank objects.
10: interface BankServer {
11:
```

```
12:      // Register the given Bank with this BankServer. The Bank will
13:      // be listed by getBanks() until unregisterBank() is called with
14:      // that Bank.
15:      void registerBank(in Bank bank)
16:          raises (InvalidBankException);
17:
18:      // Unregister the given Bank from this BankServer. If the Bank
19:      // was not previously registered, this operation does nothing.
20:      void unregisterBank(in Bank bank)
21:          raises (InvalidBankException);
22:
23:      // Return a list of all Banks currently registered with this
24:      // BankServer.
25:      BankList getBanks();
26: };
27:
28: #endif
```

Listing 7.9. Modified `Bank.idl`.

```
 1: // Bank.idl
 2:
 3: // Forward declaration of Bank interface.
 4: interface Bank;
 5:
 6: #ifndef Bank_idl
 7: #define Bank_idl
 8:
 9: // sequence of Banks
10: typedef sequence<Bank> BankList;
11:
12: #include "Customer.idl"
13: #include "Account.idl"
14: #include "Exceptions.idl"
15:
16: // A Bank provides access to Accounts. It can create an Account
17: // on behalf of a Customer, delete an Account, or list the current
18: // Accounts with the Bank.
19: interface Bank {
20:
21:      // This Bank's name.
22:      attribute string name;
23:
24:      // This Bank's address.
25:      attribute string address;
26:
27:      // Create an Account on behalf of the given Customer, with the
28:      // given account type ("savings" or "checking", where case is
29:      // significant), and the given opening balance.
30:      Account createAccount(in Customer customer, in string
31:              accountType, in float openingBalance);
32:
33:      // Delete the given Account. If the Account is not with this
```

7

continues

Listing 7.9. continued

```
34:     // Bank, this operation does nothing.
35:     void deleteAccount(in Account account)
36:             raises (InvalidAccountException);
37:
38:     // List all Accounts with this Bank.
39:     AccountList getAccounts();
40: };
41:
42: #endif
```

Listing 7.10. Modified Account.idl.

```
 1: // Account.idl
 2:
 3: // Forward declaration of Account interface.
 4: interface Account;
 5:
 6: #ifndef Account_idl
 7: #define Account_idl
 8:
 9: // sequence of Accounts
10: typedef sequence<Account> AccountList;
11:
12: #include "Customer.idl"
13: #include "Exceptions.idl"
14:
15: // An Account is an entity owned by a Bank and held by a Customer
16: // (or multiple Customers). An Account has a balance which can be
17: // affected by deposits and withdrawals.
18: interface Account {
19:
20:     // This Account's account number.
21:     readonly attribute string accountNumber;
22:
23:     // This Account's creation date.
24:     readonly attribute string creationDate;
25:
26:     // This Account's current balance.
27:     readonly attribute float balance;
28:
29:     // Return a list of Customers who hold this Account.
30:     CustomerList getCustomers();
31:
32:     // Withdraw the given amount from this Account. Returns the new
33:     // account balance.
34:     float withdraw(in float amount)
35:             raises (InvalidAmountException,
36:             InsufficientFundsException);
37:
38:     // Deposit the given amount into this Account. Returns the new
39:     // account balance.
```

```
40:     float deposit(in float amount)
41:            raises (InvalidAmountException);
42: };
43:
44: #endif
```

Listing 7.11. Modified `CheckingAccount.idl`.

```
1: // CheckingAccount.idl
2:
3: #ifndef CheckingAccount_idl
4: #define CheckingAccount_idl
5:
6: #include "Account.idl"
7:
8: // A CheckingAccount is an Account which supports checking. It
9: // does not gain any interest, as its sibling, the SavingsAccount,
10: // does.
11: interface CheckingAccount : Account {
12:
13: };
14:
15: #endif
```

Listing 7.12. Modified `SavingsAccount.idl`.

```
1: // SavingsAccount.idl
2:
3: #ifndef SavingsAccount_idl
4: #define SavingsAccount_idl
5:
6: #include "Account.idl"
7: #include "Exceptions.idl"
8:
9: // A SavingsAccount is an Account which supports savings
10: // account semantics, such as gaining interest.
11: interface SavingsAccount : Account {
12:
13:     // This Account's interest rate.
14:     readonly attribute float interestRate;
15:
16:     // Set this Account's interest rate to the given rate.
17:     // Returns the previous rate.
18:     float setInterestRate(in float rate)
19:            raises (InvalidAmountException);
20: };
21:
22: #endif
```

7

Listing 7.13. Modified `Customer.idl`.

```
 1: // Customer.idl
 2:
 3: // Forward declaration of Customer interface.
 4: interface Customer;
 5:
 6: #ifndef Customer_idl
 7: #define Customer_idl
 8:
 9: // sequence of Customers
10: typedef sequence<Customer> CustomerList;
11:
12: #include "Account.idl"
13:
14: // A Customer can hold one or more Accounts. Presumably, the
15: // Customer is what drives the rest of this application.
16: interface Customer {
17:
18:     // This Customer's name.
19:     attribute string name;
20:
21:     // This Customer's Social Security number.
22:     readonly attribute string socialSecurityNumber;
23:
24:     // This Customer's address.
25:     attribute string address;
26:
27:     // This Customer's mother's maiden name.
28:     readonly attribute string mothersMaidenName;
29:
30:     // Return a list of Accounts held (or co-held) by this
31:     // Customer.
32:     AccountList getAccounts();
33: };
34:
35: #endif
```

After you have modified the IDL interface definitions to raise the proper exceptions in the proper methods, you can recompile the IDL files to generate new client stubs and server skeletons. When you have generated those, you can begin modifying the code to use the new exceptions.

Modifying Server Code to Throw Exceptions

The IDL interface definitions specify *which* exceptions can be thrown by which methods, but they don't specify *when,* or under what circumstances, those exceptions are thrown. Thus, after modifying the IDL definitions, you need to modify the server code to throw the proper exception at the proper time.

BankServerImpl

You can start with the simpler server, the BankServer. Recall that the BankServer interface contains two methods that raise exceptions: registerBank() and unregisterBank(). The changes need to be made in BankServerImpl.h as well as BankServerImpl.cpp as they appear in Listings 7.14 and 7.15, again highlighted in **bold.**

NOTE

In C++, it is legal for a method to throw an exception without declaring that it does so (with the throw clause in the method signature). However, this practice is considered poor style in some circles. It is recommended that all exceptions thrown by a C++ method be declared in that method's header; this makes it more apparent to the caller of the method that a particular set of exceptions might be raised. (Unlike C++, Java enforces this practice.)

Listing 7.14. Modified BankServerImpl.h.

```
 1: // BankServerImpl.h
 2:
 3: #ifndef BankServerImpl_h
 4: #define BankServerImpl_h
 5:
 6: #include <vector>
 7:
 8: #include "../BankServer_s.h"
 9:
10: class BankServerImpl : public _sk_BankServer {
11:
12: public:
13:
14:     // Constructor.
15:     BankServerImpl(const char* name);
16:
17:     // Destructor.
18:     ~BankServerImpl();
19:
20:     // These methods are described in BankServer.idl.
21:     virtual void registerBank(Bank_ptr bank) throw
22:             (InvalidBankException);
23:     virtual void unregisterBank(Bank_ptr bank) throw
24:             (InvalidBankException);
25:     virtual BankList* getBanks();
26:
27: private:
28:
29:     // Default constructor.
30:     BankServerImpl();
```

7

continues

Listing 7.14. continued

```
31:
32:        // This BankServer's list of Banks.
33:        std::vector<Bank_ptr> myBanks;
34: };
35:
36: #endif
```

Listing 7.15. Modified BankServerImpl.cpp.

```
1: // BankServerImpl.cpp
2:
3: #include "BankServerImpl.h"
4:
5: #include <algorithm>
6: #include <functional>
7:
8: // STL-derived unary function which returns TRUE if Banks are equal.
9: class IsBankEqual : public std::unary_function<Bank_ptr, bool> {
10: public:
11:        IsBankEqual(argument_type bank) { myBank = bank; }
12:        result_type operator()(argument_type bank) { return bank->
13:                _is_equivalent(myBank) != 0; }
14: private:
15:        argument_type myBank;
16: };
17:
18: // Constructor.
19: BankServerImpl::BankServerImpl(const char* name) :
20:        _sk_BankServer(name), myBanks() {
21:
22: }
23:
24: // Destructor.
25: BankServerImpl::~BankServerImpl() {
26:
27: }
28:
29: void BankServerImpl::registerBank(Bank_ptr bank) throw
30:        (InvalidBankException) {
31:
32:        // First, ensure that the given Bank doesn't exist already.
33:        std::vector<Bank_ptr>::iterator first = myBanks.begin();
34:        std::vector<Bank_ptr>::iterator last = myBanks.end();
35:        IsBankEqual predicate(bank);
36:
37:        std::vector<Bank_ptr>::iterator matchedBank = std::
38:                find_if(first, last, predicate);
39:        if (matchedBank == last) {
40:
41:                // Bank was not found, so add the given Bank to the end of
42:                // the list.
```

```
43:            cout << "BankServerImpl: Registering Bank \"" << bank->
44:                  name() << "\"." << endl;
45:         myBanks.push_back(Bank::_duplicate(bank));
46:         return;
47:     } else {
48:
49:         // The Bank was already registered, so throw an exception.
50:         throw InvalidBankException();
51:     }
52: }
53:
54: void BankServerImpl::unregisterBank(Bank_ptr bank) throw
55:         (InvalidBankException) {
56:
57:     std::vector<Bank_ptr>::iterator first = myBanks.begin();
58:     std::vector<Bank_ptr>::iterator last = myBanks.end();
59:     IsBankEqual predicate(bank);
60:
61:     std::vector<Bank_ptr>::iterator matchedBank = std::
62:             find_if(first, last, predicate);
63:     if (matchedBank == last) {
64:
65:         // Invalid Bank; throw an exception.
66:         cout << "BankServerImpl: Attempted to unregister invalid "
67:                  "Bank." << endl;
68:         throw InvalidBankException();
69:     }
70:     cout << "BankServerImpl: Unregistering Bank \"" << bank->name()
71:             << "\"." << endl;
72:
73:     // Delete the given Bank.
74:     myBanks.erase(matchedBank);
75:     bank->_release();
76: }
77:
78: BankList* BankServerImpl::getBanks() {
79:
80:     BankList* list = new BankList(myBanks.size());
81:     CORBA::Long i;
82:
83:     for (i = 0; i < myBanks.size(); i++) {
84:         (*list)[i] = Bank::_duplicate(myBanks[i]);
85:     }
86:
87:     return list;
88: }
```

Note that the pre-exception version of registerBank() did nothing when a client attempted to register a duplicate Bank object. The new and improved version, however, treats this as an error condition; a duplicate Bank registration results in an InvalidBankException being thrown. Similarly, unregisterBank() now throws an InvalidBankException when a client attempts to unregister a Bank that is not registered with the BankServer.

7

AccountImpl

Having dealt with the BankServer implementation, you can now turn your attention to the various interfaces contained in the Bank application, starting with AccountImpl.h and AccountImpl.cpp. As with BankServerImpl.h, modify the method signatures in AccountImpl.h to specify the exceptions thrown by AccountImpl methods. Similarly, AccountImpl.cpp will specify the conditions under which those exceptions are thrown. The modified AccountImpl.h and AccountImpl.cpp appear in Listings 7.16 and 7.17.

Listing 7.16. Modified AccountImpl.h.

```
 1: // AccountImpl.h
 2:
 3: #ifndef AccountImpl_h
 4: #define AccountImpl_h
 5:
 6: #include "../Account_s.h"
 7:
 8: class AccountImpl : public _sk_Account {
 9:
10: // Allow CheckingAccountImpl and SavingsAccountImpl access to the
11: // protected constructor.
12: friend class CheckingAccountImpl;
13: friend class SavingsAccountImpl;
14:
15: public:
16:
17:     // Destructor.
18:     ~AccountImpl();
19:
20:     // These methods are described in Account.idl.
21:     virtual char* accountNumber();
22:     virtual char* creationDate();
23:     virtual CORBA::Float balance();
24:     virtual CustomerList* getCustomers();
25:     virtual CORBA::Float withdraw(CORBA::Float amount) throw
26:         (InvalidAmountException, InsufficientFundsException);
27:     virtual CORBA::Float deposit(CORBA::Float amount) throw
28:         (InvalidAmountException);
29:
30: protected:
31:
32:     // Constructor.
33:     //
34:     // accountNumber - Account number.
35:     // creationDate - Account creation date.
36:     // initialBalance - Initial Account balance.
37:     // customer - Initial Account owner.
38:     AccountImpl(const char* accountNumber, const char*
39:             creationDate, CORBA::Float initialBalance, Customer_ptr
40:             customer);
41:
```

```
42: private:
43:
44:     // Default constructor.
45:     AccountImpl();
46:
47:     // This Account's account number.
48:     char* myAccountNumber;
49:
50:     // This Account's creation date.
51:     char* myCreationDate;
52:
53:     // This Account's current balance.
54:     CORBA::Float myBalance;
55:
56:     // This Account's owners.
57:     CustomerList myOwners;
58: };
59:
60: #endif
```

Listing 7.17. Modified `AccountImpl.cpp`.

```
 1: // AccountImpl.cpp
 2:
 3: #include "AccountImpl.h"
 4:
 5: #include <iostream.h>
 6: #include <string.h>
 7:
 8: // Constructor.
 9: //
10: // accountNumber - Account number.
11: // creationDate - Account creation date.
12: // initialBalance - Initial Account balance.
13: // customer - Initial Account owner.
14: AccountImpl::AccountImpl(const char* accountNumber, const char*
15:         creationDate, CORBA::Float initialBalance, Customer_ptr
16:         customer) : _sk_Account(accountNumber),
17:         myAccountNumber(strdup(accountNumber)),
18:         myCreationDate(strdup(creationDate)),
19:         myBalance(initialBalance), myOwners() {
20:
21:     // Add the Customer to the owner list.
22:     myOwners.length(1);
23:     myOwners[0] = Customer::_duplicate(customer);
24: }
25:
26: // Default constructor.
27: AccountImpl::AccountImpl() : myAccountNumber(NULL),
28:         myCreationDate(NULL), myBalance(0.0), myOwners() {
29:
30: }
31:
```

continues

Listing 7.17. continued

```
32: // Destructor.
33: AccountImpl::~AccountImpl() {
34:
35:     free(myAccountNumber);
36:     free(myCreationDate);
37: }
38:
39: char* AccountImpl::accountNumber() {
40:
41:     return CORBA::strdup(myAccountNumber);
42: }
43:
44: char* AccountImpl::creationDate() {
45:
46:     return CORBA::strdup(myCreationDate);
47: }
48:
49: CORBA::Float AccountImpl::balance() {
50:
51:     return myBalance;
52: }
53:
54: CustomerList* AccountImpl::getCustomers() {
55:
56:     return &myOwners;
57: }
58:
59: CORBA::Float AccountImpl::withdraw(CORBA::Float amount) throw
60:         (InvalidAmountException, InsufficientFundsException) {
61:
62:     // Disallow the withdrawal of negative amounts and throw an
63:     // exception if this is attempted.
64:     if (amount < 0.0) {
65:         cout << "AccountImpl: Attempted to withdraw invalid "
66:                 << "amount." << endl;
67:         throw InvalidAmountException();
68:     }
69:
70:     // Disallow withdrawal of an amount greater than the current
71:     // balance and throw an exception if this is attempted.
72:     if (amount > myBalance) {
73:         cout << "AccountImpl: Insufficient funds to withdraw "
74:                 << "specified amount." << endl;
75:         throw InsufficientFundsException();
76:     }
77:
78:     myBalance -= amount;
79:
80:     return myBalance;
81: }
82:
83: CORBA::Float AccountImpl::deposit(CORBA::Float amount) throw
84:         (InvalidAmountException) {
85:
```

7

```
86:     // Disallow the deposit of negative amounts and throw an
87:     // exception if this is attempted.
88:     if (amount < 0.0) {
89:         cout << "AccountImpl: Attempted to deposit invalid amount."
90:                 << endl;
91:         throw InvalidAmountException();
92:     }
93:
94:     myBalance += amount;
95:
96:     return myBalance;
97: }
```

The modified `withdraw()` method in `AccountImpl` first checks the amount that the client wishes to withdraw. If the amount is negative, it is rejected by the `withdraw()` method, and an `InvalidAmountException` is thrown. If the amount is non-negative, the `Account` balance is checked to see whether sufficient funds are available to withdraw the requested amount. (Recall that overdraft protection is not a current feature of the system.) If there are insufficient funds to cover the withdrawal, `withdraw()` throws an `InsufficientFundsException`.

The `deposit()` method of `AccountImpl` works similarly; an `InvalidAmountException` is thrown if the caller attempts to deposit a negative amount into an `Account` (which would really be a withdrawal). Any amount can be deposited into an `Account`, so there is no need for `deposit()` to ever throw an `InsufficientFundsException`.

CheckingAccountImpl

Listings 7.18 and 7.19 contain further changes required to add exception capability to the `Bank` application.

Listing 7.18. Modified `CheckingAccountImpl.h`.

```
1: // CheckingAccountImpl.h
2:
3: #ifndef CheckingAccountImpl_h
4: #define CheckingAccountImpl_h
5:
6: #include "../CheckingAccount_s.h"
7: #include "AccountImpl.h"
8:
9: class CheckingAccountImpl : public _sk_CheckingAccount {
10:
11: public:
12:
13:     // Constructor.
14:     //
15:     // accountNumber - Account number.
16:     // creationDate - Account creation date.
```

continues

Listing 7.18. continued

```
17:      // initialBalance - Initial Account balance.
18:      // customer - Initial Account owner.
19:      CheckingAccountImpl(const char* accountNumber, const char*
20:              creationDate, CORBA::Float initialBalance, Customer_ptr
21:              customer);
22:
23:      // Destructor.
24:      ~CheckingAccountImpl();
25:
26:      // These methods are described in Account.idl.
27:      virtual char* accountNumber();
28:      virtual char* creationDate();
29:      virtual CORBA::Float balance();
30:      virtual CustomerList* getCustomers();
31:      virtual CORBA::Float withdraw(CORBA::Float amount) throw
32:              (InvalidAmountException, InsufficientFundsException);
33:      virtual CORBA::Float deposit(CORBA::Float amount) throw
34:              (InvalidAmountException);
35:
36: private:
37:
38:      // Default constructor.
39:      CheckingAccountImpl();
40:
41:      // My associated AccountImpl object.
42:      AccountImpl myAccount;
43: };
44:
45: #endif
```

Listing 7.19. Modified `CheckingAccountImpl.cpp`.

```
1: // CheckingAccountImpl.cpp
2:
3: #include "CheckingAccountImpl.h"
4:
5: // Constructor.
6: //
7: // accountNumber - Account number.
8: // creationDate - Account creation date.
9: // initialBalance - Initial Account balance.
10: // customer - Initial Account owner.
11: CheckingAccountImpl::CheckingAccountImpl(const char* accountNumber,
12:         const char* creationDate, CORBA::Float initialBalance,
13:         Customer_ptr customer) : myAccount(accountNumber,
14:         creationDate, initialBalance, customer) {
15:
16: }
17:
18: // Default constructor.
```

7

```
19: CheckingAccountImpl::CheckingAccountImpl() : myAccount(NULL, NULL,
20:         0.0, Customer::_nil()) {
21:
22: }
23:
24: // Destructor.
25: CheckingAccountImpl::~CheckingAccountImpl() {
26:
27: }
28:
29: char* CheckingAccountImpl::accountNumber() {
30:
31:     return myAccount.accountNumber();
32: }
33:
34: char* CheckingAccountImpl::creationDate() {
35:
36:     return myAccount.creationDate();
37: }
38:
39: CORBA::Float CheckingAccountImpl::balance() {
40:
41:     return myAccount.balance();
42: }
43:
44: CustomerList* CheckingAccountImpl::getCustomers() {
45:
46:     return myAccount.getCustomers();
47: }
48:
49: CORBA::Float CheckingAccountImpl::withdraw(CORBA::Float amount)
50:         throw (InvalidAmountException, InsufficientFundsException)
51:         {
52:
53:     return myAccount.withdraw(amount);
54: }
55:
56: CORBA::Float CheckingAccountImpl::deposit(CORBA::Float amount)
57:         throw (InvalidAmountException) {
58:
59:     return myAccount.deposit(amount);
60: }
```

Again, the withdraw() and deposit() methods can throw the InvalidAmountException or InsufficientFundsException, or the InvalidAmountException, respectively. Note, however, that none of these exceptions are explicitly thrown within the methods themselves. Recall that the withdraw() and deposit() operations on the myAccount member (which is an AccountImpl object) can throw these exceptions. Because these exceptions are not caught by the methods in CheckingAccountImpl, the exceptions are simply passed back to the caller of the CheckingAccountImpl method.

7

SavingsAccountImpl

The changes for `SavingsAccountImpl`, as shown in Listings 7.20 and 7.21, closely resemble the changes made in `CheckingAccountImpl`.

Listing 7.20. Modified `SavingsAccountImpl.h`.

```
 1: // SavingsAccountImpl.h
 2:
 3: #ifndef SavingsAccountImpl_h
 4: #define SavingsAccountImpl_h
 5:
 6: #include "../SavingsAccount_s.h"
 7: #include "AccountImpl.h"
 8:
 9: class SavingsAccountImpl : public AccountImpl {
10:
11: public:
12:
13:     // Constructor.
14:     //
15:     // accountNumber - Account number.
16:     // creationDate - Account creation date.
17:     // initialBalance - Initial Account balance.
18:     // customer - Initial Account owner.
19:     // interestRate - Initial Account interest rate.
20:     SavingsAccountImpl(const char* accountNumber, const char*
21:             creationDate, CORBA::Float initialBalance, Customer_ptr
22:             customer, CORBA::Float interestRate);
23:
24:     // Destructor.
25:     ~SavingsAccountImpl();
26:
27:     // These methods are described in Account.idl.
28:     virtual char* accountNumber();
29:     virtual char* creationDate();
30:     virtual CORBA::Float balance();
31:     virtual CustomerList* getCustomers();
32:     virtual CORBA::Float withdraw(CORBA::Float amount) throw
33:             (InvalidAmountException, InsufficientFundsException);
34:     virtual CORBA::Float deposit(CORBA::Float amount) throw
35:             (InvalidAmountException);
36:
37:     // These methods are described in SavingsAccount.idl.
38:         virtual CORBA::Float interestRate();
39:     virtual CORBA::Float setInterestRate(CORBA::Float rate) throw
40:             (InvalidAmountException);
41:
42: private:
43:
44:     // Default constructor.
45:     SavingsAccountImpl();
46:
47:     // This Account's interest rate.
48:     CORBA::Float myInterestRate;
```

```
49:
50:     // My associated AccountImpl object.
51:     AccountImpl myAccount;
52: };
53:
54: #endif
```

Listing 7.21. Modified `SavingsAccountImpl.cpp`.

```
1: // SavingsAccountImpl.cpp
2:
3: #include "SavingsAccountImpl.h"
4:
5: // Constructor.
6: //
7: // accountNumber - Account number.
8: // creationDate - Account creation date.
9: // initialBalance - Initial Account balance.
10: // customer - Initial Account owner.
11: // interestRate - Initial Account interest rate.
12: SavingsAccountImpl::SavingsAccountImpl(const char* accountNumber,
13:         const char* creationDate, CORBA::Float initialBalance,
14:         Customer_ptr customer, CORBA::Float interestRate) :
15:         myAccount(accountNumber, creationDate, initialBalance,
16:         customer), myInterestRate(interestRate) {
17:
18: }
19:
20: // Default constructor.
21: SavingsAccountImpl::SavingsAccountImpl() : myAccount(NULL, NULL,
22:         0.0, Customer::_nil()), myInterestRate(0.0) {
23:
24: }
25:
26: // Destructor.
27: SavingsAccountImpl::~SavingsAccountImpl() {
28:
29: }
30:
31: char* SavingsAccountImpl::accountNumber() {
32:
33:     return myAccount.accountNumber();
34: }
35:
36: char* SavingsAccountImpl::creationDate() {
37:
38:     return myAccount.creationDate();
39: }
40:
41: CORBA::Float SavingsAccountImpl::balance() {
42:
43:     return myAccount.balance();
44: }
45:
```

continues

Listing 7.21. continued

```
46: CustomerList* SavingsAccountImpl::getCustomers() {
47:
48:     return myAccount.getCustomers();
49: }
50:
51: CORBA::Float SavingsAccountImpl::withdraw(CORBA::Float amount)
52:         throw (InvalidAmountException, InsufficientFundsException)
53:         {
54:
55:     return myAccount.withdraw(amount);
56: }
57:
58: CORBA::Float SavingsAccountImpl::deposit(CORBA::Float amount) throw
59:         (InvalidAmountException) {
60:
61:     return myAccount.deposit(amount);
62: }
63:
64: CORBA::Float SavingsAccountImpl::interestRate() {
65:
66:     return myInterestRate;
67: }
68:
69: CORBA::Float SavingsAccountImpl::setInterestRate(CORBA::Float rate) throw
70:         (InvalidAmountException) {
71:
72:     // Disallow negative interest rates and throw an exception if this is
73:     // attempted.
74:     if (rate < 0.0) {
75:
76:         throw InvalidAmountException();
77:     }
78:
79:     CORBA::Float oldInterestRate = myInterestRate;
80:
81:     myInterestRate = rate;
82:
83:     return oldInterestRate;
84: }
```

The changes in the withdraw() and deposit() methods in SavingsAccountImpl copy their counterparts in CheckingAccountImpl exactly. In addition, the setInterestRate() method is modified to disallow negative interest rates (which would correspond to a savings account that loses money over time). If a client attempts to set a negative interest rate for the SavingsAccount, an InvalidAmountException is thrown.

BankImpl

The final server component to modify is the BankImpl itself. Only a single method, deleteAccount(), is modified to throw an exception. The modified BankImpl.h and BankImpl.cpp appear in Listings 7.22 and 7.23.

Listing 7.22. Modified `BankImpl.h`.

```
1: // BankImpl.h
2:
3: #ifndef BankImpl_h
4: #define BankImpl_h
5:
6: #include <vector>
7:
8: #include "../Bank_s.h"
9:
10: class BankImpl : public _sk_Bank {
11:
12: public:
13:
14:      // Constructor.
15:      //
16:      // name - This Bank's name.
17:      BankImpl(const char* name);
18:
19:      // Destructor.
20:      ~BankImpl();
21:
22:      // These methods are described in Bank.idl.
23:      virtual char* name();
24:      virtual void name(const char* val);
25:      virtual char* address();
26:      virtual void address(const char* val);
27:      virtual Account_ptr createAccount(Customer_ptr customer,
28:              const char* accountType, CORBA::Float openingBalance);
29:      virtual void deleteAccount(Account_ptr account) throw
30:              (InvalidAccountException);
31:      virtual AccountList* getAccounts();
32:
33: protected:
34:
35:      // Return the next available account number. The result is
36:      // returned in a static buffer.
37:      char* getNextAccountNumber();
38:
39:      // Return the current date in the form "Mmm DD YYYY". The result
40:      // is returned in a static buffer.
41:      char* getCurrentDate();
42:
43: private:
44:
45:      // Default constructor.
46:      BankImpl();
47:
48:      // This Bank's name.
49:      char* myName;
50:
51:      // This Bank's address.
52:      char* myAddress;
53:
```

7

continues

Listing 7.22. continued

```
54:      // This Bank's Accounts.
55:      std::vector<Account_ptr> myAccounts;
56:
57:      // The next available account number.
58:      unsigned int myNextAccountNumber;
59: };
60:
61: #endif
```

Listing 7.23. Modified BankImpl.cpp.

```cpp
1: // BankImpl.cpp
2:
3: #include "BankImpl.h"
4:
5: #include <time.h>
6: #include <string.h>
7: #include <iostream.h>
8: #include <algorithm>
9: #include <functional>
10:
11: #include "SavingsAccountImpl.h"
12: #include "CheckingAccountImpl.h"
13:
14: extern CORBA::BOA_var boa;
15:
16: // STL-derived unary function which returns TRUE if Accounts are
17: // equal.
18: class IsAccountEqual : public std::unary_function<Account_ptr,
19:          bool> {
20: public:
21:      IsAccountEqual(argument_type account) { myAccount = account; }
22:      result_type operator()(argument_type account) { return account->
23:              _is_equivalent(myAccount) != 0; }
24: private:
25:      argument_type myAccount;
26: };
27:
28: // Constructor.
29: //
30: // name - This Bank's name.
31: BankImpl::BankImpl(const char* name) : _sk_Bank(name), myAccounts(),
32:          myName(strdup(name)), myAddress(strdup("123 Elm Street, "
33:          "Anywhere USA 12345")), myNextAccountNumber(0) {
34:
35: }
36:
37: // Default constructor.
38: BankImpl::BankImpl() : myAccounts(), myName(NULL), myAddress(NULL),
39:          myNextAccountNumber(0) {
40:
```

```
41: }
42:
43: // Destructor.
44: BankImpl::~BankImpl() {
45:
46:     cout << "Bank \"" << name() << "\" being destroyed." << endl;
47:     free(myName);
48:     free(myAddress);
49: }
50:
51: char* BankImpl::name() {
52:
53:     return CORBA::strdup(myName);
54: }
55:
56: void BankImpl::name(const char* val) {
57:
58:     free(myName);
59:     myName = strdup(val);
60: }
61:
62: char* BankImpl::address() {
63:
64:     return CORBA::strdup(myAddress);
65: }
66:
67: void BankImpl::address(const char* val) {
68:
69:     free(myAddress);
70:     myAddress = strdup(val);
71: }
72:
73: Account_ptr BankImpl::createAccount(Customer_ptr customer,
74:         const char* accountType, CORBA::Float openingBalance) {
75:
76:     Account_ptr newAccount;
77:
78:     if (strcmp(accountType, "savings") == 0) {
79:
80:         // Create a new SavingsAccountImpl object for the Account.
81:         cout << "BankImpl: Creating new SavingsAccount for "
82:                 "Customer " << customer->name() << "." << endl;
83:         newAccount = new SavingsAccountImpl(getNextAccountNumber(),
84:                 getCurrentDate(), openingBalance, customer, 10.0);
85:     } else if (strcmp(accountType, "checking") == 0) {
86:
87:         // Create a new CheckingAccountImpl object for the Account.
88:         cout << "BankImpl: Creating new CheckingAccount for "
89:                 "Customer " << customer->name() << "." << endl;
90:         newAccount = new CheckingAccountImpl(getNextAccountNumber(),
91:                 getCurrentDate(), openingBalance, customer);
92:     } else {
93:
94:         // Invalid Account type; do nothing.
95:         cout << "BankImpl: Customer " << customer->name() <<
96:                 " requested invalid Account type \"" << accountType
```

7

continues

Listing 7.23. continued

```
97:                      << "\"." << endl;
98:             return Account::_nil();
99:         }
100:
101:     // Add the created Account at the end of the list and return it.
102:     ::boa->obj_is_ready(newAccount);
103:     myAccounts.push_back(Account::_duplicate(newAccount));
104:     return newAccount;
105: }
106:
107: void BankImpl::deleteAccount(Account_ptr account) throw
108:         (InvalidAccountException) {
109:
110:     std::vector<Account_ptr>::iterator first = myAccounts.begin();
111:     std::vector<Account_ptr>::iterator last = myAccounts.end();
112:     IsAccountEqual predicate(account);
113:
114:     std::vector<Account_ptr>::iterator matchedAccount = std::
115:             find_if(first, last, predicate);
116:     if (matchedAccount == last) {
117:
118:         // Invalid Account; throw an exception.
119:         cout << "BankImpl: Attempted to delete invalid Account." <<
120:                 endl;
121:         throw InvalidAccountException();
122:     }
123:     cout << "BankImpl: Deleting Account \"" << account->
124:             accountNumber() << "\"." << endl;
125:
126:     // Delete the given Account.
127:     myAccounts.erase(matchedAccount);
128:     account->_release();
129: }
130:
131: AccountList* BankImpl::getAccounts() {
132:
133:     AccountList* list = new AccountList(myAccounts.size());
134:     CORBA::Long i;
135:
136:     for (i = 0; i < myAccounts.size(); i++) {
137:         (*list)[i] = Account::_duplicate(myAccounts[i]);
138:     }
139:
140:     return list;
141: }
142:
143: // Return the next available account number. The result is returned
144: // in a static buffer.
145: char* BankImpl::getNextAccountNumber() {
146:
147:     static char accountNumber[16] = "Account       ";
148:
```

```
149:      sprintf(accountNumber + 7, "%08u", myNextAccountNumber++);
150:
151:      return accountNumber;
152: }
153:
154: // Return the current date in the form "Mmm DD YYYY". The result is
155: // returned in a static buffer.
156: char* BankImpl::getCurrentDate() {
157:
158:      static char currentDate[12] = "            ";
159:
160:      time_t ltime;
161:      time(&ltime);
162:      char* ctimeResult = ctime(&ltime);
163:
164:      memcpy(currentDate, ctimeResult + 4, 3);
165:      memcpy(currentDate + 4, ctimeResult + 8, 2);
166:      memcpy(currentDate + 7, ctimeResult + 20, 4);
167:
168:      return currentDate;
169: }
```

The logic in deleteAccount() is identical to that seen previously in BankServerImpl's unregisterBank() method: If a client attempts to delete an Account that does not exist in the Bank, deleteAccount() throws an InvalidAccountException.

Congratulations—you have successfully completed the enhancements to the server side of the Bank application!

Modifying Client Code to Catch Exceptions

So far you've seen only half the picture. Now that the server code has been modified to throw exceptions on given occasions, the client code must be modified to handle those exceptions when they are raised. Although exception-handling code often permeates a client application, you'll see relatively little exception-handling code here, due to the simplicity of the Bank application's client.

First of all, note that no changes are required to CustomerImpl.h or CustomerImpl.cpp. Methods in the CustomerImpl class neither raise nor catch any exceptions, and thus no changes are necessary to these source files. However, NewCustomerMain.cpp—the end-user client application—needs to catch various exceptions. Just to make things interesting, NewCustomerMain.cpp performs some illegal actions on purpose, just to demonstrate the exception mechanism. The modified NewCustomerMain.cpp appears in Listing 7.24.

7

Listing 7.24. Modified `NewCustomerMain.cpp`.

```cpp
 1: // NewCustomerMain.cpp
 2:
 3: #include <iostream.h>
 4:
 5: #include "../Customer/CustomerImpl.h"
 6:
 7: #include "../Bank_c.h"
 8:
 9: int main(int argc, char *const *argv) {
10:
11:     // Check the number of arguments; there should be exactly four
12:     // (five counting the executable name itself).
13:     if (argc != 5) {
14:         cout << "Usage: NewCustomer <name> <social security number>"
15:                 " <address> <mother's maiden name>" << endl;
16:         return 1;
17:     }
18:
19:     // Assign the command line arguments to the Customer attributes.
20:     const char* name = argv[1];
21:     const char* socialSecurityNumber = argv[2];
22:     const char* address = argv[3];
23:     const char* mothersMaidenName = argv[4];
24:
25:     // Initialize the ORB and BOA.
26:     CORBA::ORB_var orb = CORBA::ORB_init(argc, argv);
27:     CORBA::BOA_var boa = orb->BOA_init(argc, argv);
28:
29:     // Create a Customer object.
30:     cout << "NewCustomer: Creating new Customer:" << endl;
31:     cout << "  name: " << name << endl;
32:     cout << "  Social Security number: " << socialSecurityNumber <<
33:             endl;
34:     cout << "  address: " << address << endl;
35:     cout << "  mother's maiden name: " << mothersMaidenName << endl;
36:     CustomerImpl customer(name, socialSecurityNumber, address,
37:             mothersMaidenName);
38:
39:     // Notify the BOA that the CustomerImpl object is ready.
40:     boa->obj_is_ready(&customer);
41:
42:     // Locate a Bank object and register with it.
43:     Bank_var bank;
44:     try {
45:         bank = Bank::_bind();
46:     } catch (const CORBA::Exception& ex) {
47:
48:         // The bind attempt failed...
49:         cout << "NewCustomer: Unable to bind to a Bank." << endl;
50:         cout << ex << endl;
51:         return 1;
52:     }
53:
```

7

```
54:     // Do some cool stuff.
55:
56:     cout << "NewCustomer: Connected to Bank \"" << bank->name() <<
57:             "\"." << endl;
58:     Account_var account;
59:
60:     try {
61:         account = bank->createAccount(&customer, "checking", 0.0);
62:     } catch (const CORBA::Exception& ex) {
63:
64:         // The createAccount() attempt failed...
65:         cout << "NewCustomer: Unable to create Account." << endl;
66:         cout << ex << endl;
67:         return 1;
68:     }
69:
70:     try {
71:
72:         // Print out some Account statistics.
73:         cout << "NewCustomer: Opened new Account:" << endl;
74:         cout << "  account number: " << account->accountNumber() <<
75:                 endl;
76:         cout << "  creation date: " << account->creationDate() <<
77:                 endl;
78:         cout << "  account balance: " << account->balance() << endl;
79:
80:         // Perform some transactions on the Account.
81:         cout << "NewCustomer: Performing transactions." << endl;
82:         cout << "  Depositing $250.00; new balance is $" <<
83:                 account->deposit(250.00) << endl;
84:         cout << "  Withdrawing $500.00...; new balance is $";
85:         try {
86:             cout << account->withdraw(500.00) << endl;
87:         } catch (const InsufficientFundsException&) {
88:
89:             // Insufficient funds were available for the withdraw()
90:             // operation.
91:             cout << endl << "NewCustomer: Exception caught: " <<
92:                     "Insufficient funds" << endl;
93:         }
94:
95:         // Get rid of the Account.
96:         cout << "  Deleting Account." << endl;
97:         bank->deleteAccount(account);
98:
99:         // Attempt to delete the Account again, just for kicks.
100:        // This should result in an exception being thrown.
101:        cout << "  Attempting to cause an exception by deleting" <<
102:                " Account again." << endl;
103:        try {
104:            bank->deleteAccount(account);
105:        } catch (const InvalidAccountException&) {
106:
107:            // Sure enough, the exception was thrown.
108:            cout << "NewCustomer: Exception caught: Invalid " <<
```

continues

Listing 7.24. continued

```
109:                    "Account (as expected)" << endl;
110:            }
111:        } catch (const CORBA::Exception& ex) {
112:
113:            // Some operation on the Account failed...
114:            cout << endl << "NewCustomer: Error accessing Account." <<
115:                    endl;
116:            cout << ex << endl;
117:            return 1;
118:        }
119:
120:        // When this point is reached, the application is finished.
121:        return 0;
122: }
```

Notice the additional try and catch statements appearing in lines 85-93 and 99-110 in NewCustomerMain.cpp. Earlier, try and catch were used to catch CORBA::Exceptions, now there are user exceptions to check for as well. The first of these appears with the use of the withdraw() method; note that $250.00 was deposited to the Account, but the program attempts to withdraw $500.00. Expect to see an exception thrown here when the application is run. Also, note that deleteAccount() is called twice for the same Account (once in line 97 and again in line 104). The first call will be successful, but expect the second to result in another exception being thrown because the Account, having already been deleted, no longer exists in the Bank. In the next section, you'll verify that the program results are what you expect.

NOTE

In this example, the first call to deleteAccount() is not contained in a try ... catch block for InvalidAccountException. Although this behavior might be acceptable for this application—because the exception would be handled by the catch (const CORBA::Exception ex) handler—you might consider wrapping the call into its own try ... catch block. The arrangement of these exception handlers is highly dependent on the intent of the application, but there will be few times when you'll want a user exception to be handled by a catchall exception handler such as the CORBA::Exception handler in the previous example. Good exception-handling techniques come with practice and with careful design.

Running the Enhanced Example

Congratulations—you have now successfully added an exception-handling mechanism to the Bank application! All that remains now is to compile and run the application to verify that the results are what you expect. Make sure you run the IDL compiler on all the new and modified IDL source files; also, your IDL compiler might require special command-line arguments to generate code for exception handling. (Incidentally, Visigenic's VisiBroker for C++, version 3.0, does not.) Also, check your C++ compiler's settings to ensure that exception handling is enabled (some compilers don't enable this feature by default).

The order for starting the application components is the same as on Day 6: First start the Naming Service (or osagent, in the case of VisiBroker), followed by the BankServer server, the Bank server, and finally the NewCustomer client application.

Again, starting the BankServer application results in the following output:

```
BankServer ready.
```

On seeing this message, start a Bank server, which produces output similar to the following:

```
Bank "First Bank" ready.
```

Meanwhile, the BankServer will have output this:

```
BankServerImpl: Registering Bank "First Bank".
```

You are now ready to start the NewCustomer application, which produces output similar to the following:

```
NewCustomer: Creating new Customer:
  name: Jeremy Rosenberger
  Social Security number: 123456789
  address: 123 Main Street
  mother's maiden name: Sams
NewCustomer: Connected to Bank "First Bank".
NewCustomer: Opened new Account:
  account number: Account00000000
  creation date: Oct 14 1997
  account balance: 0
NewCustomer: Performing transactions.
  Depositing $250.00; new balance is $250
  Withdrawing $500.00...; new balance is $
NewCustomer: Exception caught: Insufficient funds
  Deleting Account.
  Attempting to cause an exception by deleting Account again.
NewCustomer: Exception caught: Invalid Account (as expected)
```

Meanwhile, you might notice the following output from the Bank server:

```
BankImpl: Creating new CheckingAccount for Customer Jeremy Rosenberger.
AccountImpl: Insufficient funds to withdraw specified amount.
BankImpl: Deleting Account "Account00000000".
```

7

Is this the output you expect? Recall that NewCustomer opens a new Account with the information given on the command line, deposits $250 into that account, and then attempts to withdraw $500. Sure enough, NewCustomer reports that the Account had insufficient funds for the withdrawal (thanks to the InsufficientFundsException). Furthermore, you'd expect to see trouble from the attempt to delete the same Account twice. Sure enough, NewCustomer indicates that it tried to delete an invalid Account the second time deleteAccount() was called. In other words, the exception mechanism worked!

Summary

In this chapter, you modified the Bank application to handle exceptions. You started by determining what exceptions might reasonably be raised in various parts of the application, and you modified the IDL interfaces of the application to use those exceptions. At this point, you specified what exceptions could be raised by what methods. You then modified the corresponding C++ header and implementation files for the CORBA server components, specifying the exact conditions under which a particular exception would be thrown. Finally, you wrote a CORBA client application that could handle those exceptions intelligently. The net result is an application that demonstrates a robust design, in the sense that it can deal with exceptional situations—that is, circumstances that should not occur during normal application execution.

 NOTE

> Although in this book you designed and built a working application before giving a thought to exception handling, typically you will think about exceptions at the same time that you design an application. When deciding which methods belong in an interface, also think about how those methods might be used erroneously, and what mechanisms—in the form of exceptions—might be used to communicate error conditions back to the client. You'll always be able to go back and add exception handling later, but it is wise to at least think about such issues early on in the application development phase.

In the next few chapters you'll continue to modify the Bank application, adding still more functionality. On Day 8, in particular, you will define additional requirements for the system—the capability to support Automated Teller Machines (ATMs). Of course, you'll only be dealing with virtual ATMs rather than real ones, but this will expose you to the development process with a non-trivial CORBA application.

Q&A

Q How do I know whether an abnormal condition is important enough to warrant an exception? In other words, should exceptions be reserved only for fatal error conditions?

A There are two schools of thought regarding exceptions. One camp suggests that exceptions should be used only to signal a serious error condition—if an exception occurs, the best an application can hope to do is clean up and try to exit gracefully. The alternative approach—and the one that CORBA architecture seems to embrace—is that exceptions might be used to signal just about any abnormal condition. For instance, in the example from this chapter, an account having insufficient funds for a withdrawal is hardly fatal to the application—it simply requires the current transaction to be aborted. This approach can be taken to an extreme, however. Because CORBA exceptions can propagate across networks, they can potentially incur a great amount of overhead compared to native C++ exceptions. As with anything else, use exceptions judiciously.

Q How do I choose exception names?

A Exception names should be self-describing; that is, an exception name should succinctly describe the specific condition being handled. On the other hand, though, exception names shouldn't be so specific that you find yourself defining multiple exceptions that have almost the same meaning. For instance, `InvalidDepositAmountException`, `InvalidWithdrawalAmountException`, `InvalidTransferAmountException`, `InvalidInterestRateAmountException`, and so on could reasonably be merged into a single `InvalidAmountException`, whose name still provides enough information to determine what triggered the exception.

Workshop

The following section will help you test your comprehension of the material presented in this chapter and put what you've learned into practice. You'll find the answers to the quiz and exercises in Appendix A.

Quiz

1. What does it mean to *raise* (or *throw*) an exception?
2. What does it mean to *catch* an exception?
3. Why are exceptions useful?

7

Exercises

1. Modify the following interface definition so that appropriate exceptions are raised in appropriate places.

```
exception InvalidNumberException { };
exception NoIncomingCallException { };
exception NotOffHookException { };

interface Telephone {

    void offHook();

    void onHook();

    void dialNumber(in string phoneNumber);

    void answerCall();
};
```

2. Implement the interface from Exercise 1, raising the appropriate exceptions under the appropriate conditions. (Most of the methods probably won't do anything, except for `dialNumber()`, which will likely check the validity of the given phone number).

WEEK

1

1

2

3

4

5

6

7

In Review

You kicked off the first week of this book by delving into the basic concepts of CORBA on Day 1. Following that, you studied various aspects of the CORBA architecture on Days 2 and 3 and cemented some of that knowledge in place on Day 4, when you built your first sample CORBA application. On Day 5 you began design and development of a more complex CORBA application, which you continued to develop through the rest of the week (and which you'll work on a little more in the following week).

Getting Started

Day 1 introduced you to the Common Object Request Broker Architecture (CORBA), its history, and the fundamentals of the architecture. Day 2 took you into greater detail concerning the various aspects of the CORBA architecture, such as the Object Request Broker (ORB), the

Interface Definition Language (IDL), and the CORBA network and object models. On Day 3 you learned everything you'd ever want to know about IDL, and finally, on Day 4, you applied the knowledge you acquired by building your first CORBA application.

Developing a CORBA Application, Part 1

Day 5 put you in the design stage of a sample CORBA application, one that you will be working with for the rest of this week and partly into the next. This chapter also introduces you to the concepts of object-oriented analysis and design, the Unified Modeling Language (UML), and the overall design of the simulated banking system. Day 6 took you through the process of developing the initial capabilities of this application, and on Day 7 you made the first enhancements to the application, increasing its robustness by adding exception handling.

At a Glance

During the first part of the second week of this book, you continue to develop the sample application you began in the first week. Days 8 and 9 continue this process. On Day 10 you move on to some more advanced CORBA topics, such as the various design issues associated with CORBA development. Day 11 introduces you to the Dynamic Invocation Interface (DII), and on Day 12 you familiarize yourself with the many CORBAservices and CORBAfacilities available to CORBA applications. You wrap up the week—and the book—by developing a Java version of the sample application on Days 13 and 14.

8

9

10

11

12

13

14

Developing a CORBA Application, Part 2

On Day 8 you further enhance the sample application capability by adding simulated Automated Teller Machines (ATMs). Then, on Day 9, you implement push capability by using what are known as callbacks, allowing bank customers to receive account updates automatically.

Advanced CORBA

Day 10 brings you to the level of advanced CORBA topics, starting with various design issues associated with CORBA. For example, you'll see some of the issues involved with using CORBA in single-threaded applications. Day 11 introduces you to the Dynamic Invocation Interface (DII), a mechanism that enables clients to learn about server interfaces at runtime rather than be limited to server interfaces that were known at the time the client was compiled. On Day 12 you learn about the multitude of CORBAservices and CORBAfacilities, horizontal services such as naming and directory services, transaction monitoring, and persistent object services, as well as vertical facilities for the health care, finance, and telecommunications industries, to name a few. Day 13 introduces you to the Java programming language and shows you how Java can interoperate with CORBA; on Day 14 you create a Java applet that can bring the functionality of the sample application to the World Wide Web.

Day **8**

Adding Automated Teller Machine (ATM) Capability

On Day 7, you started with the basic Bank application and made the first set of enhancements to it, adding error-checking functionality through the CORBA exception mechanism. The end result was an application with the same basic functionality that you implemented on Day 6 but with more robust error handling. Today you'll build on that same application, adding more features. Specifically, you'll define the interface for a virtual Automated Teller Machine (ATM) device and enhance the Bank application to interact with this device. The process you'll follow is this:

☐ *Define additional requirements.* The original requirements for the Bank application said nothing about ATMs, so you will modify the requirements to define this new feature.

□ *Modify the system design.* Adding ATM functionality will result in a number of new classes being added to the system. You'll identify these classes in the analysis and design phase. (Revisiting this phase will reinforce the concept that software design is an iterative process.)

□ *Modify the IDL definitions.* After you have defined the new classes to be added and have modified some existing classes, you'll create or update the interface definitions for those classes.

□ *Implement the new functionality.* After the design is finished and realized in IDL, you'll be ready to implement the new functionality and see how the new application works.

Defining Additional Requirements

First of all, as a review, recall that on Day 5 you defined the following system requirements for the Bank application:

□ Supports multiple banks

□ Supports multiple accounts within banks

□ Supports multiple customers holding accounts

□ Supports customers holding multiple accounts

□ Supports the capability to open (create) new accounts

□ Supports the capability to close (delete) existing accounts

□ Supports the capability to enumerate a bank's accounts

□ Supports the capability to determine an account's owner(s)

□ Supports the capability to withdraw funds from an account

□ Supports the capability to deposit funds into an account

□ Supports the capability to transfer funds between accounts within a single bank

□ Supports the capability to transfer funds between accounts in different banks

□ Supports checking accounts (which don't gain interest)

□ Supports savings accounts (which do gain interest)

The original requirements said nothing about the support of Automated Teller Machines (ATMs). But what if you want to modify the application to support the ATM concept? Certainly it is possible to add this capability to the application; this chapter demonstrates just how to do this.

8

To add ATM capability, you first define a set of requirements that describes exactly what functionality is necessary. To support ATM functionality, the requirements might look something like this:

☐ Supports the capability for a customer to deposit funds into an existing account through an ATM

☐ Supports the capability for a customer to withdraw funds from an existing account through an ATM

☐ Supports the capability for a customer to obtain the balance of an existing account through an ATM

☐ Supports the capability for an ATM to authorize customers through the use of an ATM card and a Personal Identification Number (PIN)

☐ Supports the capability for an ATM card to access multiple accounts belonging to a customer in a particular bank

In other words, an ATM provides three basic functions: depositing funds, withdrawing funds, and obtaining account balances. The ATM is accessed via an ATM card that, in conjunction with the customer's PIN, authorizes that customer to access the account (or accounts) for which the ATM card is authorized.

Of course, you won't be dealing with an actual ATM; rather, you'll be simulating the operation of an ATM through IDL interfaces. The operation of the ATM will thus be greatly simplified compared to an actual ATM, which must interface with a cash dispenser, video screen, keypad input, network, and other components. Your ATM interface will abstract the entire ATM, assuming that these components all work together as a single unit.

Modifying the Class Diagram

Now that you've identified the requirements associated with providing ATM functionality, you're ready to decide which existing classes in the system need to be modified, which classes need to be added, and what the new classes should do.

Two New Classes: ATM and ATMCard

Naturally, the expansion of the Bank application to include ATM functionality introduces some new classes into the system. An obvious class is the ATM itself; another class is ATMCard—the device the customer uses to identify himself or herself to the ATM. Now, take a look at the operations that these classes must support. Recall that the ATM needs to support deposit, withdraw, and account balance operations, in addition to authenticating the customer through the ATM card. ATMCard, in turn, needs to indicate the accounts that it is authorized to use, ought to support the capability to add and remove accounts to and from its list of authorized accounts, and—for the purposes of this application, anyway—must include the PIN associated with that ATMCard as a member data item.

The interface for the ATM class looks like this:

```
name : string

withdraw(card : ATMCard, account : Account, pin : integer,
        amount : float) : float
deposit(card : ATMCard, account : Account, pin : integer,
        amount : float) : float
getBalance(card : ATMCard, account : Account, pin : integer)
        : float
```

Note that each of the operations in the ATM class requires an ATMCard to identify the customer and the Accounts for which he or she is authorized access, an Account on which to operate, and a pin (which for the purposes of this application is simply an integer) to authenticate the customer.

ATMCard's interface resembles the following:

```
pin : integer

getAccounts() : Account[]
addAccount(account : Account) : void
removeAccount(account : Account) : void
isAuthorized(account : Account) : boolean
```

Modifying Existing Classes

Of course, you can't just create the ATM and ATMCard classes and expect the ATM capability to be integrated with the rest of the application; you must also modify some of the existing classes. For example, an ATMCard has to come from somewhere; typically, it is issued by a Bank. Also, a Customer would have some knowledge of the ATMCard because the ATMCard is intended to be used by Customers in the first place. Finally, a Customer should be able to locate and access ATMs, so it would be reasonable to modify BankServer to provide locations of ATMs as well as Banks.

First, consider the Bank class, which must be able to issue ATMCards to Customers. A reasonable way to achieve this functionality is to add the following method to Bank:

```
issueATMCard(pin : integer, account : Account) : ATMCard
```

Here, it is assumed that when the ATMCard is issued, an initial pin will be set; that ATMCard will also be authorized initially to access the given Account. Note that for this application, it is the responsibility of the caller (presumably a Customer) to retain the ATMCard after it is created.

Customer, again, should be modified to become aware of ATMCards so that a Customer can make use of them. It turns out that the only addition required to Customer is an internal list of the ATMCards held by that Customer; for the sake of convenience, you might add a method that enables other objects to access that list of ATMCards. However, for the purposes of this application, you can assume that other objects don't need access to this information (besides, people don't usually share information about their ATM cards with other people!). For your purposes, no changes are required to the `Customer` interface itself (changes to the `Customer` implementation come later).

Finally, `BankServer` should be modified to facilitate access to `ATM`s as well as `Bank`s. Recall the operations provided in the BankServer interface that enable access to `Bank`s:

```
registerBank(bank : Bank) : void
unregisterBank(bank : Bank) : void
getBanks() : Bank[]
```

It seems reasonable to mimic this interface for `ATM`s, yielding the following operations:

```
registerATM(atm : ATM) : void
unregisterATM(atm : ATM) : void
getATMs() : ATM[]
```

The modified class diagram—expanded to include the new `ATM` and `ATMCard` classes, along with the modified `Bank` class—appears in Figure 8.1.

Figure 8.1.

The modified `Bank` *application class diagram.*

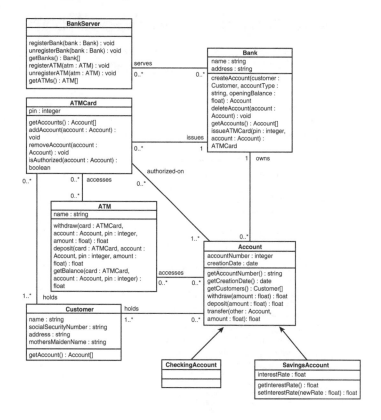

Two New Exceptions: AuthorizationException and InvalidATMException

The operations in the ATM class suggest the need for a new exception. To meet this need, define a new exception (call it AuthorizationException) that can be thrown by any of the ATM methods. Later, you'll implement these methods to raise an AuthorizationException if there is a problem authenticating the customer (for example, the customer-supplied PIN doesn't match the pin stored in the ATMCard) or authorizing the customer (for example, if the Account passed to a method in ATM is not authorized on the given ATMCard).

Also, recall the new methods added to the BankServer interface. Because they essentially duplicate the Bank-related operations, which raise InvalidBankExceptions, it follows that there ought to be an analogous exception for the ATM-related operations. Therefore, you'll want to define the InvalidATMException, which is used just as you might expect.

Modifying the IDL Specification

The modification of the IDL specifications is straightforward. Start with the modified Bank interface, which appears in Listing 8.1 with changes highlighted in **bold.**

Listing 8.1. Modified Bank.idl.

```
 1: // Bank.idl
 2:
 3: // Forward declaration of Bank interface.
 4: interface Bank;
 5:
 6: #ifndef Bank_idl
 7: #define Bank_idl
 8:
 9: // sequence of Banks
10: typedef sequence<Bank> BankList;
11:
12: #include "Customer.idl"
13: #include "Account.idl"
14: #include "ATMCard.idl"
15: #include "Exceptions.idl"
16:
17: // A Bank provides access to Accounts. It can create an Account
18: // on behalf of a Customer, delete an Account, or list the current
19: // Accounts with the Bank.
20: interface Bank {
21:
22:     // This Bank's name.
23:     attribute string name;
24:
25:     // This Bank's address.
26:     attribute string address;
27:
```

```
28:      // Create an Account on behalf of the given Customer, with the
29:      // given account type ("savings" or "checking", where case is
30:      // significant), and the given opening balance.
31:      Account createAccount(in Customer customer, in string
32:              accountType, in float openingBalance);
33:
34:      // Delete the given Account. If the Account is not with this
35:      // Bank, this operation does nothing.
36:      void deleteAccount(in Account account)
37:              raises (InvalidAccountException);
38:
39:      // List all Accounts with this Bank.
40:      AccountList getAccounts();
41:
42:      // Issue an ATMCard with the initial PIN and initially
43:      // authorized on the given Account. If the Account is not with
44:      // this Bank, this operation does nothing.
45:      ATMCard issueATMCard(in short pin, in Account account)
46:              raises (InvalidAccountException);
47: };
48:
49: #endif
```

Turn your attention to the modified Exceptions.idl, which now contains the newly created AuthorizationException and InvalidATMException. The modified file appears in Listing 8.2.

Listing 8.2. Modified Exceptions.idl.

```
 1: // Exceptions.idl
 2:
 3: #ifndef Exceptions_idl
 4: #define Exceptions_idl
 5:
 6: // This exception is thrown when an authorization fails; for
 7: // instance, if a Customer-entered PIN does not match the PIN for
 8: // the supplied ATMCard.
 9: exception AuthorizationException {
10:
11: };
12:
13: // This exception is thrown when an invalid amount is passed to a
14: // method; for instance, if an account is asked to deposit a
15: // negative amount of funds.
16: exception InvalidAmountException {
17:
18: };
19:
20: // This exception is thrown when an invalid Account is passed to a
21: // method expecting an Account object.
22: exception InvalidAccountException {
23:
24: };
25:
```

continues

Listing 8.2. continued

```
26: // This exception is thrown when an invalid Bank is passed to a
27: // method expecting a Bank object.
28: exception InvalidBankException {
29:
30: };
31:
32: // This exception is thrown when an invalid ATM is passed to a
33: // method expecting an ATM object.
34: exception InvalidATMException {
35:
36: };
37:
38: // This exception is thrown when there are insufficient funds to
39: // cover a transaction; for instance, if a withdrawal attempts to
40: // remove more funds than are available in an account.
41: exception InsufficientFundsException {
42:
43: };
44:
45: #endif
```

Now consider the IDL mappings for the newly created classes ATM and ATMCard, which appear in Listings 8.3 and 8.4. There are no surprises in the IDL interface definitions; all member data and methods map to IDL as you might expect.

Listing 8.3. ATM.idl.

```
 1: // ATM.idl
 2:
 3: // Forward declaration of ATM interface.
 4: interface ATM;
 5:
 6: #ifndef ATM_idl
 7: #define ATM_idl
 8:
 9: // sequence of ATMs
10: typedef sequence<ATM> ATMList;
11:
12: #include "Account.idl"
13: #include "ATMCard.idl"
14: #include "Exceptions.idl"
15:
16: // An ATM is used to (indirectly) access Accounts. Each operation
17: // through the ATM is verified through the ATMCard given; for
18: // example, an Account being operated on must be authorized by the
19: // given ATMCard.
20: interface ATM {
21:
22:     // This ATM's name.
23:     attribute string name;
24:
```

8

```
25:     // Withdraw the given amount from the given Account. Returns
26:     // the new account balance. If the given ATMCard is not
27:     // authorized on the given Account, or the given PIN does not
28:     // match the ATMCard's PIN, this operation does nothing.
29:     float withdraw(in ATMCard card, in Account account, in short
30:             pin, in float amount) raises (AuthorizationException,
31:             InvalidAmountException, InsufficientFundsException);
32:
33:     // Deposit the given amount into the given Account. Returns the
34:     // new account balance. If the given ATMCard is not authorized
35:     // on the given Account, or the given PIN does not match the
36:     // ATMCard's PIN, this operation does nothing.
37:     float deposit(in ATMCard card, in Account account, in short
38:             pin, in float amount) raises (AuthorizationException,
39:             InvalidAmountException);
40:
41:     // Return the current balance of the given Account. If the
42:     // given ATMCard is not authorized on the given Account, or the
43:     // given PIN does not match the ATMCard's PIN, this operation
44:     // does nothing.
45:     float getBalance(in ATMCard card, in Account account, in short
46:             pin) raises (AuthorizationException);
47: };
48:
49: #endif
```

Listing 8.4. ATMCard.idl.

```
1: // ATMCard.idl
2:
3: // Forward declaration of ATMCard interface.
4: interface ATMCard;
5:
6: #ifndef ATMCard_idl
7: #define ATMCard_idl
8:
9: // sequence of ATMCards
10: typedef sequence<ATMCard> ATMCardList;
11:
12: #include "Account.idl"
13: #include "Exceptions.idl"
14:
15: // An ATMCard is used to access an ATM. It maintains a list of
16: // Accounts which it is authorized to access, as well as a PIN
17: // which must be provided when the ATMCard is used.
18: interface ATMCard {
19:
20:     // This ATMCard's PIN.
21:     attribute short pin;
22:
23:     // List all Accounts which this ATMCard is authorized to use.
24:     AccountList getAccounts();
25:
```

continues

Listing 8.4. continued

```
26:     // Add the given Account to the list of Accounts which this
27:     // ATMCard is authorized to use.
28:     void addAccount(in Account account)
29:             raises (InvalidAccountException);
30:
31:     // Remove the given Account from the list of Accounts which
32:     // this ATMCard is authorized to use.
33:     void removeAccount(in Account account)
34:             raises (InvalidAccountException);
35:
36:     // Return true if the given Account is authorized on this
37:     // ATMCard.
38:     boolean isAuthorized(in Account account);
39: };
40:
41: #endif
```

This concludes the analysis and design portion of the ATM functionality enhancements; you're now ready to begin implementing the changes in the code itself.

Implementing the New Functionality

To implement the ATM-related enhancements, you must modify the implementation files to provide the new functionality. As a quick overview, the changes you need to make are as follows:

- [ ] *Enhance the* BankServer. Essentially, everything that the BankServer currently does for Banks, you will extend it to do for ATMs as well.

- [ ] *Enhance the* Bank. In addition to requiring the capability to issue ATMCards, the Bank also provides the implementation for the ATMCard as well.

- [ ] *Implement the* ATM *server.* Essentially, the ATM accepts transaction requests from Customers, validates the Customer's authorization against an ATMCard, and, if authorized, forwards the requests to the appropriate Accounts.

- [ ] *Implement the* ATM *client.* This application is an extension of the previous Bank client, modified to create an Account and subsequently access that Account through an ATM rather than directly.

Enhancing the BankServer

The first step in the implementation of ATM functionality is to enhance the BankServer to support ATMs as well as Banks. Because the support is exactly the same for each type of object (for example, ATMs and Banks can both register and unregister with the BankServer), the ATM-related methods can be copied almost directly from their Bank-related counterparts. The necessary modifications to the BankServer implementation files appear in Listings 8.5–8.7, with changes from the previous version highlighted in **bold.**

Listing 8.5. `BankServerImpl.h.`

```
 1: // BankServerImpl.h
 2:
 3: #ifndef BankServerImpl_h
 4: #define BankServerImpl_h
 5:
 6: #include <vector>
 7:
 8: #include "../BankServer_s.h"
 9:
10: class BankServerImpl : public _sk_BankServer {
11:
12: public:
13:
14:     // Constructor.
15:     BankServerImpl(const char* name);
16:
17:     // Destructor.
18:     ~BankServerImpl();
19:
20:     // These methods are described in BankServer.idl.
21:     virtual void registerBank(Bank_ptr bank) throw
22:             (InvalidBankException);
23:     virtual void unregisterBank(Bank_ptr bank) throw
24:             (InvalidBankException);
25:     virtual BankList* getBanks();
26:     virtual void registerATM(ATM_ptr atm) throw
27:             (InvalidATMException);
28:     virtual void unregisterATM(ATM_ptr atm) throw
29:             (InvalidATMException);
30:     virtual ATMList* getATMs();
31:
32: private:
33:
34:     // Default constructor.
35:     BankServerImpl();
36:
37:     // This BankServer's list of Banks.
38:     std::vector<Bank_ptr> myBanks;
39:
40:     // This BankServer's list of ATMs.
41:     std::vector<ATM_ptr> myATMs;
42: };
43:
44: #endif
```

In Listing 8.5, note the similarity between the `registerBank()` method (lines 21-22) and the `registerATM()` method (lines 26-27), as well as the other pairs of corresponding methods. Also, just as the `BankServerImpl` uses a `std::vector<Bank_ptr>` to store references to `Bank` objects (as seen in lines 37-38), it now uses a `std::vector<ATM_ptr>` to store references to ATM objects (lines 40-41).

Listing 8.6 illustrates the further similarities between the previously existing method implementations in BankServerImpl and the ATM-related methods being added. The implementations are exactly the same, with references to Banks changed to references to ATMs, and so on. (Because the semantics of the operations are the same for ATMs as for Banks, it isn't surprising that the implementations are nearly identical.)

Listing 8.6. `BankServerImpl.cpp.`

```
 1: // BankServerImpl.cpp
 2:
 3: #include "BankServerImpl.h"
 4:
 5: #include <algorithm>
 6: #include <functional>
 7:
 8: // STL-derived unary function which returns TRUE if Banks are equal.
 9: class IsBankEqual : public std::unary_function<Bank_ptr, bool> {
10: public:
11:     IsBankEqual(argument_type bank) { myBank = bank; }
12:     result_type operator()(argument_type bank) { return bank->
13:             _is_equivalent(myBank) != 0; }
14: private:
15:     argument_type myBank;
16: };
17:
18: // STL-derived unary function which returns TRUE if ATMs are equal.
19: class IsATMEqual : public std::unary_function<ATM_ptr, bool> {
20: public:
21:     IsATMEqual(argument_type atm) { myATM = atm; }
22:     result_type operator()(argument_type atm) { return atm->
23:             _is_equivalent(myATM) != 0; }
24: private:
25:     argument_type myATM;
26: };
27:
28: // Constructor.
29: BankServerImpl::BankServerImpl(const char* name) :
30:         _sk_BankServer(name), myBanks(), myATMs() {
31:
32: }
33:
34: // Destructor.
35: BankServerImpl::~BankServerImpl() {
36:
37: }
38:
39: void BankServerImpl::registerBank(Bank_ptr bank) throw
40:         (InvalidBankException) {
41:
42:     // First, ensure that the given Bank doesn't exist already.
43:     std::vector<Bank_ptr>::iterator first = myBanks.begin();
44:     std::vector<Bank_ptr>::iterator last = myBanks.end();
45:     IsBankEqual predicate(bank);
46:
```

```
47:      std::vector<Bank_ptr>::iterator matchedBank = std::
48:           find_if(first, last, predicate);
49:      if (matchedBank == last) {
50:
51:          // Bank was not found, so add the given Bank to the end of
52:          // the list.
53:          cout << "BankServerImpl: Registering Bank \"" << bank->
54:               name() << "\"." << endl;
55:          myBanks.push_back(Bank::_duplicate(bank));
56:          return;
57:      } else {
58:
59:          // The Bank was already registered, so throw an exception.
60:          throw InvalidBankException();
61:      }
62: }
63:
64: void BankServerImpl::unregisterBank(Bank_ptr bank) throw
65:          (InvalidBankException) {
66:
67:      std::vector<Bank_ptr>::iterator first = myBanks.begin();
68:      std::vector<Bank_ptr>::iterator last = myBanks.end();
69:      IsBankEqual predicate(bank);
70:
71:      std::vector<Bank_ptr>::iterator matchedBank = std::
72:           find_if(first, last, predicate);
73:      if (matchedBank == last) {
74:
75:          // Invalid Bank; throw an exception.
76:          cout << "BankServerImpl: Attempted to unregister invalid "
77:               "Bank." << endl;
78:          throw InvalidBankException();
79:      }
80:      cout << "BankServerImpl: Unregistering Bank \"" << bank->name()
81:           << "\"." << endl;
82:
83:      // Delete the given Bank.
84:      myBanks.erase(matchedBank);
85:      bank->_release();
86: }
87:
88: BankList* BankServerImpl::getBanks() {
89:
90:      BankList* list = new BankList();
91:      CORBA::Long i;
92:
93:      list->length(myBanks.size());
94:      for (i = 0; i < myBanks.size(); i++) {
95:          (*list)[i] = Bank::_duplicate(myBanks[i]);
96:      }
97:
98:      cout << "BankServerImpl: Returning list of " << myBanks.size()
99:           << " Banks." << endl;
100:
101:      return BankList::_duplicate(list);
102: }
103:
```

continues

Listing 8.6. continued

```
104: void BankServerImpl::registerATM(ATM_ptr atm) throw
105:        (InvalidATMException) {
106:
107:     // First, ensure that the given ATM doesn't exist already.
108:     std::vector<ATM_ptr>::iterator first = myATMs.begin();
109:     std::vector<ATM_ptr>::iterator last = myATMs.end();
110:     IsATMEqual predicate(atm);
111:
112:     std::vector<ATM_ptr>::iterator matchedATM = std::find_if(first,
113:            last, predicate);
114:     if (matchedATM == last) {
115:
116:         // ATM was not found, so add the given ATM to the end of
117:         // the list.
118:         cout << "BankServerImpl: Registering ATM \"" << atm->
119:                name() << "\"." << endl;
120:         myATMs.push_back(ATM::_duplicate(atm));
121:         return;
122:     } else {
123:
124:         // The ATM was already registered, so throw an exception.
125:         throw InvalidATMException();
126:   }
127: }
128:
129: void BankServerImpl::unregisterATM(ATM_ptr atm) throw
130:        (InvalidBankException) {
131:
132:     std::vector<ATM_ptr>::iterator first = myATMs.begin();
133:     std::vector<ATM_ptr>::iterator last = myATMs.end();
134:     IsATMEqual predicate(atm);
135:
136:     std::vector<ATM_ptr>::iterator matchedATM = std::find_if(first,
137:            last, predicate);
138:     if (matchedATM == last) {
139:
140:         // Invalid ATM; throw an exception..
141:         cout << "BankServerImpl: Attempted to unregister invalid "
142:                "ATM." << endl;
143:         throw InvalidATMException();
144:     }
145:     cout << "BankServerImpl: Unregistering ATM \"" << atm->name()
146:            << "\"." << endl;
147:
148:     // Delete the given ATM.
149:     myATMs.erase(matchedATM);
150:     atm->_release();
151: }
152:
153: ATMList* BankServerImpl::getATMs() {
154:
155:     ATMList* list = new ATMList();
156:     CORBA::Long i;
157:
```

8

```
158:        list->length(myATMs.size());
159:        for (i = 0; i < myATMs.size(); i++) {
160:            (*list)[i] = ATM::_duplicate(myATMs[i]);
161:        }
162:
163:        cout << "BankServerImpl: Returning list of " << myATMs.size()
164:                << " ATMs." << endl;
165:
166:        return ATMList::_duplicate(list);
167: }
```

As shown in Listing 8.7, no changes are necessary to BankServerMain.cpp; the BankServer application starts up in exactly the same way it did on Day 7.

Listing 8.7. BankServerMain.cpp.

```
1: // BankServerMain.cpp
2:
3: #include "BankServerImpl.h"
4: #include <iostream.h>
5:
6: int main(int argc, char *const *argv) {
7:
8:        // Initialize the ORB and BOA.
9:        CORBA::ORB_var orb = CORBA::ORB_init(argc, argv);
10:       CORBA::BOA_var boa = orb->BOA_init(argc, argv);
11:
12:       // Create a BankServerImpl object.
13:       BankServerImpl bankServer("BankServer");
14:
15:       // Notify the BOA that the BankServerImpl object is ready.
16:       boa->obj_is_ready(&bankServer);
17:
18:       // Wait for CORBA events.
19:       cout << "BankServer ready." << endl;
20:       boa->impl_is_ready();
21:
22:       // When this point is reached, the application is finished.
23:       return 0;
24: }
```

Enhancing the Bank

In Listings 8.8 and 8.9, the BankImpl class is largely unchanged, except for the addition of issueATMCard() in lines 32-33. This method accepts a request to issue an ATMCard for a given Account. issueATMCard() first checks the Account object to see whether it exists in this Bank. If it does, the ATMCard is issued; if not, an InvalidAccountException is thrown.

Listing 8.8. `BankImpl.h`.

```
 1: // BankImpl.h
 2:
 3: #ifndef BankImpl_h
 4: #define BankImpl_h
 5:
 6: #include <vector>
 7:
 8: #include "../Bank_s.h"
 9:
10: class BankImpl : public _sk_Bank {
11:
12: public:
13:
14:     // Constructor.
15:     //
16:     // name - This Bank's name.
17:     BankImpl(const char* name);
18:
19:     // Destructor.
20:     ~BankImpl();
21:
22:     // These methods are described in Bank.idl.
23:     virtual char* name();
24:     virtual void name(const char* val);
25:     virtual char* address();
26:     virtual void address(const char* val);
27:     virtual Account_ptr createAccount(Customer_ptr customer,
28:             const char* accountType, CORBA::Float openingBalance);
29:     virtual void deleteAccount(Account_ptr account) throw
30:             (InvalidAccountException);
31:     virtual AccountList* getAccounts();
32:     virtual ATMCard_ptr issueATMCard(CORBA::Short pin, Account_ptr
33:             account) throw (InvalidAccountException);
34:
35: protected:
36:
37:     // Return the next available account number. The result is
38:     // returned in a static buffer.
39:     char* getNextAccountNumber();
40:
41:     // Return the current date in the form "Mmm DD YYYY". The result
42:     // is returned in a static buffer.
43:     char* getCurrentDate();
44:
45: private:
46:
47:     // Default constructor.
48:     BankImpl();
49:
50:     // This Bank's name.
51:     char* myName;
52:
53:     // This Bank's address.
54:     char* myAddress;
55:
```

8

```
56:     // This Bank's Accounts.
57:     std::vector<Account_ptr> myAccounts;
58:
59:     // The next available account number.
60:     unsigned int myNextAccountNumber;
61: };
62:
63: #endif
```

Listing 8.9. BankImpl.cpp.

```
 1: // BankImpl.cpp
 2:
 3: #include "BankImpl.h"
 4:
 5: #include <time.h>
 6: #include <string.h>
 7: #include <iostream.h>
 8: #include <algorithm>
 9: #include <functional>
10:
11: #include "SavingsAccountImpl.h"
12: #include "CheckingAccountImpl.h"
13: #include "ATMCardImpl.h"
14:
15: extern CORBA::BOA_var boa;
16:
17: // STL-derived unary function which returns TRUE if Accounts are
18: // equal.
19: class IsAccountEqual : public std::unary_function<Account_ptr,
20:         bool> {
21: public:
22:     IsAccountEqual(argument_type account) { myAccount = account; }
23:     result_type operator()(argument_type account) { return account->
24:         _is_equivalent(myAccount) != 0; }
25: private:
26:     argument_type myAccount;
27: };
28:
29: // Constructor.
30: //
31: // name - This Bank's name.
32: BankImpl::BankImpl(const char* name) : _sk_Bank(name), myAccounts(),
33:         myName(strdup(name)), myAddress(strdup("123 Elm Street, "
34:         "Anyware USA 12345")), myNextAccountNumber(0) {
35:
36: }
37:
38: // Default constructor.
39: BankImpl::BankImpl() : myAccounts(), myName(NULL), myAddress(NULL),
40:         myNextAccountNumber(0) {
41:
42: }
43:
```

continues

Listing 8.9. continued

```
44: // Destructor.
45: BankImpl::~BankImpl() {
46:
47:     cout << "Bank \"" << name() << "\" being destroyed." << endl;
48:     free(myName);
49:     free(myAddress);
50: }
51:
52: char* BankImpl::name() {
53:
54:     return CORBA::strdup(myName);
55: }
56:
57: void BankImpl::name(const char* val) {
58:
59:     free(myName);
60:     myName = strdup(val);
61: }
62:
63: char* BankImpl::address() {
64:
65:     return CORBA::strdup(myAddress);
66: }
67:
68: void BankImpl::address(const char* val) {
69:
70:     free(myAddress);
71:     myAddress = strdup(val);
72: }
73:
74: Account_ptr BankImpl::createAccount(Customer_ptr customer,
75:         const char* accountType, CORBA::Float openingBalance) {
76:
77:     Account_ptr newAccount;
78:
79:     if (strcmp(accountType, "savings") == 0) {
80:
81:         // Create a new SavingsAccountImpl object for the Account.
82:         cout << "BankImpl: Creating new SavingsAccount for "
83:                 "Customer " << customer->name() << "." << endl;
84:         newAccount = new SavingsAccountImpl(getNextAccountNumber(),
85:                 getCurrentDate(), openingBalance, customer, 10.0);
86:     } else if (strcmp(accountType, "checking") == 0) {
87:
88:         // Create a new CheckingAccountImpl object for the Account.
89:         cout << "BankImpl: Creating new CheckingAccount for "
90:                 "Customer " << customer->name() << "." << endl;
91:         newAccount = new CheckingAccountImpl(getNextAccountNumber(),
92:                 getCurrentDate(), openingBalance, customer);
93:     } else {
94:
95:         // Invalid Account type; do nothing.
96:         cout << "BankImpl: Customer " << customer->name() <<
97:                 " requested invalid Account type \"" << accountType
98:                 << "\"." << endl;
```

8

```
 99:            return Account::_nil();
100:        }
101:
102:        // Add the created Account at the end of the list and return it.
103:        ::boa->obj_is_ready(newAccount);
104:        myAccounts.push_back(Account::_duplicate(newAccount));
105:        return newAccount;
106: }
107:
108: void BankImpl::deleteAccount(Account_ptr account) throw
109:        (InvalidAccountException) {
110:
111:        std::vector<Account_ptr>::iterator first = myAccounts.begin();
112:        std::vector<Account_ptr>::iterator last = myAccounts.end();
113:        IsAccountEqual predicate(account);
114:
115:        std::vector<Account_ptr>::iterator matchedAccount = std::
116:              find_if(first, last, predicate);
117:        if (matchedAccount == last) {
118:
119:            // Invalid Account; throw an exception.
120:            cout << "BankImpl: Attempted to delete invalid Account." <<
121:                 endl;
122:            throw InvalidAccountException();
123:        }
124:        cout << "BankImpl: Deleting Account \"" << account->
125:              accountNumber() << "\"." << endl;
126:
127:        // Delete the given Account.
128:        myAccounts.erase(matchedAccount);
129:        account->_release();
130: }
131:
132: AccountList* BankImpl::getAccounts() {
133:
134:        AccountList* list = new AccountList(myAccounts.size());
135:        CORBA::Long i;
136:
137:        for (i = 0; i < myAccounts.size(); i++) {
138:            (*list)[i] = Account::_duplicate(myAccounts[i]);
139:        }
140:
141:        return list;
142: }
143:
144: ATMCard_ptr BankImpl::issueATMCard(CORBA::Short pin, Account_ptr
145:        account) throw (InvalidAccountException) {
146:
147:        // First check to see if the Account is with this Bank.
148:        std::vector<Account_ptr>::iterator first = myAccounts.begin();
149:        std::vector<Account_ptr>::iterator last = myAccounts.end();
150:        IsAccountEqual predicate(account);
151:
152:        std::vector<Account_ptr>::iterator matchedAccount = std::
153:              find_if(first, last, predicate);
154:        if (matchedAccount == last) {
155:
```

continues

Listing 8.9. continued

```
156:            // Invalid Account; throw an exception.
157:            throw InvalidAccountException();
158:     }
159:
160:     // If we got this far, the Account must exist with this Bank,
161:     // so we can proceed.
162:     ATMCard_ptr newCard = new ATMCardImpl(pin, account);
163:
164:     return ATMCard::_duplicate(newCard);
165: }
166:
167: // Return the next available account number. The result is returned
168: // in a static buffer.
169: char* BankImpl::getNextAccountNumber() {
170:
171:     static char accountNumber[16] = "Account        ";
172:
173:     sprintf(accountNumber + 7, "%08u", myNextAccountNumber++);
174:
175:     return accountNumber;
176: }
177:
178: // Return the current date in the form "Mmm DD YYYY". The result is
179: // returned in a static buffer.
180: char* BankImpl::getCurrentDate() {
181:
182:     static char currentDate[12] = "            ";
183:
184:     time_t ltime;
185:     time(&ltime);
186:     char* ctimeResult = ctime(&ltime);
187:
188:     memcpy(currentDate, ctimeResult + 4, 3);
189:     memcpy(currentDate + 4, ctimeResult + 8, 2);
190:     memcpy(currentDate + 7, ctimeResult + 20, 4);
191:
192:     return currentDate;
193: }
```

The logic of ATMCardImpl (Listings 8.10 and 8.11) is very similar to that in BankImpl; addAccount(), removeAccount(), and getAccounts() are implemented in exactly the same way as they are in BankImpl (with the exception that removeAccount() and addAccount() call isAuthorized() to determine whether the Account is in the list of Accounts, rather than duplicate this functionality).

Listing 8.10. `ATMCardImpl.h.`

```
1: // ATMCardImpl.h
2:
3: #ifndef ATMCardImpl_h
4: #define ATMCardImpl_h
5:
6: #include <vector>
7:
8: #include "../ATMCard_s.h"
9:
10: class ATMCardImpl : public _sk_ATMCard {
11:
12: public:
13:     // Constuctor.
14:     //
15:     // pin - the initial PIN to use for this ATMCard.
16:     // initialAccount - the Account for which this ATMCard is
17:     // initially authorized.
18:     ATMCardImpl(CORBA::Short pin, Account_ptr initialAccount);
19:
20:     // Destructor.
21:     ~ATMCardImpl();
22:
23:     // These methods are described in ATMCard.idl.
24:     virtual CORBA::Boolean isAuthorized(Account_ptr account);
25:     virtual CORBA::Short pin();
26:     virtual void pin(CORBA::Short val);
27:     virtual void removeAccount(Account_ptr account) throw
28:             (InvalidAccountException);
29:     virtual void addAccount(Account_ptr account) throw
30:             (InvalidAccountException);
31:     virtual AccountList* getAccounts();
32:
33: private:
34:
35:     // Default constructor.
36:     ATMCardImpl();
37:
38:     // This ATMCard's PIN.
39:     CORBA::Short myPIN;
40:
41:     // A list of Accounts on which this ATM is authorized.
42:     std::vector<Account_ptr> myAccounts;
43: };
44:
45: #endif
```

Listing 8.11. `ATMCardImpl.cpp`.

```cpp
 1: // ATMCardImpl.cpp
 2:
 3: #include "ATMCardImpl.h"
 4:
 5: #include <iostream.h>
 6: #include <algorithm>
 7: #include <functional>
 8:
 9: // STL-derived unary function which returns TRUE if Accounts are
10: // equal.
11: class IsAccountEqual : public std::unary_function<Account_ptr,
12:         bool> {
13: public:
14:     IsAccountEqual(argument_type account) { myAccount = account; }
15:     result_type operator()(argument_type account) { return account->
16:             _is_equivalent(myAccount) != 0; }
17: private:
18:     argument_type myAccount;
19: };
20:
21: // Constuctor.
22: //
23: // pin - the initial PIN to use for this ATMCard.
24: // initialAccount - the Account for which this ATMCard is
25: // initially authorized.
26: ATMCardImpl::ATMCardImpl(CORBA::Short pin, Account_ptr
27:         initialAccount) : myPIN(pin), myAccounts() {
28:
29:     // Add the Account to the authorized Account list.
30:     myAccounts.push_back(Account::_duplicate(initialAccount));
31: }
32:
33: // Default constructor.
34: ATMCardImpl::ATMCardImpl() : myPIN(0), myAccounts() {
35:
36: }
37:
38: // Destructor.
39: ATMCardImpl::~ATMCardImpl() {
40:
41: }
42:
43: CORBA::Short ATMCardImpl::pin() {
44:
45:     return myPIN;
46: }
47:
48: void ATMCardImpl::pin(CORBA::Short val) {
49:
50:     myPIN = val;
51: }
52:
53: CORBA::Boolean ATMCardImpl::isAuthorized(Account_ptr account) {
54:
```

8

```
55:     std::vector<Account_ptr>::iterator first = myAccounts.begin();
56:     std::vector<Account_ptr>::iterator last = myAccounts.end();
57:     IsAccountEqual predicate(account);
58:
59:     std::vector<Account_ptr>::iterator matchedAccount = std::
60:             find_if(first, last, predicate);
61:     if (matchedAccount == last) {
62:
63:         // Account not found; return false.
64:         return 0;
65:     } else {
66:
67:         // Account found; return true.
68:         return 1;
69:     }
70: }
71:
72: void ATMCardImpl::removeAccount(Account_ptr account) throw
73:         (InvalidAccountException) {
74:
75:     if (!isAuthorized(account)) {
76:
77:         // Invalid Account; throw an exception.
78:         throw InvalidAccountException();
79:     }
80:
81:     // Delete the given Account.
82:     myAccounts.erase(&account);
83:     account->_release();
84: }
85:
86: void ATMCardImpl::addAccount(Account_ptr account) throw
87:         (InvalidAccountException) {
88:
89:     if (isAuthorized(account)) {
90:
91:         // Account has already been added, so throw an exception.
92:         throw InvalidAccountException();
93:     }
94:
95:     // Add the created Account at the end of the list.
96:     myAccounts.push_back(Account::_duplicate(account));
97: }
98:
99: AccountList* ATMCardImpl::getAccounts() {
100:
101:     AccountList* list = new AccountList(myAccounts.size());
102:     CORBA::Long i;
103:
104:     for (i = 0; i < myAccounts.size(); i++) {
105:         (*list)[i] = Account::_duplicate(myAccounts[i]);
106:     }
107:
108:     return list;
109: }
```

Because nothing different needs to be done when a BankImpl object is created, no changes are necessary from the original BankMain.cpp, but, for good measure, it appears in Listing 8.12.

Listing 8.12. BankMain.cpp.

```cpp
 1: // BankMain.cpp
 2:
 3: #include "BankImpl.h"
 4:
 5: #include <iostream.h>
 6:
 7: #include "../BankServer_c.h"
 8:
 9: CORBA::BOA_var boa;
10:
11: int main(int argc, char *const *argv) {
12:
13:     // Check the number of arguments; there should be exactly one
14:     // (two counting the executable name itself).
15:     if (argc != 2) {
16:         cout << "Usage: Bank <bankname>" << endl;
17:         return 1;
18:     }
19:
20:     // Assign the bank name to the first argument.
21:     const char* bankName = argv[1];
22:
23:     // Initialize the ORB and BOA.
24:     CORBA::ORB_var orb = CORBA::ORB_init(argc, argv);
25:     ::boa = orb->BOA_init(argc, argv);
26:
27:     // Create a Bank object.
28:     BankImpl bank(bankName);
29:
30:     // Notify the BOA that the BankImpl object is ready.
31:     ::boa->obj_is_ready(&bank);
32:
33:     // Locate a BankServer object and register with it.
34:     BankServer_var bankServer;
35:        try {
36:            bankServer = BankServer::_bind();
37:     } catch (const CORBA::Exception& ex) {
38:
39:         // The bind attempt failed...
40:         cout << "BankImpl: Unable to bind to a BankServer." << endl;
41:         cout << ex << endl;
42:         return 1;
43:     }
44:     try {
45:         bankServer->registerBank(&bank);
46:     } catch (const CORBA::Exception& ex) {
47:
48:         // The registerBank() attempt failed...
49:         cout << "BankImpl: Unable to register Bank." << endl;
```

8

```
50:          cout << ex << endl;
51:          return 1;
52:      }
53:
54:      // Wait for CORBA events.
55:      cout << "Bank \"" << bankName << "\" ready." << endl;
56:      ::boa->impl_is_ready();
57:
58:      // When this point is reached, the application is finished.
59:      return 0;
60: }
```

Implementing the ATM Server

The implementation of ATMImpl (see Listings 8.13 and 8.14) is clear-cut. The ATMImpl simply forwards requests to withdraw funds into an Account, to deposit funds into an Account, and to get the current balance of an Account. Each operation uses the ATMCard to authorize the transaction, and if the ATMCard approves, the transaction is forwarded to the Account. Because the transaction itself is performed by the Account, the implementations for withdraw(), deposit(), and getBalance() are simple.

Listing 8.13. ATMImpl.h.

```
 1: // ATMImpl.h
 2:
 3: #ifndef ATMImpl_h
 4: #define ATMImpl_h
 5:
 6: #include "../ATM_s.h"
 7:
 8: class ATMImpl : public _sk_ATM {
 9:
10: public:
11:      // Constuctor.
12:      //
13:      // name - the name of this ATM.
14:      ATMImpl(const char* name);
15:
16:      // Destructor.
17:      ~ATMImpl();
18:
19:      // These methods are described in ATM.idl.
20:      virtual char* name();
21:      virtual void name(const char* val);
22:      virtual CORBA::Float withdraw(ATMCard_ptr card, Account_ptr
23:              account, CORBA::Short pin, CORBA::Float amount) throw
24:              (AuthorizationException, InvalidAmountException,
25:              InsufficientFundsException);
26:      virtual CORBA::Float deposit(ATMCard_ptr card, Account_ptr
27:              account, CORBA::Short pin, CORBA::Float amount) throw
28:              (AuthorizationException, InvalidAmountException);
```

continues

Listing 8.13. continued

```
29:     virtual CORBA::Float getBalance(ATMCard_ptr card, Account_ptr
30:             account, CORBA::Short pin) throw
31:             (AuthorizationException);
32:
33: private:
34:
35:     // Default constuctor.
36:     ATMImpl();
37:
38:     // This ATM's name.
39:     char* myName;
40: };
41:
42: #endif
```

Listing 8.14. ATMImpl.cpp.

```
1: // ATMImpl.cpp
2:
3: #include "ATMImpl.h"
4:
5: #include <iostream.h>
6:
7: // Constuctor.
8: //
9: // name - the name of this ATM.
10: ATMImpl::ATMImpl(const char* name) : _sk_ATM(name),
11:         myName(strdup(name)) {
12:
13: }
14:
15: // Default constuctor.
16: ATMImpl::ATMImpl() : _sk_ATM(""), myName(NULL) {
17:
18: }
19:
20: // Destructor.
21: ATMImpl::~ATMImpl() {
22:
23:     free(myName);
24: }
25:
26: char* ATMImpl::name() {
27:
28:     return CORBA::strdup(myName);
29: }
30:
31: void ATMImpl::name(const char* val) {
32:
33:     free(myName);
34:     myName = strdup(val);
35: }
36:
```

8

```
37: CORBA::Float ATMImpl::withdraw(ATMCard_ptr card, Account_ptr
38:         account, CORBA::Short pin, CORBA::Float amount) throw
39:         (AuthorizationException, InvalidAmountException,
40:         InsufficientFundsException) {
41:
42:     cout << "ATM: Authorizing Account for withdrawal." << endl;
43:     if (pin != card->pin() || !card->isAuthorized(account)) {
44:
45:         // Incorrect PIN or card not authorized; throw an
46:         // exception.
47:         cout << " Authorization failed." << endl;
48:         throw AuthorizationException();
49:     }
50:
51:     cout << " Authorization succeeded; forwarding withdrawal " <<
52:             "request to Account." << endl;
53:     return account->withdraw(amount);
54: }
55:
56: CORBA::Float ATMImpl::deposit(ATMCard_ptr card, Account_ptr
57:         account, CORBA::Short pin, CORBA::Float amount) throw
58:         (AuthorizationException, InvalidAmountException) {
59:
60:     cout << "ATM: Authorizing Account for deposit." << endl;
61:     if (pin != card->pin() || !card->isAuthorized(account)) {
62:
63:         // Incorrect PIN or card not authorized; throw an
64:         // exception.
65:         cout << " Authorization failed." << endl;
66:         throw AuthorizationException();
67:     }
68:
69:     cout << " Authorization succeeded; forwarding deposit " <<
70:             "request to Account." << endl;
71:     return account->deposit(amount);
72: }
73:
74: CORBA::Float ATMImpl::getBalance(ATMCard_ptr card, Account_ptr
75:         account, CORBA::Short pin) throw (AuthorizationException) {
76:
77:     cout << "ATM: Authorizing Account for balance." << endl;
78:     if (pin != card->pin() || !card->isAuthorized(account)) {
79:
80:         // Incorrect PIN or card not authorized; throw an
81:         // exception.
82:         cout << " Authorization failed." << endl;
83:         throw AuthorizationException();
84:     }
85:
86:     cout << " Authorization succeeded; forwarding balance " <<
87:             "request to Account." << endl;
88:     return account->balance();
89: }
```

Again, the implementation in ATMMain.cpp is one that can be mostly borrowed from somewhere else. In this case, because an ATM interacts with the BankServer much the same way as a Bank does, you can borrow the code from BankMain.cpp and modify it slightly (to create and register an ATMImpl rather than a BankImpl). ATMMain.cpp appears in Listing 8.15, but compare it with BankMain.cpp (see Listing 8.12) and notice the similarity.

Listing 8.15. ATMMain.cpp.

```
 1: // ATMMain.cpp
 2:
 3: #include "ATMImpl.h"
 4:
 5: #include <iostream.h>
 6:
 7: #include "../BankServer_c.h"
 8:
 9: CORBA::BOA_var boa;
10:
11: int main(int argc, char *const *argv) {
12:
13:     // Check the number of arguments; there should be exactly one
14:     // (two counting the executable name itself).
15:     if (argc != 2) {
16:         cout << "Usage: ATM <atmname>" << endl;
17:         return 1;
18:     }
19:
20:     // Assign the ATM name to the first argument.
21:     const char* atmName = argv[1];
22:
23:     // Initialize the ORB and BOA.
24:     CORBA::ORB_var orb = CORBA::ORB_init(argc, argv);
25:     ::boa = orb->BOA_init(argc, argv);
26:
27:     // Create an ATM object.
28:     ATMImpl atm(atmName);
29:
30:     // Notify the BOA that the ATMImpl object is ready.
31:     ::boa->obj_is_ready(&atm);
32:
33:     // Locate a BankServer object and register with it.
34:     BankServer_var bankServer;
35:     try {
36:         bankServer = BankServer::_bind();
37:     } catch (const CORBA::Exception& ex) {
38:
39:         // The bind attempt failed...
40:         cout << "ATMImpl: Unable to bind to a BankServer." << endl;
41:         cout << ex << endl;
42:         return 1;
43:     }
44:     try {
45:         bankServer->registerATM(&atm);
46:     } catch (const CORBA::Exception& ex) {
47:
```

8

```
48:          // The registerATM() attempt failed...
49:          cout << "ATMImpl: Unable to register ATM." << endl;
50:          cout << ex << endl;
51:          return 1;
52:      }
53:
54:      // Wait for CORBA events.
55:      cout << "ATM \"" << atmName << "\" ready." << endl;
56:      ::boa->impl_is_ready();
57:
58:      // When this point is reached, the application is finished.
59:      return 0;
60: }
```

Note that in line 36 the _bind() method call reappears. Again, while this functionality appears in many ORBs, it is not standard CORBA. On Day 12 you'll replace this call to the nonstandard _bind() with the use of the CORBA Naming Service, but in the meantime, you'll continue to use _bind() for the sake of simplicity.

Implementing the ATM Client

The next step is to implement a client application that uses the newly added ATM functionality. The client can be similar in function to the BankClient application from previous chapters, except that rather than accessing an Account directly, it will do so through the ATM interface. The implementation of the ATMClient appears in Listing 8.16.

Listing 8.16. ATMClientMain.cpp.

```
 1: // ATMClientMain.cpp
 2:
 3: #include <iostream.h>
 4: #include <stdlib.h>
 5:
 6: #include "../Customer/CustomerImpl.h"
 7:
 8: #include "../Bank_c.h"
 9: #include "../BankServer_c.h"
10: #include "../ATM_c.h"
11:
12: int main(int argc, char *const *argv) {
13:
14:      // Check the number of arguments; there should be exactly five
15:      // (six counting the executable name itself).
16:      if (argc != 6) {
17:          cout << "Usage: ATMClient <name> <social security number>"
18:                  " <address> <mother's maiden name> <PIN>" << endl;
19:          return 1;
20:      }
21:
```

continues

Listing 8.16. continued

```
22:     // Assign the command line arguments to the Customer attributes.
23:     const char* name = argv[1];
24:     const char* socialSecurityNumber = argv[2];
25:     const char* address = argv[3];
26:     const char* mothersMaidenName = argv[4];
27:     CORBA::Short pin = atoi(argv[5]);
28:
29:     // Initialize the ORB and BOA.
30:     CORBA::ORB_var orb = CORBA::ORB_init(argc, argv);
31:     CORBA::BOA_var boa = orb->BOA_init(argc, argv);
32:
33:     // Create a Customer object.
34:     cout << "ATMClient: Creating new Customer:" << endl;
35:     cout << "  name: " << name << endl;
36:     cout << "  Social Security number: " << socialSecurityNumber <<
37:             endl;
38:     cout << "  address: " << address << endl;
39:     cout << "  mother's maiden name: " << mothersMaidenName << endl;
40:     CustomerImpl customer(name, socialSecurityNumber, address,
41:             mothersMaidenName);
42:
43:     // Notify the BOA that the CustomerImpl object is ready.
44:     boa->obj_is_ready(&customer);
45:
46:     // Locate a BankServer object and try to get a list of Banks
47:     // and ATMs from it.
48:     BankServer_var bankServer;
49:     try {
50:         bankServer = BankServer::_bind();
51:     } catch (const CORBA::Exception& ex) {
52:
53:         // The bind attempt failed...
54:         cout << "ATMClient: Unable to bind to a BankServer:" <<
55:                 endl;
56:         cout << ex << endl;
57:         return 1;
58:     }
59:     cout << "ATMClient: Successfully bound to a BankServer." <<
60:             endl;
61:
62:     BankList_ptr banks;
63:     ATMList_ptr ATMs;
64:
65:     try {
66:         banks = bankServer->getBanks();
67:         ATMs = bankServer->getATMs();
68:     } catch (const CORBA::Exception& ex) {
69:
70:         // The attempt failed...
71:         cout << "ATMClient: Unable to get lists of Banks and ATMs:"
72:                 << endl;
73:         cout << ex << endl;
74:         return 1;
75:     }
76:
```

8

```
77:     // Use the first Bank and the first ATM that appear in the
78:     // lists.
79:     if (banks->length() == 0) {
80:
81:         // No Banks were available.
82:         cout << "ATMClient: No Banks available." << endl;
83:         return 1;
84:     }
85:     if (ATMs->length() == 0) {
86:
87:         // No ATMs were available.
88:         cout << "ATMClient: No ATMs available." << endl;
89:         return 1;
90:     }
91:     Bank_var bank = (*banks)[0];
92:     ATM_var atm = (*ATMs)[0];
93:     cout << "ATMClient: Using Bank \"" << bank->name() << "\" and"
94:             << " ATM \"" << atm->name() << "\"." << endl;
95:
96:     // Do some cool stuff.
97:
98:     Account_var account;
99:     ATMCard_var atmCard;
100:
101:     try {
102:         account = bank->createAccount(&customer, "checking", 0.0);
103:     } catch (const CORBA::Exception& ex) {
104:
105:         // The createAccount() attempt failed...
106:         cout << "ATMClient: Unable to create Account." << endl;
107:         cout << ex << endl;
108:         return 1;
109:     }
110:
111:     try {
112:
113:         // Print out some Account statistics.
114:         cout << "ATMClient: Opened new Account:" << endl;
115:         cout << "   account number: " << account->accountNumber() <<
116:                 endl;
117:         cout << "   creation date: " << account->creationDate() <<
118:                 endl;
119:         cout << "   account balance: " << account->balance() << endl;
120:
121:         // Ask the Bank to issue an ATMCard for the newly-created
122:         // Account.
123:         cout << "ATMClient: Getting ATMCard from Bank." << endl;
124:         try {
125:             atmCard = bank->issueATMCard(pin, account);
126:         } catch (const InvalidAccountException&) {
127:
128:             // For some reason, the Account was invalid (this
129:             // shouldn't happen).
130:             cout << "ATMClient: Exception caught: Invalid Account"
131:                     << endl;
```

continues

Listing 8.16. continued

```
132:            return 1;
133:        }
134:
135:        // Perform some transactions on the Account through the
136:        // ATM.
137:        cout << "ATMClient: Performing transactions." << endl;
138:        try {
139:            cout << "  Depositing $250.00..." << endl;
140:            cout << "  New balance is $" << atm->deposit(atmCard,
141:                    account, pin, 250.00) << endl;
142:
143:            // This will throw an exception since we're trying to
144:            // withdraw too much.
145:            cout << "  Withdrawing $500.00..." << endl;
146:            cout << "  New balance is $" << atm->withdraw(atmCard,
147:                    account, pin, 500.00) << endl;
148:        } catch (AuthorizationException&) {
149:            cout << "ATMClient: Exception caught: Invalid PIN or "
150:                    << "No authorization (as expected)" << endl;
151:        } catch (InvalidAmountException&) {
152:            cout << "ATMClient: Exception caught: Invalid amount"
153:                    << endl;
154:        } catch (InsufficientFundsException&) {
155:            cout << "ATMClient: Exception caught: Insufficient " <<
156:                    "funds" << endl;
157:        }
158:
159:        // Perform some more transactions on the Account through
160:        // the ATM.
161:        cout << "ATMClient: Performing more transactions." << endl;
162:        try {
163:            cout << "  Depositing $500.00..." << endl;
164:            cout << "  New balance is $" <<
165:                    atm->deposit(atmCard, account, pin, 500.00) <<
166:                    endl;
167:
168:            // This will throw an exception since we're using the
169:            // wrong PIN.
170:            cout << "  Withdrawing $250.00 with incorrect PIN..."
171:                    << endl;
172:            cout << "  New balance is $" << atm->withdraw(atmCard,
173:                    account, pin + 1, 250.00) << endl;
174:        } catch (AuthorizationException&) {
175:            cout << "ATMClient: Exception caught: Invalid PIN or "
176:                    << "No authorization (as expected)" << endl;
177:        } catch (InvalidAmountException&) {
178:            cout << "ATMClient: Exception caught: Invalid amount"
179:                    << endl;
180:        } catch (InsufficientFundsException&) {
181:            cout << "ATMClient: Exception caught: Insufficient " <<
182:                    "funds" << endl;
183:        }
184:
```

8

```
185:        // Get rid of the Account.
186:        try {
187:            cout << "  Deleting Account." << endl;
188:            bank->deleteAccount(account);
189:
190:            // Attempt to delete the Account again, just for kicks.
191:            // This should result in an exception being thrown.
192:            cout << "  Attempting to cause an exception by " <<
193:                    "deleting Account again." << endl;
194:            bank->deleteAccount(account);
195:        } catch (const InvalidAccountException&) {
196:
197:            // Sure enough, the exception was thrown.
198:            cout << "ATMClient: Exception caught: Invalid " <<
199:                    "Account (as expected)" << endl;
200:        }
201:    } catch (const CORBA::Exception& ex) {
202:
203:        // Some operation on the Account failed...
204:        cout << "ATMClient: Error accessing Account:" << endl;
205:        cout << ex << endl;
206:        return 1;
207:    }
208:
209:    // When this point is reached, the application is finished.
210:    return 0;
211: }
```

ATMClient.cpp is more involved than the NewCustomer.cpp application from the previous chapters (refer to Listing 8.16). It might be instructive to step through the code to see exactly what is going on:

The first three #includes (lines 3-6) will look familiar to you by now. Because the ATMClient is a client of a Bank, a BankServer, and an ATM, the header files for those client stubs are #included as well in lines 8-10.

In the first few lines of main() (lines 12-20), the ATMClient first checks the number of arguments passed on the command line. The five arguments are the Customer's name, Social Security number, address, mother's maiden name, and Personal Identification Number (PIN). If the number of arguments is not correct, the program exits.

In lines 22-31, ATMClient sets its internal parameters to the values passed on the command line and then initializes the ORB and BOA. (This section of code almost exactly duplicates the corresponding code in the NewCustomer application.)

Next, ATMClient creates a Customer object (lines 33-41) and registers it with the BOA (lines 43-44). Because there are no changes to the Customer interface from Day 7, the creation of a Customer object is exactly the same as in NewCustomer.

ATMClient's next step, in lines 46-60, is to locate a BankServer object and bind to it (in line 50). If a BankServer cannot be located, the ATMClient cannot continue and thus exits (a condition handled by the catch construct in lines 51-58).

In lines 62-75, ATMClient gets the list of available Banks and ATMs from the BankServer it previously located. Again, if there is a problem retrieving this information, the ATMClient exits.

Next, in lines 77-94, ATMClient chooses the first Bank and ATM that occur in the lists received from the BankServer. If there isn't at least one of each available (the actual checks are made in lines 79 and 85), ATMClient exits.

The next step is to open an Account with the chosen Bank, using the Customer object created previously, which the ATMClient accomplishes in lines 96-109. In lines 111-119, ATMClient prints out some statistics of the Account—account number, creation date, and current balance (which should be zero).

In lines 121-133, ATMClient requests an ATMCard from the Bank, using the pin that was passed on the command line. Because the ATMCard is being issued for the Account just opened by the same Bank, don't expect to get an InvalidAccountException here, but just as a safe practice, ATMClient tries to catch this exception anyway in line 126.

ATMClient proceeds to perform a few transactions on the Account, such as depositing and withdrawing funds, as in lines 135-157. Like the NewCustomer application, ATMClient attempts to withdraw too much from the Account (in line 146), eliciting an InsufficientFundsException (caught in line 154).

Next, in lines 159-183, ATMClient performs another transaction; this time it attempts to make a deposit into the Account, but using the wrong PIN. (It obtains an incorrect PIN by taking the PIN and adding one to it, as can be seen in line 173.) As expected, this causes an AuthorizationException to be raised (which is caught in line 174).

Finally, in lines 185-211, the ATMClient deletes the Account. Again, because the Account was created by the same Bank that ATMClient uses to delete the Account, don't expect the InvalidAccountException to be thrown, but the catch is added anyway, for good measure. Like its predecessor, ATMClient also attempts to delete the Account twice (line 194) for the purpose of demonstrating the InvalidAccountException (caught in line 195).

Running the Application

After you've successfully compiled the various application components, you're ready to run them together to see the results. As on Day 7, start by running the BankServer application; type the following:

```
BankServer
```

Again, the output of BankServer will be this:

```
BankServer ready.
```

You're now ready to start the Bank application. Actually, you can start the ATM application first because Bank and ATM objects are independent of each other (but both depend on locating a BankServer object). Start the BankServer by typing this:

```
BankServer "First Bank"
```

which in turn outputs this:

```
Bank "First Bank" ready.
```

Meanwhile, the BankServer will have output this:

```
BankServerImpl: Registering Bank "First Bank".
```

Then you'll want to start the ATM application:

```
ATM "First Bank ATM"
```

The ATM application displays the following:

```
ATM "First Bank ATM" ready.
```

The BankServer also pipes in with this message:

```
BankServerImpl: Registering ATM "First Bank ATM".
```

Finally, you're ready to run the ATMClient application. You can do so by typing

```
ATMClient "Jeremy Rosenberger" 123456789 "123 Main Street" Doe 1234
```

The ATMClient will then do its magic, displaying the following:

```
ATMClient: Creating new Customer:
  name: Jeremy Rosenberger
  Social Security number: 123456789
  address: 123 Main Street
  mother's maiden name: Doe
ATMClient: Successfully bound to a BankServer.
ATMClient: Using Bank "First Bank" and ATM "First Bank ATM".
ATMClient: Opened new Account:
  account number: Account00000000
  creation date: Oct 20 1997
  account balance: 0
ATMClient: Getting ATMCard from Bank.
ATMClient: Performing transactions.
  Depositing $250.00...
  New balance is $250
  Withdrawing $500.00...
ATMClient: Exception caught: Insufficient funds
ATMClient: Performing more transactions.
  Depositing $500.00...
  New balance is $750
  Withdrawing $250.00 with incorrect PIN...
ATMClient: Exception caught: Invalid PIN or No authorization (as expected)
  Deleting Account.
  Attempting to cause an exception by deleting Account again.
ATMClient: Exception caught: Invalid Account (as expected)
```

All this will go by very quickly, but after it's all over, you'll be able to go to the other application windows and see some evidence of what transpired here. Looking first at the BankServer application, you'll see this (with new output messages highlighted in **bold**):

```
BankServer ready.
BankServerImpl: Returning list of 1 Banks.
BankServerImpl: Returning list of 1 ATMs.
```

Recalling the implementation of BankServerImpl, you will notice that these messages are displayed when the getBanks() and getATMs() methods are called.

Turning your attention now to the Bank application, you'll see the following messages:

```
Bank "First Bank" ready.
BankImpl: Creating new CheckingAccount for Customer Jeremy Rosenberger.
AccountImpl: Insufficient funds to withdraw specified amount.
BankImpl: Deleting Account "Account00000000".
BankImpl: Attempted to delete invalid Account.
```

Examining the output of the Bank application, you can trace the actions of the ATMClient application: A new CheckingAccount is created; at some point later, an unsuccessful attempt is made to withdraw funds from the Account, and later the Account is deleted. Recall also that the ATMClient, like the NewCustomer application before it, attempts to delete the Account twice, and a message to this effect is also displayed by the Bank application.

You will recall that the ATMClient also attempted to perform a transaction with the incorrect PIN. Notice that there is no such message to that effect here; indeed, the Bank never even saw the transaction attempt because the ATM blocked the transaction from occurring when the Customer could not be authorized by the ATMCard.

Finally, turn your attention to the output of the ATM application:

```
ATM "First Bank ATM" ready.
ATM: Authorizing Account for deposit.
  Authorization succeeded; forwarding deposit request to Account.
ATM: Authorizing Account for withdrawal.
  Authorization succeeded; forwarding withdrawal request to Account.
ATM: Authorizing Account for deposit.
  Authorization succeeded; forwarding deposit request to Account.
ATM: Authorizing Account for withdrawal.
  Authorization failed.
```

The output from the ATM provides the most insight into what the ATMClient is doing. Each operation, whether successful or not, is logged by the ATM application. As you see, each transaction is successful except the last, in which the ATMClient deliberately attempts to use the wrong PIN for the transaction.

Summary

In this chapter, you added a fair amount of functionality to the Bank application. Most of it was added in the form of a new system component, the ATM application, and its counterpart, the ATMCard. You also modified the other components of the system to work with the ATM: Notably, the BankServer was modified to enable ATMs to register, the Bank was modified to issue ATMCards on request, and, of course, the NewCustomer application was revised to use an ATM and ATMCard for all its transactions. This chapter gives you the opportunity to work with a more complex CORBA application, involving a number of components that interact with each other.

On Day 9, you'll implement the final installment of the Bank application. So far, the client portion of the application (NewCustomer yesterday, ATMClient today) controls most of the process. In other words, the server components spend their time waiting for a transaction to be initiated by the client component. This is commonly referred to as a *pull* model because the client "pulls" information from the servers as it is needed.

On Day 9, you'll add a new capability: Through callbacks, the server components can "push" messages to the client. In other words, if a server (for instance, a Bank) wants to send a message to the Customer, it won't have to wait for the Customer to pull that information from the Bank; it can push the information to the Customer at any time. This is useful if the Customer subscribes through the Bank to a service that, for example, periodically provides stock updates.

Q&A

Q It seems to me that the ATM interface is little more than a pass-through for Customers to access their Accounts.

A If you noticed this property of the ATM interface, give yourself a pat on the back. The ATM doesn't actually introduce any new functionality to the application—at least where Account operations are concerned—but simply provides another way to access Accounts.

Q If this application were to actually be deployed, wouldn't security be a major issue? For instance, it looks like it would be easy to guess a customer's PIN through brute force.

A If you're asking this question, you've no doubt observed the complete lack of a security mechanism in the application (other than the PIN mechanism itself). Of course, in a production application, you'd need to make additional security considerations to prevent password snooping, brute force attacks, and so on. (You might want to use the CORBA Security Service or your own mechanisms to implement and enforce security policies.)

Workshop

The following section will help you test your comprehension of the material presented in this chapter and put what you've learned into practice. You'll find the answers to the quiz and exercise in Appendix A.

Quiz

What are the four steps you'll typically follow to make enhancements to a CORBA application?

Exercise

Add an operation to the ATM interface that allows funds to be transferred between Accounts. Be sure to provide appropriate exceptions as well.

Day **9**

Using Callbacks to Add Push Capability

On Day 8, "Adding Automated Teller Machine (ATM) Capability," you continued development of the sample Bank application by adding Automated Teller Machine (ATM) capabilities. Now, you'll make the final enhancements, this time adding push capability.

NOTE

Although *push* appears to be one of the latest buzzwords in the industry (particularly where the Internet is concerned), the concept has been around for quite some time. (The Internet is simply one of the more visible applications for it.) Client/server applications typically follow the pull model, in which the client *pulls* information from the server when it so desires (in other words, the client initiates the transaction). In the push model, the server *pushes* information to the client—that is, the server initiates the transaction. For example, when a stock price changes, a

> server can push the updated information to its clients. Push can be much more efficient than pull when information is updated infrequently, especially when there are a number of clients in a system.

Push capability can be utilized in many ways, but in the Bank application you'll use it to implement an account update system. Through this system, customers receive account balance updates every minute. (Of course, this would probably be useless in an actual bank application, but it serves to demonstrate the concept.) The process you'll follow is the same as in the previous chapter:

☐ *Define additional requirements.* Modify the system requirements to specify a requirement for the account update capability.

☐ *Modify the system design.* Translate the additional requirements into changes in system design, again reinforcing the notion of software design as an iterative process.

☐ *Modify the IDL definitions.* Create or update the interface definitions for new classes or classes that have changed since the previous iteration.

☐ *Implement the new functionality.* After the design is finished and then realized in IDL, implement the new functionality and see how the new application works.

Defining Additional Requirements

Recall the system requirements for the Bank application from Day 8. As you did when you added ATM capability to the application, you'll define a set of requirements that describes the desired functionality. For the account update capability, assume the following requirements:

☐ Supports the capability for a server to send account balance updates periodically and automatically to customers

☐ Supports the capability for customers to request the account update feature

The requirements are straightforward; they formalize the functionality already described. Note that there is only a requirement to request the account update feature; there is no requirement to cancel the feature. Adding such a capability is not difficult, but to keep the sample application simple, this feature is omitted. (Perhaps it would make a good exercise…)

9

Modifying the Class Diagram

Again, you're ready to translate a modified set of requirements into an updated system design. This time, you won't need to create any additional classes, and you'll need to modify some existing classes only slightly.

Modifying Existing Classes

The modifications required to add account updating to the application are clear-cut. First, a Customer must subscribe to the service, so the Bank must be modified to enable this. The only information required to subscribe to the service is the Account, so the method should take this as a parameter. No other parameters are strictly necessary; the Bank can obtain the Customer(s) from the Account when necessary. Also, no return value is required. The signature for the new method is this:

```
requestUpdateService(account : Account) : void
```

The other requirement is to add a method to the Customer class that enables the Bank to send updates when necessary. So that the Customer knows which Account the update is for (Customers can have multiple Accounts, after all), the Account should be a parameter. With just the Account information, the Customer can determine the current balance, but for the sake of convenience, the method will take the balance as a parameter as well. Again, no return value is necessary—and just for fun, make the method oneway as well, so the Bank will be able to send updates without having to wait for responses from the Customers. Here is the signature for the method:

```
updateAccountBalance(account : Account, balance : float) : void
```

 NOTE

> For the updateAccountBalance() operation, using the oneway calling mechanism is a reasonable choice. Recall that the oneway mechanism is unreliable—that is, delivery of oneway messages is not guaranteed. This is acceptable for updateAccountBalance() because the account update messages are not considered critical. In other words, if an occasional update message is not delivered, the impact on the operation of the application is minimal.

Appearing in Figure 9.1 is the modified class diagram for the Bank application, reflecting these additions.

Figure 9.1.

The modified Bank *application class diagram.*

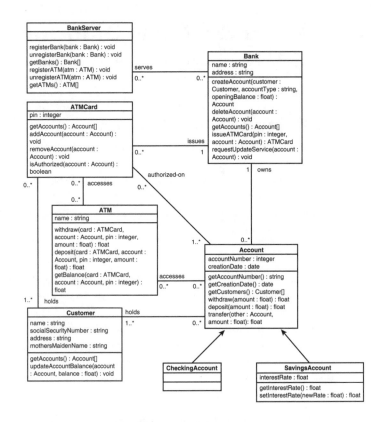

Modifying the IDL Specification

As on Day 8, the modifications to the IDL interface specifications are obvious. Start with the modified Bank interface, appearing in Listing 9.1, with changes highlighted in **bold.**

Listing 9.1. Modified Bank.idl.

```
 1: // Bank.idl
 2:
 3: // Forward declaration of Bank interface.
 4: interface Bank;
 5:
 6: #ifndef Bank_idl
 7: #define Bank_idl
 8:
 9: // sequence of Banks
10: typedef sequence<Bank> BankList;
11:
```

```
12: #include "Customer.idl"
13: #include "Account.idl"
14: #include "ATMCard.idl"
15: #include "Exceptions.idl"
16:
17: // A Bank provides access to Accounts. It can create an Account
18: // on behalf of a Customer, delete an Account, or list the current
19: // Accounts with the Bank.
20: interface Bank {
21:
22:     // This Bank's name.
23:     attribute string name;
24:
25:     // This Bank's address.
26:     attribute string address;
27:
28:     // Create an Account on behalf of the given Customer, with the
29:     // given account type ("savings" or "checking", where case is
30:     // significant), and the given opening balance.
31:     Account createAccount(in Customer customer, in string
32:             accountType, in float openingBalance);
33:
34:     // Delete the given Account. If the Account is not with this
35:     // Bank, this operation does nothing.
36:     void deleteAccount(in Account account)
37:             raises (InvalidAccountException);
38:
39:     // List all Accounts with this Bank.
40:     AccountList getAccounts();
41:
42:     // Issue an ATMCard with the initial PIN and initially
43:     // authorized on the given Account. If the Account is not with
44:     // this Bank, this operation does nothing.
45:     ATMCard issueATMCard(in short pin, in Account account)
46:             raises (InvalidAccountException);
47:
48:     // Request the automatic update service on the given Account.
49:     // Account balances will be sent periodically to the Customers
50:     // owning the Account.
51:     void requestUpdateService(in Account account)
52:             raises (InvalidAccountException);
53: };
54:
55: #endif
```

Note that the changes to Bank.idl are minimal, consisting only of the new requestUpdateService() method. Also, notice that the InvalidAccountException comes into play again here, in case an Account is passed that does not belong to the Bank.

The other changes are made to Customer.idl, which appears in Listing 9.2.

Listing 9.2. Modified Customer.idl.

```
 1: // Customer.idl
 2:
 3: // Forward declaration of Customer interface.
 4: interface Customer;
 5:
 6: #ifndef Customer_idl
 7: #define Customer_idl
 8:
 9: // sequence of Customers
10: typedef sequence<Customer> CustomerList;
11:
12: #include "Account.idl"
13:
14: // A Customer can hold one or more Accounts. Presumably, the
15: // Customer is what drives the rest of this application.
16: interface Customer {
17:
18:     // This Customer's name.
19:     attribute string name;
20:
21:     // This Customer's Social Security number.
22:     readonly attribute string socialSecurityNumber;
23:
24:     // This Customer's address.
25:     attribute string address;
26:
27:     // This Customer's mother's maiden name.
28:     readonly attribute string mothersMaidenName;
29:
30:     // Return a list of Accounts held (or co-held) by this
31:     // Customer.
32:     AccountList getAccounts();
33:
34:     // Send an update message to this Customer regarding the given
35:     // Account and its new balance.
36:     oneway void updateAccountBalance(in Account account, in float
37:             balance);
38: };
39:
40: #endif
```

Again, changes to Customer.idl are minimal, adding only the updateAccountBalance() method. Note the use of the oneway modifier, indicating that when this method is called, it will return to the caller immediately.

You're now ready to proceed with the changes to the implementation itself.

Implementing the New Functionality

Implementing the account update functionality is also a simple process. Given that only two methods have been added to the entire system, there are only a couple of steps involved:

☐ Implement requestUpdateService() in the BankImpl class. The BankImpl must keep track of all Accounts for which the service is activated; when it comes time to send update messages to the Accounts' Customers, the BankImpl can simply traverse this list of Accounts.

☐ Implement updateAccountBalance() in the CustomerImpl class. This method can be as trivial as simply printing a message indicating the Account and its new balance.

Enhancing the BankImpl

First, you'll modify BankImpl to provide the requestUpdateService() functionality. As already mentioned, the BankImpl must maintain a list of Accounts for which the automatic update service is activated. You'll see how this is done in Listing 9.3, BankImpl.h, with changes highlighted in **bold**.

Listing 9.3. BankImpl.h.

```
 1: // BankImpl.h
 2:
 3: #ifndef BankImpl_h
 4: #define BankImpl_h
 5:
 6: #include <vector>
 7:
 8: #include "../Bank_s.h"
 9:
10: class BankImpl : public _sk_Bank {
11:
12: public:
13:
14:     // Constructor.
15:     //
16:     // name - This Bank's name.
17:     BankImpl(const char* name);
18:
19:     // Destructor.
20:     ~BankImpl();
21:
22:     // These methods are described in Bank.idl.
23:     virtual char* name();
24:     virtual void name(const char* val);
25:     virtual char* address();
26:     virtual void address(const char* val);
27:     virtual Account_ptr createAccount(Customer_ptr customer,
28:             const char* accountType, CORBA::Float openingBalance);
```

continues

Listing 9.3. continued

```
29:      virtual void deleteAccount(Account_ptr account) throw
30:             (InvalidAccountException);
31:      virtual AccountList* getAccounts();
32:      virtual ATMCard_ptr issueATMCard(CORBA::Short pin, Account_ptr
33:             account) throw (InvalidAccountException);
34:      virtual void requestUpdateService(Account_ptr account) throw
35:             (InvalidAccountException);
36:
37: protected:
38:
39:      // Return the next available account number. The result is
40:      // returned in a static buffer.
41:      char* getNextAccountNumber();
42:
43:      // Return the current date in the form "Mmm DD YYYY". The result
44:      // is returned in a static buffer.
45:      char* getCurrentDate();
46:
47: private:
48:
49:      // Default constructor.
50:      BankImpl();
51:
52:      // This Bank's name.
53:      char* myName;
54:
55:      // This Bank's address.
56:      char* myAddress;
57:
58:      // This Bank's Accounts.
59:      std::vector<Account_ptr> myAccounts;
60:
61:      // The Accounts which are subscribed to the automatic update
62:      // service.
63:      std::vector<Account_ptr> mySubscribedAccounts;
64:
65:      // The next available account number.
66:      unsigned int myNextAccountNumber;
67: };
68:
69: #endif
```

In `BankImpl.h`, note the addition of the `requestUpdateService()` method and the `mySubscribedAccounts` data member. `mySubscribedAccounts` is a C++ Standard Template Library `vector`, just like the `myAccounts` member, which contains all the `Account`s held by a particular `Bank`. In Listing 9.4, `BankImpl.cpp`, you'll observe how the elements of `mySubscribedAccounts` are managed.

9

Listing 9.4. `BankImpl.cpp`.

```cpp
 1: // BankImpl.cpp
 2:
 3: #include "BankImpl.h"
 4:
 5: #include <process.h>
 6:
 7: #include <time.h>
 8: #include <string.h>
 9: #include <iostream.h>
10: #include <algorithm>
11: #include <functional>
12:
13: #include "SavingsAccountImpl.h"
14: #include "CheckingAccountImpl.h"
15: #include "ATMCardImpl.h"
16:
17: extern CORBA::BOA_var boa;
18:
19: // STL-derived unary function which returns TRUE if Accounts are
20: // equal.
21: class IsAccountEqual : public std::unary_function<Account_ptr,
22:         bool> {
23: public:
24:     IsAccountEqual(argument_type account) { myAccount = account; }
25:     result_type operator()(argument_type account) { return account->
26:             _is_equivalent(myAccount) != 0; }
27: private:
28:     argument_type myAccount;
29: };
30:
31: void updateAccountThreadFunction(LPVOID pParam) {
32:
33:     std::vector<Account_ptr>* accounts = (std::
34:             vector<Account_ptr>*)pParam;
35:
36:     while (1) {
37:         Sleep(60000);
38:         cout << "BankImpl: Updating Accounts." << endl;
39:
40:         // Iterate through the list of Accounts.
41:         for (int i = 0; i < accounts->size(); i++) {
42:
43:             // For each Account, get the list of Customers and send
44:             // an update message to each.
45:             CustomerList* customers = (*accounts)[i]->
46:                     getCustomers();
47:             for (CORBA::Long j = 0; j < customers->length(); j++) {
48:                 try {
49:                     (*customers)[i]->
50:                             updateAccountBalance((*accounts)[i],
51:                             (*accounts)[i]->balance());
52:                 } catch (const CORBA::Exception&) {
53:
```

continues

Listing 9.4. continued

```
54:                          // Ignore the exception; we don't care if
55:                          // there's a problem with the update.
56:                  }
57:              }
58:          }
59:      }
60: }
61:
62: // Constructor.
63: //
64: // name - This Bank's name.
65: BankImpl::BankImpl(const char* name) : _sk_Bank(name), myAccounts(),
66:          mySubscribedAccounts(), myName(strdup(name)),
67:          myAddress(strdup("123 Elm Street, Anywhere USA 12345")),
68:          myNextAccountNumber(0) {
69:
70:      _beginthread(&updateAccountThreadFunction, 0,
71:              &mySubscribedAccounts);
72: }
73:
74: // Default constructor.
75: BankImpl::BankImpl() : myAccounts(), mySubscribedAccounts(),
76:          myName(NULL), myAddress(NULL), myNextAccountNumber(0) {
77:
78: }
79:
80: // Destructor.
81: BankImpl::~BankImpl() {
82:
83:      cout << "Bank \"" << name() << "\" being destroyed." << endl;
84:      free(myName);
85:      free(myAddress);
86: }
87:
88: char* BankImpl::name() {
89:
90:      return CORBA::strdup(myName);
91: }
92:
93: void BankImpl::name(const char* val) {
94:
95:      free(myName);
96:      myName = strdup(val);
97: }
98:
99: char* BankImpl::address() {
100:
101:      return CORBA::strdup(myAddress);
102: }
103:
104: void BankImpl::address(const char* val) {
105:
```

```
106:      free(myAddress);
107:      myAddress = strdup(val);
108: }
109:
110: Account_ptr BankImpl::createAccount(Customer_ptr customer,
111:         const char* accountType, CORBA::Float openingBalance) {
112:
113:      Account_ptr newAccount;
114:
115:      if (strcmp(accountType, "savings") == 0) {
116:
117:          // Create a new SavingsAccountImpl object for the Account.
118:          cout << "BankImpl: Creating new SavingsAccount for "
119:              "Customer " << customer->name() << "." << endl;
120:          newAccount = new SavingsAccountImpl(getNextAccountNumber(),
121:              getCurrentDate(), openingBalance, customer, 10.0);
122:      } else if (strcmp(accountType, "checking") == 0) {
123:
124:          // Create a new CheckingAccountImpl object for the Account.
125:          cout << "BankImpl: Creating new CheckingAccount for "
126:              "Customer " << customer->name() << "." << endl;
127:          newAccount = new CheckingAccountImpl(getNextAccountNumber(),
128:              getCurrentDate(), openingBalance, customer);
129:      } else {
130:
131:          // Invalid Account type; do nothing.
132:          cout << "BankImpl: Customer " << customer->name() <<
133:              " requested invalid Account type \"" << accountType
134:              << "\"." << endl;
135:          return Account::_nil();
136:      }
137:
138:      // Add the created Account at the end of the list and return it.
139:      ::boa->obj_is_ready(newAccount);
140:      myAccounts.push_back(Account::_duplicate(newAccount));
141:      return newAccount;
142: }
143:
144: void BankImpl::deleteAccount(Account_ptr account) throw
145:         (InvalidAccountException) {
146:
147:      std::vector<Account_ptr>::iterator first = myAccounts.begin();
148:      std::vector<Account_ptr>::iterator last = myAccounts.end();
149:      IsAccountEqual predicate(account);
150:
151:      std::vector<Account_ptr>::iterator matchedAccount = std::
152:              find_if(first, last, predicate);
153:      if (matchedAccount == last) {
154:
155:          // Invalid Account; throw an exception.
156:          cout << "BankImpl: Attempted to delete invalid Account." <<
157:              endl;
158:          throw InvalidAccountException();
159:      }
160:      cout << "BankImpl: Deleting Account \"" << account->
161:          accountNumber() << "\"." << endl;
162:
```

continues

Listing 9.4. continued

```
163:     // Delete the given Account.
164:     myAccounts.erase(matchedAccount);
165:     account->_release();
166: }
167:
168: AccountList* BankImpl::getAccounts() {
169:
170:     AccountList* list = new AccountList(myAccounts.size());
171:     CORBA::Long i;
172:
173:     for (i = 0; i < myAccounts.size(); i++) {
174:         (*list)[i] = Account::_duplicate(myAccounts[i]);
175:     }
176:
177:     return list;
178: }
179:
180: ATMCard_ptr BankImpl::issueATMCard(CORBA::Short pin, Account_ptr
181:         account) throw (InvalidAccountException) {
182:
183:     // First check to see if the Account is with this Bank.
184:     std::vector<Account_ptr>::iterator first = myAccounts.begin();
185:     std::vector<Account_ptr>::iterator last = myAccounts.end();
186:     IsAccountEqual predicate(account);
187:
188:     std::vector<Account_ptr>::iterator matchedAccount = std::
189:             find_if(first, last, predicate);
190:     if (matchedAccount == last) {
191:
192:         // Invalid Account; throw an exception.
193:         throw InvalidAccountException();
194:     }
195:
196:     // If we got this far, the Account must exist with this Bank,
197:     // so we can proceed.
198:     ATMCard_ptr newCard = new ATMCardImpl(pin, account);
199:
200:     return ATMCard::_duplicate(newCard);
201: }
202:
203: void BankImpl::requestUpdateService(Account_ptr account) throw
204:         (InvalidAccountException) {
205:
206:     // First check to see if the Account is with this Bank.
207:     std::vector<Account_ptr>::iterator first = myAccounts.begin();
208:     std::vector<Account_ptr>::iterator last = myAccounts.end();
209:     IsAccountEqual predicate(account);
210:
211:     std::vector<Account_ptr>::iterator matchedAccount = std::
212:             find_if(first, last, predicate);
213:     if (matchedAccount == last) {
214:
215:         // Invalid Account; throw an exception.
216:         throw InvalidAccountException();
217:     }
218:
```

```
219:     // If we got this far, the Account must exist with this Bank,
220:     // so we can proceed.
221:         mySubscribedAccounts.push_back(Account::_duplicate(account));
222: }
223:
224: // Return the next available account number. The result is returned
225: // in a static buffer.
226: char* BankImpl::getNextAccountNumber() {
227:
228:     static char accountNumber[16] = "Account         ";
229:
230:     sprintf(accountNumber + 7, "%08u", myNextAccountNumber++);
231:
232:     return accountNumber;
233: }
234:
235: // Return the current date in the form "Mmm DD YYYY". The result is
236: // returned in a static buffer.
237: char* BankImpl::getCurrentDate() {
238:
239:     static char currentDate[12] = "           ";
240:
241:     time_t ltime;
242:     time(&ltime);
243:     char* ctimeResult = ctime(&ltime);
244:
245:     memcpy(currentDate, ctimeResult + 4, 3);
246:     memcpy(currentDate + 4, ctimeResult + 8, 2);
247:     memcpy(currentDate + 7, ctimeResult + 20, 4);
248:
249:     return currentDate;
250: }
```

WARNING

BankImpl.cpp, as it appears in Listing 9.4, introduces the use of threads in the server application. Depending on your operating system, however, the file will not compile as listed. BankImpl.cpp makes use of the Win32 APIs for using threads, so it will compile on Windows 95 and NT. Users of other platforms, particularly UNIX platforms, need to modify the code slightly to use the thread API (such as POSIX threads) for their operating system. This is a trivial matter because only one new thread is created in the BankImpl.cpp implementation.

Also, as a reminder, the code presented here is not thread-safe—for the sake of clarity, no checks are made to ensure that both threads don't access the mySubscribedAccounts vector simultaneously. This non-thread-safe code works for demonstration purposes, but for a production system, you'll definitely want to ensure that all code is thread-safe when using multithreading in an application.

Now take a closer look at Listing 9.4. The first thing you'll notice, in lines 31–60, is the addition of a function called updateAccountThreadFunction() that executes in a second thread.

First of all, as you can see in lines 31–34, updateAccountThreadFunction() expects its argument to be a pointer to an STL vector of Accounts (you'll see later that this is the argument with which the function is actually called).

What is happening in lines 36–37 is that the thread is being set up to run for as long as the server application is running (hence, the while (1), which will never exit). Also, the loop is set up to sleep for 60,000 milliseconds (one minute) between executions.

Every minute, the for statement in line 41 will cause the thread to iterate through its list of Accounts (lines 43–46), and then to iterate through each of the Customers belonging to those Accounts, as you can see in lines 47–51. Also, in line 51 you see that the updateAccountBalance() message is sent to each of the Customers.

Finally, if for some reason an exception is thrown by the remote method call, it is ignored, as you can see in lines 52–56. (updateAccountThreadFunction() catches the exception but does nothing with it.)

Enhancing the CustomerImpl

The enhancements to CustomerImpl are simple. CustomerImpl need only accept the updateAccountBalance() message and print a message indicating the new Account balance. The modified CustomerImpl.h and CustomerImpl.cpp appear in Listings 9.5 and 9.6.

Listing 9.5. CustomerImpl.h.

```
 1: // CustomerImpl.h
 2:
 3: #ifndef CustomerImpl_h
 4: #define CustomerImpl_h
 5:
 6: #include "../Customer_s.h"
 7: #include "../ATMCard_c.h"
 8:
 9: class CustomerImpl : public _sk_Customer {
10:
11: public:
12:
13:     // Constructor.
14:     //
15:     // name - Customer's name.
16:     // socialSecurityNumber - Customer's Social Security number.
17:     // address - Customer's address.
18:     // mothersMaidenName - Customer's mother's maiden name.
19:     CustomerImpl(const char* name, const char* socialSecurityNumber,
20:             const char* address, const char* mothersMaidenName);
21:
```

```
22:     // Destructor.
23:     ~CustomerImpl();
24:
25:     // These methods are described in Customer.idl.
26:     virtual char* name();
27:     virtual void name(const char* val);
28:     virtual char* socialSecurityNumber();
29:     virtual char* address();
30:     virtual void address(const char* val);
31:     virtual char* mothersMaidenName();
32:     virtual AccountList* getAccounts();
33:     virtual void updateAccountBalance(Account_ptr account, CORBA::
34:             Float balance);
35:
36: private:
37:
38:     // Default constructor.
39:     CustomerImpl();
40:
41:     // This Customer's name.
42:     char* myName;
43:
44:     // This Customer's Social Security number.
45:     char* mySocialSecurityNumber;
46:
47:     // This Customer's address.
48:     char* myAddress;
49:
50:     // This Customer's mother's maiden name.
51:     char* myMothersMaidenName;
52:
53:     // This Customer's Accounts.
54:     AccountList myAccounts;
55:
56:     // This Customer's ATMCards.
57:     ATMCardList myATMCards;
58: };
59:
60: #endif
```

Listing 9.6. CustomerImpl.cpp.

```
1: // CustomerImpl.cpp
2:
3: #include "CustomerImpl.h"
4:
5: #include <iostream.h>
6: #include <string.h>
7:
8: // Constructor.
9: //
10: // name - Customer's name.
11: // socialSecurityNumber - Customer's Social Security number.
```

continues

Listing 9.6. continued

```
12: // address - Customer's address.
13: // mothersMaidenName - Customer's mother's maiden name.
14: CustomerImpl::CustomerImpl(const char* name, const char*
15:        socialSecurityNumber, const char* address, const char*
16:        mothersMaidenName) : _sk_Customer(socialSecurityNumber),
17:        myName(strdup(name)),
18:        mySocialSecurityNumber(strdup(socialSecurityNumber)),
19:        myAddress(strdup(address)),
20:        myMothersMaidenName(strdup(mothersMaidenName)),
21:        myAccounts(), myATMCards() {
22:
23: }
24:
25: // Default constructor.
26: CustomerImpl::CustomerImpl() : myName(NULL),
27:        mySocialSecurityNumber(NULL), myAddress(NULL),
28:        myMothersMaidenName(NULL), myAccounts(), myATMCards() {
29:
30: }
31:
32: // Destructor.
33: CustomerImpl::~CustomerImpl() {
34:
35:     free(myName);
36:     free(mySocialSecurityNumber);
37:     free(myAddress);
38:     free(myMothersMaidenName);
39: }
40:
41: char* CustomerImpl::name() {
42:
43:     return CORBA::strdup(myName);
44: }
45:
46: void CustomerImpl::name(const char* val) {
47:
48:     free(myName);
49:     myName = strdup(val);
50: }
51:
52: char* CustomerImpl::socialSecurityNumber() {
53:
54:     return CORBA::strdup(mySocialSecurityNumber);
55: }
56:
57: char* CustomerImpl::address() {
58:
59:     return CORBA::strdup(myAddress);
60: }
61:
62: void CustomerImpl::address(const char* val) {
63:
64:     free(myAddress);
65:     myAddress = strdup(val);
66: }
67:
```

9

```
68: char* CustomerImpl::mothersMaidenName() {
69:
70:     return CORBA::strdup(myMothersMaidenName);
71: }
72:
73: AccountList* CustomerImpl::getAccounts() {
74:
75:     return &myAccounts;
76: }
77:
78: void CustomerImpl::updateAccountBalance(Account_ptr account,
79:         CORBA::Float balance) {
80:
81:     cout << "CustomerImpl: Received account update:" << endl <<
82:             "  New balance is $" << balance << endl;
83: }
```

Enhancing the ATMClient

The modifications to ATMClientMain.cpp are easy to follow (see Listing 9.7). The only additions are that the ATMClient now requests the account update service from the Bank when the Account is created, and when the ATMClient is finished, it waits for two minutes to give the Bank a chance to call updateAccountBalance() once or twice before the ATMClient exits. (Like BankImpl, ATMClient uses the Win32 API to cause the current thread to sleep; again, non-Windows developers need to substitute the appropriate method call here.)

Listing 9.7. ATMClientMain.cpp.

```
 1: // ATMClientMain.cpp
 2:
 3: #include <iostream.h>
 4: #include <stdlib.h>
 5:
 6: #include "../Customer/CustomerImpl.h"
 7:
 8: #include "../Bank_c.h"
 9: #include "../BankServer_c.h"
10: #include "../ATM_c.h"
11:
12: int main(int argc, char *const *argv) {
13:
14:     // Check the number of arguments; there should be exactly five
15:     // (six counting the executable name itself).
16:     if (argc != 6) {
17:         cout << "Usage: ATMClient <name> <social security number>"
18:                 " <address> <mother's maiden name> <PIN>" << endl;
19:         return 1;
20:     }
21:
22:     // Assign the command line arguments to the Customer attributes.
23:     const char* name = argv[1];
```

continues

Listing 9.7. continued

```
24:        const char* socialSecurityNumber = argv[2];
25:        const char* address = argv[3];
26:        const char* mothersMaidenName = argv[4];
27:        CORBA::Short pin = atoi(argv[5]);
28:
29:        // Initialize the ORB and BOA.
30:        CORBA::ORB_var orb = CORBA::ORB_init(argc, argv);
31:        CORBA::BOA_var boa = orb->BOA_init(argc, argv);
32:
33:        // Create a Customer object.
34:        cout << "ATMClient: Creating new Customer:" << endl;
35:        cout << "  name: " << name << endl;
36:        cout << "  Social Security number: " << socialSecurityNumber <<
37:                endl;
38:        cout << "  address: " << address << endl;
39:        cout << "  mother's maiden name: " << mothersMaidenName << endl;
40:        CustomerImpl customer(name, socialSecurityNumber, address,
41:                mothersMaidenName);
42:
43:        // Notify the BOA that the CustomerImpl object is ready.
44:        boa->obj_is_ready(&customer);
45:
46:        // Locate a BankServer object and try to get a list of Banks
47:        // and ATMs from it.
48:        BankServer_var bankServer;
49:        try {
50:            bankServer = BankServer::_bind();
51:        } catch (const CORBA::Exception& ex) {
52:
53:            // The bind attempt failed...
54:            cout << "ATMClient: Unable to bind to a BankServer:" <<
55:                    endl;
56:            cout << ex << endl;
57:            return 1;
58:        }
59:        cout << "ATMClient: Successfully bound to a BankServer." <<
60:                endl;
61:
62:        BankList_ptr banks;
63:        ATMList_ptr ATMs;
64:
65:        try {
66:            banks = bankServer->getBanks();
67:            ATMs = bankServer->getATMs();
68:        } catch (const CORBA::Exception& ex) {
69:
70:            // The attempt failed...
71:            cout << "ATMClient: Unable to get lists of Banks and ATMs:"
72:                    << endl;
73:            cout << ex << endl;
74:            return 1;
75:        }
76:
```

9

```
77:     // Use the first Bank and the first ATM that appear in the
78:     // lists.
79:     if (banks->length() == 0) {
80:
81:         // No Banks were available.
82:         cout << "ATMClient: No Banks available." << endl;
83:         return 1;
84:     }
85:     if (ATMs->length() == 0) {
86:
87:         // No ATMs were available.
88:         cout << "ATMClient: No ATMs available." << endl;
89:         return 1;
90:     }
91:     Bank_var bank = (*banks)[0];
92:     ATM_var atm = (*ATMs)[0];
93:     cout << "ATMClient: Using Bank \"" << bank->name() << "\" and"
94:             << " ATM \"" << atm->name() << "\"." << endl;
95:
96:     // Do some cool stuff.
97:
98:     Account_var account;
99:     ATMCard_var atmCard;
100:
101:     try {
102:         account = bank->createAccount(&customer, "checking", 0.0);
103:     } catch (const CORBA::Exception& ex) {
104:
105:         // The createAccount() attempt failed...
106:         cout << "ATMClient: Unable to create Account." << endl;
107:         cout << ex << endl;
108:         return 1;
109:     }
110:
111:     try {
112:
113:         // Request the automatic account update service from the
114:         // Bank.
115:         bank->requestUpdateService(account);
116:     } catch (const CORBA::Exception& ex) {
117:
118:         // The requestUpdateService() attempt failed...
119:         cout << "ATMClient: Unable to create Account." << endl;
120:         cout << ex << endl;
121:         return 1;
122:     }
123:
124:     try {
125:
126:         // Print out some Account statistics.
127:         cout << "ATMClient: Opened new Account:" << endl;
128:         cout << "  account number: " << account->accountNumber() <<
129:                 endl;
130:         cout << "  creation date: " << account->creationDate() <<
131:                 endl;
132:         cout << "  account balance: " << account->balance() << endl;
133:
```

continues

Listing 9.7. continued

```
134:        // Ask the Bank to issue an ATMCard for the newly-created
135:        // Account.
136:        cout << "ATMClient: Getting ATMCard from Bank." << endl;
137:        try {
138:            atmCard = bank->issueATMCard(pin, account);
139:        } catch (const InvalidAccountException&) {
140:
141:            // For some reason, the Account was invalid (this
142:            // shouldn't happen).
143:            cout << "ATMClient: Exception caught: Invalid Account"
144:                    << endl;
145:            return 1;
146:        }
147:
148:        // Perform some transactions on the Account through the
149:        // ATM.
150:        cout << "ATMClient: Performing transactions." << endl;
151:        try {
152:            cout << "  Depositing $250.00..." << endl;
153:            cout << "  New balance is $" << atm->deposit(atmCard,
154:                    account, pin, 250.00) << endl;
155:
156:            // This will throw an exception since we're trying to
157:            // withdraw too much.
158:            cout << "  Withdrawing $500.00..." << endl;
159:            cout << "  New balance is $" << atm->withdraw(atmCard,
160:                    account, pin, 500.00) << endl;
161:        } catch (AuthorizationException&) {
162:            cout << "ATMClient: Exception caught: Invalid PIN or "
163:                    << "No authorization (as expected)" << endl;
164:        } catch (InvalidAmountException&) {
165:            cout << "ATMClient: Exception caught: Invalid amount"
166:                    << endl;
167:        } catch (InsufficientFundsException&) {
168:            cout << "ATMClient: Exception caught: Insufficient " <<
169:                    "funds" << endl;
170:        }
171:
172:        // Perform some more transactions on the Account through
173:        // the ATM.
174:        cout << "ATMClient: Performing more transactions." << endl;
175:        try {
176:            cout << "  Depositing $500.00..." << endl;
177:            cout << "  New balance is $" <<
178:                    atm->deposit(atmCard, account, pin, 500.00) <<
179:                    endl;
180:
181:            // This will throw an exception since we're using the
182:            // wrong PIN.
183:            cout << "  Withdrawing $250.00 with incorrect PIN..."
184:                    << endl;
185:            cout << "  New balance is $" << atm->withdraw(atmCard,
186:                    account, pin + 1, 250.00) << endl;
187:        } catch (AuthorizationException&) {
```

9

```
188:             cout << "ATMClient: Exception caught: Invalid PIN or "
189:                     << "No authorization (as expected)" << endl;
190:         } catch (InvalidAmountException&) {
191:             cout << "ATMClient: Exception caught: Invalid amount"
192:                     << endl;
193:         } catch (InsufficientFundsException&) {
194:             cout << "ATMClient: Exception caught: Insufficient " <<
195:                     "funds" << endl;
196:         }
197:
198:         // Get rid of the Account.
199:         try {
200:             cout << "  Deleting Account." << endl;
201:             bank->deleteAccount(account);
202:
203:             // Attempt to delete the Account again, just for kicks.
204:             // This should result in an exception being thrown.
205:             cout << "  Attempting to cause an exception by " <<
206:                     "deleting Account again." << endl;
207:             bank->deleteAccount(account);
208:         } catch (const InvalidAccountException&) {
209:
210:             // Sure enough, the exception was thrown.
211:             cout << "ATMClient: Exception caught: Invalid " <<
212:                     "Account (as expected)" << endl;
213:         }
214:     } catch (const CORBA::Exception& ex) {
215:
216:         // Some operation on the Account failed...
217:         cout << "ATMClient: Error accessing Account:" << endl;
218:         cout << ex << endl;
219:         return 1;
220:     }
221:
222:     // Sleep for long enough to catch an Account update message or
223:     // two.
224:     Sleep(120000);
225:
226:     // When this point is reached, the application is finished.
227:     return 0;
228: }
```

Running the Application

Once again, you're ready to run the modified application. The process is exactly the same as in the previous chapter, but the output from the various applications will be slightly different, as you would expect. Again, start by running the BankServer application:

```
BankServer
```

Again, the output of the BankServer will be this:

```
BankServer ready.
```

You're now ready to start the Bank application

```
Bank "First Bank"
```

which, again, will output this:

```
Bank "First Bank" ready.
```

Meanwhile, the BankServer will output this:

```
BankServerImpl: Registering Bank "First Bank".
```

Now you'll start the ATM application:

```
ATM "First Bank ATM"
```

The ATM application will display the following:

```
ATM "First Bank ATM" ready.
```

The BankServer, again, will output the message:

```
BankServerImpl: Registering ATM "First Bank ATM".
```

Finally, you're ready to run the ATMClient application. You can do so by typing the following:

```
ATMClient "Jeremy Rosenberger" 123456789 "123 Main Street" Doe 1234
```

The ATMClient will again display the following:

```
ATMClient: Creating new Customer:
  name: Jeremy Rosenberger
  Social Security number: 123456789
  address: 123 Main Street
  mother's maiden name: Doe
ATMClient: Successfully bound to a BankServer.
ATMClient: Using Bank "First Bank" and ATM "First Bank ATM".
ATMClient: Opened new Account:
  account number: Account00000000
  creation date: Oct 20 1997
  account balance: 0
ATMClient: Getting ATMCard from Bank.
ATMClient: Performing transactions.
  Depositing $250.00...
  New balance is $250
  Withdrawing $500.00...
ATMClient: Exception caught: Insufficient funds
ATMClient: Performing more transactions.
  Depositing $500.00...
  New balance is $750
  Withdrawing $250.00 with incorrect PIN...
ATMClient: Exception caught: Invalid PIN or No authorization (as expected)
  Deleting Account.
  Attempting to cause an exception by deleting Account again.
ATMClient: Exception caught: Invalid Account (as expected)
```

At this point, the ATMClient will sleep for two minutes while waiting for messages from the Bank. Be patient, and the ATMClient will eventually output

```
CustomerImpl: Received account update:
  New balance is $750
```

All this will go by very quickly, but after it's all over, you can go to the other application windows and see some evidence of what transpired here. Looking first at the BankServer application, you'll see this (with new output messages highlighted in **bold**):

```
BankServer ready.
BankServerImpl: Returning list of 1 Banks.
BankServerImpl: Returning list of 1 ATMs.
```

The output of the other applications will be the same as last time, except for the Bank application. Turn your attention to the window in which the Bank is running and you will see the following, familiar output:

```
Bank "First Bank" ready.
BankImpl: Creating new CheckingAccount for Customer Jeremy Rosenberger.
AccountImpl: Insufficient funds to withdraw specified amount.
BankImpl: Deleting Account "Account00000000".
BankImpl: Attempted to delete invalid Account.
```

Stay tuned for a few moments, and you will see the following (if it took you a minute or so to bring the Bank output window up, this might already be on your screen):

```
BankImpl: Updating Accounts.
```

Recall that this message is output just before the second thread in the Bank application sends the update messages to all the Account owners.

Ideas for Future Enhancements

You've only begun to scratch the surface of what can be done with CORBA. As far as the Bank application is concerned, there are a number of possible enhancements. As you progress into advanced CORBA topics in the upcoming days, you'll make a few more enhancements to the Bank application, but the possibilities for enhancements are limitless. If you want to further experiment with the Bank application, here are a few ideas:

- ☐ SavingsAccounts already support an interest rate, but the interest is never added to the account balances. Implement a mechanism—probably using a separate thread in the Bank application—that periodically adds interest to each SavingsAccount.

- ☐ CheckingAccounts typically feature overdraft protection; that is, withdrawing a greater amount than is available in the account automatically dips into the customer's line of credit.

- ☐ As mentioned numerous times before, the sample code presented here is not thread-safe. Modify the code so that it is thread-safe.

☐ Add a new type of account—perhaps a mutual fund or stock market account. As an added feature, make it possible for customers to subscribe to a service that will automatically inform them—using push messaging—of the account's performance.

Again, the possibilities for enhancements are endless. Adding features or robustness to the Bank application on your own will help you to hone your skills for developing CORBA applications.

Summary

Today you added a simple capability to the Bank application—for the Bank server to push updated information to the bank customers. Although the implementation for this capability is simple, the potential of the push architecture is very great. Indeed, as this book is being written, a number of companies are vying to create the de facto standard for pushing content to users on the Internet.

You were also reminded—albeit briefly—of the importance of writing thread-safe code in a multithreaded environment. Although this book takes a "do as I say, not as I do" approach to writing thread-safe code, it is very important that when writing multithreaded applications, you take care to ensure thread safety. In a sample application with only one user, thread safety is not likely to be an issue because chances are small that two threads will use the same data at the same time. However, in a production system—particularly an enterprisewide system—the penalty for writing non-thread-safe code can be stiff, usually resulting in the corruption of data.

On Day 10 you'll shift gears into some more advanced CORBA topics—a number of design issues that are involved with CORBA, along with a few suggestions about how to deal with those issues. You'll get a small break from further developing the Bank application, but the example does return in future chapters when you study additional advanced CORBA topics, such as the use of the Dynamic Invocation Interface (DII), CORBAservices and CORBAfacilities, and using Java with CORBA.

Q&A

Q What's the big deal about push technology anyway?

A Properly implemented, a push architecture can save users the trouble of actively searching for desired information. (However, if the application goes overboard with the information pushed to the user, the user might suffer from the new problem of information overload.) Also, push technology has the potential to conserve system resources. Information can be delivered to users as it is updated (as opposed to requiring users to periodically check for updated data, which can be inefficient if the data doesn't change very often).

Q It seems to me that push method calls can almost always be oneway calls. Is this accurate?

A To the extent that the pushed information is not considered essential for the purposes of the application, this is true. Using oneway calls allows for more efficient server implementations (because the server does not have to wait for a reply from the clients), at the expense of reliability of message delivery. In the case of a server that delivers account balance updates or stock quote updates to casual subscribers, it usually doesn't matter if an occasional update message is lost. When the information being updated is considered essential, oneway is usually not a good choice.

Workshop

The following section will help you test your comprehension of the material presented in this chapter and put what you've learned into practice. You'll find the answers to the quiz and exercises in Appendix A.

Quiz

1. Why does the issue of thread safety become important in the sample application developed in this chapter?

2. Instead of using oneway methods to notify clients of updates, can you think of another way to efficiently send update messages to clients? (**Hint:** Multithreading could come in handy here.)

Exercises

1. It was noted earlier in the chapter that no facility currently exists to cancel the automatic account update service. Provide an IDL method signature for such an operation. Don't forget to include appropriate exceptions, if any.

2. Implement the account update cancellation method from Exercise 1.

Day **10**

Learning About CORBA Design Issues

By now you have probably determined for yourself that CORBA is a complex architecture. Like any complex architecture, CORBA comes with its own set of issues that affect the design and implementation of CORBA systems. For example, the fact that all interfaces in CORBA are specified in IDL has an effect on developers who want to integrate existing systems with CORBA—usually, IDL interfaces have to be written for a number of existing classes (not a trivial undertaking). This chapter introduces you to such design issues and offers suggestions on how to deal with them.

IDL Creep

The term *IDL creep* does not refer to that guy in the office down the hall who thinks he knows everything about the Interface Definition Language. Rather, it is a term coined to refer to the tendency for IDL to permeate a system design— and permeate it does. Think about it: For a class to be understood by CORBA, its interface must be expressed in IDL. Furthermore, if the classes referenced or otherwise used by that class also need to be accessible to CORBA components, then those classes must also have their interfaces expressed in IDL. Consequently, it is not uncommon for most, if not all, classes in a system to require IDL specifications.

If you're designing an application from the ground up, having to define IDL interfaces for most (or even all) classes isn't terribly demanding. However, if you're converting an existing application to CORBA, the process can be an arduous one indeed. Because the existing classes were probably not written with CORBA—or a distributed architecture of any kind—in mind, the interfaces for those classes might have to be modified somewhat to mesh well with IDL. Although the modifications themselves might not require a great deal of effort, remember that if the interface of an object changes, any code that uses that object might have to be modified as well. This cascade effect can easily turn a few interface changes in a relatively few classes into a frustrating mess of changes throughout an application.

This scenario doesn't even take into consideration the possibility that the non-CORBA application's very architecture might not be amenable to the CORBA architecture. In particular, CORBA's current lack of the capability to pass objects by value can especially affect the design of an application (discussed later in this chapter). Sometimes, modifying an existing application to use CORBA can be like trying to fit a square peg into a round hole.

The moral is that IDL is pervasive—it has a way of creeping into a system design and slowly taking it over. This is not necessarily a bad thing in itself, but it can potentially make the "CORBAtization" of legacy applications a difficult prospect. Be prepared to write IDL for any class in an application that might need to be shared between application components.

It is not always possible to avoid introducing IDL into most classes of an existing application without entailing a significant redesign of portions (or all!) of the application. However, when designing an application from the ground up, there is one guideline in particular for minimizing the impact of IDL on the rest of the application: Pay close attention to which classes will likely need to be shared between application components and which will not. The underlying classes (e.g., classes that aren't part of any interfaces between components) generally will not require IDL interfaces.

Single-Threaded Applications

Although most modern operating systems support multithreaded applications—that is, applications in which multiple threads of control might be executing in a single program at the same time—the use of multithreading is still limited. There are several reasons for this: Not all operating systems fully support threading, not all developers use the later versions of operating systems, which do support threading, and not all developers feel comfortable with it anyway. In addition, using multiple threads in applications introduces new issues—not the least of which is the need to manage concurrent access to objects—that complicate application design and development. Consequently, the use of multithreading is not as widespread as it could be.

10

CORBA does not force developers into a multithreaded development paradigm; indeed, it is perfectly feasible to create single-threaded CORBA applications. However, due to the nature of the operation of distributed applications, great care must be taken when designing and developing CORBA applications for a single-threaded environment. This chapter tells you why, covering issues on both the server and client ends of the application.

Server Applications

The justification for using multiple threads in server applications is simple: A CORBA server might have multiple clients accessing it at any given time. If the server is single-threaded, it can only process a request from one client at a time—if another client attempts to access the server while the server is busy processing a second client's request, the first client must wait until the server is finished (see Figure 10.1). The obvious disadvantage to this architecture is that if the server performs transactions that take time to complete, the apparent responsiveness of the system (as far as the end users are concerned) suffers.

10

Figure 10.1.

Single-threaded server operation.

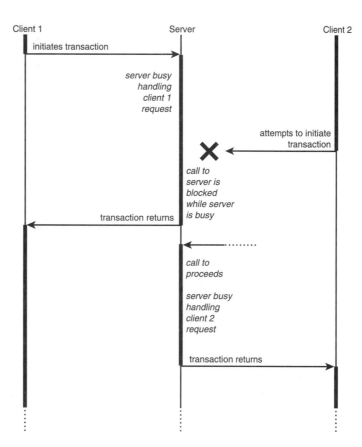

One approach to mitigating this problem is to employ the use of multiple servers in an application. Normally, an enterprise-scale application employs multiple servers anyway, for reasons such as load balancing and redundancy. However, it is simply not practical to provide a server per concurrent client, given the amount of overhead required by each server application. It is much more efficient for a single server to handle multiple simultaneous clients, and this is precisely the capability afforded by a multithreaded architecture.

In a multithreaded server architecture (see Figure 10.2), rather than process only one client request at a time, the server can start a new thread of execution for each transaction. Because there is always a thread listening for new requests, other clients no longer need to wait for the server to complete a transaction before it can accept the next one. The result is that the server appears more responsive because it can respond immediately to incoming requests.

Figure 10.2.

Multithreaded server operation.

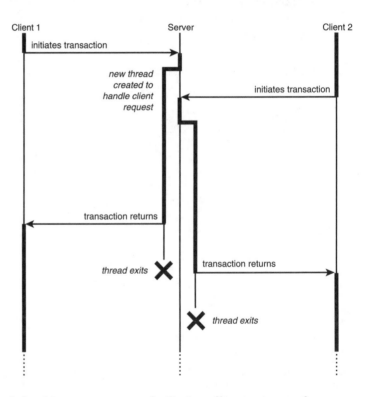

Although the multithreaded architecture can create the illusion of better server performance by enhancing server responsiveness, the architecture does not magically make servers faster. If the server is processing several transactions simultaneously, the speed at which each transaction is processed is likely to decrease relative to a server processing only one transaction at a time. (Multithreaded applications can be more efficient than single-threaded applications, however, so a server processing only one transaction at a time might not be twice as fast

10

as a server processing two transactions simultaneously.) So, although the use of multithreading is not intended to replace the use of multiple servers, it is usually preferable to deploy multiple multithreaded servers than multiple single-threaded servers. Furthermore, in most cases, fewer multithreaded servers are required to deliver the same end user responsiveness.

Because multithreading does not come for free, it is important to understand when it is appropriate. Managing multiple threads, especially when it is necessary (as it often is) to prevent multiple threads from simultaneously accessing the same data, can result in costly overhead. Consequently, on a machine with a single CPU, adding multiple threads to an application that is already CPU-bound will only make it slower (although response time to individual clients, as discussed previously, might still improve). On the other hand, on a multiprocessing machine, because each thread can potentially run on its own CPU, performance when using multithreading might increase, even on a CPU-bound application. Where multiprocessing truly shines, however, is in I/O-bound server applications or in applications that act as clients and servers simultaneously (as you will see in the next section). In an I/O-bound server application with multiple client connections, the likelihood that a given thread will be blocked while waiting for I/O increases. Hence, other threads will be given the opportunity to do useful work, thus using the available CPU(s) more efficiently.

The bottom line regarding the use of threads in CORBA servers is this: If the server can process transactions quickly enough so that response time is not a concern, a single-threaded server will probably suffice. If the response time of a single-threaded server is not adequate, the use of multithreading is probably a better alternative. Note that this is true only if the server does not also act as a client. If it performs both roles, there might be additional issues involved, as you will soon see.

Client Applications

Unlike a server application, a client application does not need to concern itself with providing a reasonable response time to other clients. In most cases, when a client calls a remote method on a server, it is perfectly reasonable for the client to wait for the server's response before continuing. This is true as long as one assumption holds true—that the client application is a *pure* client; that is, the application does not create any CORBA objects and pass references to those objects to other applications.

Mixed Server/Client Applications

The guidelines for the use of threads in pure servers (applications that behave as servers only, never as clients) are clear-cut: If the response time requirements warrant it, multithreading is preferred; otherwise, single threading is adequate. The guidelines for pure clients are simple as well: Under most circumstances, multithreading is not required. Therefore, you can conclude that single-threaded architectures are adequate for most CORBA applications. If your applications were all pure servers and clients, you'd be right.

10

When an application demonstrates behaviors of a server and a client—call it a *mixed server/ client application* for lack of a better term—the design issues associated with using a single-threaded architecture become insidious. Illustrated in Figure 10.3 is the basic problem: If a single-threaded, mixed server/client application passes one of its objects to a second application in a remote method call, and the second application, in turn, tries to access the object passed to it, both applications become blocked.

Figure 10.3.

Single-threaded mixed server/client application operation.

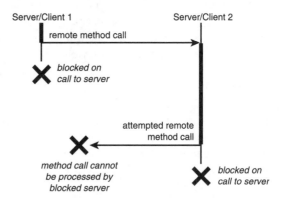

Of course, this problem is neatly solved by the use of multithreading in the mixed server/ client application, as illustrated in Figure 10.4. If multithreading is not an option for whatever reason, another solution is required. The remainder of this section discusses potential solutions to the problems involved in developing single-threaded applications that need to assume the roles of both client and server.

Presented here are two useful design patterns for designing CORBA applications using only single-threaded components. Again, the use of multithreading is probably the cleanest method of implementing CORBA applications, but when multithreading is not an option, you will want to consider one of these design patterns.

Object Factory Pattern

Recall that single-threaded applications that are pure servers or pure clients don't suffer from the deadlock problem illustrated in Figure 10.3. The *Object Factory pattern* capitalizes on this property of pure client and pure server applications by moving functionality to the appropriate component of the application, resulting in application components that are either pure clients or pure servers.

NOTE

In the *Object Factory design pattern,* a factory object is responsible for creating objects of a particular type. For example, the Bank object can be thought of as an Account factory, since Banks are responsible for creating all Account objects in the system.

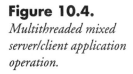

Figure 10.4.

Multithreaded mixed server/client application operation.

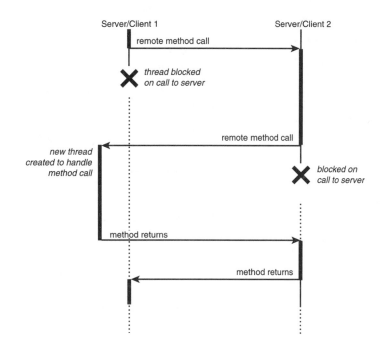

To understand how this is feasible, consider the following scenario: A client wishes to call a remote method on a server. The method takes a particular type of object as a parameter; call it a Widget. Now assume that the Widget is created by the client. If the client were to pass a Widget that it created to the server through a remote method, and that method attempted to call a method on the Widget, the result would be a deadlock scenario, as described in Figure 10.3. These are the typical application semantics over which single-threaded applications stumble. It would be most useful if these types of semantics could be achieved in a way that worked with single-threaded applications.

This is where the Object Factory pattern steps in (see Figure 10.5). This pattern takes the place of the object creation step. Rather than create the Widget itself, the client requests the Factory (which is the same object as the server whose method the client wishes to invoke) to create the Widget on the client's behalf. The client can then manipulate the Widget, if desired, and can finally invoke the desired remote method on the server, passing the Widget as a parameter. Now, because the Widget exists in the same address space as the rest of the server, the server can manipulate the Widget as it sees fit.

Figure 10.5.

Object Factory pattern.

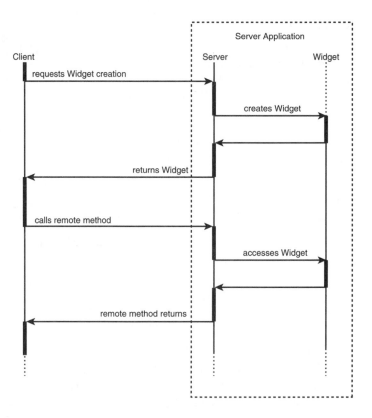

The Object Factory pattern boasts the advantage of enabling single-threaded clients to pass objects as parameters to remote methods. This capability comes at a price: The server must provide methods for creating every type of CORBA object that a client might want to create. Although providing implementations for these methods is simple, it can be tedious, particularly in applications containing large numbers of classes. Also, it can be more inconvenient for clients to call additional methods to create objects rather than to directly use constructors, although this inconvenience might be minimal. These drawbacks, however, are often outweighed by the advantages offered by the Object Factory pattern.

Exclusive oneway Call Pattern

Another approach to creating harmony between single-threaded applications and CORBA is what you might call the *Exclusive* oneway *Call pattern*. This pattern calls for the exclusive use of oneway invocations throughout the application. Because oneway methods don't block, the deadlock issue associated with single-threaded CORBA applications is eliminated. However, this advantage comes at a price, as you'll soon find out.

NOTE   The *Exclusive* oneway *Call design pattern* calls for the exclusive use of oneway methods for communication between CORBA objects.

NOTE   For a review of CORBA oneway methods, refer to Day 3, "Mastering the Interface Definition Language (IDL)."

The exclusive use of oneway method calls throughout a CORBA application exacts a potentially stiff penalty: First, the concept of a clearly laid-out program flow is lost. Consider a typical client application. There is generally a well-defined flow of control through the program. That is, there is a main method—it might very well be C/C++/Java's main()—at which the program begins and proceeds to call other methods. Usually, the flow of the program can be determined by tracing the sequence of method calls. In other words, the behavior of the application is at least somewhat predictable because the execution flow can be traced relatively easily.

Using oneway methods exclusively, however, radically alters the landscape of an application, as illustrated in Figure 10.6. Instead of a well-defined flow of control traceable throughout the application, the client features a series of seemingly disjointed oneway methods. The exchange between client and server, rather than following the familiar pattern of "client calls server/server returns result" is transformed into a volley of oneway calls from one application to the other. The client starts by calling a method on the server. That method, when completed, calls a method on the client that performs the second step in the application. That method, in turn, calls another method on the server, which eventually calls a method on the client, and so on.

Again, because each method called is oneway, there is no blocking due to the client or server being busy. Consequently, each application is free to pass any CORBA objects—including objects created by itself—without fear of blocking. The downside of this architecture is that because the flow of control is now shared between two applications, it is much more difficult to trace.

Another penalty that must be paid by developers wanting to use the Exclusive oneway Call pattern stems from a characteristic of oneway methods which you should recall—namely, that oneway messages are not guaranteed to be delivered to their destination. Building an entire application based on this mechanism is certain to be a trying experience, primarily because if there are any methods in the application which require reliable delivery, the developer must implement a mechanism to determine whether a oneway method call actually executed successfully. In other words, the developer essentially must implement reliable delivery semantics on top of the unreliable oneway mechanism, in addition to implementing all the usual application functionality.

Figure 10.6.

Exclusive oneway *Call pattern.*

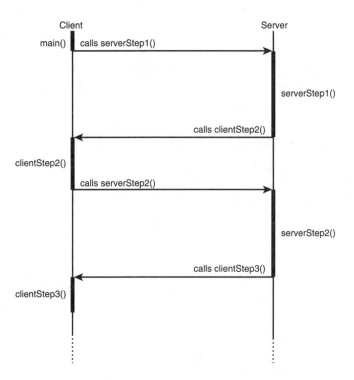

To summarize the Exclusive oneway Call design pattern, it should be stressed that this pattern would be extremely difficult to implement for most real-world production systems. Consequently, developers are strongly encouraged to pursue a different method of marrying client and server functionality in a single-threaded application if at all possible.

Object Lifetime

In a non-distributed application, management of object lifetime is a non-issue: When the application is finished using an object, it simply destroys it. With garbage-collected languages like Java, the developer does not even need to write code to do this—the application handles it automatically. If the application crashes, the memory used by its objects is reclaimed by the operating system. Because all objects are self-contained in the application, there are no issues associated with object lifetime.

10

In a distributed application, circumstances are different. An application might use objects that are local to the application—that is, objects that live in the same address space as the application—or it might use remote objects, which might reside in a different process on the same machine or on a different machine somewhere on the network. Many CORBA ORB products use reference counting for managing object lifetime—a mechanism which works well when applications behave normally. Although the use of a reference-counting mechanism is not dictated by CORBA, its inclusion into some major ORB products merits some discussion here. Recall that in such a reference-counting mechanism, object references are duplicated—that is, their reference count is incremented—when the reference is passed to an application. Similarly, when an application is finished using an object, it releases the object reference, that is, decrements the reference count. When the reference count reaches zero, the object is no longer in use and can safely be destroyed.

But what happens when an application holding an object reference crashes before it can release that object reference? This is where the reference-counting mechanism begins to break down. Under these circumstances, the object's reference count never reaches zero, and thus the object is never destroyed. This can be thought of as a sort of memory leak in a distributed application. Consequently, developers might need to think beyond the reference counting mechanism and consider a contingency mechanism that picks up where reference counting leaves off.

Because a distributed application cannot truly know when all other applications are finished using its objects (because it doesn't know whether any of those applications have crashed), a mechanism over and above the basic reference-counting mechanism is required. Such a mechanism manages the lifetime of CORBA objects, automatically determining whether an object is in use and, if not, destroying that object. But how does this mechanism determine whether an object is still in use? Actually, it can only *guess*. To understand how such a mechanism works, consider the following case study.

One such mechanism, known as the Evictor, manages object lifetime by tracking the usage of each CORBA object within a server (each CORBA server would contain its own Evictor). When an object has not been in use for a predetermined period of time (for example, a day), the Evictor *evicts* that object. Although it's possible for the eviction process to simply destroy the unused object, recall that the Evictor does not know for certain that the object is no longer in use. It is possible that one of the clients using that object could be dormant for a period of time, and if the object were destroyed, the client, on waking up, would no longer be able to access that object. To accommodate this possibility, the Evictor does not actually destroy a CORBA object after a period of non-use but evicts it into a persistent store, such as a database. If that object is needed later, it can be resurrected from the persistent store. All this occurs transparently to clients, which are completely unaware that objects are being evicted and resurrected as necessary.

Of course, a mechanism such as the Evictor, rather than enabling potentially unused objects to consume memory in a server process's address space, simply moves the unused objects to some form of persistent storage. The result is that unused objects still exist somewhere—in this case, the persistent storage rather than the server application address space. Using persistent storage for this purpose, in addition to offering the advantage of freeing up a server machine's memory resources, provides for simpler maintenance. That is, the objects in persistent storage can be cleaned up periodically, perhaps as a part of the system's periodic maintenance cycle. Purging the database of unused objects in this way would not require system administrators to bring down the server, thus enhancing the server availability.

Lack of Pass-by-Value Semantics

Perhaps one of the trickiest issues associated with CORBA development is that CORBA does not currently support the capability to pass objects by value. (This limitation is expected to be removed in a later version of CORBA; see Appendix C, "What Lies Ahead? The Future of CORBA," for more details on this and other future enhancements to the CORBA architecture.) Sometimes it is far more efficient for a server to return an object by value to a client so that the client can act on the object locally rather than call a series of remote methods—each of which incurs the overhead of executing a method remotely—on the object. See Figure 10.7 for an illustration of this scenario.

Clearly, if a client is to invoke a large number of methods on an object, it is preferable, in terms of efficiency, to act on a local copy of the object rather than a remote one. This is particularly true if the parameters or return value of the method(s) are complex values. Such values are even more expensive to transmit across the network, as is the case with remote methods.

If passing objects by value is sometimes a good idea, but CORBA doesn't offer the capability, then isn't the entire discussion a moot point anyway? As it turns out, even though CORBA doesn't offer this capability directly, there are several approaches that emulate this behavior.

Rogue Wave `ORBstreams.h++`

Rogue Wave Software offers a product that enables CORBA applications to pass C++ objects by value. The product, which builds on Rogue Wave's `Tools.h++` product, provides the capability to pass many of the `Tools.h++` classes by value, as well as user-defined classes that derive from certain `Tools.h++` classes or conform to the proper Rogue Wave-supplied interfaces.

Figure 10.7.

Pass-by-reference versus pass-by-value.

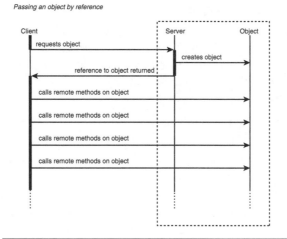

Passing an object by reference

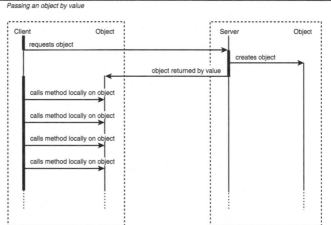

Passing an object by value

10

ORBstreams.h++ does have some disadvantages. For one, it only supports C++. (If you're implementing a CORBA application entirely in C++—which isn't altogether unlikely—this probably isn't of concern to you.) Also, the product currently supports only one ORB— IONA Technologies' Orbix—further limiting your choice of development tools. Finally, because ORBstreams.h++ builds on the Tools.h++ product, you might be saddled with additional baggage associated with using Tools.h++, if you didn't originally plan on using that product. For all its drawbacks, however, ORBstreams.h++ is a good stopgap solution to the current lack of pass-by-value capability in CORBA.

Using **CORBA** structs

Another approach to achieving a pass-by-value–like behavior is the strategic use of CORBA structs. For each CORBA interface that needs to be passed by value, the developer creates a struct that contains members corresponding to all the data members of the class implementing the interface. After these structs are defined, the mechanism works something like this:

1. A method that ordinarily uses interface types for parameters and return value instead uses the corresponding struct types.

2. Before calling such a method, the client creates struct versions of the objects it wants to pass by value. It then invokes the method with these parameters.

3. The server creates objects corresponding to the structs (if necessary), performs its processing, and creates structs for any output parameters or return values that are to be passed by value.

4. The client receives the output parameters and/or return value from the server and, if necessary, creates objects that correspond to the struct parameters.

There are a few disadvantages to this approach. The most significant is that inheritance is not a feature of structs; therefore, polymorphism is not supported. In other words, if a particular method takes a certain kind of struct as a parameter, it is not possible to pass another type of struct in its place. Referring to the Bank example, this is akin to creating a CheckingAccount object and passing it back in the place of an Account parameter. However, the CORBA any type might be of use here, at the expense of increased complexity.

Using Conversion Constructors

A third approach that emulates pass-by-value capability in CORBA is to pass an object normally, but then for the client (or server, depending on whether the object is an input or output parameter) to copy the object's state immediately on receipt. The process is as follows:

1. A client calls a method on a server, which returns an object reference. The server simply returns the object reference as usual.

2. On receiving the object reference, the client creates a new object of the same type, copying the remote object's state into the local one. This is generally done through the use of a constructor that takes the remote object as an argument, converting that object into a local one (hence the term *conversion constructor.*)

3. The client releases the remote object and continues working with the local one.

Compared to the struct approach, the conversion constructor approach has the advantage of being able to work with objects of inherited class types. Additionally, this approach does not require the development of separate IDL interfaces and structs—it is possible to use the exact same implementation classes for local and remote objects. One potential disadvantage to this mechanism is that the local object must call a number of methods on the remote object to obtain its initial state (often preferential to making a number of remote calls over the life of the object). Furthermore, this approach requires that for an object to be passed by value, its interface must provide methods that enable its entire state to be read by another object. This requirement goes against the concept of encapsulation, one of the goals of object-oriented design. It might also require the developer to write more code.

CORBA and X Window System

One last issue involves the use of CORBA with applications written for the X Window System. In both single-threaded and multithreaded applications, using CORBA and X raises a number of concerns.

Single-Threaded Applications Using CORBA and X

The primary issue in writing single-threaded applications that use CORBA and X is that both these products try to install what is known as an *event loop*. An event loop is what the name suggests: a loop in the application code (actually in the windowing system code which is linked with the application code, in the case of X) that waits for an event, processes it, and loops back to wait for another event, and so on, ad nauseum. Such an event loop exists for X as well as for CORBA. In the case of X, the event loop receives and processes events from the X server; in the case of CORBA, the event loop processes events from other CORBA applications. In either case, the event loop is the main loop of the application, designed such that it expects to be running in its own thread all the time. Therein lies the problem with single-threaded applications: Both CORBA and X expect to use their own event loops, each of which expects to be run in its own thread, but there is only one thread in the application.

Fortunately, ORB products usually have a mechanism for integrating the CORBA event loop with an X event loop. In these cases, the CORBA events are registered with the X event loop, so the single-event loop can handle events for both products. You can refer to your product's documentation for more information on how this is accomplished.

Multithreaded Applications Using CORBA and X

In a multithreaded environment, it is perfectly viable to run separate event loops for X and CORBA, so the issues applying to single-threaded applications don't apply to multithreaded applications. However, there are a couple of issues to be aware of: Older revisions of X—versions prior to X11R6.1—are not thread-safe and therefore must be used with care in a multithreading environment. This means that the developer must take additional steps to ensure that multiple threads don't access X library calls at the same time. (As of X11R6.1, however, X is thread-safe and does not suffer from this restriction.)

A related issue is Motif, a common user interface library for X. As of the time of this writing, there is not yet a thread-safe version of the Motif library. Thus, even with the thread-safe X11R6.1 or greater, developers still need to take care that multiple threads don't execute Motif library calls at the same time. As a result, integrating CORBA with a Motif application in a multithreaded environment, at least with the current version of Motif, takes as much effort as integrating CORBA with a non–thread-safe X library in a multithreaded environment.

Integrating multithreading, CORBA, and non-thread-safe X and/or Motif is certainly possible, although you can expect it to take some work. All non-thread-safe calls need to be wrapped in methods that ensure that only one thread can call such a method at any given time. One way of ensuring this is through a *thread queue,* a mechanism enabling multiple threads to be queued (in other words, wait in line) for access to non-thread-safe code. As thread-safe versions of X and Motif proliferate, this will become less of an issue, but for now, CORBA developers should be aware.

Summary

Today you examined several issues associated with developing CORBA applications. The most significant are those associated with developing CORBA applications in a single-threaded environment and those raised by CORBA's current lack of pass-by-value capability. You also learned a few, and by no means an exhaustive list of, workarounds for these issues.

On Day 11, you'll move on to the next topic in advanced CORBA development: use of the Dynamic Invocation Interface (DII). The DII enables CORBA applications to learn about each other dynamically (in other words, at runtime) and access newly discovered services.

Q&A

Q If non-trivial single-threaded CORBA applications raise so many design issues, why wouldn't someone just use multithreading?

A Although multithreading is often the preferable alternative to wrestling with the issues raised by single-threaded applications, there are times when multithreading simply isn't available, such as when single-threading is dictated by choices of other applications or development tools. It is for cases such as these that the design patterns dealing with single-threaded applications are intended.

Q It was mentioned earlier in the chapter that some CORBA products implement reference counting to manage object lifetime. What other way can this be accomplished?

10

A Another mechanism that can be used to manage object lifetime is for each remote object to have a heartbeat. Other objects, or the ORBs themselves, can ping each remote object to determine whether that object is still alive. If an object doesn't respond to the ping within a preset period of time, the other object can assume that the application containing that object has crashed. (As it turns out, a mechanism similar to this one is used by other ORB-like products such as Microsoft's DCOM and ObjectSpace's Voyager.)

Workshop

The following section will help you test your comprehension of the material presented today and put what you've learned into practice. You'll find the answers to the quiz in Appendix A. On most days, a few exercises will accompany the quiz; today, because no real "working knowledge" material was presented, there are no exercises.

Quiz

1. What is the major issue associated with mixing client and server functionality in a single-threaded CORBA application?

2. How can the use of reference counting in a CORBA application lead to problems?

3. Which version of X11 (the X Window System) would be required to safely run multithreaded X-based applications?

4. Why is the capability to pass objects by value sometimes useful?

5. Why is it usually inadvisable to use the Exclusive oneway Call design pattern introduced earlier in this chapter?

10

Day 11

Using the Dynamic Invocation Interface (DII)

On Day 10, "Learning About CORBA Design Issues," you took a short break from developing the sample Bank application to study some design issues raised by the CORBA architecture. As you saw, using CORBA sometimes requires you to rethink parts (or all!) of the design of some applications because CORBA introduces some restrictions of its own.

Today you'll continue your hiatus from the sample Bank application—this time to study a simple client that accesses a server object through the Dynamic Invocation Interface (DII). DII enables a client to access services without having been compiled with a client stub for those services. (Recall in the past that with your applications you had to compile and link client stubs that used CORBA object services.) How does this work? The DII enables CORBA clients to discover interfaces dynamically (in other words, at runtime rather than compile time) and invoke methods on objects that implement those interfaces. Today you'll learn about DII and why it is useful, and then you'll see how a client application is implemented to use DII services.

Introducing the Dynamic Invocation Interface

Until now, the CORBA clients you've implemented have been static in some respect, aware of only the interfaces whose client stubs had been included with the rest of the client application at compile time. Thus, the BankClient and ATMClient applications only knew about the Bank interface, the ATM interface, the Account interface, and so on. For the purposes of the Bank application, static knowledge of interfaces works well; there is no reason for a client to access other types of objects unknown to it at compile time. However, there are times when more dynamic client applications are called for, and this is where DII comes in. (You'll see very soon the situations which call for the capability provided by DII.)

It should be stressed that the Dynamic Invocation Interface could quite possibly be the least useful feature of CORBA. You'll see later in this chapter that there are only a handful of types of applications which really benefit from using DII; in almost all other cases, chances are that you'll never have to use DII. However, for the sake of completeness—and just in case, by some freak chance, you might ever find yourself needing to use it—a discussion of DII is included here.

The Purpose of DII

As stated earlier, DII enables a CORBA client application to discover interfaces at runtime. This means that such a client application can be compiled with no client stubs at all, thus having no prior knowledge of any type of CORBA server object. (The client need not discover all server interfaces dynamically, though; it can be compiled with client stubs for some interfaces and find other interfaces dynamically.) In any case, DII is the enabling feature of CORBA that lets clients use services of objects that were unknown to the client at compile time. (Note that the use of DII only applies to a client; when a server method is invoked, that server has no knowledge of whether a method was invoked via the conventional static mechanism or through DII.)

So why is the Dynamic Invocation Interface useful? After all, shouldn't the designer of an application know what kind of objects the application will need to access? In most cases, this is true, but some types of applications, although uncommon, do benefit from the capability to discover new object types and use them. There are at least two practical examples: a CORBA design tool and a generic object browser application.

A Hypothetical CORBA Design Tool Using DII

One potential use for DII is in a design tool for creating CORBA applications. Such a tool would have access to the IDL interfaces used to create the CORBA objects, because developers don't generally deal with CORBA objects for which they have no source code or IDL. However, because you can never be sure what developers are going to do, it would be a nice touch for the tool to have the capability to discover existing CORBA interfaces and generate client code to use those objects. The tool could also enable the developer to plug in CORBA server objects based on either their IDL interfaces or the interfaces as determined through DII (much as controls can be plugged in to development tools such as Visual Basic and JavaBeans-aware Java development tools).

A Generic Object Browser Using DII

Another possible use for the Dynamic Invocation Interface is in an esoteric, but sometimes practical, application: one that browses objects on the network. There are many reasons why you might want to do this in some types of applications. For example, envision an automated test application that discovers objects, learns their interfaces, and invokes each method in the interface with a set of dummy parameters. The results could then be recorded and later analyzed to determine objects' compliance with a test plan. Because the test application would discover object interfaces dynamically using DII, it would not need to be recompiled to handle new types of objects, making it useful as a generic testing tool.

Yet another type of object browsing tool could look for objects that implement particular methods and then enable a user to access those objects. This would be helpful if a particular design called for a set of standard methods that should be implemented by all objects in the system, but for some reason it did not define a base class from which all interfaces would derive (this is not always possible when mixing together interfaces from various sources, such as different products or different projects). For example, if each object were to define a killObject() method, an object browser could use DII to look for objects that defined such a method, which would in turn enable users to kill objects at will. Although this is a trivial example, it sets the stage for a more complex set of methods that could, for example, provide remote system administration features.

Taking this idea one step further, it would be possible to design a Web object browser that could browse objects, instead of Web pages consisting of static HTML, Dynamic HTML, Java applications, and so on. Objects could support a basic interface and also, optionally, offer additional capabilities in the form of methods that the browser could discover through DII. Because such an application would most likely be interactive, the user could determine which methods were interesting through inspection. In fact, a clever browser application could determine which methods are interesting, based on their names and parameter lists.

As a final example, consider an interpreted scripting language such as Perl or Tcl (or some other fictitious scripting language). DII could be used to interface such a language with CORBA objects. When a script accessed an operation on a CORBA object, the interpreter could use DII to "assemble" a remote method invocation from the IDL interface definition, pass the proper arguments to the method, and return the result to the script. Here the language interpreter would essentially replace the IDL compiler, which as you should recall is usually responsible for interfacing CORBA objects with various languages. However, the language interpreter would also have to become an IDL compiler of sorts, since it would have to translate IDL definitions into DII method calls.

11

Comparison with Static Interfaces/IDL

By now it has been established that DII offers at least one advantage over the conventional static process of invoking methods on objects. You have also seen some potential applications in which DII would prove useful. Although this range of applications is admittedly limited, DII is instrumental in making them possible—without DII, such applications could not exist at all. To review the advantages of DII:

☐ A client need not be aware of server interfaces at compile time; in fact, the interface definition for the server object does not need to even exist at the time that the client is compiled. This makes possible enormous flexibility in applications using DII (if you can find an application that requires such flexibility).

☐ The DII offers several options for obtaining return parameters from a method. The client application can obtain the result normally, invoke the method using oneway semantics (even if the interface's IDL did not declare the method as oneway, although this may not be advisable), or poll for a result. These options enable even greater flexibility in DII applications than in their static invocation-making counterparts.

There are, however, some disadvantages associated with using the Dynamic Invocation Interface:

☐ Applications using DII are more complex than their client stub-using counterparts. This is because a method call through DII must push each of the input arguments one at a time, invoke the method, and then pull each of the return arguments back. If this is done by hand, it can be a tedious and error-prone process.

☐ While static type-checking capability is built into the static method invocation mechanism, there essentially is none for DII method calls. Consequently, subtle differences in interface definitions may cause an application to inadvertently invoke incorrect methods—even if the application code compiles correctly! Such errors can be difficult to track down, making them especially insidious.

☐ Because each argument to a method must be pushed one at a time, additional overhead is incurred in each DII method call.

☐ Of course, there is also the overhead associated with the actual discovery of interfaces. A DII client will typically need to "negotiate" with a server (or a number of servers) to locate the interface (or interfaces) in which that client is interested.

Using DII: An Overview

Now that you know what the DII is designed for, you need to see how it is used. The process of issuing a DII method invocation differs from issuing a static method invocation, as you might expect. There are three major concepts associated with using the DII: the Request

object, the use of Anys and TypeCodes (which you will recall from Day 3), and available options
for sending requests and receiving replies.

Introducing the Request

The Request is a "pseudo-object" (that is, it does not represent a CORBA object, but is
implemented as an object as far as the implementation language is concerned) that invokes
a method on a CORBA object. To invoke a method using DII, you first obtain a reference
to the object on which the method is to be invoked. Then, using the object's request() or
create_request() method, you create a Request object. Depending on which method you
choose, you populate the Request with arguments, return types, and exceptions, using the
add_value() and result() methods of the Request object. Then you invoke the method
(using one of the methods discussed later in this section) and finally retrieve the result of the
method invocation (again using one of the methods discussed later).

The purpose of the Request is to encapsulate input parameters to method invocations and
return result values from them. A Request can be created in one of two ways, depending on
how you intend to use the Request. (Note that a Request object can be used for only one
method invocation on one object; to call a method twice, call two separate methods on the
same object, or to call methods on two different objects, you need to create two Request
objects.) The two methods for creating a Request object are as follows:

☐ Invoke the request() method on the CORBA object. The request() method
takes the name of the method to be invoked as a parameter, for instance,
request("getBanks"). You then call add_value() on the returned Request object to
add input parameters. Finally, you call result() on the Request object to specify
the type of the return parameter.

☐ Invoke the create_request() method on the CORBA object. This method takes
several parameters that populate the Request object before it is returned. The
arguments used in the call to create_request() can be reused, possibly enhancing
performance.

Anys and TypeCodes: A Review

You recall from Day 3 the discussion about the Any and TypeCode types. An object of type Any
can contain any type of object; a TypeCode is an object that describes an object's type. An Any
consists of a TypeCode (describing the type of the Any) and the value itself. Most likely, when
using the DII, you'll obtain TypeCodes through the ORB methods create_struct_tc() and
create_exception_tc().

Another object you'll encounter when using DII is the NVList (NV stands for *Named Value*).
An NVList is a list of corresponding names, values, and flags that specify whether its value is
an in or out parameter. The values stored in the NVList are Anys. When using the request()
method of an object to generate a Request, you simply add the arguments one at a time using

11

add_value(); however, when using the create_request() method, you use an NVList to specify the input arguments to the method being called. In either case, the return value from the method invocation is always supplied in an NVList.

Request and Reply Options

A variety of options exist for sending a Request to a CORBA object. After the Request psuedo-object is created and the arguments for the method are specified, you invoke the method in one of the following ways:

- [ ] Call the invoke() method on the Request. This method behaves in a way you're most likely accustomed to (with non-oneway calls), blocking until the reply is received.

- [ ] Call the send_deferred() method on the Request. This method invokes the request but returns immediately; you can then retrieve the reply using one of the following methods:

    Call the send_oneway()method on the Request. You should do this only if the method being invoked is declared as a oneway method in the IDL definition.

    You can also use send_multiple_requests_deferred() and send_multiple_requests_oneway() on the ORB to invoke a number of methods on different objects in parallel.

Depending on how a method is invoked, there are several possible ways to obtain the results of the method invocation:

- [ ] First, call the env() method on the Request to determine whether an exception was raised. If there was no exception, call the result() method on the Request object to obtain the NVList that contains the results of the method invocation. Use this method if you invoked the method using the invoke() method on the Request.

- [ ] Call the poll_response()method on the Request to periodically check for a response from the method invocation. After poll_response() indicates that the result has been received or the client wants to block while waiting for the result, call the get_response() method on the Request object. Use this method if you invoked the method using the send_deferred() method.

- [ ] Of course, if you used the send_oneway() method, there is no return result, and thus you don't call any method to get it.

Now that you're familiar with the process of invoking a method via DII, it's time for an example.

DII Example

Using DII in a simple example is more straightforward than it might sound. You can obtain an object reference in much the same way as you have in the past, using the ORB's bind() mechanism (keeping in mind that bind(), while being nonstandard, is useful for developing simple examples). However, the object reference you obtain will be a generic object reference, pointing to a generic CORBA::Object, rather than an instance of a specific object type. The following are some highlights from a CORBA client that uses DII:

```
CORBA::ORB_ptr orb;
CORBA::Object_ptr helloWorld;
```

Of course, first of all, you need a pointer to an ORB object. You also want a pointer to the object to which you'll be connecting. In this case, the object is a fictitious "Hello World" object, featuring a single method helloWorld() that takes a CORBA::String as a parameter and returns a CORBA::Long. The method does not raise any exceptions (but remember that a CORBA System Exception can be raised by any remote method). Note that the pointer to the HelloWorld object is a generic CORBA::Object pointer.

```
CORBA::NamedValue_ptr resultVal;
CORBA::Any_ptr resultValAny;
CORBA::Long returnValue = 0;
CORBA::Request_ptr request;
CORBA::Any string;
```

Next, you need a few other pointers. One holds the NamedValue returned by the DII method invocation. Another pointer holds the Any value contained in the NamedValue. A CORBA::Long variable is created to hold the actual return value. Also, a pointer is created to hold the Request object returned by the invoke() call. Finally, a pointer is created to hold the input parameter (which is the string "Hello World").

```
orb = CORBA::ORB_init(argc, argv);
```

You should be familiar with this call by now; it simply initializes the ORB. This much is the same in a DII application as in a static invocation application.

```
try {
    helloWorld = orb->bind("IDL:HelloWorld:1.0");
} catch (const CORBA::Exception& ex) {
    cout << "Could not bind to HelloWorld" << endl;
    cout << ex << endl;
    return 1;
}
```

Now the client application attempts to bind to the desired HelloWorld object. Note that, because the application does not have a client stub for the HelloWorld object, rather than use the HelloWorld::_bind() method, it uses the ORB::bind() method with a slightly revised syntax to obtain a reference to a HelloWorld object.

```
try {
    request = helloWorld->_request("helloWorld");
    string <<= "Hello World";
    CORBA::NVList_ptr arguments = request->arguments();
    arguments->add_value("string", string, CORBA::ARG_IN );
```

The client application asks the HelloWorld object to create a Request object by calling the request() method. The name of the method that the client wants to invoke on the HelloWorld object is the helloWorld() method, which is used as the parameter to the request() method. Then the client gets a parameter list (an NVList) from the Request object through its arguments() method and proceeds to populate the NVList with the single argument to the helloWorld() method: a CORBA::String with the value "Hello World". This argument is added as an input parameter using the add_value() method on the NVList.

```
    resultVal = request->result();
    resultValAny = result->value();
    resultAny->replace(CORBA::_tc_long, &resultVal);
} catch (const CORBA::Exception& ex) {
    cout << "Could not create request" << endl;
    cout << ex << endl;
    return 1;
}
```

Before submitting the Request, the client must do one more thing: Specify the expected return type for the method. As the method is expected to return a CORBA::Long, the TypeCode for this type is pushed into the result. To do this, the client calls result() on the Request object, gets the value() (which is an Any) from the result, and sets the type and value of the Any returned to be CORBA::Long. The client is now ready to invoke the method through DII.

```
try {
    request->invoke();
    CORBA::Environment_ptr env = request->env();
    if (env->exception()) {
        cout << "An exception occurred: " << *env->exception() <<
                endl;
        returnValue = 0;
    } else {
        returnValue = *(CORBA::Long*)resultValAny->value();
    }
} catch (const CORBA::Exception& ex) {
    cout << "Could not invoke request" << endl;
    cout << ex << endl;
    return 1;
}

cout << "The return value was " << returnValue << endl;
```

Finally, the client invokes the helloWorld() method on the HelloWorld object through the invoke() method on the Request. The client then checks for any exceptions that were raised by calling env() on the Request object and checking the returned environment by calling exception(). If this call returns a non-NULL result, then an exception was raised by the method call, and the exception is reported. If there is no exception, the client can call `value()` on the `Any` that was previously returned by the `result()` method, casting the value of the `Any` (obtained by calling `value()`) to a `CORBA::Long`, which is what the type of the `Any` should be.

Compared to the equivalent static invocation, you can see that the Dynamic Invocation Interface is much more involved. It is for this reason that most CORBA developers avoid the DII; the added flexibility often does not justify the added programming complexity. When the functionality offered by the DII is required, DII is necessary; otherwise, it is probably best left alone.

It is probably worth reiterating once more that most developers will never need to touch DII. Aside from the sort of examples provided earlier in this chapter, DII is not useful for most applications, and would generally only add unnecessary complexity to most applications. If you're developing tools—such as development and system management tools—that need to work with unknown CORBA objects in a generic way, you might find DII useful; otherwise, you'll find that it provides little, if any, benefit.

Summary

Today you learned a new way to invoke methods on remote CORBA objects—through the Dynamic Invocation Interface (DII). You also learned about the advantages and disadvantages of the DII mechanism compared to the traditional method of static invocation, as well as some potential practical applications of the DII mechanism. You then learned how to employ the DII features in an application, witnessing firsthand its extreme complexity compared to the static invocation to which you're accustomed.

On Day 12, "Exploring CORBAservices and CORBAfacilities," you'll explore the next in the series of advanced CORBA topics—the use of CORBAservices and CORBAfacilities. Because a great number of features are offered by these services, there is space in this book for only a short description of each. However, you will also return to the sample `Bank` application and get the opportunity to integrate the use of a CORBAservice—namely, the CORBA Naming Service—with the `Bank` application.

Q&A

Q I think I need to use DII.

A You don't. Actually, this answer is only partly tongue-in-cheek. DII invites many opportunities for confusion and difficult-to-trace errors in your application development efforts. Unless you're developing an application similar to those described in the examples in this chapter and absolutely need to take advantage of a feature offered by DII, it is almost certain that you don't want to even *think* about DII.

Q If DII is so useless for most applications, why does the CORBA specification bother with it in the first place?

A In the early days of CORBA, there were two camps with opposing views regarding how methods should be invoked. From one camp's view evolved the static invocation mechanism, and from the other came the DII.

Workshop

The following section will help you test your comprehension of the material presented today and put what you've learned into practice. You'll find the answers to the quiz in Appendix A. On most days, a few exercises will accompany the quiz; today, because no real "working knowledge" material was presented, there are no exercises.

Quiz

1. Would you expect DII to be useful to most CORBA application developers? Why or why not?

2. What are the advantages of DII over static method invocation?

3. What are the disadvantages of DII compared to static method invocation?

Day **12**

Exploring CORBAservices and CORBAfacilities

By now you are very familiar with the basic mechanisms provided by CORBA to enable the development of distributed object-oriented applications. The ORB mechanism facilitates the communication between CORBA objects and enables objects to locate each other, and the BOA provides the core functionality for all CORBA objects.

The functionality provided by the ORB and the BOA alone is not nearly enough on which to build robust, enterprise-class–distributed applications. Additional capabilities would definitely be advantageous—such as directory services, persistent object capability, a transaction mechanism, user interface and presentation facilities, and so on—regardless of the industry in which they are used. Many industries—such as health care, finance, and telecommunications—require applications that are especially well-suited to CORBA, so functionality that caters to these vertical markets is a good idea. As it turns out, the OMG offers such horizontal and vertical functionality in the form of CORBAservices and CORBAfacilities.

You've already been introduced, albeit briefly, to CORBAservices and CORBAfacilities. Today you'll learn about these in greater detail, as well as get the chance to apply some of the CORBAservices to the Bank application you've been developing.

CORBAservices

The Object Management Architecture (OMA), of which CORBA is a part, defines a number of services that are useful to applications in general. These services range from the nearly indispensable Naming Service to higher level services such as the Transaction Service. As with all its specifications (including CORBA), the Object Management Group (OMG) does not define the implementations for these services but provides the interfaces by which the services are offered. It is up to the various CORBA product vendors to supply implementations. Note that products implementing CORBAservices are often provided separately from CORBA ORB products and that implementation of CORBAservices is not necessary for CORBA 2 compliance.

This section briefly describes each of the CORBAservices. In Appendix B, "CORBA Tools and Utilities," you'll see which vendors are currently providing implementations for these services.

Concurrency Control Service

The Concurrency Control Service provides an interface for managing concurrency in shared CORBA objects. This is done through the use of locks, several types of which are supported by the service. For example, readers-writer locks are supported, as are intention locks. Developers who have worked with multithreaded applications are probably familiar with the features provided by the Concurrency Control Service.

Event Service

The Event Service provides a mechanism through which CORBA objects can send and receive events. The service includes such features as these:

☐ Reliable delivery, which (simply put) ensures that an event will reach its destination(s)

☐ Support for push and pull models of event delivery

☐ Anonymous messaging, when suppliers need not know the identities of event consumers, or vice versa

☐ Event channels, a mechanism similar to publish/subscribe, through which consumers can subscribe to certain types of events

Externalization Service

The Externalization Service provides interfaces for externalizing (that is, serializing) and internalizing objects. When an object is externalized, it can be internalized within the same process or a different process. In addition, objects can be externalized into a portable file format (one that is defined with the Externalization Service Specification). One possible application for the Externalization Service is in a pass-by-value mechanism for CORBA objects.

Licensing Service

The Licensing Service enables the provider to define policies that control the use of services. The service supports three types of licensing policies:

- ☐ *Time* enables a license to set a start date, expiration date, and duration.
- ☐ *Value mapping* enables licensing based on units (resource usage metering, number of concurrent users, and so on).
- ☐ *Consumer* assigns services for use by a particular user or machine.

Facilities like those provided by the Licensing Service will become more widely used as concepts such as pay-as-you-go or rentable software are realized. For example, an occasional user of image editing software might pay per use of a certain image filter. As a framework for electronic commerce becomes available, it is possible that you'll see more software made available in this way.

Life Cycle Service

The Life Cycle Service offers facilities for creating, deleting, copying, and moving CORBA objects. The service also supports the notion of an object factory, which is a CORBA object that creates other CORBA objects.

Naming Service

The Naming Service enables CORBA objects to register and be located by name. This service uses the notion of a *naming context*, which contains a set of unique names. The Naming Service also supports a *federated* architecture, meaning that name servers can be distributed across the network and work in conjunction with each other.

You recall that, as a part of the standard bind mechanism, CORBA objects are given names by which other objects can look them up. Although you can think of this feature as a miniature Naming Service, the actual Naming Service is much more scalable.

Object Trader Service

The Trader Service, like the Naming Service, enables other objects to locate CORBA objects. Rather than use a name to locate an object, a client object looks for services based on operation names, parameters, and result types.

The major difference between the Trader Service and the Naming Service is analogous to the difference between the yellow pages and the white pages of a telephone directory. The Naming Service can be thought of as the white pages, in which you look up a particular service if you know its exact name. The Trader Service, on the other hand, resembles the yellow

12

pages, in which you locate a service, based on its location, function, or even name. For example, in the white pages you can look up "Bob's Dry Cleaning;" in the yellow pages you can look for all dry cleaning services in, say, Littleton, Colorado. In the Bank example from previous chapters, an application might use the Naming Service to locate a Bank by its name (such as FirstBank) or use the Trader Service to locate objects by function (such as a bank or an ATM).

Persistent Object Service

The Persistent Object Service provides a set of interfaces for managing the persistence of objects. Typically, implementations for this service are provided by database vendors.

Persistent objects are objects that *persist* over a period of time; that is, the lifetime of the object can transcend the lifetime of any one application. While not in use, the object resides in a persistent store, such as a database or a flat file; the object can then be retrieved, or *resurrected*, when needed. For example, a document created by a word processor can be thought of as a persistent object because the word processor application can be closed and run again later, allowing the document to be retrieved. In a CORBA application, it will sometimes be useful to provide persistent capability to CORBA objects. For example, in the sample Bank application, the Bank objects could conceivably be persistent objects. A Bank could be resurrected as needed, and then when it is no longer processing transactions, it could be *put to sleep*, meaning that its state could be stored in a database until the Bank was needed again.

Property Service

The Property Service enables objects to define sets of properties, which are name/value pairs. The name in a pair is simply a CORBA string; the value is a CORBA any. Access to properties can be restricted. For example, a property can be read-only or fixed.

The use of properties to describe objects is becoming more widespread, particularly as object models such as JavaBeans gain momentum. A large application, or set of applications, could define a number of standard properties for its objects, thereby potentially easing management. For example, if the Bank application defined a location property for each object, the location of Banks, ATMs, Customers, and other objects could be determined in a uniform way anywhere in the application code.

Query Service

The Query Service supports the use of queries on objects. Queries can contain predicates that specify objects to act on, based on attribute values. The service also supports object indexing as well as nested queries. Query capability provides database-like semantics to CORBA objects. Just as an application can perform queries on tables and rows in a relational database, the Query Service allows an application to perform queries on CORBA objects.

Relationship Service

The Relationship Service enables the representation of relationships between objects. It provides for full constraint checking of relationship type and cardinality (one-to-many, one-to-one, and so on) and also works in conjunction with the Life Cycle Service to copy, move, and remove related objects. Managing relationships between objects is, of course, possible without the Relationship Service, but this service reduces the complexity of managing complex relationships.

Security Service

The Security Service specifies the interfaces for security features:

- [ ] *Identification* and *authentication* of users, which verify that a user is who he or she claims to be.
- [ ] *Authorization* and *access control* determine which users are enabled access to which services or objects.
- [ ] *Security auditing*, which provides records of users' actions.
- [ ] *Security of communication*, which includes authentication of users to services (and vice versa), integrity protection, and confidentiality protection.
- [ ] *Non-repudiation*, which provides capabilities similar to those offered by digital signatures; that is, the origin of data or the receipt of data can be proven irrefutably.
- [ ] *Administration* of various security policies.

Security is a paramount issue in a number of applications; for example, in a production bank application, virtually all aspects of the system must be made secure, from authentication and identification of customers to security of communication between banks and ATMs.

12

Time Service

The Time Service enables a user to obtain the current time; it can determine event ordering and can generate events based on timers.

Transaction Service

The Transaction Service provides the interfaces to support transaction capabilities. It supports flat and nested transaction models as well as external TP monitors. Transaction services can also interoperate with each other.

Transaction semantics are an integral part of almost every non-trivial application. For example, in the sample Bank application, to coordinate a transfer between accounts at different banks, a transaction should be initiated that would cause the banks involved either to both commit the transaction or to both abort the transaction; otherwise, inconsistent data (such as account balances) would result.

CORBAfacilities

CORBAfacilities cover both horizontal facilities (features useful to all types of CORBA applications across various industries) and vertical facilities (functionality that is especially useful to applications within particular vertical markets and industries). Horizontal facilities include user interface and system management facilities because this functionality is useful to most types of applications, regardless of the industry in which they are used. Vertical facilities might include, for example, general ledger and amortization functionality for use within the accounting industry, or automated shop floor control facilities for use in the manufacturing industry. Like CORBAservices, the OMG only specifies the interfaces for these facilities; the implementations, where applicable, are provided by CORBA vendors. Additionally, some CORBAfacilities only suggest interfaces to be used for particular services and types of applications.

Horizontal Facilities

The horizontal CORBAfacilities are categorized into four types of facilities: user interface, information management, systems management, and task management. These categories are further broken down into other facilities (listed in the next section). Again, horizontal facilities are advantageous to all types of applications, regardless of industry. For example, most applications require user interfaces, methods of information storage and retrieval, security facilities, workflow and process management, and so on.

User Interface Common Facilities

The User Interface Common Facilities cover all that relates to user interfaces, from the tools used to develop them to the way they are presented to the user. CORBAfacilities defines the following components of user interfaces:

User Interface Style is the "look and feel" presented to the user by the application.

User Interface Enablers present the user interface to the user. Enablers are grouped into the following facilities:

- ☐ *Rendering Management*, for abstracting user interface objects
- ☐ *Compound Presentation*, for displaying compound documents
- ☐ *User Support*, for spell checking, online help, and so on

Work Management System maintains a user's work environment and consists of the user's desktop, single sign-on to the system, and information used by the user.

Task and Process Automation enables users to write scripts to automate their tasks and use workflows.

Information Management Common Facilities

The Information Management Common Facilities consist of the following:

Information Modeling deals primarily with the way data is structured.

Information Storage and Retrieval includes databases, information retrieval systems, and repositories.

Information Interchange enables the exchange of data between users and between applications, consisting of the Compound Interchange Facility, the Data Interchange Facility, and the Information Exchange Facility.

Data Encoding and Representation deals with how information is stored, down to the bit level, if necessary. The primary reason for addressing this is to enable portability of data between applications, processes, hardware and software architectures, and so on.

Systems Management Common Facilities

The Systems Management Common Facilities provide interfaces for system administration.

Policy Management controls the creation, deletion, and modification of manageable components.

Quality of Service Management supports the selection of service levels for availability, performance, reliability, and recovery.

Instrumentation provides the capability to gather and analyze data regarding system load, object location, system responsiveness, and so on.

Data Collection includes capabilities such as logging and data archival.

Security provides for the management of security of system resources.

Collection Management enables administrators to deal with collections of objects to be managed.

Instance Management enables objects to be associated with other objects for management purposes.

Scheduling Management enables tasks to be performed in a controlled manner (for example, to occur at a certain time or as a response to a particular event).

Customization enables objects to be extended dynamically while retaining type safety.

Event Management provides for various manipulations of events in the system.

Task Management Common Facilities

Task Management Common Facilities support the processing of user tasks. Among the Task Management Common Facilities are the following:

Workflow provides management and coordination of objects that are part of a work process, for example, a purchase process. It supports production-based workflows as well as ad hoc (coordination-based) workflows.

12

Agent supports both static and mobile agent types. Although the definition and discussion of the use of agents are beyond the scope of this chapter, the agent-related facilities include the Content Service, the Communication Service, the Message Service, the Basic Information Services, the Simple Query Services, the Multi-Response Query Services, the Assertion Services, the Generation Services, the Capability Definition Services, the Notification Services, the Networking Services, the Facilitation Services, the Database Services, the Adaptation Services, the Error Correction Services, the Automatic Re-Transmission Services, the Registration Service, Security Services, and Management Services. (The sheer number of services suggests that the topic of agents is far beyond the scope of this book.)

Rule Management provides for the specification and processing of rules, which in turn are based on events, conditions, and actions.

Automation provides the capability to use scripts and macros to manipulate large-grained CORBA objects.

Vertical Market Facilities

In addition to the horizontal services and facilities offered by the OMA, there are also a number of vertical CORBAfacilities—facilities intended for the unique requirements of specific markets. Also, the OMG continually adds new Vertical Market Facilities, depending on the interest in a particular specialty area. The remainder of this section gives a brief overview of the Vertical Market Facilities specifications available at the time of this writing.

NOTE

> Although now a part of the OMG's Facilities Architecture, the Vertical Market Facilities are largely being superceded by work done by the OMG's various Domain Task Forces. Each of these Task Forces produces specifications for the vertical application domain to which it is assigned. An overview of the work completed (or in progress) by the Task Forces at the time of this writing appears in Appendix C, "What Lies Ahead? The Future of CORBA."

Imagery supports the access and interchange of imagery and related data.

Information Superhighways consists of a set of networks, protocols, and rules, information repositories connected through these networks, and a collection of tools for transparent access to this information.

Manufacturing represents the integration of manufacturing functions and resources with other aspects of the business enterprise.

Distributed Simulation supports distributed simulations of air traffic control, video games and entertainment, and other needs.

Oil and Gas Industry Exploration and Production provides a foundation for defining specifications for exploration and production (E&P). Requirements for E&P include dealing with large quantities of data, complex algorithms, and long-term data storage.

Accounting provides an interoperable approach to accounting interfaces and seeks to remove the complexity from accounting service providers and end users.

Application Development covers the selection, development, building, and evolution of the applications needed to support an enterprise's information systems strategy.

Mapping provides a cohesive means of manipulating the flow of data from databases through constructed analysis modules into either presentation tools or secondary data applications.

Enhancing the Bank Example with CORBAservices

Of course, today wouldn't be complete without a discussion and example of how to integrate CORBAservices and CORBAfacilities with the Bank example. This section will do just that. First, you'll examine which CORBAservices are of use to the Bank application; then, you'll modify the application to employ those services. There isn't room in this chapter (or this book, for that matter) to make use of all the CORBAservices and CORBAfacilities that might be applicable, so you will focus on just a couple.

Choosing CORBAservices

Now, briefly review the available CORBAservices for a moment and analyze the suitability of each service to the Bank application:

☐ *The Concurrency Control Service.* Because it is quite feasible that objects in the Bank application (particularly Banks) might be accessed by different objects simultaneously, the use of the Concurrency Control Service has merit. However, the type of concurrency used might be better serviced by the Transaction Service.

☐ *The Event Service.* If the Bank application were to expand to include messages other than those used by the account update service added on Day 9, "Using Callbacks to Add Push Capability," the Event Service would prove beneficial.

☐ *The Externalization Service.* Externalization of objects isn't a terribly important feature to the Bank application.

☐ *The Licensing Service.* Bank services are generally not licensed, so you can safely overlook the Licensing Service for the purposes of the Bank application.

☐ *The Life Cycle Service.* The Bank application would theoretically benefit from the use of the Life Cycle Service but is served well enough by the standard CORBA mechanisms for managing object life cycle.

12

☐ *The Naming Service.* If the Bank application were to grow into a highly distributed system, it would benefit greatly from the use of the Naming Service. Rather than use the standard CORBA bind mechanism, you could locate Banks through a federated Naming Service.

☐ *The Object Trader Service.* Because the Bank application components are well-known and localized, it is unlikely that components will need to locate objects based on the services they provide. The Trader Service is geared more towards applications that require richer facilities for locating services. (Had the scope of the Bank application been more extensive, it might have been worthwhile to provide the capability to look up Banks based on location, for example.)

☐ *The Persistent Object Service.* The Persistent Object Service would be worthwhile, for example, to a Bank that needs to store customer and account data in persistent storage while the information is not in use.

☐ *The Property Service.* Although the Property Service can be used, for example, to represent customer or account information, it is not particularly advantageous to the Bank application.

☐ *The Query Service.* As it stands, the Bank application would not benefit greatly from the Query Service. However, if reporting tools were developed to work with the Bank application, the Query Service would prove useful.

☐ *The Relationship Service.* For the Bank application, there is little value in using the Relationship Service to model the relationships between objects (for example, between Banks and Accounts or between Customers and Accounts). However, if new objects were added that might increase the complexity of relationships, the Relationship Service would be helpful.

☐ *The Security Service.* Because a Bank needs to be a highly secure institution, the Security Service is indispensable to a production Bank application. Numerous aspects of the Security Service can be utilized, such as user identification and authorization, security auditing, communication security, and non-repudiation. The Security Service is a perfect choice for the Bank application.

☐ *The Time Service.* The Time Service is valuable; it ensures that various Banks are in sync with each other with respect to time.

☐ *The Transaction Service.* The Transaction Service is another service that is highly useful to a Bank application. In particular, the interoperability with a TP monitor can coordinate transactions between Accounts and between Banks.

Looking at the CORBAservices from the perspective of what would provide the most utility for the Bank application, the answer would probably be the Security Service and the Transaction Service. However, looking at the services from the perspective of what's readily available (and what space is available in this book) a more practical choice would be the Naming Service.

12

Implementing the New Functionality

Deciding where to use the functionality provided by the Naming Service is easy. The Naming Service can replace the use of the standard CORBA bind mechanism; rather than bind to objects directly by name, CORBA objects can use the Naming Service to look up other objects. In the Bank application, the only object that is located in this manner is the BankServer; all other server objects (Banks and ATMs) are located through the BankServer itself. Because these changes aren't major, they fit well within the scope of this chapter.

Using the CORBA Naming Service

Rather than bind directly to the BankServer using the CORBA bind mechanism, application components instead bind to a Naming Context and then use that Naming Context to resolve a BankServer by name. A Naming Context object makes the functionality of the CORBA Naming Service available to applications. Note that the Naming Context is simply a CORBA object: Its interface is expressed in IDL, and it is manipulated by an application just as any other CORBA object is.

 NEW TERM A *Naming Context* is simply a collection of naming structures that associate names with either CORBA object references or other Naming Contexts. Taken together, these collections of associations form a hierarchical naming structure that CORBA objects use to locate other objects.

NOTE

> In previous chapters, you built on the application source code developed in the preceding chapter. This chapter is an exception, however, using the code from Day 9, not Day 11, as a baseline. This spares you the complexity of using the DII and CORBAservices in the same application.

12

The first modification to the Bank application is to change the BankServer application so that it registers itself with the Naming Service. None of the changes, to either the BankServer or any other application component, need to be made in the object implementations themselves. The only changes required are in the main section of each application, where the object is created. The first such modifications, in BankServerMain.cpp, are highlighted in **bold** in Listing 12.1.

Listing 12.1. BankServerMain.cpp.

```cpp
1: // BankServerMain.cpp
2:
3: #include <CosNaming_c.hh>
4:
5: #include "BankServerImpl.h"
6: #include <iostream.h>
7:
8: int main(int argc, char *const *argv) {
9:
10:     // Check the number of arguments; there should be exactly one
11:     // (two counting the executable name itself).
12:     if (argc != 2) {
13:         cout << "Usage: BankServer <bankservername>" << endl;
14:         return 1;
15:     }
16:
17:     // Assign the BankServer name to the first argument.
18:     const char* bankServerName = argv[1];
19:
20:     // Initialize the ORB and BOA.
21:     CORBA::ORB_var orb = CORBA::ORB_init(argc, argv);
22:     CORBA::BOA_var boa = orb->BOA_init(argc, argv);
23:
24:     // Create a BankServerImpl object.
25:     BankServerImpl bankServer(bankServerName);
26:
27:     // Notify the BOA that the BankServerImpl object is ready.
28:     boa->obj_is_ready(&bankServer);
29:
30:     // Locate a Naming Service and register the BankServer object
31:     // with it.
32:     CosNaming::NamingContext_var context;
33:     try {
34:         CORBA::Object_ptr contextObj = orb->
35:                 resolve_initial_references("NameService");
36:         CosNaming::NamingContext_var context = CosNaming::
37:                 NamingContext::_narrow(contextObj);
38:     } catch (const CORBA::Exception& ex) {
39:         cout << "BankServerMain: Could not connect to Naming "
40:                 "Service:" << endl << ex << endl;
41:         return 1;
42:     }
43:     CosNaming::Name name;
44:     name.length(1);
45:     name[0].id = bankServerName;
46:     name[0].kind = "BankServer";
47:     context->bind(name, &bankServer);
48:
49:     // Wait for CORBA events.
50:     cout << "BankServer ready." << endl;
51:     boa->impl_is_ready();
52:
53:     // When this point is reached, the application is finished.
54:     return 0;
55: }
```

12

Note the process of binding the object to the Naming Service. Previously, a name was not required for the BankServer; now the BankServer takes its name as a command-line argument. The BankServer then locates the default Naming Context (created by the Naming Service when it is started), creates a Name entry corresponding to the BankServer object, and finally binds to the Naming Service using that Name entry. Note also that the kind of the object, which can be any arbitrary string, uses the name "BankServer".

Now direct your attention to the next file to be changed, BankMain.cpp, in Listing 12.2. Again, rather than bind directly to a BankServer, the Bank (and, similarly, the ATM) locates a BankServer object through the Naming Service. Note that when the Name object is created, it is given the ID of "BankServer1" and the kind of "BankServer". This means that the Bank expects to connect to an object whose kind is "BankServer" (which you can verify is the case in BankServerMain.cpp, Listing 12.1) and whose ID is "BankServer1". Because the BankServer gets its ID (also called the Name) from the command line, you'll want to start the BankServer with the argument "BankServer1" when the time comes.

Listing 12.2. BankMain.cpp.

```
1: // BankMain.cpp
2:
3: #include "BankImpl.h"
4:
5: #include <iostream.h>
6:
7: #include <CosNaming_c.hh>
8:
9: #include "../BankServer_c.h"
10:
11: CORBA::BOA_var boa;
12:
13: int main(int argc, char *const *argv) {
14:
15:     // Check the number of arguments; there should be exactly one
16:     // (two counting the executable name itself).
17:     if (argc != 2) {
18:         cout << "Usage: Bank <bankname>" << endl;
19:         return 1;
20:     }
21:
22:     // Assign the bank name to the first argument.
23:     const char* bankName = argv[1];
24:
25:     // Initialize the ORB and BOA.
26:     CORBA::ORB_var orb = CORBA::ORB_init(argc, argv);
27:     ::boa = orb->BOA_init(argc, argv);
28:
29:     // Create a Bank object.
30:     BankImpl bank(bankName);
31:
```

continues

12

Listing 12.2. continued

```
32:      // Notify the BOA that the BankImpl object is ready.
33:      ::boa->obj_is_ready(&bank);
34:
35:      // Locate a BankServer object in the Naming Service.
36:      BankServer_var bankServer;
37:      try {
38:         CORBA::Object_ptr contextObj = orb->
39:                  resolve_initial_references("NameService");
40:         CosNaming::NamingContext_var context = CosNaming::
41:                  NamingContext::_narrow(contextObj);
42:         CosNaming::Name name;
43:         name.length(1);
44:         name[0].id = "BankServer1";
45:         name[0].kind = "BankServer";
46:         CORBA::Object_var object = context->resolve(name);
47:         bankServer = BankServer::_narrow(object);
48:      } catch (const CORBA::Exception& ex) {
49:
50:         // The bind attempt failed...
51:         cout << "BankImpl: Unable to bind to a BankServer:" << endl;
52:         cout << ex << endl;
53:         return 1;
54:      }
55:
56:      // Register with the BankServer.
57:      try {
58:         bankServer->registerBank(&bank);
59:      } catch (const CORBA::Exception& ex) {
60:
61:         // The registerBank() attempt failed...
62:         cout << "BankImpl: Unable to register Bank." << endl;
63:         cout << ex << endl;
64:         return 1;
65:      }
66:
67:      // Wait for CORBA events.
68:      cout << "Bank \"" << bankName << "\" ready." << endl;
69:      ::boa->impl_is_ready();
70:
71:      // When this point is reached, the application is finished.
72:      return 0;
73: }
```

The changes for ATMMain.cpp, similar to those in BankMain.cpp, appear in Listing 12.3. You will readily see that the two implementations are nearly identical.

Listing 12.3. ATMMain.cpp.

```
1: // ATMMain.cpp
2:
3: #include "ATMImpl.h"
4:
```

```
 5: #include <iostream.h>
 6:
 7: #include <CosNaming_c.hh>
 8:
 9: #include "../BankServer_c.h"
10:
11: CORBA::BOA_var boa;
12:
13: int main(int argc, char *const *argv) {
14:
15:     // Check the number of arguments; there should be exactly one
16:     // (two counting the executable name itself).
17:     if (argc != 2) {
18:         cout << "Usage: ATM <atmname>" << endl;
19:         return 1;
20:     }
21:
22:     // Assign the ATM name to the first argument.
23:     const char* atmName = argv[1];
24:
25:     // Initialize the ORB and BOA.
26:     CORBA::ORB_var orb = CORBA::ORB_init(argc, argv);
27:     ::boa = orb->BOA_init(argc, argv);
28:
29:     // Create an ATM object.
30:     ATMImpl atm(atmName);
31:
32:     // Notify the BOA that the ATMImpl object is ready.
33:     ::boa->obj_is_ready(&atm);
34:
35:     // Locate a BankServer object in the Naming Service.
36:     BankServer_var bankServer;
37:     try {
38:        CORBA::Object_ptr contextObj = orb->
39:                resolve_initial_references("NameService");
40:        CosNaming::NamingContext_var context = CosNaming::
41:                NamingContext::_narrow(contextObj);
42:        CosNaming::Name name;
43:        name.length(1);
44:        name[0].id = "BankServer1";
45:        name[0].kind = "BankServer";
46:        CORBA::Object_var object = context->resolve(name);
47:        bankServer = BankServer::_narrow(object);
48:     } catch (const CORBA::Exception& ex) {
49:
50:         // The bind attempt failed...
51:         cout << "ATMImpl: Unable to bind to a BankServer:" << endl;
52:         cout << ex << endl;
53:         return 1;
54:     }
55:
56:     // Register with the BankServer.
57:     try {
58:         bankServer->registerATM(&atm);
59:     } catch (const CORBA::Exception& ex) {
60:
```

continues

Listing 12.3. continued

```
61:          // The registerATM() attempt failed...
62:          cout << "ATMImpl: Unable to register ATM." << endl;
63:          cout << ex << endl;
64:          return 1;
65:     }
66:
67:     // Wait for CORBA events.
68:     cout << "ATM \"" << atmName << "\" ready." << endl;
69:     ::boa->impl_is_ready();
70:
71:     // When this point is reached, the application is finished.
72:     return 0;
73: }
```

The modified ATMClientMain.cpp, appearing in Listing 12.4, demonstrates similar changes.
Again, the ATMClient searches the Naming Service for an object named "BankServer1" of type
"BankServer". The remaining code for ATMClientMain.cpp is unchanged.

Listing 12.4. ATMClientMain.cpp.

```
 1: // ATMClientMain.cpp
 2:
 3: #include <iostream.h>
 4: #include <stdlib.h>
 5:
 6: #include "../Customer/CustomerImpl.h"
 7:
 8: #include <CosNaming_c.hh>
 9:
10: #include "../Bank_c.h"
11: #include "../BankServer_c.h"
12: #include "../ATM_c.h"
13:
14: int main(int argc, char *const *argv) {
15:
16:     // Check the number of arguments; there should be exactly five
17:     // (six counting the executable name itself).
18:     if (argc != 6) {
19:         cout << "Usage: ATMClient <name> <social security number>"
20:                 " <address> <mother's maiden name> <PIN>" << endl;
21:         return 1;
22:     }
23:
24:     // Assign the command line arguments to the Customer attributes.
25:     const char* name = argv[1];
26:     const char* socialSecurityNumber = argv[2];
27:     const char* address = argv[3];
28:     const char* mothersMaidenName = argv[4];
29:     CORBA::Short pin = atoi(argv[5]);
30:
```

```
31:     // Initialize the ORB and BOA.
32:     CORBA::ORB_var orb = CORBA::ORB_init(argc, argv);
33:     CORBA::BOA_var boa = orb->BOA_init(argc, argv);
34:
35:     // Create a Customer object.
36:     cout << "ATMClient: Creating new Customer:" << endl;
37:     cout << "  name: " << name << endl;
38:     cout << "  Social Security number: " << socialSecurityNumber <<
39:           endl;
40:     cout << "  address: " << address << endl;
41:     cout << "  mother's maiden name: " << mothersMaidenName << endl;
42:     CustomerImpl customer(name, socialSecurityNumber, address,
43:           mothersMaidenName);
44:
45:     // Notify the BOA that the CustomerImpl object is ready.
46:     boa->obj_is_ready(&customer);
47:
48:     // Locate a BankServer object in the Naming Service,
49:     BankServer_var bankServer;
50:     try {
51:         CORBA::Object_ptr contextObj = orb->
52:               resolve_initial_references("NameService");
53:         CosNaming::NamingContext_var context = CosNaming::
54:               NamingContext::_narrow(contextObj);
55:         CosNaming::Name name;
56:         name.length(1);
57:         name[0].id = "BankServer1";
58:         name[0].kind = "BankServer";
59:         CORBA::Object_var object = context->resolve(name);
60:         bankServer = BankServer::_narrow(object);
61:     } catch (const CORBA::Exception& ex) {
62:
63:         // The bind attempt failed...
64:         cout << "ATMClient: Unable to bind to a BankServer:" <<
65:               endl;
66:         cout << ex << endl;
67:         return 1;
68:     }
69:
70:     cout << "ATMClient: Successfully bound to a BankServer." <<
71:           endl;
72:
73:     // Try to get a list of Banks and ATMs from the BankServer.
74:     BankList_ptr banks;
75:     ATMList_ptr ATMs;
76:
77:     try {
78:         banks = bankServer->getBanks();
79:         ATMs = bankServer->getATMs();
80:     } catch (const CORBA::Exception& ex) {
81:
82:         // The attempt failed...
83:         cout << "ATMClient: Unable to get lists of Banks and ATMs:"
84:               << endl;
```

continues

12

Listing 12.4. continued

```
85:            cout << ex << endl;
86:            return 1;
87:    }
88:
89:    // Use the first Bank and the first ATM that appear in the
90:    // lists.
91:    if (banks->length() == 0) {
92:
93:            // No Banks were available.
94:            cout << "ATMClient: No Banks available." << endl;
95:            return 1;
96:    }
97:    if (ATMs->length() == 0) {
98:
99:            // No ATMs were available.
100:           cout << "ATMClient: No ATMs available." << endl;
101:           return 1;
102:   }
103:   Bank_var bank = (*banks)[0];
104:   ATM_var atm = (*ATMs)[0];
105:   cout << "ATMClient: Using Bank \"" << bank->name() << "\" and"
106:           << " ATM \"" << atm->name() << "\"." << endl;
107:
108:   // Do some cool stuff.
109:
110:   Account_var account;
111:   ATMCard_var atmCard;
112:
113:   try {
114:           account = bank->createAccount(&customer, "checking", 0.0);
115:   } catch (const CORBA::Exception& ex) {
116:
117:           // The createAccount() attempt failed...
118:           cout << "ATMClient: Unable to create Account." << endl;
119:           cout << ex << endl;
120:           return 1;
121:   }
122:
123:   try {
124:
125:           // Request the automatic account update service from the
126:           // Bank.
127:           bank->requestUpdateService(account);
128:   } catch (const CORBA::Exception& ex) {
129:
130:           // The requestUpdateService() attempt failed...
131:           cout << "ATMClient: Unable to create Account." << endl;
132:           cout << ex << endl;
133:           return 1;
134:   }
135:
136:   try {
137:
```

12

```
138:        // Print out some Account statistics.
139:        cout << "ATMClient: Opened new Account:" << endl;
140:        cout << "  account number: " << account->accountNumber() <<
141:             endl;
142:        cout << "  creation date: " << account->creationDate() <<
143:             endl;
144:        cout << "  account balance: " << account->balance() << endl;
145:
146:        // Ask the Bank to issue an ATMCard for the newly created
147:        // Account.
148:        cout << "ATMClient: Getting ATMCard from Bank." << endl;
149:        try {
150:            atmCard = bank->issueATMCard(pin, account);
151:        } catch (const InvalidAccountException&) {
152:
153:            // For some reason, the Account was invalid (this
154:            // shouldn't happen).
155:            cout << "ATMClient: Exception caught: Invalid Account"
156:                 << endl;
157:            return 1;
158:        }
159:
160:        // Perform some transactions on the Account through the
161:        // ATM.
162:        cout << "ATMClient: Performing transactions." << endl;
163:        try {
164:            cout << "  Depositing $250.00..." << endl;
165:            cout << "  New balance is $" << atm->deposit(atmCard,
166:                    account, pin, 250.00) << endl;
167:
168:            // This will throw an exception since we're trying to
169:            // withdraw too much.
170:            cout << "  Withdrawing $500.00..." << endl;
171:            cout << "  New balance is $" << atm->withdraw(atmCard,
172:                    account, pin, 500.00) << endl;
173:        } catch (AuthorizationException&) {
174:            cout << "ATMClient: Exception caught: Invalid PIN or "
175:                    << "No authorization (as expected)" << endl;
176:        } catch (InvalidAmountException&) {
177:            cout << "ATMClient: Exception caught: Invalid amount"
178:                    << endl;
179:        } catch (InsufficientFundsException&) {
180:            cout << "ATMClient: Exception caught: Insufficient " <<
181:                    "funds" << endl;
182:        }
183:
184:        // Perform some more transactions on the Account through
185:        // the ATM.
186:        cout << "ATMClient: Performing more transactions." << endl;
187:        try {
188:            cout << "  Depositing $500.00..." << endl;
189:            cout << "  New balance is $" <<
190:                    atm->deposit(atmCard, account, pin, 500.00) <<
191:                    endl;
192:
```

continues

Listing 12.4. continued

```
193:          // This will throw an exception because we're using the
194:          // wrong PIN.
195:          cout << "  Withdrawing $250.00 with incorrect PIN..."
196:                  << endl;
197:          cout << "  New balance is $" << atm->withdraw(atmCard,
198:                  account, pin + 1, 250.00) << endl;
199:      } catch (AuthorizationException&) {
200:          cout << "ATMClient: Exception caught: Invalid PIN or "
201:                  << "No authorization (as expected)" << endl;
202:      } catch (InvalidAmountException&) {
203:          cout << "ATMClient: Exception caught: Invalid amount"
204:                  << endl;
205:      } catch (InsufficientFundsException&) {
206:          cout << "ATMClient: Exception caught: Insufficient " <<
207:                  "funds" << endl;
208:      }
209:
210:      // Get rid of the Account.
211:      try {
212:          cout << "  Deleting Account." << endl;
213:          bank->deleteAccount(account);
214:
215:          // Attempt to delete the Account again, just for kicks.
216:          // This should result in an exception being thrown.
217:          cout << "  Attempting to cause an exception by " <<
218:                  "deleting Account again." << endl;
219:          bank->deleteAccount(account);
220:      } catch (const InvalidAccountException&) {
221:
222:          // Sure enough, the exception was thrown.
223:          cout << "ATMClient: Exception caught: Invalid " <<
224:                  "Account (as expected)" << endl;
225:      }
226:  } catch (const CORBA::Exception& ex) {
227:
228:      // Some operation on the Account failed...
229:      cout << "ATMClient: Error accessing Account:" << endl;
230:      cout << ex << endl;
231:      return 1;
232:  }
233:
234:  // Sleep for long enough to catch an Account update message or
235:  // two.
236:  Sleep(120000);
237:
238:  // When this point is reached, the application is finished.
239:  return 0;
240: }
```

That's it for modifications—you're now ready to run the modified code.

12

Running the Application

The various components of the Bank application should be run in exactly the same manner as on Day 9, with one exception: Before running anything else, you need to start the CORBA Naming Service and let it create a default Naming Context. To do this with Visigenic's implementation of the Naming Service, type the following:

```
NameExtF <factory name> <logfile>
```

For the purposes of the Bank application, the following will do just fine:

```
NameExtF NameServer naming.log
```

The output of the Naming Service application will be the Interoperable Object Reference (IOR) assigned to the Naming Service. Your output will vary but will look something like this:

```
IOR:012020203700000049444c3a6f72672e6f6d672f436f734e616d696e672f457
874656e6465644e616d696e67436f6e74657874446163746f72793a312e30002002
0000000153495680000000010101201400000069767939362e626577656c6c6c6e657
42e636f6d005750f8ff0100000005300000001504d43000000003700000049444c3a
6f72672e6f6d672f436f734e616d696e672f457874656e6465644e616d696e6743436
f6e74657874446163746f72793a312e3000200b0000004e616d6553657276657200
2000000000000000006f00000001010200200e0000003135332e33362e3234302e373
9000206530000000001504d4300000003700000049444c3a6f72672e6f6d672f436f
734e616d696e672f457874656e6465644e616d696e67436f6e74657874446163746
f72793a312e3000200b0000004e616d6553657276657200
```

You're now ready to run the application as you did on Day 9. Because you didn't modify any of the functionality, the output of all the application components will be exactly the same.

Summary

In this chapter you became aware of the many CORBAservices and CORBAfacilities specified by the OMG. You also determined which of the CORBAservices are appropriate for use with the Bank application from previous chapters. Finally, you modified the Bank application to use some of the features offered in the CORBA Naming Service.

Additional information on the CORBAservices (the information provided in this chapter is a condensed version) is available from the OMG's Web site at http://www.omg.org/.

On Day 13, you'll shift gears again, this time turning your attention to the Java programming language/platform. As you are no doubt aware, the CORBA architecture spans many programming languages, of which Java is just one. However, Java is an especially interesting language to use with CORBA, given such features as interfaces and garbage collection (features you'll learn more about, if you're not already familiar with them). The next chapter, "Developing for the Internet Using CORBA and Java," briefly introduces you to the Java programming language and discusses the use of Java with CORBA. Finally, on Day 14, "Web-Enabling the Bank Example with Java," you'll apply Java and CORBA development to the Web, deploying an applet-based front end to the Bank application with which you're so familiar by now.

Q&A

Q I didn't see any mention of vertical CORBAfacilities for [insert my pet industry here]. Is the OMG neglecting us?

A The OMG is actively working in an ever-increasing number of vertical domains. If you are interested in developing standard facility interfaces for a particular industry, you should contact the OMG for more information.

Q What is that weird-looking IOR thing anyway?

A The Interoperable Object Reference is a string that uniquely identifies a CORBA object. The IOR is defined in such a way that any vendor's ORB can accept an IOR and resolve it, yielding the object's location. Generally, you won't need to deal with these, though occasionally they can be a convenient mechanism for objects to locate each other. Because they are plain strings, they are easily transmitted across a network, stored in a file, and so on.

Q When using the Naming Service, the application components had the ID, "BankServer1", hardcoded. Could I make the applications search the Naming Service for a registered BankServer instead?

A Yes. The Naming Context supports a list() operation that returns a BindingList and BindingIterator, which in turn can be used to iterate over the contents of the Naming Context. In this way, objects are located by name or by type, or the application simply uses the first object that is found. Although the Naming Service can be used for this purpose, a better choice might be to use the Trader Service, which is intended for precisely this use.

Workshop

The following section will help you test your comprehension of the material presented in this chapter and put what you've learned into practice. You'll find the answers to the quiz and exercises in Appendix A.

Quiz

1. Who defines the specifications for CORBAservices and CORBAfacilities?
2. Who provides the implementations for CORBAservices and CORBAfacilities?

3. What CORBAservices and/or CORBAfacilities, if any, must a vendor provide with an ORB product in order to be considered CORBA 2.0-compliant?

4. Why are vertical market facilities useful?

Exercises

1. Provide an overview of how the Object Trader Service could be used to replace the BankServer in the sample Bank application.

2. Describe how the Event Service could be used within the Bank application (hint: consider the automatic account update feature added on Day 9). What would be the benefit of using this approach?

3. (Extra Credit) If you have any products available to you that implement one or more CORBAservices, try to integrate the functionality provided by a service of your choice with the sample Bank application. (See the section of this chapter labeled "Choosing CORBAservices" to determine which services might integrate well with the sample application.) Because of the numerous possibilities available to you, no answer is provided for this exercise.

12

Day **13**

Developing for the Internet Using CORBA and Java

On Day 12 "Exploring CORBAservices and CORBAfacilities," you first studied the various CORBAservices and CORBAfacilities and learned what sort of functionality is provided by these specifications. You then got a crack at modifying the Bank application to use the CORBA Naming Service. By now, the Bank application has grown into a complex system.

Today you'll take a step back with the Bank application in terms of functionality, but you'll step out in a completely new direction at the same time. Taking the baseline Bank application from Day 9, "Using Callbacks to Add Push Capability," you'll port the application to Java (not as hard as it might sound). In case you're not familiar with Java already, this chapter first gives you a picture of what Java is all about, along with insights into the relationship between Java and CORBA. Java and CORBA are a very good match for each other, and you'll find out why.

Introducing Java

Java is still a relative newcomer to the computer industry, but this language-cum-platform has already seen significant increases in maturity and utility, both in the reliability of the platform itself (in most cases) and in the availability of development tools. Since its introduction in 1995 (when it metamorphosed from its predecessor, known as Oak), Java has enjoyed explosive growth, and despite some legal squabbles at the time of this writing, its growth is continuing.

For those unfamiliar with the Java language/platform, the best way to learn about it is to visit the Web page of the JavaSoft division of Sun Microsystems at http://www.javasoft.com/ or to peruse one of numerous texts available on the language. What these sources will tell you is that Java is characterized by the following:

☐ An object-oriented language whose syntax resembles a simplified C++; it borrows various concepts from other languages such as Smalltalk and Objective C.

☐ A compiler that translates Java source code into a platform-neutral format known as bytecode. The bytecode files, also known as class files, can be distributed to various machines and executed by the Java runtime environment (see the next bullet).

☐ A runtime environment that insulates Java applications from the underlying hardware and operating system. To this aspect, Java applications mostly owe their cross-platform portability.

☐ A set of class libraries encompassing a variety of capabilities, from file and socket I/O, to multimedia and 3D, to graphical user interface objects.

☐ The capability to be run inside a Web browser as an *applet*. An applet is an application that, in addition to being run inside a Web browser (as a component to a Web page, perhaps), is subject to various security restrictions. Security is a feature built into the Java language that makes this possible and makes Java particularly well suited to Internet-based applications.

Java has the potential to make the operating system into a commodity, providing a consistent API across all platforms. Whether this potential will ever be realized remains to be seen. Java is not perfect, of course, and still must face challenges in the way of performance, portability, and, of course, political opposition. For the time being, however, it appears that Java is here to stay, and as it turns out, Java is very well suited for use in CORBA application development.

Discovering the Symbiosis Between CORBA and Java

Why do CORBA and Java make a good match for each other? How is this so? What does the CORBA architecture have to offer the Java language/platform, and vice versa? What symbiosis exists between the two? This section discusses some of the factors that make development with CORBA and Java an attractive proposition.

Architectural Similarities

To Java programmers, developing in CORBA feels surprisingly natural and intuitive, almost as if Java and CORBA were designed for each other. (Of course, this isn't the case; Java and CORBA have completely separate design goals.) Most responsible for the near seamlessness between Java and CORBA are the similarities in architecture:

☐ CORBA's `module` construct, which groups together interfaces that perform related tasks, is analogous to Java's `package` construct.

☐ Java's garbage-collected memory management model eases application development in general, and the development of CORBA applications is no exception. Such niceties as not having to manage strings passed across CORBA interfaces make the CORBA developer's life just a little bit easier.

☐ Java's exception model also works well with CORBA. Unlike C++, Java forces methods to handle exceptions or explicitly throw them (and declare this in the method signature). Therefore, CORBA exceptions are easier to use without the worry of exceptions falling through the cracks.

☐ Last, but perhaps the most convenient, is the almost direct correspondence between Java's use of interfaces and CORBA's. Mapping CORBA interfaces to C++ classes can become hairy at times; the mapping to Java interfaces is much cleaner.

CORBA Versus Java RMI

Those familiar with Java are already aware of its Remote Method Interface (RMI) feature. The functionality provided by RMI is very CORBA-like; indeed, both CORBA and RMI share the common goal of enabling the development of distributed, object-oriented applications. Other than some superficial architectural similarities, CORBA and RMI are quite different, and, thus, each is better suited for different purposes.

One major difference between CORBA and RMI is that, whereas CORBA is language-independent, RMI is limited to Java only. This is a major consideration when choosing an architecture, even for an application implemented entirely in Java. Although such an application can use RMI, an architect must consider the possible need for a system to interact in the future with other, non-Java applications. However, Sun has indicated that later

13

versions of RMI will be interoperable with IIOP (CORBA's Internet Inter-ORB Protocol) so interoperability between the RMI and CORBA architectures might not be far away.

CORBA also holds an advantage over RMI in terms of robustness. Not only has CORBA had a number of years head start on RMI, but also CORBA provides a more enterprise-ready solution. Whereas RMI consists of a communications layer and simple naming services, CORBA is part of an architecture that offers many more services valuable for developing enterprise-class applications. (Review Chapter 12 for an overview of the services and facilities provided by the Object Management Architecture.) Offering capabilities such as hierarchical naming services, transaction management facilities, event services, and a wealth of vertical market facilities, CORBA holds a clear advantage over RMI in terms of robustness.

CORBA does not hold all the cards, though; RMI currently has at least one significant advantage over the CORBA architecture. Because RMI is a Java-only technology, it can take advantage of features of the Java platform. Most notably, RMI integrates seamlessly with Java's Object Serialization technology, enabling objects to be passed by value (as well as by reference) between remote components. In addition, not only can objects be passed by value, but also, because Java employs a platform-independent bytecode, new classes can be sent across the network via RMI for use by client or server components. The capability to dynamically (at runtime) introduce new classes into a system opens up a wealth of potential for new breeds of applications.

Other Considerations

Other factors exist that lend credibility to the marriage of Java and CORBA. Perhaps one of the most compelling features of Java is its portability—the capability to run on various types of computer hardware and operating systems. One characteristic you're certain to find in a distributed application is the need to run on a variety of hardware and OS platforms. Also, there is likely greater diversity on the client end of the application, where numerous types of desktop machines abound—from low-end Network Computers, to midrange PCs, to high-end UNIX workstations. Certainly, being able to deliver client applications on all potential end-user platforms is a boon to developers of enterprise-class applications. This is what Java offers to CORBA: the capability to write a client-side application once and run it on a multitude of platforms. (As Java continues to make strides in performance and robustness, it will see more use on the server side of distributed applications, but that's another story.)

Not only does CORBA benefit from Java by gaining cross-platform client applications, but also Java gains from CORBA. The benefit to Java is that CORBA offers cross-language interoperability. Recall that Java's Remote Method Invocation facility works only between Java applications; to communicate with non-Java applications, developers must implement their own communications layer, possibly involving low-level network sockets. CORBA makes this unnecessary, providing an object-oriented abstraction that enables Java applications to communicate with applications written in almost any language.

Developing a CORBA Application in Java: An Overview

Developing a CORBA application in Java is not unlike developing the same application in C++. You still use an IDL compiler to translate IDL definitions into server skeletons and client stubs; the only difference is that the compiler generates Java code rather than C++ code. The process, however, remains the same.

To develop the Java version of the Bank application presented in this chapter, you need a few additional tools:

☐ A CORBA product that supports Java. The example in this chapter (and the next, "Web-Enabling the Bank Example with Java") uses Visigenic Software's VisiBroker for Java, but you can also use other products, such as Sun's Java IDL or IONA Technologies' OrbixWeb, with little or no modification to the provided code.

☐ A Java development tool. This can be an Integrated Development Environment (IDE) such as Microsoft's Visual J++ or Symantec's Café or Visual Café, or it can be the Java Development Kit (JDK) from Sun. Depending on the CORBA product you choose, you need a tool that supports JDK 1.1 or higher, but you might be able to get by with JDK 1.0.2.

☐ A machine (or machines) capable of running these products. Chances are, though, that if you have the products, you probably have the machine, too.

When you have all these items, you're ready to begin developing in Java.

Using the IDL Compiler

As already mentioned, the use of the IDL compiler is exactly the same when you're writing a CORBA application in C++ or in Java. The command to run the IDL compiler, though, might be different. For the compiler included with VisiBroker for Java, use the following command:

```
idl2java -package idlGlobal filename
```

where *filename* is the name of the IDL file to be compiled. Also, here the `-package idlGlobal` switch tells the IDL compiler to place the generated code into a directory named `idlGlobal`, and the generated Java classes will be placed in the `idlGlobal` package. The VisiBroker IDL compiler will generate code for both servers and clients.

13

WARNING

Before attempting to use the Java IDL compiler, make sure you have installed the product according to the vendor's documentation. In particular, you need to set the PATH and CLASSPATH environment

> variables. For example, VisiBroker requires *VisiBroker-directory/*
> vbj30.jar to be added to the CLASSPATH. If you encounter errors when
> trying to use the IDL compiler, consult your vendor's documentation.

To prepare for development of the Java Bank application, copy the IDL source files from Day 9 into a new directory, and then compile them with the Java IDL compiler. It's convenient to create a batch file, shell script file, or Makefile to perform this step automatically. When you complete this step, you will have a directory named idlGlobal containing a number of files with the .java extension. You're now ready to proceed with development, starting with the server functionality.

Implementing the Server Functionality

Because you have made no changes to the Bank application, other than using a different development language, the architecture has not altered from previous chapters. Consequently, all the application components will look very familiar to you by now.

BankServer

The BankServer is now implemented in two files, BankServerImpl.java and BankServerMain.java, appearing in Listings 13.1 and 13.2, respectively. Also, there is the file CORBAAlgorithms.java, which contains some utility methods, appearing in Listing 13.3.

Listing 13.1. BankServerImpl.java.

```
 1: // BankServerImpl.java
 2:
 3: import java.util.Enumeration;
 4: import java.util.Vector;
 5:
 6: import idlGlobal.ATM;
 7: import idlGlobal.Bank;
 8:
 9: import idlGlobal.InvalidATMException;
10: import idlGlobal.InvalidBankException;
11:
12: import util.CORBAAlgorithms;
13:
14: public class BankServerImpl extends idlGlobal._BankServerImplBase {
15:
16:     // This BankServer's list of Banks.
17:     private Vector myBanks;
18:
19:     // This BankServer's list of ATMs.
20:     private Vector myATMs;
21:
22:     public BankServerImpl(String name) {
23:
```

13

```
24:            super(name);
25:
26:            myBanks = new Vector();
27:            myATMs = new Vector();
28:        }
29:
30:    public void registerBank(Bank bank) throws InvalidBankException
31:            {
32:
33:            // First, ensure that the given Bank doesn't exist already.
34:            if (!CORBAAlgorithms.contains(myBanks, bank)) {
35:
36:                // Bank was not found, so add the given Bank to the end
37:                // of the list.
38:                System.out.println("BankServerImpl: Registering Bank "
39:                        + "\"" + bank.name() + "\".");
40:                myBanks.addElement(bank._duplicate());
41:                return;
42:            }
43:
44:            // The Bank was already registered, so throw an exception.
45:            System.out.println("BankServerImpl: Attempted to " +
46:                    "register duplicate Bank.");
47:            throw new InvalidBankException();
48:        }
49:
50:    public void unregisterBank(Bank bank) throws
51:            InvalidBankException {
52:
53:            if (!CORBAAlgorithms.contains(myBanks, bank)) {
54:
55:                // Invalid Bank; throw an exception.
56:                System.out.println("BankServerImpl: Attempted to " +
57:                        "unregister invalid Bank.");
58:                throw new InvalidBankException();
59:            }
60:
61:            System.out.println("BankServerImpl: Unregistering Bank \""
62:                    + bank.name() + "\".");
63:
64:            // Delete the given Bank.
65:            CORBAAlgorithms.removeElement(myBanks, bank);
66:            bank._release();
67:        }
68:
69:    public Bank[] getBanks() {
70:
71:            Bank[] list = new Bank[myBanks.size()];
72:            myBanks.copyInto(list);
73:
74:            Enumeration e = myBanks.elements();
75:            while (e.hasMoreElements()) {
76:                ((Bank)e.nextElement())._duplicate();
77:            }
78:
```

13

continues

Listing 13.1. continued

```
79:          return list;
80:      }
81:
82:      public void registerATM(ATM atm) throws InvalidATMException {
83:
84:          // First, ensure that the given ATM doesn't exist already.
85:          if (!CORBAAlgorithms.contains(myATMs, atm)) {
86:
87:              // ATM was not found, so add the given ATM to the end of
88:              // the list.
89:              System.out.println("BankServerImpl: Registering ATM "
90:                      + "\"" + atm.name() + "\".");
91:              myATMs.addElement(atm._duplicate());
92:              return;
93:          }
94:
95:          // The ATM was already registered, so throw an exception.
96:          System.out.println("BankServerImpl: Attempted to " +
97:                  "register duplicate ATM.");
98:          throw new InvalidATMException();
99:      }
100:
101:     public void unregisterATM(ATM atm) throws InvalidATMException {
102:
103:
104:         if (!CORBAAlgorithms.contains(myATMs, atm)) {
105:
106:             // Invalid ATM; throw an exception.
107:             System.out.println("BankServerImpl: Attempted to " +
108:                     "unregister invalid ATM.");
109:             throw new InvalidATMException();
110:         }
111:
112:         System.out.println("BankServerImpl: Unregistering ATM \""
113:                 + atm.name() + "\".");
114:
115:         // Delete the given ATM.
116:         CORBAAlgorithms.removeElement(myATMs, atm);
117:         atm._release();
118:     }
119:
120:     public ATM[] getATMs() {
121:
122:         ATM[] list = new ATM[myATMs.size()];
123:         myATMs.copyInto(list);
124:
125:         Enumeration e = myATMs.elements();
126:         while (e.hasMoreElements()) {
127:             ((ATM)e.nextElement())._duplicate();
128:         }
129:
130:         return list;
131:     }
132: }
```

Listing 13.2. `BankServerMain.java.`

```
1: // BankServerMain.java
2:
3: import org.omg.CORBA.BOA;
4: import org.omg.CORBA.ORB;
5:
6: public class BankServerMain {
7:
8:     public static ORB myORB;
9:     public static BOA myBOA;
10:
11:     public static void main(String[] args) {
12:
13:         try {
14:
15:             // Initialize the ORB and BOA.
16:             myORB = ORB.init(args, null);
17:             myBOA = myORB.BOA_init();
18:
19:             // Create a BankServerImpl object and register it with
20:             // the ORB.
21:             BankServerImpl bankServer = new
22:                     BankServerImpl("BankServer");
23:             myBOA.obj_is_ready(bankServer);
24:
25:             // Wait for CORBA events.
26:             System.out.println("BankServer ready.");
27:             myBOA.impl_is_ready();
28:         } catch (Exception ex) {
29:
30:             // Something failed...
31:             System.out.println("BankServerImpl: Unable to bind " +
32:                     "BankServer:");
33:             System.out.println(ex);
34:             return;
35:         }
36:
37:         // When this point is reached, the application is finished.
38:         return;
39:     }
40: }
```

Listing 13.3. `CORBAAlgorithms.java.`

```
1: // CORBAAlgorithms.java
2:
3: package util;
4:
5: import java.util.Enumeration;
6: import java.util.Vector;
7:
```

continues

Listing 13.3. continued

```
 8: public class CORBAAlgorithms {
 9:
10:     // Return true if the given Vector contains the given CORBA
11:     // object, that is, if there is an element in the Vector for
12:     // which obj._is_equivalent() returns true.
13:     public static boolean contains(Vector vector, org.omg.CORBA.
14:             Object obj) {
15:
16:         Enumeration e = vector.elements();
17:
18:         while (e.hasMoreElements()) {
19:             if (obj._is_equivalent((org.omg.CORBA.Object)e.
20:                     nextElement())) {
21:
22:                 // A match was found.
23:                 return true;
24:             }
25:         }
26:
27:         // A match was not found.
28:         return false;
29:     }
30:
31:     // Remove the first element from the given Vector for which the
32:     // obj._is_equivalent() returns true for that element. If no
33:     // such element is found, this method does nothing.
34:     public static void removeElement(Vector vector, org.omg.CORBA.
35:             Object obj) {
36:
37:         Enumeration e = vector.elements();
38:
39:         while (e.hasMoreElements()) {
40:             org.omg.CORBA.Object cobj = (org.omg.CORBA.Object)e.
41:                     nextElement();
42:             if (obj._is_equivalent(cobj)) {
43:
44:                 // A match was found; remove the element.
45:                 vector.removeElement(cobj);
46:                 return;
47:             }
48:         }
49:     }
50: }
```

The logic of the BankServer implementation is identical to its C++ counterpart. Here are
some highlights of the Java implementation.

The import statement in Java, as seen in lines 3-12 of Listing 13.1, is a distant cousin to C++'s
#include preprocessor directive. The #include directive imports information about other
classes into a source file; Java's import statement serves the same purpose. Note that the import
statement uses the *fully qualified class name* of the class—that is, the class's package name plus

13

the class name itself. For instance, the Enumeration class from the preceding listings is in the java.util package.

Note the imports of classes in the idlGlobal package (in lines 6 and 7 of Listing 13.1). These are the classes generated by the IDL compiler in the previous step.

Now notice the class declaration in line 14. In the Java language mapping for IDL, implementation classes for CORBA interfaces extend a certain base class. For the BankServerImpl class, this base class is idlGlobal._BankServerImplBase.

Vector (or more specifically, java.util.Vector) is a built-in Java class that provides the semantics of a resizable array. The BankServerImpl uses Vectors to store the Banks and ATMs that register with the BankServer, as seen in lines 16-20.

Note that in the constructor for BankServerImpl (appearing in lines 22-28), a call is made to super(). This is a special method name denoting a constructor in the superclass (in this case, _BankServerImplBase) that accepts the given arguments (or argument, in this case). Also, note that the BankServerImpl constructor creates the two Vectors declared earlier.

The remainder of the BankServerImpl implementation is self-explanatory. You'll now move on to BankServerMain.java, which creates a BankServerImpl and registers the object in the CORBA environment.

Now turn your attention to Listing 13.2. Note first the import statements appearing in line 3 and 4. These import statements import two important classes in a CORBA application: the Basic Object Adapter (BOA) and the Object Request Broker (ORB). In a moment, you'll see what they are used for.

You might have already guessed this, but static class members in Java (such as those that appear in lines 8 and 9) behave like static members in C++: They are available independently of a particular instance of that class.

Every Java application must have a public static void main() in at least one class (actually, every class can have a main() method, but only one can invoke the application at any given time). This method always takes String[] args as a parameter (or the semantically equivalent String args[]). The main() method of BankServerMain begins in line 11.

Before any CORBA objects are created, the ORB and BOA must be initialized, as shown in lines 13-17.

Then the BankServerImpl object is created and registered with the BOA, through the obj_is_ready() method, as seen in lines 19-23.

The impl_is_ready() method, called in line 27, enters the CORBA event loop, passing incoming CORBA events to the appropriate objects.

Finally, in lines 28-35, a catch handler is added in case exceptions are thrown by any of the methods called. The try...catch mechanism works the same in Java as in C++.

13

`CORBAAlgorithms.java`, appearing in Listing 13.3, contains a couple of useful methods.

Note the use of the `package` statement in line 3. This indicates that the `CORBAAlgorithms` class belongs to the `util` package.

Note also that `contains()`, which begins in line 10, is declared as a `static` method. Such methods behave the same as in C++—that is, they exist independently of any object instance and are invoked as freestanding functions rather than as methods on objects.

As seen in lines 16-29, this method iterates through the provided `Vector`, searching for an object for which `_is_equivalent()` (a standard CORBA method) returns `true`. The next method, `removeElement()`, behaves similarly.

WARNING

Remember that the `_is_equivalent()` method returns `true` if it is known that two object references refer to the same object. It is possible for `_is_equivalent()` to return `false` even if two references are in fact equivalent; the only guarantee is that the method will never return `true` if the references are not equivalent. Use this method with caution.

Bank

Listings 13.4-10 contain the definitions of the Java classes that implement the `Bank` functionality. You'll see that the functionality provided by these classes mirrors their counterparts from previous chapters.

Listing 13.4. `AccountImpl.java`.

```
 1: // AccountImpl.java
 2:
 3: import java.util.Enumeration;
 4: import java.util.Vector;
 5:
 6: import idlGlobal.Customer;
 7:
 8: import idlGlobal.InsufficientFundsException;
 9: import idlGlobal.InvalidAmountException;
10:
11: public class AccountImpl extends idlGlobal._AccountImplBase {
12:
13:     // This Account's account number.
14:     private String myAccountNumber;
15:
16:     // This Account's creation date.
17:     private String myCreationDate;
18:
```

```
19:      // This Account's balance.
20:      private float myBalance;
21:
22:      // This Account's list of owners (which are Customers).
23:      private Vector myOwners;
24:
25:      public AccountImpl(String accountNumber, String creationDate,
26:              float initialBalance, Customer customer) {
27:
28:          super(accountNumber);
29:
30:          myAccountNumber = new String(accountNumber);
31:          myCreationDate = new String(creationDate);
32:          myBalance = initialBalance;
33:          myOwners = new Vector();
34:          myOwners.addElement(customer._duplicate());
35:      }
36:
37:      protected AccountImpl() {
38:
39:          myAccountNumber = new String();
40:          myCreationDate = new String();
41:          myBalance = 0.0f;
42:          myOwners = new Vector();
43:      }
44:
45:      public String accountNumber() {
46:
47:          return myAccountNumber;
48:      }
49:
50:      public String creationDate() {
51:
52:          return myCreationDate;
53:      }
54:
55:      public float balance() {
56:
57:          return myBalance;
58:      }
59:
60:      public Customer[] getCustomers() {
61:
62:          Customer[] list = new Customer[myOwners.size()];
63:          myOwners.copyInto(list);
64:
65:          Enumeration e = myOwners.elements();
66:          while (e.hasMoreElements()) {
67:              ((Customer)e.nextElement())._duplicate();
68:          }
69:
70:          return list;
71:      }
72:
73:      public float withdraw(float amount) throws
74:              InvalidAmountException, InsufficientFundsException {
75:
```

13

continues

Listing 13.4. continued

```
76:        // Disallow the withdrawal of negative amounts and throw an
77:        // exception if this is attempted.
78:        if (amount < 0.0) {
79:            System.out.println("AccountImpl: Attempted to " +
80:                    "withdraw invalid amount.");
81:            throw new InvalidAmountException();
82:        }
83:
84:        // Disallow withdrawal of an amount greater than the
85:        // current balance and throw an exception if this is
86:        // attempted.
87:        if (amount > myBalance) {
88:            System.out.println("AccountImpl: Insufficient funds to"
89:                    + " withdraw specified amount.");
90:            throw new InsufficientFundsException();
91:        }
92:
93:        myBalance -= amount;
94:
95:        return myBalance;
96:    }
97:
98:    public float deposit(float amount) throws
99:            InvalidAmountException {
100:
101:        // Disallow the deposit of negative amounts and throw an
102:        // exception if this is attempted.
103:        if (amount < 0.0) {
104:            System.out.println("AccountImpl: Attempted to deposit "
105:                    + "invalid amount.");
106:            throw new InvalidAmountException();
107:        }
108:
109:        myBalance += amount;
110:
111:        return myBalance;
112:    }
113: }
```

Listing 13.5. ATMCardImpl.java.

```
1: // ATMCardImpl.java
2:
3: import java.util.Enumeration;
4: import java.util.Vector;
5:
6: import idlGlobal.Account;
7:
8: import idlGlobal.InvalidAccountException;
9:
10: import util.CORBAAlgorithms;
11:
```

13

```
12: public class ATMCardImpl extends idlGlobal._ATMCardImplBase {
13:
14:     // This ATMCard's Personal Identification Number (PIN).
15:     private short myPIN;
16:
17:     // The Accounts which are authorized for use with this ATMCard.
18:     private Vector myAccounts;
19:
20:     public ATMCardImpl(short pin, Account initialAccount) {
21:
22:         myPIN = pin;
23:         myAccounts = new Vector();
24:         myAccounts.addElement(initialAccount._duplicate());
25:     }
26:
27:     private ATMCardImpl() {
28:
29:         myPIN = 0;
30:         myAccounts = new Vector();
31:     }
32:
33:     public void pin(short pin) {
34:
35:         myPIN = pin;
36:     }
37:
38:     public short pin() {
39:
40:         return myPIN;
41:     }
42:
43:     public Account[] getAccounts() {
44:
45:         Account[] list = new Account[myAccounts.size()];
46:         myAccounts.copyInto(list);
47:
48:         Enumeration e = myAccounts.elements();
49:         while (e.hasMoreElements()) {
50:             ((Account)e.nextElement())._duplicate();
51:         }
52:
53:         return list;
54:     }
55:
56:     public void addAccount(Account account) throws
57:             InvalidAccountException {
58:
59:         if (isAuthorized(account)) {
60:
61:             // Account has already been added, so throw an
62:             // exception.
63:             throw new InvalidAccountException();
64:         }
65:
```

continues

13

Listing 13.5. continued

```
66:         // Add the created Account at the end of the list.
67:         myAccounts.addElement(account._duplicate());
68:     }
69:
70:     public void removeAccount(Account account) throws
71:             InvalidAccountException {
72:
73:         if (!isAuthorized(account)) {
74:
75:             // Invalid Account; throw an exception.
76:             throw new InvalidAccountException();
77:         }
78:
79:         // Delete the given Account.
80:         CORBAAlgorithms.removeElement(myAccounts, account);
81:         account._release();
82:     }
83:
84:     public boolean isAuthorized(Account account) {
85:
86:         return CORBAAlgorithms.contains(myAccounts, account);
87:     }
88: }
```

Listing 13.6. CheckingAccountImpl.java.

```
1: // CheckingAccountImpl.java
2:
3: import idlGlobal.Customer;
4:
5: import idlGlobal.InsufficientFundsException;
6: import idlGlobal.InvalidAmountException;
7:
8: public class CheckingAccountImpl extends idlGlobal.
9:         _CheckingAccountImplBase {
10:
11:     // The AccountImpl to which most of this CheckingAccountImpl's
12:     // functionality is delegated.
13:     private AccountImpl myAccount;
14:
15:     public CheckingAccountImpl(String accountNumber, String
16:             creationDate, float initialBalance, Customer customer)
17:             {
18:
19:         myAccount = new AccountImpl(accountNumber, creationDate,
20:                 initialBalance, customer);
21:     }
22:
23:     protected CheckingAccountImpl() {
24:
25:     }
26:
```

13

```
27:     public String accountNumber() {
28:
29:         return myAccount.accountNumber();
30:     }
31:
32:     public String creationDate() {
33:
34:         return myAccount.creationDate();
35:     }
36:
37:     public float balance() {
38:
39:         return myAccount.balance();
40:     }
41:
42:     public Customer[] getCustomers() {
43:
44:         return myAccount.getCustomers();
45:     }
46:
47:     public float withdraw(float amount) throws
48:             InvalidAmountException, InsufficientFundsException {
49:
50:         return myAccount.withdraw(amount);
51:     }
52:
53:     public float deposit(float amount) throws
54:             InvalidAmountException {
55:
56:         return myAccount.deposit(amount);
57:     }
58: }
```

Listing 13.7. `SavingsAccountImpl.java`.

```
 1: // SavingsAccountImpl.java
 2:
 3: import idlGlobal.Customer;
 4:
 5: import idlGlobal.InsufficientFundsException;
 6: import idlGlobal.InvalidAmountException;
 7:
 8: public class SavingsAccountImpl extends idlGlobal.
 9:         _SavingsAccountImplBase {
10:
11:     // The AccountImpl to which most of this SavingsAccountImpl's
12:     // functionality is delegated.
13:     private AccountImpl myAccount;
14:
15:     // This account's interest rate.
16:     private float myInterestRate;
17:
```

13

continues

Listing 13.7. continued

```
18:    public SavingsAccountImpl(String accountNumber, String
19:            creationDate, float initialBalance, Customer customer,
20:            float interestRate) {
21:
22:        myAccount = new AccountImpl(accountNumber, creationDate,
23:                initialBalance, customer);
24:        myInterestRate = interestRate;
25:    }
26:
27:    protected SavingsAccountImpl() {
28:
29:    }
30:
31:    public String accountNumber() {
32:
33:        return myAccount.accountNumber();
34:    }
35:
36:    public String creationDate() {
37:
38:        return myAccount.creationDate();
39:    }
40:
41:    public float balance() {
42:
43:        return myAccount.balance();
44:    }
45:
46:    public Customer[] getCustomers() {
47:
48:        return myAccount.getCustomers();
49:    }
50:
51:    public float withdraw(float amount) throws
52:            InvalidAmountException, InsufficientFundsException {
53:
54:        return myAccount.withdraw(amount);
55:    }
56:
57:    public float deposit(float amount) throws
58:            InvalidAmountException {
59:
60:        return myAccount.deposit(amount);
61:    }
62:
63:    public float interestRate() {
64:
65:        return myInterestRate;
66:    }
67:
68:    public float setInterestRate(float rate) throws
69:            InvalidAmountException {
70:
```

13

```
71:          // Disallow negative interest rates and throw an exception
72:          // if this is attempted.
73:          if (rate < 0.0) {
74:
75:              throw new InvalidAmountException();
76:          }
77:
78:          float oldInterestRate = myInterestRate;
79:          myInterestRate = rate;
80:          return oldInterestRate;
81:     }
82: }
```

Listing 13.8. BankImpl.java.

```
 1: // BankImpl.java
 2:
 3: import java.text.SimpleDateFormat;
 4: import java.util.Date;
 5: import java.util.Enumeration;
 6: import java.util.Vector;
 7:
 8: import idlGlobal.Account;
 9: import idlGlobal.ATMCard;
10: import idlGlobal.Customer;
11:
12: import idlGlobal.InvalidAccountException;
13:
14: import util.CORBAAlgorithms;
15:
16: public class BankImpl extends idlGlobal._BankImplBase {
17:
18:     // This Bank's name.
19:     private String myName;
20:
21:     // This Bank's address.
22:     private String myAddress;
23:
24:     // This Bank's list of Accounts.
25:     Vector myAccounts;
26:
27:     // This Bank's list of Accounts that are subscribed to the
28:     // automatic account update service.
29:     Vector mySubscribedAccounts;
30:
31:     // This Bank's next Account number to assign.
32:     int myNextAccountNumber;
33:
34:     public BankImpl(String name) {
35:
36:         myName = new String(name);
37:         myAddress = new String("123 Elm Street, Anywhere USA "
38:                 + "12345");
```

continues

Listing 13.8. continued

```
39:          myNextAccountNumber = 0;
40:          myAccounts = new Vector();
41:          mySubscribedAccounts = new Vector();
42:
43:          Thread updateThread = new
44:                  UpdateAccountThread(mySubscribedAccounts);
45:          updateThread.start();
46:      }
47:
48:      private BankImpl() {
49:
50:          myName = new String();
51:          myAddress = new String();
52:          myAccounts = new Vector();
53:          mySubscribedAccounts = new Vector();
54:          myNextAccountNumber = 0;
55:      }
56:
57:      public void name(String name) {
58:
59:          myName = new String(name);
60:      }
61:
62:      public String name() {
63:
64:          return myName;
65:      }
66:
67:      public void address(String address) {
68:
69:          myAddress = new String(address);
70:      }
71:
72:      public String address() {
73:
74:          return myAddress;
75:      }
76:
77:      public Account createAccount(Customer customer, String
78:              accountType, float openingBalance) {
79:
80:          Account newAccount;
81:
82:          if (accountType.compareTo("savings") == 0) {
83:
84:              // Create a new SavingsAccountImpl object for the
85:              // Account.
86:              System.out.println("BankImpl: Creating new " +
87:                      "SavingsAccount for Customer " + customer.
88:                      name() + ".");
89:              newAccount = new
90:                      SavingsAccountImpl(getNextAccountNumber(),
91:                      getCurrentDate(), openingBalance, customer,
92:                      10.0f);
93:          } else if (accountType.compareTo("checking") == 0) {
94:
```

13

```
 95:                    // Create a new CheckingAccountImpl object for the
 96:                    // Account.
 97:                    System.out.println("BankImpl: Creating new " +
 98:                            "CheckingAccount for Customer " + customer.
 99:                            name() + ".");
100:                    newAccount = new
101:                            CheckingAccountImpl(getNextAccountNumber(),
102:                            getCurrentDate(), openingBalance, customer);
103:            } else {
104:
105:                    // Invalid Account type; do nothing.
106:                    System.out.println("BankImpl: Customer " + customer.
107:                            name() + " requested invalid Account type \"" +
108:                            accountType + "\".");
109:                    return null;
110:            }
111:
112:            // Add the created Account at the end of the list and
113:            // return it.
114:            BankMain.myBOA.obj_is_ready(newAccount);
115:            myAccounts.addElement(newAccount._duplicate());
116:            return newAccount;
117:    }
118:
119:    public void deleteAccount(Account account) throws
120:            InvalidAccountException {
121:
122:            if (!CORBAAlgorithms.contains(myAccounts, account)) {
123:
124:                    // Invalid Account; throw an exception.
125:                    System.out.println("BankImpl: Attempted to delete " +
126:                            "invalid Account.");
127:                    throw new InvalidAccountException();
128:            }
129:
130:            System.out.println("BankImpl: Deleting Account \"" +
131:                    account.accountNumber() + "\".");
132:
133:            // Delete the given Account.
134:            CORBAAlgorithms.removeElement(myAccounts, account);
135:            account._release();
136:    }
137:
138:    public Account[] getAccounts() {
139:
140:            Account[] list = new Account[myAccounts.size()];
141:            myAccounts.copyInto(list);
142:
143:            Enumeration e = myAccounts.elements();
144:            while (e.hasMoreElements()) {
145:                    ((Account)e.nextElement())._duplicate();
146:            }
147:
148:            return list;
149:    }
150:
```

13

continues

Listing 13.8. continued

```
151:    public ATMCard issueATMCard(short pin, Account account) throws
152:            InvalidAccountException {
153:
154:        // First check to see if the Account is with this Bank.
155:        if (!CORBAAlgorithms.contains(myAccounts, account)) {
156:
157:            // Invalid Account; throw an exception.
158:            System.out.println("BankImpl: Attempted to delete " +
159:                    "invalid Account.");
160:            throw new InvalidAccountException();
161:        }
162:
163:        // If we got this far, the Account must exist with this
164:        // Bank, so we can proceed.
165:        ATMCard newCard = new ATMCardImpl(pin, account);
166:        BankMain.myBOA.obj_is_ready(newCard);
167:
168:        System.out.println("BankImpl: Issuing new ATMCard on " +
169:                "Account " + account.accountNumber());
170:        newCard._duplicate();
171:        return newCard;
172:    }
173:
174:    public void requestUpdateService(Account account) throws
175:            InvalidAccountException {
176:
177:        // First check to see if the Account is with this Bank.
178:        if (!CORBAAlgorithms.contains(myAccounts, account)) {
179:
180:            // Invalid Account; throw an exception.
181:            System.out.println("BankImpl: Attempted to delete " +
182:                    "invalid Account.");
183:            throw new InvalidAccountException();
184:        }
185:
186:        // If we got this far, the Account must exist with this
187:        // Bank, so we can proceed.
188:        mySubscribedAccounts.addElement(account._duplicate());
189:    }
190:
191:    // Return the next available account number.
192:    protected String getNextAccountNumber() {
193:
194:        return "Account" + myNextAccountNumber++;
195:    }
196:
197:    // Return the current date in the form "Mmm DD YYYY".
198:    protected String getCurrentDate() {
199:
200:        SimpleDateFormat format = new SimpleDateFormat("MMM dd " +
201:                "yyyy");
202:        return format.format(new Date());
203:    }
204: }
```

13

Listing 13.9. `UpdateAccountThread.java`.

```
 1: // UpdateAccountThread.java
 2:
 3: import java.util.Enumeration;
 4: import java.util.Vector;
 5:
 6: import idlGlobal.Account;
 7: import idlGlobal.Customer;
 8:
 9: public class UpdateAccountThread extends Thread {
10:
11:     // The Accounts to be updated by this thread.
12:     Vector myAccounts;
13:
14:     public UpdateAccountThread(Vector accounts) {
15:
16:         myAccounts = accounts;
17:     }
18:
19:     protected UpdateAccountThread() {
20:
21:     }
22:
23:     public void run() {
24:
25:         // Do this forever (or until the thread is killed).
26:         while (true) {
27:
28:             // Sleep for one minute between updates.
29:             try {
30:                 sleep(60000);
31:             } catch (InterruptedException ex) {
32:             }
33:
34:             // Iterate through each Account...
35:             Enumeration e = myAccounts.elements();
36:             while (e.hasMoreElements()) {
37:                 Account account = (Account)e.nextElement();
38:
39:                 // Iterate through each Customer associated with
40:                 // the Account...
41:                 Customer[] customers = account.getCustomers();
42:                 for (int i = 0; i < customers.length; i++) {
43:
44:                     try {
45:                         // Send an update message to each Customer.
46:                         customers[i].updateAccountBalance(account,
47:                             account.balance());
48:                     } catch (Exception ex) {
49:
50:                         // Ignore any exceptions that occur.
51:                     }
52:                 }
53:             }
54:         }
55:     }
56: }
```

13

Listing 13.10. `BankMain.java`.

```
 1: // BankMain.java
 2:
 3: import org.omg.CORBA.BOA;
 4: import org.omg.CORBA.ORB;
 5:
 6: import idlGlobal.BankServer;
 7: import idlGlobal.BankServerHelper;
 8:
 9: public class BankMain {
10:
11:     public static ORB myORB;
12:     public static BOA myBOA;
13:
14:     public static void main(String[] args) {
15:
16:         // Check the number of arguments; there should be exactly
17:         // one.
18:         if (args.length != 1) {
19:             System.out.println("Usage: Bank <bankname>");
20:             return;
21:         }
22:
23:         // Assign the Bank name to the first argument.
24:         String bankName = args[0];
25:
26:         BankServer bankServer;
27:         BankImpl bank;
28:
29:         try {
30:
31:             // Initialize the ORB and BOA.
32:             myORB = ORB.init(args, null);
33:             myBOA = myORB.BOA_init();
34:
35:             // Create an BankImpl object and register it with the
36:             // ORB.
37:             bank = new BankImpl(bankName);
38:             myBOA.obj_is_ready(bank);
39:
40:             // Bind to a BankServer.
41:             bankServer = BankServerHelper.bind(myORB);
42:             System.out.println("BankImpl: Successfully bound to " +
43:                     "BankServer.");
44:         } catch (Exception ex) {
45:
46:             // The bind attempt failed...
47:             System.out.println("BankImpl: Unable to bind to " +
48:                     "BankServer.");
49:             return;
50:         }
51:
52:         try {
53:
```

```
54:             // Register with the BankServer.
55:             bankServer.registerBank(bank);
56:
57:             // Wait for CORBA events.
58:             myBOA.impl_is_ready();
59:         } catch (Exception ex) {
60:
61:             // The registerBank() attempt failed...
62:             System.out.println("BankImpl: Unable to register " +
63:                     "Bank:");
64:             System.out.println(ex);
65:             return;
66:         }
67:
68:         // When this point is reached, the application is finished.
69:         return;
70:     }
71: }
```

Here are highlights from the various classes that implement the Bank server application. First, note the implementation for getCustomers() in AccountImpl.java (refer to lines 60-71 of Listing 13.4).

Notice the relative simplicity with which objects are copied from Vectors into arrays. First, an array of the appropriate size is created (in line 62), and the contents of the Vector are copied into it with a single method call: copyInto() (line 63). Because these are outbound CORBA objects, they must be _duplicate()d, which is the reason for the subsequent iteration across the Vector, as in lines 65-68.

Next, note the constructor of BankImpl (lines 34-46 of Listing 13.8).

In the constructor, an UpdateAccountThread object is created (which you'll get a closer look at in a moment) and started. For simple threads, this is all that Java requires: Create a Thread object, and call start() on that object. Now, look at the UpdateAccountThread itself, beginning in line 9 of Listing 13.9.

One way to implement threads in Java is to create a class that derives from java.lang.Thread (or simply Thread), as UpdateAccountThread does. The next step is to implement the run() method. The actual workings of the UpdateAccountThread.run() method are self-explanatory.

Finally, notice in BankMain.java how an application binds to a CORBA object (refer to Listing 13.10). Again, the ORB is initialized (lines 31-33).

Sometime after the ORB and BOA are initialized, BankMain uses the bind() method of BankServerHelper to bind to a BankServer object, as in line 41. (Recall again that bind() is nonstandard and is used here for simplicity.)

13

ATM

The implementation of the ATM server, consisting of ATMImpl.java and ATMMain.java, appears in Listings 13.11 and 13.12. This is clear-cut and contains no surprises.

Listing 13.11. ATMImpl.java.

```
 1: // ATMImpl.java
 2:
 3: import idlGlobal.Account;
 4: import idlGlobal.ATMCard;
 5:
 6: import idlGlobal.AuthorizationException;
 7: import idlGlobal.InsufficientFundsException;
 8: import idlGlobal.InvalidAmountException;
 9:
10: public class ATMImpl extends idlGlobal._ATMImplBase {
11:
12:     private String myName;
13:
14:     public ATMImpl(String name) {
15:
16:         myName = new String(name);
17:     }
18:
19:     private ATMImpl() {
20:
21:         myName = new String();
22:     }
23:
24:     public String name() {
25:
26:         return myName;
27:     }
28:
29:     public void name(String name) {
30:
31:         myName = new String(name);
32:     }
33:
34:     public float withdraw(ATMCard card, Account account, short pin,
35:             float amount) throws AuthorizationException,
36:             InvalidAmountException, InsufficientFundsException {
37:
38:         System.out.println("ATM: Authorizing Account for " +
39:                 "withdrawal.");
40:         if (pin != card.pin() || !card.isAuthorized(account)) {
41:
42:             // Incorrect PIN or card not authorized; throw an
43:             // exception.
44:             System.out.println("  Authorization failed.");
45:             throw new AuthorizationException();
46:         }
47:
```

```
48:            System.out.println("  Authorization succeeded; forwarding "
49:                    + "withdrawal request to Account.");
50:            return account.withdraw(amount);
51:        }
52:
53:    public float deposit(ATMCard card, Account account, short pin,
54:            float amount) throws AuthorizationException,
55:            InvalidAmountException {
56:
57:        System.out.println("ATM: Authorizing Account for " +
58:                "deposit.");
59:        if (pin != card.pin() || !card.isAuthorized(account)) {
60:
61:            // Incorrect PIN or card not authorized; throw an
62:            // exception.
63:            System.out.println("  Authorization failed.");
64:            throw new AuthorizationException();
65:        }
66:
67:        System.out.println("  Authorization succeeded; forwarding "
68:                + "deposit request to Account.");
69:        return account.deposit(amount);
70:    }
71:
72:    public float getBalance(ATMCard card, Account account, short
73:            pin) throws AuthorizationException {
74:
75:        System.out.println("ATM: Authorizing Account for " +
76:                "balance.");
77:        if (pin != card.pin() || !card.isAuthorized(account)) {
78:
79:            // Incorrect PIN or card not authorized; throw an
80:            // exception.
81:            System.out.println("  Authorization failed.");
82:            throw new AuthorizationException();
83:        }
84:
85:        System.out.println("  Authorization succeeded; forwarding "
86:                + "balance request to Account.");
87:        return account.balance();
88:    }
89: }
```

13

Listing 13.12. ATMMain.java.

```
1: // ATMMain.java
2:
3: import org.omg.CORBA.BOA;
4: import org.omg.CORBA.ORB;
5:
6: import idlGlobal.BankServer;
7: import idlGlobal.BankServerHelper;
8:
```

continues

Listing 13.12. continued

```
 9: public class ATMMain {
10:
11:     public static ORB myORB;
12:     public static BOA myBOA;
13:
14:     public static void main(String[] args) {
15:
16:         // Check the number of arguments; there should be exactly
17:         // one.
18:         if (args.length != 1) {
19:             System.out.println("Usage: ATM <atmname>");
20:             return;
21:         }
22:
23:         // Assign the ATM name to the first argument.
24:         String atmName = args[0];
25:
26:         BankServer bankServer;
27:         ATMImpl atm;
28:         try {
29:
30:             // Initialize the ORB and BOA.
31:             myORB = ORB.init(args, null);
32:             myBOA = myORB.BOA_init();
33:
34:             // Create an ATMImpl object and register it with the
35:             // ORB.
36:             atm = new ATMImpl(atmName);
37:             myBOA.obj_is_ready(atm);
38:
39:             // Bind to a BankServer.
40:             bankServer = BankServerHelper.bind(myORB);
41:             System.out.println("ATMImpl: Successfully bound to " +
42:                     "BankServer.");
43:         } catch (Exception ex) {
44:
45:             // The bind attempt failed...
46:             System.out.println("ATMImpl: Unable to bind to " +
47:                     "BankServer.");
48:             return;
49:         }
50:
51:         try {
52:
53:             // Register with the BankServer.
54:             bankServer.registerATM(atm);
55:
56:             // Wait for CORBA events.
57:             myBOA.impl_is_ready();
58:         } catch (Exception ex) {
59:
60:             // The registerATM() attempt failed...
61:             System.out.println("ATMImpl: Unable to register ATM:");
```

```
62:            System.out.println(ex);
63:            return;
64:        }
65:
66:        // When this point is reached, the application is finished.
67:        return;
68:    }
69: }
```

Implementing the Client Functionality

The client pieces—CustomerImpl.java and ATMClientMain.java—carry over almost exactly from their C++ counterparts. The implementations appear in Listings 13.13 and 13.14, respectively.

Listing 13.13. CustomerImpl.java.

```
 1: // CustomerImpl.java
 2:
 3: import java.util.Enumeration;
 4: import java.util.Vector;
 5:
 6: import idlGlobal.Account;
 7:
 8: public class CustomerImpl extends idlGlobal._CustomerImplBase {
 9:
10:     // This Customer's name.
11:     private String myName;
12:
13:     // This Customer's Social Security number.
14:     private String mySocialSecurityNumber;
15:
16:     // This Customer's address.
17:     private String myAddress;
18:
19:     // This Customer's mother's maiden name.
20:     private String myMothersMaidenName;
21:
22:     // This Customer's list of Accounts.
23:     private Vector myAccounts;
24:
25:     // This Customer's list of ATMCards.
26:     private Vector myATMCards;
27:
28:     public CustomerImpl(String name, String socialSecurityNumber,
29:             String address, String mothersMaidenName) {
30:
31:         super(socialSecurityNumber);
32:
33:         myName = new String(name);
34:         mySocialSecurityNumber = new
35:                 String(socialSecurityNumber);
```

continues

Listing 13.13. continued

```
36:                    myAddress = new String(address);
37:                    myMothersMaidenName = new String(mothersMaidenName);
38:                    myAccounts = new Vector();
39:                    myATMCards = new Vector();
40:        }
41:
42:        protected CustomerImpl() {
43:
44:            myName = new String();
45:            mySocialSecurityNumber = new String();
46:            myAddress = new String();
47:            myMothersMaidenName = new String();
48:            myAccounts = new Vector();
49:            myATMCards = new Vector();
50:        }
51:
52:        public void name(String name) {
53:
54:            myName = new String(name);
55:        }
56:
57:        public String name() {
58:
59:            return myName;
60:        }
61:
62:        public String socialSecurityNumber() {
63:
64:            return mySocialSecurityNumber;
65:        }
66:
67:        public void address(String address) {
68:
69:            myAddress = new String(address);
70:        }
71:
72:        public String address() {
73:
74:            return myAddress;
75:        }
76:
77:        public java.lang.String mothersMaidenName() {
78:
79:            return myMothersMaidenName;
80:        }
81:
82:        public Account[] getAccounts() {
83:
84:            Account[] list = new Account[myAccounts.size()];
85:            myAccounts.copyInto(list);
86:
87:            Enumeration e = myAccounts.elements();
88:            while (e.hasMoreElements()) {
89:                ((Account)e.nextElement())._duplicate();
90:            }
91:
```

13

```
 92:            return list;
 93:        }
 94:
 95:        public void updateAccountBalance(Account account, float
 96:                balance) {
 97:
 98:            System.out.println("CustomerImpl: Received account " +
 99:                    "update:");
100:            System.out.println("  New balance is $" + balance);
101:        }
102: }
```

Listing 13.14. ATMClientMain.java.

```
 1: // ATMClientMain.java
 2:
 3: import org.omg.CORBA.BOA;
 4: import org.omg.CORBA.ORB;
 5:
 6: import idlGlobal.Account;
 7: import idlGlobal.ATM;
 8: import idlGlobal.ATMCard;
 9: import idlGlobal.Bank;
10: import idlGlobal.BankServer;
11: import idlGlobal.BankServerHelper;
12:
13: import idlGlobal.AuthorizationException;
14: import idlGlobal.InsufficientFundsException;
15: import idlGlobal.InvalidAccountException;
16: import idlGlobal.InvalidAmountException;
17:
18: public class ATMClientMain {
19:
20:     public static ORB myORB;
21:     public static BOA myBOA;
22:
23:     public static void main(String[] args) {
24:
25:         // Check the number of arguments; there should be exactly
26:         // five.
27:         if (args.length != 5) {
28:             System.out.println("Usage: ATMClient <name> <social " +
29:                     "security number> <address> <mother's maiden" +
30:                     " name> <PIN>");
31:             return;
32:         }
33:
34:         // Assign the command line arguments to the Customer
35:         // attributes.
36:         String name = args[0];
37:         String socialSecurityNumber = args[1];
38:         String address = args[2];
```

continues

13

Listing 13.14. continued

```
39:          String mothersMaidenName = args[3];
40:          short pin = Short.decode(args[4]).shortValue();
41:
42:          // Initialize the ORB and BOA.
43:          myORB = ORB.init(args, null);
44:          myBOA = myORB.BOA_init();
45:
46:          // Create a Customer object.
47:          System.out.println("ATMClient: Creating new Customer:");
48:          System.out.println("  name: " + name);
49:          System.out.println("  Social Security number: " +
50:              socialSecurityNumber);
51:          System.out.println("  address: " + address);
52:          System.out.println("  mother's maiden name: " +
53:              mothersMaidenName);
54:          CustomerImpl customer = new CustomerImpl(name,
55:              socialSecurityNumber, address, mothersMaidenName);
56:
57:          // Notify the BOA that the CustomerImpl object is ready.
58:          myBOA.obj_is_ready(customer);
59:
60:          // Locate a BankServer object and try to get a list of Banks
61:          // and ATMs from it.
62:          BankServer bankServer;
63:          try {
64:              bankServer = BankServerHelper.bind(myORB);
65:          } catch (Exception ex) {
66:
67:              // The bind attempt failed...
68:              System.out.println("ATMClient: Unable to bind to a " +
69:                  "BankServer:");
70:              System.out.println(ex);
71:              return;
72:          }
73:          System.out.println("ATMClient: Successfully bound to a " +
74:              "BankServer.");
75:
76:          Bank[] banks;
77:          ATM[] ATMs;
78:
79:          try {
80:              banks = bankServer.getBanks();
81:              ATMs = bankServer.getATMs();
82:          } catch (Exception ex) {
83:
84:              // The attempt failed...
85:              System.out.println("ATMClient: Unable to get lists of "
86:                  + "Banks and ATMs:");
87:              System.out.println(ex);
88:              return;
89:          }
90:
91:          // Use the first Bank and the first ATM that appear in the
92:          // lists.
93:          if (banks.length == 0) {
94:
```

13

```
 95:                    // No Banks were available.
 96:                    System.out.println("ATMClient: No Banks available.");
 97:                    return;
 98:            }
 99:            if (ATMs.length == 0) {
100:
101:                    // No ATMs were available.
102:                    System.out.println("ATMClient: No ATMs available.");
103:                    return;
104:            }
105:            Bank bank = banks[0];
106:            ATM atm = ATMs[0];
107:            System.out.println("ATMClient: Using Bank \"" + bank.
108:                    name() + "\" and ATM \"" + atm.name() + "\".");
109:
110:            // Do some cool stuff.
111:
112:            Account account;
113:            ATMCard atmCard;
114:
115:            try {
116:                account = bank.createAccount(customer, "checking",
117:                        0.0f);
118:            } catch (Exception ex) {
119:
120:                // The createAccount() attempt failed...
121:                System.out.println("ATMClient: Unable to create " +
122:                        "Account:");
123:                System.out.println(ex);
124:                return;
125:            }
126:
127:            try {
128:
129:                // Request the automatic account update service from the
130:                // Bank.
131:                bank.requestUpdateService(account);
132:            } catch (Exception ex) {
133:
134:                // The requestUpdateService() attempt failed...
135:                System.out.println("ATMClient: Unable to request "
136:                        + "Account update service:");
137:                System.out.println(ex);
138:                return;
139:            }
140:
141:            try {
142:
143:                // Print out some Account statistics.
144:                System.out.println("ATMClient: Opened new Account:");
145:                System.out.println("  account number: " + account.
146:                        accountNumber());
147:                System.out.println("  creation date: " + account.
148:                        creationDate());
149:                System.out.println("  account balance: " + account.
150:                        balance());
151:
```

13

continues

Listing 13.14. continued

```
152:                    // Ask the Bank to issue an ATMCard for the newly created
153:                    // Account.
154:                    System.out.println("ATMClient: Getting ATMCard from " +
155:                            "Bank.");
156:                    try {
157:                        atmCard = bank.issueATMCard(pin, account);
158:                    } catch (InvalidAccountException ex) {
159:
160:                        // For some reason, the Account was invalid (this
161:                        // shouldn't happen).
162:                        System.out.println("ATMClient: Exception caught: "
163:                                + "Invalid Account");
164:                        return;
165:                    }
166:
167:                    // Perform some transactions on the Account through the
168:                    // ATM.
169:                    System.out.println("ATMClient: Performing " +
170:                            "transactions.");
171:                    try {
172:                        System.out.println("  Depositing $250.00...");
173:                        System.out.println("  New balance is $" + atm.
174:                                deposit(atmCard, account, pin, 250.00f));
175:
176:                        // This will throw an exception since we're trying to
177:                        // withdraw too much.
178:                        System.out.println("  Withdrawing $500.00...");
179:                        System.out.println("  New balance is $" + atm.
180:                                withdraw(atmCard, account, pin, 500.00f));
181:                    } catch (AuthorizationException ex) {
182:                        System.out.println("ATMClient: Exception caught:" +
183:                                " Invalid PIN or No authorization (as " +
184:                                "expected)");
185:                    } catch (InvalidAmountException ex) {
186:                        System.out.println("ATMClient: Exception caught:" +
187:                                " Invalid amount");
188:                    } catch (InsufficientFundsException ex) {
189:                        System.out.println("ATMClient: Exception caught:" +
190:                                " Insufficient funds");
191:                    }
192:
193:                    // Perform some more transactions on the Account
194:                    // through the ATM.
195:                    System.out.println("ATMClient: Performing more " +
196:                            "transactions.");
197:                    try {
198:                        System.out.println("  Depositing $500.00...");
199:                        System.out.println("  New balance is $" + atm.
200:                                deposit(atmCard, account, pin, 500.00f));
201:
202:                        // This will throw an exception since we're using the
203:                        // wrong PIN.
```

13

```
204:                    System.out.println("  Withdrawing $250.00 with " +
205:                            "incorrect PIN...");
206:                    System.out.println("  New balance is $" + atm.
207:                            withdraw(atmCard, account, (short)(pin +
208:                            1), 250.00f));
209:                } catch (AuthorizationException ex) {
210:                    System.out.println("ATMClient: Exception caught:" +
211:                            " Invalid PIN or No authorization (as " +
212:                            "expected)");
213:                } catch (InvalidAmountException ex) {
214:                    System.out.println("ATMClient: Exception caught:" +
215:                            " Invalid amount");
216:                } catch (InsufficientFundsException ex) {
217:                    System.out.println("ATMClient: Exception caught:" +
218:                            " Insufficient funds");
219:                }
220:
221:                // Get rid of the Account.
222:                try {
223:                    System.out.println("  Deleting Account.");
224:                    bank.deleteAccount(account);
225:
226:                    // Attempt to delete the Account again, just for kicks.
227:                    // This should result in an exception being thrown.
228:                    System.out.println("  Attempting to cause an " +
229:                            "exception by deleting Account again.");
230:                    bank.deleteAccount(account);
231:                } catch (InvalidAccountException ex) {
232:
233:                    // Sure enough, the exception was thrown.
234:                    System.out.println("ATMClient: Exception caught:" +
235:                            " Invalid Account (as expected)");
236:                }
237:            } catch (Exception ex) {
238:
239:                // Some operation on the Account failed...
240:                System.out.println("ATMClient: Error accessing " +
241:                        "Account:");
242:                System.out.println(ex);
243:                return;
244:            }
245:
246:            // Sleep for long enough to catch an Account update message or
247:            // two.
248:            try {
249:                Thread.currentThread().sleep(120000);
250:            } catch (InterruptedException ex) {
251:            }
252:
253:            // When this point is reached, the application is finished.
254:            return;
255:    }
256: }
```

13

Running the Application

Except for being ported to Java, the application is precisely the same as on Day 9. The output, save for slight differences between formatting in C++ and Java, is nearly identical. The only difference is the way the application components are invoked (the exception being that, if you're using a Java development tool that produces native executables, there is no difference at all in the way the components are invoked).

Start by running the `BankServer` application:

```
java BankServerMain
```

Again, the output of the `BankServer` is this:

```
BankServer ready.
```

You're now ready to start the `Bank` application:

```
java BankMain "First Bank"
```

which, again, outputs this:

```
Bank "First Bank" ready.
```

Meanwhile, the `BankServer` will have output this:

```
BankServerImpl: Registering Bank "First Bank".
```

Then you start the `ATM` application:

```
java ATMMain "First Bank ATM"
```

The `ATM` application displays the following:

```
ATM "First Bank ATM" ready.
```

The `BankServer`, again, outputs the message:

```
BankServerImpl: Registering ATM "First Bank ATM".
```

Finally, you're ready to run the `ATMClient` application. You can do so by typing the following:

```
java ATMClientMain "Jeremy Rosenberger" 123456789 "123 Main Street" Doe 1234
```

The `ATMClient` again displays the following:

```
ATMClient: Creating new Customer:
  name: Jeremy Rosenberger
  Social Security number: 123456789
  address: 123 Main Street
  mother's maiden name: Doe
```

```
ATMClient: Successfully bound to a BankServer.
ATMClient: Using Bank "First Bank" and ATM "First Bank ATM".
ATMClient: Opened new Account:
  account number: Account0
  creation date: Oct 20 1997
  account balance: 0.0
ATMClient: Getting ATMCard from Bank.
ATMClient: Performing transactions.
  Depositing $250.00...
  New balance is $250.0
  Withdrawing $500.00...
ATMClient: Exception caught: Insufficient funds
ATMClient: Performing more transactions.
  Depositing $500.00...
  New balance is $750.0
  Withdrawing $250.00 with incorrect PIN...
ATMClient: Exception caught: Invalid PIN or No authorization (as expected)
  Deleting Account.
  Attempting to cause an exception by deleting Account again.
ATMClient: Exception caught: Invalid Account (as expected)
```

At this point, the ATMClient sleeps for two minutes while waiting for messages from the Bank. Be patient, and the ATMClient will eventually output this:

```
CustomerImpl: Received account update:
  New balance is $750.0
```

All this goes by very quickly. After it's over, you can go to the other application windows and see some evidence of what transpired here. Looking first at the BankServer application, you'll see this (with new output messages highlighted in **bold**):

```
BankServer ready.
BankServerImpl: Returning list of 1 Banks.
BankServerImpl: Returning list of 1 ATMs.
```

The output of the other applications is the same as last time, except for the Bank application. Turn your attention to the window in which the Bank is running and you will see the following familiar output:

```
Bank "First Bank" ready.
BankImpl: Creating new CheckingAccount for Customer Jeremy Rosenberger.
AccountImpl: Insufficient funds to withdraw specified amount.
BankImpl: Deleting Account "Account00000000".
BankImpl: Attempted to delete invalid Account.
```

Stay tuned for a few moments, and you will see the following (if it took you a minute or so to bring the Bank output window up, this might already be on your screen):

```
BankImpl: Updating Accounts.
```

Recall that this message is output just before the second thread in the Bank application sends the update messages to all the Account owners.

13

Summary

Today you were first introduced to the Java language/platform; you then ported the Bank application from C++ to Java. This was a pretty straight port: Most of the code could be translated almost line for line from C++. If you're already familiar with Java, this should have been a fairly trivial exercise. If you're new to Java, you've learned a bit about the language and, more importantly, witnessed the ease with which CORBA applications are implemented in Java.

Because the port of the Bank application from C++ to Java didn't add anything novel, you might have found this exercise uninteresting. However, on Day 14, "Web-Enabling the Bank Example with Java," the Java port will be developed further, so read on.

On Day 14, you'll take the Java version of the Bank application to its next logical step. Because one of Java's strengths is its capability to deploy graphical applications through Web browsers to end users, it makes sense to develop a graphical front end to the Bank application, rather than continue with the (rather boring) character-based interface. This is exactly what you'll do on the next and final day of this book. This exercise will give you insight into what can be accomplished using CORBA and Java.

Q&A

Q I thought Java was just for making cute animations on Web pages. What gives?

A Although Java initially rose in popularity because of its suitability for the Web, and the first-generation Java development tools were mostly geared toward developing simple Web applets, Java is much more than a language for writing cute but useless software. Indeed, Java is entirely suitable for general-purpose software development, much like C++. Java's integration with CORBA is a testament to the fact that Java is not just a toy programming language.

Q Much of the Java code in this chapter looks an awful lot like the C++ code from the previous chapters. Is this typical?

A Because there is a good deal of similarity in the syntax of C++ and Java, it is not uncommon for simple applications in Java to strongly resemble their C++ counterparts. When the application starts making use of various class libraries, however, the apparent similarity will quickly end.

Workshop

The following section will help you test your comprehension of the material presented in this chapter and put what you've learned into practice (there are no exercises for this chapter; they'll return in the next). You'll find the answers to the quiz in Appendix A.

Quiz

1. Which IDL construct resembles Java's package?

2. What is an advantage of Java Remote Method Invocation (RMI) over CORBA? Of CORBA over RMI?

3. Why might a developer want to use Java to develop a CORBA application?

13

Day 14

Web-Enabling the Bank Example with Java

On Day 13, "Developing for the Internet Using CORBA and Java," you were introduced to the Java programming language and proceeded to port the Bank application from C++ to Java. The porting process was straightforward, due to the similarities between C++ and Java and the fact that you didn't add any new functionality to the application when you ported it. The result was a CORBA application that behaved exactly like its predecessor, with no new bells or whistles.

Today, you'll take the Java version of the Bank example to its next logical evolutionary step. One of Java's greater potentials is in the development of graphical user interfaces (GUIs), and in this chapter you'll explore Java's capabilities in that area. Of course, the subject of developing GUIs in Java would by itself fill an entire book, so many of the details are omitted here. By the end of today, though, you will have built a functional Java applet that provides a GUI version of the functionality formerly provided by the ATMClient portion of the Bank application.

Developing the `BankApplet`

The process for developing the applet varies slightly from processes in previous chapters, primarily due to the inclusion of a GUI interface instead of the previous command-line interfaces. Here is the process you'll follow this time around:

- ☐ Implement the server functionality. As it turns out, you don't have to make any changes to the existing server components.
- ☐ Implement the client functionality. You'll replace the former `ATMClient` with a Java applet called, ever so originally, `BankApplet`.
- ☐ Deploy the `BankApplet`. You'll run the `BankApplet` in the `appletviewer` (a standalone application that runs Java applets) and then in a Web browser.

Implementing the Server Functionality

As on Day 13, no changes will be made to the server components of the `Bank` application. When the time comes to run the sample application, you'll run the same `BankServer`, `Bank`, and `ATM` server components as on Day 13.

Implementing the Client Functionality

Before delving into the development of the `BankApplet`, you need to make a slight modification to the existing `CustomerImpl`. The reason is that, until now, all output of the client application (and of the server applications, for that matter) has been to the system console (the `cout` stream in C++ or the `System.out` stream in Java). Previously, the `updateAccountBalance()` method of `CustomerImpl` simply printed a message to `System.out`, which is fine for a console mode application such as the former `ATMClient`. However, for a graphical client application such as `BankApplet`, you probably want to deal with messages in a more graphical way. You'll see how the `BankApplet` handles such messages, but for now, just recognize that the `CustomerImpl` forwards the update message to another object—one that implements the `AccountUpdateListener` interface (which you'll also see in a moment).

Customer

The modifications to the `CustomerImpl` class are very minor; the `CustomerImpl` constructor now accepts an `AccountUpdateListener` parameter, which is used when account update messages are later sent to the `CustomerImpl`. Also, as mentioned previously, the `updateAccountBalance()` method itself, rather than print a message to `System.out`, now forwards the update message to the registered `AccountUpdateListener` object. (You'll soon see that the `AccountUpdateListener` object, in this case, is the `BankApplet` itself.) The modified `CustomerImpl.java` appears in Listing 14.1.

Listing 14.1. `CustomerImpl.java`.

```
 1:  // CustomerImpl.java
 2:
 3:  import java.util.Enumeration;
 4:  import java.util.Vector;
 5:
 6:  import idlGlobal.Account;
 7:
 8:  public class CustomerImpl extends idlGlobal._CustomerImplBase {
 9:
10:      // This Customer's name.
11:      private String myName;
12:
13:      // This Customer's Social Security number.
14:      private String mySocialSecurityNumber;
15:
16:      // This Customer's address.
17:      private String myAddress;
18:
19:      // This Customer's mother's maiden name.
20:      private String myMothersMaidenName;
21:
22:      // This Customer's list of Accounts.
23:      private Vector myAccounts;
24:
25:      // This Customer's list of ATMCards.
26:      private Vector myATMCards;
27:
28:      // This Customer's AccountUpdateListener (for simplicity, only
29:      // one is allowed).
30:      private AccountUpdateListener myAccountUpdateListener;
31:
32:      public CustomerImpl(String name, String socialSecurityNumber,
33:              String address, String mothersMaidenName,
34:              AccountUpdateListener accountUpdateListener) {
35:
36:              super(socialSecurityNumber);
37:
38:              myName = new String(name);
39:              mySocialSecurityNumber = new
40:                      String(socialSecurityNumber);
41:              myAddress = new String(address);
42:              myMothersMaidenName = new String(mothersMaidenName);
43:              myAccounts = new Vector();
44:              myATMCards = new Vector();
45:              myAccountUpdateListener = accountUpdateListener;
46:      }
47:
48:      protected CustomerImpl() {
49:
50:          myName = new String();
51:          mySocialSecurityNumber = new String();
52:          myAddress = new String();
53:          myMothersMaidenName = new String();
```

14

continues

Listing 14.1. continued

```
54:            myAccounts = new Vector();
55:            myATMCards = new Vector();
56:        }
57:
58:    public void name(String name) {
59:
60:            myName = new String(name);
61:        }
62:
63:    public String name() {
64:
65:            return myName;
66:        }
67:
68:    public String socialSecurityNumber() {
69:
70:            return mySocialSecurityNumber;
71:        }
72:
73:    public void address(String address) {
74:
75:            myAddress = new String(address);
76:        }
77:
78:    public String address() {
79:
80:            return myAddress;
81:        }
82:
83:    public java.lang.String mothersMaidenName() {
84:
85:            return myMothersMaidenName;
86:        }
87:
88:    public Account[] getAccounts() {
89:
90:            Account[] list = new Account[myAccounts.size()];
91:            myAccounts.copyInto(list);
92:
93:            Enumeration e = myAccounts.elements();
94:            while (e.hasMoreElements()) {
95:                ((Account)e.nextElement())._duplicate();
96:            }
97:
98:            return list;
99:        }
100:
101:    public void updateAccountBalance(Account account, float
102:            balance) {
103:
104:            myAccountUpdateListener.update(account, balance);
105:        }
106: }
```

14

The AccountUpdateListener interface is simple, its only purpose being to accept update messages for Accounts. Consequently, its single method, update(), reflects the updateAccountBalance() method in CustomerImpl. Note that, as an interface, AccountUpdateListener doesn't provide an implementation for this method; the implementation is the responsibility of the class(es) implementing this interface. AccountUpdateListener.java appears in Listing 14.2.

Listing 14.2. AccountUpdateListener.java.

```
1: // AccountUpdateListener.java
2:
3: import idlGlobal.Account;
4:
5: public interface AccountUpdateListener {
6:
7:     /**
8:      * Update the given Account with the new balance.
9:      */
10:     public void update(Account account, float balance);
11: }
```

A Word About Java Development Tools

You're almost ready to begin work on the BankApplet itself. If you already took a peek at BankApplet.java (see Listing 14.3), you saw that the file is quite sizable—much larger than anything that has appeared in this book. Don't be alarmed. Much of the code was not written by hand but was generated by a development tool (a development tool, or a portion thereof, for defining GUI interfaces is often called a *GUI builder*). Symantec's Visual Café 2.0 (available at http://cafe.symantec.com/) was used to develop this particular applet, but any GUI builder for Java—such as Sun's Java Workshop (http://www.sun.com/), Microsoft's Visual J++ (http://www.microsoft.com/), Borland's JBuilder (http://www.borland.com/), IBM's Visual Age for Java (http://www.software.ibm.com/), or many others—can be used to perform the GUI design portion of this task. Each of these products generates different code, depending on the GUI components chosen, but produces a similar end result.

Although you can certainly write all the user interface code by hand, using a GUI builder makes your life a lot easier for all but the most trivial user interfaces. Describing even one of these tools is beyond the scope of this book, so it's hoped that you already have some experience with these. Many GUI builders not only enable you to place user interface components on forms (also called screens or dialogs) but also to define interactions between components without writing any code. The more work the GUI builder does, the less code you have to write by hand, and you can always take code the GUI builder generates and modify it by hand to get the exact results you want.

14

BankApplet

BankApplet.java, including code generated by Visual Café and code written by hand, appears in Listing 14.3. Again, most of this code (almost the entire init() method, for instance) was generated by Visual Café. In a few moments, you'll examine more closely the portions written by hand. You will see that the applet's behavior is similar to that of the client applications implemented in previous chapters. The structure, however, differs significantly, as the structures of GUI-based applications often differ from their console-based counterparts.

Before examining the code for the BankApplet, it's helpful to see what it produces. Figure 14.1 illustrates the main window of the BankApplet, as designed using Visual Café. Figure 14.2 shows the corresponding hierarchy of objects that make up the user interface.

Figure 14.1.

BankApplet *main window.*

Figure 14.2.

BankApplet *main window hierarchy.*

Listing 14.3. BankApplet.java.

```
1: // BankApplet.java
2:
3: import java.awt.*;
4: import java.awt.event.ItemEvent;
5: import java.applet.*;
```

14

```
 6: import java.util.Enumeration;
 7: import java.util.Hashtable;
 8:
 9: import org.omg.CORBA.BOA;
10: import org.omg.CORBA.ORB;
11:
12: import idlGlobal.Account;
13: import idlGlobal.ATM;
14: import idlGlobal.Bank;
15: import idlGlobal.BankServer;
16: import idlGlobal.BankServerHelper;
17: import idlGlobal.CheckingAccountHelper;
18: import idlGlobal.Customer;
19:
20: import idlGlobal.InsufficientFundsException;
21: import idlGlobal.InvalidAccountException;
22: import idlGlobal.InvalidAmountException;
23:
24: public class BankApplet extends Applet implements
25:         AccountUpdateListener {
26:
27:     public static ORB myORB;
28:     public static BOA myBOA;
29:
30:     // This BankApplet's BankServer.
31:     BankServer myBankServer;
32:
33:     // This BankApplet's currently selected Bank, ATM, Customer,
34:     // and Account.
35:     Bank mySelectedBank;
36:     ATM mySelectedATM;
37:     Customer mySelectedCustomer;
38:     Account mySelectedAccount;
39:
40:     // This BankApplet's list of Banks, keyed on the Bank name.
41:     Hashtable myBanks = new Hashtable();
42:
43:     // This BankApplet's list of ATMs, keyed on the ATM name.
44:     Hashtable myATMs = new Hashtable();
45:
46:     // This BankApplet's list of Customers, keyed on the Customer
47:     // name. Note that this means that Customer names must be
48:     // unique in this applet!
49:     Hashtable myCustomers = new Hashtable();
50:
51:     // This BankApplet's list of Accounts. This Hashtable is keyed
52:     // on Customer objects, which in turn point to Hashtables which
53:     // are keyed on the concatenation of Bank names and Account
54:     // numbers and identify Accounts.
55:     Hashtable myAccounts = new Hashtable();
56:
57:     // This BankApplet's map which links Accounts to Banks.
58:     Hashtable myAccountBankMap = new Hashtable();
59:
60:     public void init() {
61:
```

14

continues

Listing 14.3. continued

```
62:          //{{INIT_CONTROLS
63:          GridBagLayout gridBagLayout;
64:          gridBagLayout = new GridBagLayout();
65:          setLayout(gridBagLayout);
66:          setSize(404, 327);
67:          setBackground(new Color(-4144944));
68:          bankChoice = new java.awt.Choice();
69:          bankChoice.setBounds(112, 3, 322, 21);
70:          GridBagConstraints gbc;
71:          gbc = new GridBagConstraints();
72:          gbc.gridx = 1;
73:          gbc.gridy = 0;
74:          gbc.weightx = 1.0;
75:          gbc.fill = GridBagConstraints.HORIZONTAL;
76:          gbc.insets = new Insets(2, 2, 2, 2);
77:          gbc.ipadx = 100;
78:          ((GridBagLayout)getLayout()).setConstraints(bankChoice,
79:                  gbc);
80:          add(bankChoice);
81:          atmChoice = new java.awt.Choice();
82:          atmChoice.setBounds(112, 30, 156, 21);
83:          gbc = new GridBagConstraints();
84:          gbc.gridx = 1;
85:          gbc.gridy = 1;
86:          gbc.weightx = 1.0;
87:          gbc.fill = GridBagConstraints.HORIZONTAL;
88:          gbc.insets = new Insets(2, 2, 2, 2);
89:          ((GridBagLayout)getLayout()).setConstraints(atmChoice,
90:                  gbc);
91:          add(atmChoice);
92:          customerChoice = new java.awt.Choice();
93:          customerChoice.setBounds(112, 57, 156, 21);
94:          gbc = new GridBagConstraints();
95:          gbc.gridx = 1;
96:          gbc.gridy = 2;
97:          gbc.weightx = 1.0;
98:          gbc.fill = GridBagConstraints.HORIZONTAL;
99:          gbc.insets = new Insets(2, 2, 2, 2);
100:         ((GridBagLayout)getLayout()).setConstraints(customerChoice,
101:                 gbc);
102:         add(customerChoice);
103:         newCustomerButton = new java.awt.Button();
104:         newCustomerButton.setActionCommand("button");
105:         newCustomerButton.setLabel("New...");
106:         newCustomerButton.setBounds(272, 56, 48, 23);
107:         gbc = new GridBagConstraints();
108:         gbc.gridx = 2;
109:         gbc.gridy = 2;
110:         gbc.fill = GridBagConstraints.NONE;
111:         gbc.insets = new Insets(2, 2, 2, 2);
112:         ((GridBagLayout)getLayout()).
113:                 setConstraints(newCustomerButton, gbc);
114:         add(newCustomerButton);
115:         accountChoice = new java.awt.Choice();
```

14

```
116:        accountChoice.setBounds(112, 84, 156, 21);
117:        gbc = new GridBagConstraints();
118:        gbc.gridx = 1;
119:        gbc.gridy = 3;
120:        gbc.weightx = 1.0;
121:        gbc.fill = GridBagConstraints.HORIZONTAL;
122:        gbc.insets = new Insets(2, 2, 2, 2);
123:        ((GridBagLayout)getLayout()).setConstraints(accountChoice,
124:                gbc);
125:        add(accountChoice);
126:        accountChoice.setEnabled(false);
127:        newAccountButton = new java.awt.Button();
128:        newAccountButton.setActionCommand("button");
129:        newAccountButton.setLabel("New...");
130:        newAccountButton.setBounds(272, 83, 48, 23);
131:        gbc = new GridBagConstraints();
132:        gbc.gridx = 2;
133:        gbc.gridy = 3;
134:        gbc.fill = GridBagConstraints.NONE;
135:        gbc.insets = new Insets(2, 2, 2, 2);
136:        ((GridBagLayout)getLayout()).
137:                setConstraints(newAccountButton, gbc);
138:        add(newAccountButton);
139:        newAccountButton.setEnabled(false);
140:        autoUpdateButton = new java.awt.Button();
141:        autoUpdateButton.setActionCommand("button");
142:        autoUpdateButton.setLabel("AutoUpdate");
143:        autoUpdateButton.setBounds(324, 83, 78, 23);
144:        gbc = new GridBagConstraints();
145:        gbc.gridx = 3;
146:        gbc.gridy = 3;
147:        gbc.fill = GridBagConstraints.NONE;
148:        gbc.insets = new Insets(2, 2, 2, 2);
149:        ((GridBagLayout)getLayout()).
150:                setConstraints(autoUpdateButton, gbc);
151:        add(autoUpdateButton);
152:        autoUpdateButton.setEnabled(false);
153:        selectBankLabel = new java.awt.Label("Select Bank");
154:        selectBankLabel.setBounds(2, 2, 79, 23);
155:        gbc = new GridBagConstraints();
156:        gbc.gridx = 0;
157:        gbc.gridy = 0;
158:        gbc.anchor = GridBagConstraints.WEST;
159:        gbc.fill = GridBagConstraints.NONE;
160:        gbc.insets = new Insets(2, 2, 2, 2);
161:        ((GridBagLayout)getLayout()).
162:                setConstraints(selectBankLabel, gbc);
163:        add(selectBankLabel);
164:        selectATMLabel = new java.awt.Label("Select ATM");
165:        selectATMLabel.setBounds(2, 29, 74, 23);
166:        gbc = new GridBagConstraints();
167:        gbc.gridx = 0;
168:        gbc.gridy = 1;
169:        gbc.anchor = GridBagConstraints.WEST;
170:        gbc.fill = GridBagConstraints.NONE;
171:        gbc.insets = new Insets(2, 2, 2, 2);
```

14

continues

Listing 14.3. continued

```
172:        ((GridBagLayout)getLayout()).
173:                setConstraints(selectATMLabel, gbc);
174:        add(selectATMLabel);
175:        selectCustomerLabel = new java.awt.
176:                Label("Select Customer");
177:        selectCustomerLabel.setBounds(2, 56, 106, 23);
178:        gbc = new GridBagConstraints();
179:        gbc.gridx = 0;
180:        gbc.gridy = 2;
181:        gbc.anchor = GridBagConstraints.WEST;
182:        gbc.fill = GridBagConstraints.NONE;
183:        gbc.insets = new Insets(2, 2, 2, 2);
184:        ((GridBagLayout)getLayout()).
185:                setConstraints(selectCustomerLabel, gbc);
186:        add(selectCustomerLabel);
187:        selectAccountLabel = new java.awt.Label("Select Account");
188:        selectAccountLabel.setBounds(2, 83, 94, 23);
189:        gbc = new GridBagConstraints();
190:        gbc.gridx = 0;
191:        gbc.gridy = 3;
192:        gbc.anchor = GridBagConstraints.WEST;
193:        gbc.fill = GridBagConstraints.NONE;
194:        gbc.insets = new Insets(2, 2, 2, 2);
195:        ((GridBagLayout)getLayout()).
196:                setConstraints(selectAccountLabel, gbc);
197:        add(selectAccountLabel);
198:        accountActionPanel = new java.awt.Panel();
199:        gridBagLayout = new GridBagLayout();
200:        accountActionPanel.setLayout(gridBagLayout);
201:        accountActionPanel.setBounds(2, 110, 400, 188);
202:        gbc = new GridBagConstraints();
203:        gbc.gridx = 0;
204:        gbc.gridy = 4;
205:        gbc.gridwidth = 4;
206:        gbc.weightx = 1.0;
207:        gbc.weighty = 1.0;
208:        gbc.fill = GridBagConstraints.BOTH;
209:        gbc.insets = new Insets(2, 2, 2, 2);
210:        ((GridBagLayout)getLayout()).
211:                setConstraints(accountActionPanel, gbc);
212:        add(accountActionPanel);
213:        accountInfoPanel = new java.awt.Panel();
214:        gridBagLayout = new GridBagLayout();
215:        accountInfoPanel.setLayout(gridBagLayout);
216:        accountInfoPanel.setBounds(0, 13, 246, 162);
217:        gbc = new GridBagConstraints();
218:        gbc.weightx = 0.65;
219:        gbc.anchor = GridBagConstraints.NORTH;
220:        gbc.fill = GridBagConstraints.HORIZONTAL;
221:        gbc.insets = new Insets(0, 0, 0, 2);
222:        ((GridBagLayout)accountActionPanel.getLayout()).
223:                setConstraints(accountInfoPanel, gbc);
224:        accountActionPanel.add(accountInfoPanel);
225:        issuingBankTextField = new java.awt.TextField();
```

14

```
226:        issuingBankTextField.setEditable(false);
227:        issuingBankTextField.setBounds(136, 29, 108, 23);
228:        gbc = new GridBagConstraints();
229:        gbc.gridx = 2;
230:        gbc.gridy = 1;
231:        gbc.weightx = 1.0;
232:        gbc.fill = GridBagConstraints.HORIZONTAL;
233:        gbc.insets = new Insets(2, 2, 2, 2);
234:        ((GridBagLayout)accountInfoPanel.getLayout()).
235:                setConstraints(issuingBankTextField, gbc);
236:        accountInfoPanel.add(issuingBankTextField);
237:        accountNumberTextField = new java.awt.TextField();
238:        accountNumberTextField.setEditable(false);
239:        accountNumberTextField.setBounds(136, 56, 108, 23);
240:        gbc = new GridBagConstraints();
241:        gbc.gridx = 2;
242:        gbc.gridy = 2;
243:        gbc.weightx = 1.0;
244:        gbc.fill = GridBagConstraints.HORIZONTAL;
245:        gbc.insets = new Insets(2, 2, 2, 2);
246:        ((GridBagLayout)accountInfoPanel.getLayout()).
247:                setConstraints(accountNumberTextField, gbc);
248:        accountInfoPanel.add(accountNumberTextField);
249:        accountTypeTextField = new java.awt.TextField();
250:        accountTypeTextField.setEditable(false);
251:        accountTypeTextField.setBounds(136, 83, 108, 23);
252:        gbc = new GridBagConstraints();
253:        gbc.gridx = 2;
254:        gbc.gridy = 3;
255:        gbc.weightx = 1.0;
256:        gbc.fill = GridBagConstraints.HORIZONTAL;
257:        gbc.insets = new Insets(2, 2, 2, 2);
258:        ((GridBagLayout)accountInfoPanel.getLayout()).
259:                setConstraints(accountTypeTextField, gbc);
260:        accountInfoPanel.add(accountTypeTextField);
261:        creationDateTextField = new java.awt.TextField();
262:        creationDateTextField.setEditable(false);
263:        creationDateTextField.setBounds(136, 110, 115, 23);
264:        gbc = new GridBagConstraints();
265:        gbc.gridx = 2;
266:        gbc.gridy = 4;
267:        gbc.weightx = 1.0;
268:        gbc.fill = GridBagConstraints.HORIZONTAL;
269:        gbc.insets = new Insets(2, 2, 2, 2);
270:        ((GridBagLayout)accountInfoPanel.getLayout()).
271:                setConstraints(creationDateTextField, gbc);
272:        accountInfoPanel.add(creationDateTextField);
273:        currentBalanceTextField = new java.awt.TextField();
274:        currentBalanceTextField.setEditable(false);
275:        currentBalanceTextField.setBounds(136, 137, 115, 23);
276:        gbc = new GridBagConstraints();
277:        gbc.gridx = 2;
278:        gbc.gridy = 5;
279:        gbc.weightx = 1.0;
280:        gbc.fill = GridBagConstraints.HORIZONTAL;
281:        gbc.insets = new Insets(2, 2, 2, 2);
```

14

continues

Listing 14.3. continued

```
282:          ((GridBagLayout)accountInfoPanel.getLayout()).
283:                  setConstraints(currentBalanceTextField, gbc);
284:          accountInfoPanel.add(currentBalanceTextField);
285:          accountInfoLabel = new java.awt.
286:                  Label("Account Information", Label.CENTER);
287:          accountInfoLabel.setBounds(62, 2, 122, 23);
288:          gbc = new GridBagConstraints();
289:          gbc.gridx = 0;
290:          gbc.gridy = 0;
291:          gbc.gridwidth = 3;
292:          gbc.fill = GridBagConstraints.NONE;
293:          gbc.insets = new Insets(2, 2, 2, 2);
294:          ((GridBagLayout)accountInfoPanel.getLayout()).
295:                  setConstraints(accountInfoLabel, gbc);
296:          accountInfoPanel.add(accountInfoLabel);
297:          issuingBankLabel = new java.awt.Label("Issuing Bank");
298:          issuingBankLabel.setBounds(2, 29, 86, 23);
299:          gbc = new GridBagConstraints();
300:          gbc.gridx = 0;
301:          gbc.gridy = 1;
302:          gbc.anchor = GridBagConstraints.WEST;
303:          gbc.fill = GridBagConstraints.NONE;
304:          gbc.insets = new Insets(2, 2, 2, 2);
305:          ((GridBagLayout)accountInfoPanel.getLayout()).
306:                  setConstraints(issuingBankLabel, gbc);
307:          accountInfoPanel.add(issuingBankLabel);
308:          accountNumberLabel = new java.awt.Label("Account Number");
309:          accountNumberLabel.setBounds(2, 56, 105, 23);
310:          gbc = new GridBagConstraints();
311:          gbc.gridx = 0;
312:          gbc.gridy = 2;
313:          gbc.anchor = GridBagConstraints.WEST;
314:          gbc.fill = GridBagConstraints.NONE;
315:          gbc.insets = new Insets(2, 2, 2, 2);
316:          ((GridBagLayout)accountInfoPanel.getLayout()).
317:                  setConstraints(accountNumberLabel, gbc);
318:          accountInfoPanel.add(accountNumberLabel);
319:          accountTypeLabel = new java.awt.Label("Account Type");
320:          accountTypeLabel.setBounds(2, 83, 86, 23);
321:          gbc = new GridBagConstraints();
322:          gbc.gridx = 0;
323:          gbc.gridy = 3;
324:          gbc.anchor = GridBagConstraints.WEST;
325:          gbc.fill = GridBagConstraints.NONE;
326:          gbc.insets = new Insets(2, 2, 2, 2);
327:          ((GridBagLayout)accountInfoPanel.getLayout()).
328:                  setConstraints(accountTypeLabel, gbc);
329:          accountInfoPanel.add(accountTypeLabel);
330:          creationDateLabel = new java.awt.Label("Creation Date");
331:          creationDateLabel.setBounds(2, 110, 90, 23);
332:          gbc = new GridBagConstraints();
333:          gbc.gridx = 0;
334:          gbc.gridy = 4;
335:          gbc.anchor = GridBagConstraints.WEST;
```

```
336:        gbc.fill = GridBagConstraints.NONE;
337:        gbc.insets = new Insets(2, 2, 2, 2);
338:        ((GridBagLayout)accountInfoPanel.getLayout()).
339:              setConstraints(creationDateLabel, gbc);
340:        accountInfoPanel.add(creationDateLabel);
341:        currentBalanceLabel = new java.awt.
342:              Label("Current Balance");
343:        currentBalanceLabel.setBounds(2, 137, 103, 23);
344:        gbc = new GridBagConstraints();
345:        gbc.gridx = 0;
346:        gbc.gridy = 5;
347:        gbc.anchor = GridBagConstraints.WEST;
348:        gbc.fill = GridBagConstraints.NONE;
349:        gbc.insets = new Insets(2, 2, 2, 2);
350:        ((GridBagLayout)accountInfoPanel.getLayout()).
351:              setConstraints(currentBalanceLabel, gbc);
352:        accountInfoPanel.add(currentBalanceLabel);
353:        dollarLabel1 = new java.awt.Label("$", Label.RIGHT);
354:        dollarLabel1.setBounds(111, 137, 21, 23);
355:        gbc = new GridBagConstraints();
356:        gbc.gridx = 1;
357:        gbc.gridy = 5;
358:        gbc.anchor = GridBagConstraints.EAST;
359:        gbc.fill = GridBagConstraints.NONE;
360:        gbc.insets = new Insets(2, 2, 2, 2);
361:        ((GridBagLayout)accountInfoPanel.getLayout()).
362:              setConstraints(dollarLabel1, gbc);
363:        accountInfoPanel.add(dollarLabel1);
364:        transactionsPanel = new java.awt.Panel();
365:        gridBagLayout = new GridBagLayout();
366:        transactionsPanel.setLayout(gridBagLayout);
367:        transactionsPanel.setBounds(250, 13, 149, 162);
368:        gbc = new GridBagConstraints();
369:        gbc.weightx = 0.35;
370:        gbc.anchor = GridBagConstraints.NORTH;
371:        gbc.fill = GridBagConstraints.BOTH;
372:        gbc.insets = new Insets(0, 2, 0, 0);
373:        ((GridBagLayout)accountActionPanel.getLayout()).
374:              setConstraints(transactionsPanel, gbc);
375:        accountActionPanel.add(transactionsPanel);
376:        transactionTextField = new java.awt.TextField();
377:        transactionTextField.setBounds(27, 29, 129, 23);
378:        gbc = new GridBagConstraints();
379:        gbc.gridx = 1;
380:        gbc.gridy = 1;
381:        gbc.weightx = 1.0;
382:        gbc.anchor = GridBagConstraints.NORTH;
383:        gbc.fill = GridBagConstraints.HORIZONTAL;
384:        gbc.insets = new Insets(2, 2, 2, 2);
385:        ((GridBagLayout)transactionsPanel.getLayout()).
386:              setConstraints(transactionTextField, gbc);
387:        transactionsPanel.add(transactionTextField);
388:        transactionTextField.setEnabled(false);
389:        depositButton = new java.awt.Button();
390:        depositButton.setActionCommand("button");
391:        depositButton.setLabel("Deposit");
```

14

continues

Listing 14.3. continued

```
392:            depositButton.setBounds(2, 56, 154, 23);
393:            gbc = new GridBagConstraints();
394:            gbc.gridx = 0;
395:            gbc.gridy = 2;
396:            gbc.gridwidth = 2;
397:            gbc.anchor = GridBagConstraints.SOUTH;
398:            gbc.fill = GridBagConstraints.HORIZONTAL;
399:            gbc.insets = new Insets(2, 2, 2, 2);
400:            ((GridBagLayout)transactionsPanel.getLayout()).
401:                    setConstraints(depositButton, gbc);
402:            transactionsPanel.add(depositButton);
403:            depositButton.setEnabled(false);
404:            withdrawButton = new java.awt.Button();
405:            withdrawButton.setActionCommand("button");
406:            withdrawButton.setLabel("Withdraw");
407:            withdrawButton.setBounds(2, 83, 154, 23);
408:            gbc = new GridBagConstraints();
409:            gbc.gridx = 0;
410:            gbc.gridy = 3;
411:            gbc.gridwidth = 2;
412:            gbc.anchor = GridBagConstraints.SOUTH;
413:            gbc.fill = GridBagConstraints.HORIZONTAL;
414:            gbc.insets = new Insets(2, 2, 2, 2);
415:            ((GridBagLayout)transactionsPanel.getLayout()).
416:                    setConstraints(withdrawButton, gbc);
417:            transactionsPanel.add(withdrawButton);
418:            withdrawButton.setEnabled(false);
419:            updateAccountButton = new java.awt.Button();
420:            updateAccountButton.setActionCommand("button");
421:            updateAccountButton.setLabel("Update Account");
422:            updateAccountButton.setBounds(2, 137, 154, 23);
423:            gbc = new GridBagConstraints();
424:            gbc.gridx = 0;
425:            gbc.gridy = 4;
426:            gbc.gridwidth = 2;
427:            gbc.weighty = 1.0;
428:            gbc.anchor = GridBagConstraints.SOUTH;
429:            gbc.fill = GridBagConstraints.HORIZONTAL;
430:            gbc.insets = new Insets(2, 2, 2, 2);
431:            ((GridBagLayout)transactionsPanel.getLayout()).
432:                    setConstraints(updateAccountButton, gbc);
433:            transactionsPanel.add(updateAccountButton);
434:            updateAccountButton.setEnabled(false);
435:            transactionsLabel = new java.awt.Label("Transactions",
436:                    Label.CENTER);
437:            transactionsLabel.setBounds(31, 2, 86, 23);
438:            gbc = new GridBagConstraints();
439:            gbc.gridx = 0;
440:            gbc.gridy = 0;
441:            gbc.gridwidth = 2;
442:            gbc.anchor = GridBagConstraints.NORTH;
443:            gbc.fill = GridBagConstraints.NONE;
444:            gbc.insets = new Insets(2, 2, 2, 2);
445:            ((GridBagLayout)transactionsPanel.getLayout()).
446:                    setConstraints(transactionsLabel, gbc);
```

```
447:        transactionsPanel.add(transactionsLabel);
448:        dollarLabel2 = new java.awt.Label("$", Label.RIGHT);
449:        dollarLabel2.setBounds(2, 29, 21, 23);
450:        gbc = new GridBagConstraints();
451:        gbc.gridx = 0;
452:        gbc.gridy = 1;
453:        gbc.anchor = GridBagConstraints.EAST;
454:        gbc.fill = GridBagConstraints.NONE;
455:        gbc.insets = new Insets(2, 2, 2, 2);
456:        ((GridBagLayout)transactionsPanel.getLayout()).
457:              setConstraints(dollarLabel2, gbc);
458:        transactionsPanel.add(dollarLabel2);
459:        statusTextField = new java.awt.TextField();
460:        statusTextField.setEditable(false);
461:        statusTextField.setText("BankApplet Ready.");
462:        statusTextField.setBounds(2, 302, 400, 23);
463:        gbc = new GridBagConstraints();
464:        gbc.gridx = 0;
465:        gbc.gridy = 5;
466:        gbc.gridwidth = 4;
467:        gbc.weightx = 1.0;
468:        gbc.anchor = GridBagConstraints.SOUTH;
469:        gbc.fill = GridBagConstraints.HORIZONTAL;
470:        gbc.insets = new Insets(2, 2, 2, 2);
471:        ((GridBagLayout)getLayout()).
472:              setConstraints(statusTextField, gbc);
473:        add(statusTextField);
474:        //}}
475:
476:        //{{REGISTER_LISTENERS
477:        SymAction lSymAction = new SymAction();
478:        newCustomerButton.addActionListener(lSymAction);
479:        newAccountButton.addActionListener(lSymAction);
480:        SymItem lSymItem = new SymItem();
481:        bankChoice.addItemListener(lSymItem);
482:        atmChoice.addItemListener(lSymItem);
483:        customerChoice.addItemListener(lSymItem);
484:        accountChoice.addItemListener(lSymItem);
485:        autoUpdateButton.addActionListener(lSymAction);
486:        depositButton.addActionListener(lSymAction);
487:        withdrawButton.addActionListener(lSymAction);
488:        updateAccountButton.addActionListener(lSymAction);
489:        //}}
490:
491:        // Initialize the ORB and BOA.
492:        myORB = ORB.init(this);
493:        myBOA = myORB.BOA_init();
494:
495:        // Locate a BankServer object and try to get a list of
496:        // Banks and ATMs from it.
497:        setStatus("Binding to a BankServer...");
498:        try {
499:            myBankServer = BankServerHelper.bind(myORB);
500:        } catch (Exception ex) {
501:
```

14

continues

Listing 14.3. continued

```
502:                    // The bind attempt failed...
503:                    setStatus("Unable to bind to a BankServer.");
504:                    System.out.println(ex);
505:                    return;
506:                }
507:                setStatus("Successfully bound to a BankServer.");
508:
509:                // Get lists of Banks and ATMs from the BankServer.
510:                ATM[] atms;
511:                Bank[] banks;
512:                setStatus("Getting list of available Banks...");
513:                try {
514:                    banks = myBankServer.getBanks();
515:                } catch (Exception ex) {
516:
517:                    // The attempt failed...
518:                    setStatus("Unable to get list of Banks.");
519:                    return;
520:                }
521:                setStatus("Getting list of available ATMs...");
522:                try {
523:                    atms = myBankServer.getATMs();
524:                } catch (Exception ex) {
525:
526:                    // The attempt failed...
527:                    setStatus("Unable to get list of ATMs.");
528:                    return;
529:                }
530:                addBanks(banks);
531:                addATMs(atms);
532:                setStatus(null);
533:            }
534:
535:            //{{DECLARE_CONTROLS
536:            java.awt.Choice bankChoice;
537:            java.awt.Choice atmChoice;
538:            java.awt.Choice customerChoice;
539:            java.awt.Button newCustomerButton;
540:            java.awt.Choice accountChoice;
541:            java.awt.Button newAccountButton;
542:            java.awt.Button autoUpdateButton;
543:            java.awt.Label selectBankLabel;
544:            java.awt.Label selectATMLabel;
545:            java.awt.Label selectCustomerLabel;
546:            java.awt.Label selectAccountLabel;
547:            java.awt.Panel accountActionPanel;
548:            java.awt.Panel accountInfoPanel;
549:            java.awt.TextField issuingBankTextField;
550:            java.awt.TextField accountNumberTextField;
551:            java.awt.TextField accountTypeTextField;
552:            java.awt.TextField creationDateTextField;
553:            java.awt.TextField currentBalanceTextField;
554:            java.awt.Label accountInfoLabel;
555:            java.awt.Label issuingBankLabel;
556:            java.awt.Label accountNumberLabel;
```

14

```
557:        java.awt.Label accountTypeLabel;
558:        java.awt.Label creationDateLabel;
559:        java.awt.Label currentBalanceLabel;
560:        java.awt.Label dollarLabel1;
561:        java.awt.Panel transactionsPanel;
562:        java.awt.TextField transactionTextField;
563:        java.awt.Button depositButton;
564:        java.awt.Button withdrawButton;
565:        java.awt.Button updateAccountButton;
566:        java.awt.Label transactionsLabel;
567:        java.awt.Label dollarLabel2;
568:        java.awt.TextField statusTextField;
569:        //}}

570:
571:        /**
572:         * Set the status bar message to the given string. If the
573:         * string is null, the status message is reset to the default.
574:         */
575:        public void setStatus(String status) {
576:
577:            if (status != null) {
578:                statusTextField.setText(status);
579:            } else {
580:                statusTextField.setText("BankApplet ready.");
581:            }
582:        }
583:
584:        /**
585:         * Update the given Account with the new balance.
586:         */
587:        public void update(Account account, float balance) {
588:
589:            setStatus("Received AutoUpdate for Account \"" + ((Bank)
590:                    myAccountBankMap.get(mySelectedAccount)).name() +
591:                    ":" + account.accountNumber() + "\"");
592:
593:            // If the updated Account is currently selected, update the
594:            // display immediately.
595:            if (account._is_equivalent(mySelectedAccount)) {
596:                currentBalanceTextField.setText(String.
597:                        valueOf(balance));
598:            }
599:        }
600:
601:        /**
602:         * Add the given array of Banks to the Bank choice box and to
603:         * this BankApplet's internal data structures.
604:         */
605:        protected void addBanks(Bank[] banks) {
606:
607:            for (int i = 0; i < banks.length; i++) {
608:                String name = banks[i].name();
609:                myBanks.put(name, banks[i]);
610:                bankChoice.add(name);
```

14

continues

Listing 14.3. continued

```
611:            }
612:            if (mySelectedBank == null && banks.length > 0) {
613:                mySelectedBank = banks[0];
614:            }
615:        }
616:
617:        /**
618:         * Add the given array of ATMs to the ATM choice box and to
619:         * this BankApplet's internal data structures.
620:         */
621:        protected void addATMs(ATM[] atms) {
622:
623:            for (int i = 0; i < atms.length; i++) {
624:                String name = atms[i].name();
625:                myATMs.put(name, atms[i]);
626:                atmChoice.add(name);
627:            }
628:            if (mySelectedATM == null && atms.length > 0) {
629:                mySelectedATM = atms[0];
630:            }
631:        }
632:
633:        /**
634:         * Create a new Customer with the given name, Social Security
635:         * number, address, mother's maiden name, and PIN.
636:         */
637:        protected void createCustomer(String name, String
638:                socialSecurityNumber, String address, String
639:                mothersMaidenName) {
640:
641:            // Create a new Customer and register it with the BOA.
642:            setStatus("Creating new Customer...");
643:            CustomerImpl customer = new CustomerImpl(name,
644:                    socialSecurityNumber, address, mothersMaidenName,
645:                    this);
646:            myBOA.obj_is_ready(customer);
647:            myCustomers.put(name, customer);
648:            customerChoice.add(name);
649:            if (mySelectedCustomer == null) {
650:                mySelectedCustomer = customer;
651:            }
652:
653:            // Now that there is a Customer selected, the Account
654:            // operations can be enabled.
655:            accountChoice.setEnabled(true);
656:            newAccountButton.setEnabled(true);
657:
658:            setStatus(null);
659:        }
660:
661:        /**
662:         * Create a new Account with the given owner, Account type, and
663:         * initial balance.
664:         */
```

14

```
665:    protected void createAccount(Customer owner, String type, float
666:            initialBalance) {
667:
668:        setStatus("Creating new Account...");
669:        Account account = mySelectedBank.createAccount(owner, type,
670:            initialBalance);
671:        Hashtable accounts = (Hashtable)myAccounts.
672:            get(mySelectedCustomer);
673:
674:        // If there doesn't exist an index of Accounts for this
675:        // Customer already, create one.
676:        if (accounts == null) {
677:            accounts = new Hashtable();
678:            myAccounts.put(mySelectedCustomer, accounts);
679:        }
680:        String accountName = mySelectedBank.name() + ":" + account.
681:            accountNumber();
682:        accounts.put(accountName, account);
683:        accountChoice.add(accountName);
684:        myAccountBankMap.put(account, mySelectedBank);
685:
686:        if (mySelectedAccount == null) {
687:            mySelectedAccount = account;
688:        }
689:
690:        // Now that there is an Account selected, the Account
691:        // features can be enabled. Also update the Account info
692:        // display.
693:        enableAccountFeatures(true);
694:        updateAccountInfo();
695:
696:        setStatus(null);
697:    }
698:
699:    /**
700:     * Enable/disable the Account-related features.
701:     */
702:    protected void enableAccountFeatures(boolean enable) {
703:
704:        autoUpdateButton.enable(enable);
705:        transactionTextField.enable(enable);
706:        depositButton.enable(enable);
707:        withdrawButton.enable(enable);
708:        updateAccountButton.enable(enable);
709:        if (!enable) {
710:            issuingBankTextField.setText("");
711:            accountNumberTextField.setText("");
712:            accountTypeTextField.setText("");
713:            creationDateTextField.setText("");
714:            currentBalanceTextField.setText("");
715:            transactionTextField.setText("");
716:        }
717:    }
718:
```

14

continues

Listing 14.3. continued

```
719:      /**
720:       * Update the Account information to correspond to the
721:       * currently selected Account.
722:       */
723:      protected void updateAccountInfo() {
724:
725:          if (mySelectedAccount == null) {
726:              return;
727:          }
728:
729:          issuingBankTextField.setText(((Bank)myAccountBankMap.
730:                  get(mySelectedAccount)).name());
731:          accountNumberTextField.setText(mySelectedAccount.
732:                  accountNumber());
733:          if (CheckingAccountHelper.narrow(mySelectedAccount) !=
734:                  null) {
735:              accountTypeTextField.setText("Checking");
736:          } else {
737:
738:              // If Account is not a CheckingAccount, assume it is a
739:              // SavingsAccount
740:              accountTypeTextField.setText("Savings");
741:          }
742:          creationDateTextField.setText(mySelectedAccount.
743:                  creationDate());
744:          currentBalanceTextField.setText(String.
745:                  valueOf(mySelectedAccount.balance()));
746:      }
747:
748:      class SymAction implements java.awt.event.ActionListener {
749:
750:          public void actionPerformed(java.awt.event.ActionEvent
751:                  event) {
752:              Object object = event.getSource();
753:              if (object == newCustomerButton)
754:                  newCustomerButton_Action(event);
755:              else if (object == newAccountButton)
756:                  newAccountButton_Action(event);
757:              else if (object == autoUpdateButton)
758:                  autoUpdateButton_Action(event);
759:              else if (object == depositButton)
760:                  depositButton_Action(event);
761:              else if (object == withdrawButton)
762:                  withdrawButton_Action(event);
763:              else if (object == updateAccountButton)
764:                  updateAccountButton_Action(event);
765:          }
766:      }
767:
768:      void newCustomerButton_Action(java.awt.event.ActionEvent event)
769:          {
770:
```

14

```
771:        Container theFrame = this;
772:        do {
773:            theFrame = theFrame.getParent();
774:        } while ((theFrame != null) && !(theFrame instanceof
775:                Frame));
776:        if (theFrame == null)
777:            theFrame = new Frame();
778:
779:        CustomerDialog cd = new CustomerDialog((Frame)theFrame,
780:                true);
781:        cd.show();
782:        if (cd.myOKPressed) {
783:            createCustomer(cd.nameTextField.getText(), cd.
784:                    socialSecurityNumberTextField.getText(), cd.
785:                    addressTextField.getText(), cd.
786:                    mothersMaidenNameTextField.getText());
787:        }
788:    }
789:
790:    void newAccountButton_Action(java.awt.event.ActionEvent event)
791:        {
792:
793:        Container theFrame = this;
794:        do {
795:            theFrame = theFrame.getParent();
796:        } while ((theFrame != null) && !(theFrame instanceof
797:                Frame));
798:        if (theFrame == null)
799:            theFrame = new Frame();
800:
801:        AccountDialog ad = new AccountDialog((Frame)theFrame,
802:                true);
803:        ad.show();
804:        if (ad.myOKPressed) {
805:            createAccount(mySelectedCustomer, ad.checkingRadio.
806:                    getState() ? "checking" : "savings", new
807:                    Float(ad.initialBalanceTextField.getText()).
808:                    floatValue());
809:        }
810:    }
811:
812:    class SymItem implements java.awt.event.ItemListener {
813:
814:        public void itemStateChanged(java.awt.event.ItemEvent
815:                event) {
816:            Object object = event.getSource();
817:            if (object == bankChoice)
818:                bankChoice_ItemStateChanged(event);
819:            else if (object == atmChoice)
820:                atmChoice_ItemStateChanged(event);
821:            else if (object == customerChoice)
822:                customerChoice_ItemStateChanged(event);
823:            else if (object == accountChoice)
824:                accountChoice_ItemStateChanged(event);
825:        }
826:    }
827:
```

14

continues

Listing 14.3. continued

```
828:     void bankChoice_ItemStateChanged(java.awt.event.ItemEvent
829:           event) {
830:
831:        if (event.getStateChange() == ItemEvent.SELECTED) {
832:           mySelectedBank = (Bank)myBanks.get(bankChoice.
833:                 getSelectedItem());
834:        }
835:     }
836:
837:     void atmChoice_ItemStateChanged(java.awt.event.ItemEvent event)
838:           {
839:
840:        if (event.getStateChange() == ItemEvent.SELECTED) {
841:           mySelectedATM = (ATM)myATMs.get(atmChoice.
842:                 getSelectedItem());
843:        }
844:     }
845:
846:     void customerChoice_ItemStateChanged(java.awt.event.ItemEvent
847:           event) {
848:
849:        if (event.getStateChange() == ItemEvent.SELECTED) {
850:
851:           // Update the Account list to show the currently
852:           // selected Customer's Accounts.
853:           mySelectedCustomer = (Customer)myCustomers.
854:                 get(customerChoice.getSelectedItem());
855:           accountChoice.removeAll();
856:           Hashtable accounts = (Hashtable)myAccounts.
857:                 get(mySelectedCustomer);
858:           if (accounts != null) {
859:              Enumeration e = accounts.keys();
860:              while (e.hasMoreElements()) {
861:                 accountChoice.add((String)e.nextElement());
862:              }
863:           }
864:           mySelectedAccount = null;
865:           enableAccountFeatures(false);
866:        }
867:     }
868:
869:     void accountChoice_ItemStateChanged(java.awt.event.ItemEvent
870:           event) {
871:
872:        if (event.getStateChange() == ItemEvent.SELECTED) {
873:           Hashtable accounts = (Hashtable)myAccounts.
874:                 get(mySelectedCustomer);
875:           mySelectedAccount = (Account)accounts.
876:                 get(accountChoice.getSelectedItem());
877:           enableAccountFeatures(true);
878:           updateAccountInfo();
879:        }
880:     }
881:
```

14

```
882:    void autoUpdateButton_Action(java.awt.event.ActionEvent event)
883:            {
884:
885:        setStatus("Requesting AutoUpdate service for selected " +
886:                "Account...");
887:        try {
888:            ((Bank)myAccountBankMap.get(mySelectedAccount)).
889:                    requestUpdateService(mySelectedAccount);
890:        } catch (InvalidAccountException ex) {
891:            setStatus("Could not request AutoUpdate service for " +
892:                    "selected Account: InvalidAcccountException");
893:        }
894:        setStatus(null);
895:    }
896:
897:    void depositButton_Action(java.awt.event.ActionEvent event) {
898:
899:        String amount = transactionTextField.getText();
900:        setStatus("Depositing $" + amount + "...");
901:        float newBalance = 0.0f;
902:        try {
903:            newBalance = mySelectedAccount.deposit(new
904:                    Float(amount).floatValue());
905:        } catch (InvalidAmountException ex) {
906:            setStatus("Could not perform transaction: " +
907:                    "InvalidAmountException");
908:            return;
909:        } catch (NumberFormatException ex) {
910:            setStatus("Could not perform transaction: " +
911:                    "NumberFormatException");
912:            return;
913:        }
914:        currentBalanceTextField.setText(String.
915:                valueOf(newBalance));
916:        setStatus("Deposited $" + amount + " into selected " +
917:                "Account.");
918:    }
919:
920:    void withdrawButton_Action(java.awt.event.ActionEvent event) {
921:
922:        String amount = transactionTextField.getText();
923:        setStatus("Withdrawing $" + amount + "...");
924:        float newBalance = 0.0f;
925:        try {
926:            newBalance = mySelectedAccount.withdraw(new
927:                    Float(amount).floatValue());
928:        } catch (InvalidAmountException ex) {
929:            setStatus("Could not perform transaction: " +
930:                    "InvalidAmountException");
931:            return;
932:        } catch (InsufficientFundsException ex) {
933:            setStatus("Could not perform transaction: " +
934:                    "InsufficientFundsException");
935:            return;
936:        } catch (NumberFormatException ex) {
```

14

continues

Listing 14.3. continued

```
937:              setStatus("Could not perform transaction: " +
938:                  "NumberFormatException");
939:              return;
940:          }
941:          currentBalanceTextField.setText(String.
942:              valueOf(newBalance));
943:          setStatus("Withdrew $" + amount + " from selected " +
944:              "Account.");
945:      }
946:
947:      void updateAccountButton_Action(java.awt.event.ActionEvent
948:          event) {
949:
950:          updateAccountInfo();
951:      }
952: }
```

Now take a look at selected portions of BankApplet.java. The three import statements in lines 3-5 import the definitions of several GUI-related Java classes. The java.awt package and related packages contain the classes and interfaces that compose the Abstract Windowing Toolkit (AWT). The AWT is a collection of user interface objects and the event handling mechanism that enables those objects to interact with each other. Applications and libraries can build on the core AWT classes to create more complex user interface objects and entire user interfaces.

The java.util package includes a number of utility classes and interfaces. One interface is the Enumeration (imported in line 6), which enables the iteration across collections (such as Vector, Dictionary, Hashtable, and so on), much like a C++ Standard Template Library (STL) iterator. The Hashtable class (imported in line 7), as its name suggests, implements a *hash table* (a data structure that maps one object instance to another).

The imports in lines 9 and 10 should look familiar. Because BankApplet is a CORBA application, it must be able to access the familiar CORBA ORB and BOA.

Like the ATMClient that came before it, BankApplet makes use of the preceding CORBA objects and exceptions. (Recall that you placed all these definitions in the idlGlobal package when you ran the IDL compiler on Day 13.) Lines 12-22 import these classes into the application.

Note in lines 24 and 25 that the BankApplet class is declared to implement the AccountUpdateListener interface. This means that the BankApplet class must be able to implement the update() method from that interface, and you'll see later that this is indeed the case. It also means that a BankApplet object can be used as a parameter to any method requiring an AccountUpdateListener as a parameter.

14

For various reasons, the BankApplet keeps track of the currently selected Bank, ATM, Customer, and Account. The definitions of these member variables are found in lines 33-38.

The BankApplet must also keep track of which Bank names correspond to which Bank objects, which ATM names correspond to which ATM objects, and so on. This is so that the user can select each of these objects from a list of names, and the applet will be able to determine the actual object, given its name. The Hashtable class is ideally suited to this purpose; in most of the cases appearing in lines 40-58, it maps Strings to the appropriate object type.

Most of the init() method is omitted from this discussion because it was automatically generated by Visual Café. However, there are some additions, such as the code appearing in lines 491-493. This illustrates a second method of initializing the ORB. Recall that the first method used the command-line parameters from the Java application. Because a Java applet does not have command-line parameters, another form of initialization is used. This form of ORB.init() accepts an Applet as a parameter. From the Applet, the ORB gets its configuration information.

NOTE

Keep in mind that the ORB.init() method used in the example is a feature of VisiBroker for Java. Other products might (and almost certainly will) use a different method for initializing the ORB.

The bit of code in lines 495-507 will look familiar, but with a small twist. Rather than use System.out.println(), the code calls the setStatus() method. You'll see later exactly what this method does, but for now you only need to know that the method delivers a status message to the user.

Appearing in lines 509-533 is the familiar section of code that obtains the available Bank and ATM objects. When these lists are obtained, the addBanks() and addATMs() methods are called. Again, you'll see shortly what these methods do.

The setStatus() method (lines 571-582), alluded to before, takes a String as a parameter. If the String is null, a default status message is displayed (in this case, "BankApplet ready."); otherwise, the supplied String is displayed. Closer inspection reveals that the status message is displayed in the statusTextField object, the text field spanning the bottom of the BankApplet window.

Recall that BankApplet was required to implement the update() method as a part of implementing the AccountUpdateListener interface. The implementation, appearing in lines 584-599, displays a status message (through—what else—the setStatus() method), and if the information for the updated Account is currently being displayed, the display is updated.

14

The addBanks() method (lines 601-615), called earlier in init(), adds the names of the given Bank objects to the choice box containing names. The names, along with the Banks themselves, are then added to the myBanks hash table so that the Banks can later be retrieved by name. addATMs() is similar, except it works with ATMs.

The createCustomer() method, in lines 633-659, performs functionality similar to that in the previous ATMClient example. Note, in particular, that the method creates a new CustomerImpl object and registers the object with the BOA, using the obj_is_ready() method. In addition to performing this familiar functionality, createCustomer() adds the Customer to the internal hash table for future lookup. Finally, the method enables parts of the user interface that might have been previously disabled. For example, it doesn't make sense to create an Account before a Customer is created to be associated with that Account. Therefore, the Account creation features are disabled until there is a Customer selected.

Creating an Account is more involved, as evidenced by the longer createAccount() method in lines 661-697. The Account creation consists only of calling the createAccount() method on the currently selected Bank, but there is a bit more work involved with associating the newly created Account with the currently selected Customer. This is because there is a two-level hierarchy of Hashtables that relates Customers to their Accounts. In addition, the Hashtable of Accounts is keyed on the concatenation of the issuing Bank name and the Account number, instead of just the Account number itself (because two different Banks can issue the same Account number, but the keys must be unique). Figure 14.3 illustrates the relationship between Customers and their Accounts. Finally, if an Account is selected, certain features can be enabled, such as the Account transaction features. This is performed by the enableAccountFeatures() method, discussed next.

Figure 14.3.

Relationship between Customers *and* Accounts.

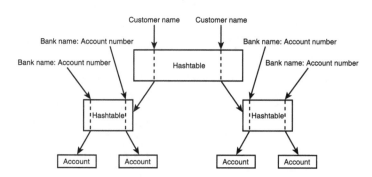

The enableAccountFeatures() method (lines 699-717) enables some Account-related user interface components if its parameter is true and disables them if the parameter is false. In addition, if the parameter is false, the text fields containing Account information are cleared.

The updateAccountInfo() method (lines 719-746) updates the display with the current information on the selected Account, such as issuing the Bank name, the account number, type, creation date, and current balance. Note in line 733 that the type of Account is determined by using the narrow() operation. In this case, CheckingAccountHelper.narrow() returns a CheckingAccount if the Account is indeed a CheckingAccount; otherwise, the operation returns null. (This is CORBA's version of what is commonly referred to as Runtime Type Information, or RTTI.)

The newCustomerButton_Action() method, which appears in lines 768-788, is called when the New Customer button is pressed. Basically, it creates a new CustomerDialog window (which you'll see later in the chapter) and calls createCustomer() with the information provided by that Dialog. The newAccountButton_Action() method operates in much the same manner.

The bankChoice_ItemStateChanged() method, which you can see in lines 828-835, is called when an item is selected in the Bank choice box. It looks up the Bank's name in the appropriate Hashtable to determine which Bank object corresponds to that name and then sets the currently selected Bank to this object. The atmChoice_ItemStateChanged() method behaves similarly. So do the customerChoice_ItemStateChanged() and accountChoice_ItemStateChanged() methods, although the latter two methods perform additional tasks when a new item is selected, such as updating the display with new information. In the case of a Customer selection, that Customer's Accounts are displayed in the Account choice box. In the case of an Account selection, the Account information display is updated with the newly selected Account.

The remaining BankApplet methods are straightforward: autoUpdateButton_Action() calls the appropriate Bank's requestUpdateService() method for the selected Account, depositButton_Action() calls deposit() on the selected Account with the amount indicated in the transaction text field, withdrawButton_Action() calls withdraw(), and updateAccountButton_Action() calls updateAccountInfo().

BankApplet **Dialogs**

In addition to the main BankApplet window, there are two other dialog boxes used in the applet. The first is the CustomerDialog, for entering information about a new Customer. The second is the AccountDialog, for entering information about a new Account. The layout of the CustomerDialog appears in Figure 14.4, with its corresponding hierarchy of interface objects appearing in Figure 14.5.

Figure 14.4.

CustomerDialog
window.

14

Figure 14.5.

CustomerDialog
window hierarchy.

Like BankApplet.java, most of CustomerDialog.java is generated by the GUI builder. Listing 14.4 shows CustomerDialog.java in its entirety. In the section following the listing, you'll pick apart the real functionality behind it.

Listing 14.4. CustomerDialog.java.

```
 1: // CustomerDialog.java
 2:
 3: import java.awt.*;
 4:
 5: public class CustomerDialog extends Dialog {
 6:
 7:     // Set to true if this dialog was completed by pressing OK.
 8:     public boolean myOKPressed = false;
 9:
10:     public CustomerDialog(Frame parent, boolean modal) {
11:
12:         super(parent, modal);
13:
14:         //{{INIT_CONTROLS
15:         GridBagLayout gridBagLayout;
16:         gridBagLayout = new GridBagLayout();
17:         setLayout(gridBagLayout);
18:         setVisible(false);
19:         setSize(insets().left + insets().right + 435, insets().top
20:                 + insets().bottom + 110);
21:         setBackground(new Color(-4144944));
22:         nameTextField = new java.awt.TextField();
23:         nameTextField.setBounds(insets().left + 148, insets().top +
24:                 3, 218, 23);
25:         GridBagConstraints gbc;
26:         gbc = new GridBagConstraints();
27:         gbc.gridx = 1;
28:         gbc.gridy = 0;
29:         gbc.weightx = 1.0;
30:         gbc.fill = GridBagConstraints.HORIZONTAL;
31:         gbc.insets = new Insets(2, 2, 2, 2);
32:         ((GridBagLayout)getLayout()).setConstraints(nameTextField,
33:                 gbc);
34:         add(nameTextField);
35:         socialSecurityNumberTextField = new java.awt.TextField();
36:         socialSecurityNumberTextField.setBounds(insets().left +
37:                 148, insets().top + 30, 218, 23);
```

14

```
38:        gbc = new GridBagConstraints();
39:        gbc.gridx = 1;
40:        gbc.gridy = 1;
41:        gbc.weightx = 1.0;
42:        gbc.fill = GridBagConstraints.HORIZONTAL;
43:        gbc.insets = new Insets(2, 2, 2, 2);
44:        ((GridBagLayout)getLayout()).
45:                setConstraints(socialSecurityNumberTextField, gbc);
46:        add(socialSecurityNumberTextField);
47:        addressTextField = new java.awt.TextField();
48:        addressTextField.setBounds(insets().left + 148, insets().
49:                top + 57, 218, 23);
50:        gbc = new GridBagConstraints();
51:        gbc.gridx = 1;
52:        gbc.gridy = 2;
53:        gbc.weightx = 1.0;
54:        gbc.fill = GridBagConstraints.HORIZONTAL;
55:        gbc.insets = new Insets(2, 2, 2, 2);
56:        ((GridBagLayout)getLayout()).
57:                setConstraints(addressTextField, gbc);
58:        add(addressTextField);
59:        mothersMaidenNameTextField = new java.awt.TextField();
60:        mothersMaidenNameTextField.setBounds(insets().left + 148,
61:                insets().top + 84, 218, 23);
62:        gbc = new GridBagConstraints();
63:        gbc.gridx = 1;
64:        gbc.gridy = 3;
65:        gbc.weightx = 1.0;
66:        gbc.fill = GridBagConstraints.HORIZONTAL;
67:        gbc.insets = new Insets(2, 2, 2, 2);
68:        ((GridBagLayout)getLayout()).
69:                setConstraints(mothersMaidenNameTextField, gbc);
70:        add(mothersMaidenNameTextField);
71:        okButton = new java.awt.Button();
72:        okButton.setActionCommand("button");
73:        okButton.setLabel("OK");
74:        okButton.setBounds(insets().left + 370, insets().top + 3,
75:                63, 23);
76:        gbc = new GridBagConstraints();
77:        gbc.gridx = 2;
78:        gbc.gridy = 0;
79:        gbc.anchor = GridBagConstraints.NORTHEAST;
80:        gbc.fill = GridBagConstraints.HORIZONTAL;
81:        gbc.insets = new Insets(2, 2, 2, 2);
82:        ((GridBagLayout)getLayout()).setConstraints(okButton, gbc);
83:        add(okButton);
84:        okButton.setEnabled(false);
85:        cancelButton = new java.awt.Button();
86:        cancelButton.setActionCommand("button");
87:        cancelButton.setLabel("Cancel");
88:        cancelButton.setBounds(insets().left + 370, insets().top +
89:                30, 63, 23);
90:        gbc = new GridBagConstraints();
91:        gbc.gridx = 2;
92:        gbc.gridy = 1;
93:        gbc.anchor = GridBagConstraints.NORTHEAST;
```

14

continues

Listing 14.4. continued

```
94:              gbc.fill = GridBagConstraints.HORIZONTAL;
95:              gbc.insets = new Insets(2, 2, 2, 2);
96:              gbc.ipadx = 10;
97:              ((GridBagLayout)getLayout()).setConstraints(cancelButton,
98:                      gbc);
99:              add(cancelButton);
100:             nameLabel = new java.awt.Label("Name");
101:             nameLabel.setBounds(insets().left + 2, insets().top + 3,
102:                     48, 23);
103:             gbc = new GridBagConstraints();
104:             gbc.gridx = 0;
105:             gbc.gridy = 0;
106:             gbc.anchor = GridBagConstraints.WEST;
107:             gbc.fill = GridBagConstraints.NONE;
108:             gbc.insets = new Insets(2, 2, 2, 2);
109:             ((GridBagLayout)getLayout()).setConstraints(nameLabel,
110:                     gbc);
111:             add(nameLabel);
112:             socialSecurityNumberLabel = new java.awt.
113:                     Label("Social Security Number");
114:             socialSecurityNumberLabel.setBounds(insets().left + 2,
115:                     insets().top + 30, 142, 23);
116:             gbc = new GridBagConstraints();
117:             gbc.gridx = 0;
118:             gbc.gridy = 1;
119:             gbc.anchor = GridBagConstraints.WEST;
120:             gbc.fill = GridBagConstraints.NONE;
121:             gbc.insets = new Insets(2, 2, 2, 2);
122:             ((GridBagLayout)getLayout()).
123:                     setConstraints(socialSecurityNumberLabel, gbc);
124:             add(socialSecurityNumberLabel);
125:             addressLabel = new java.awt.Label("Address");
126:             addressLabel.setBounds(insets().left + 2, insets().top +
127:                     57, 60, 23);
128:             gbc = new GridBagConstraints();
129:             gbc.gridx = 0;
130:             gbc.gridy = 2;
131:             gbc.anchor = GridBagConstraints.WEST;
132:             gbc.fill = GridBagConstraints.NONE;
133:             gbc.insets = new Insets(2, 2, 2, 2);
134:             ((GridBagLayout)getLayout()).setConstraints(addressLabel,
135:                     gbc);
136:             add(addressLabel);
137:             mothersMaidenNameLabel = new java.awt.
138:                     Label("Mother's Maiden Name");
139:             mothersMaidenNameLabel.setBounds(insets().left + 2,
140:                     insets().top + 84, 140, 23);
141:             gbc = new GridBagConstraints();
142:             gbc.gridx = 0;
143:             gbc.gridy = 3;
144:             gbc.anchor = GridBagConstraints.WEST;
145:             gbc.fill = GridBagConstraints.NONE;
146:             gbc.insets = new Insets(2, 2, 2, 2);
147:             ((GridBagLayout)getLayout()).
148:                     setConstraints(mothersMaidenNameLabel, gbc);
```

```
149:            add(mothersMaidenNameLabel);
150:            setTitle("New Customer Information");
151:            //}}
152:
153:            //{{REGISTER_LISTENERS
154:            SymWindow aSymWindow = new SymWindow();
155:            this.addWindowListener(aSymWindow);
156:            SymAction lSymAction = new SymAction();
157:            okButton.addActionListener(lSymAction);
158:            cancelButton.addActionListener(lSymAction);
159:            SymText lSymText = new SymText();
160:            nameTextField.addTextListener(lSymText);
161:            socialSecurityNumberTextField.addTextListener(lSymText);
162:            addressTextField.addTextListener(lSymText);
163:            mothersMaidenNameTextField.addTextListener(lSymText);
164:            //}}
165:        }
166:
167:    public void addNotify() {
168:
169:        // Record the size of the window prior to calling parent's
170:        // addNotify.
171:        Dimension d = getSize();
172:
173:        super.addNotify();
174:
175:        if (fComponentsAdjusted)
176:            return;
177:
178:        // Adjust components according to the insets
179:        setSize(insets().left + insets().right + d.width, insets().
180:                top + insets().bottom + d.height);
181:        Component components[] = getComponents();
182:        for (int i = 0; i < components.length; i++)
183:        {
184:            Point p = components[i].getLocation();
185:            p.translate(insets().left, insets().top);
186:            components[i].setLocation(p);
187:        }
188:        fComponentsAdjusted = true;
189:    }
190:
191:    // Used for addNotify check.
192:    boolean fComponentsAdjusted = false;
193:
194:    public CustomerDialog(Frame parent, String title, boolean
195:            modal) {
196:
197:        this(parent, modal);
198:        setTitle(title);
199:    }
200:
201:    public synchronized void show() {
202:
203:        Rectangle bounds = getParent().bounds();
204:        Rectangle abounds = bounds();
205:
```

14

continues

Listing 14.4. continued

```
206:            move(bounds.x + (bounds.width - abounds.width) / 2,
207:                bounds.y + (bounds.height - abounds.height) /2);
208:
209:            super.show();
210:        }
211:
212:        //{{DECLARE_CONTROLS
213:        java.awt.TextField nameTextField;
214:        java.awt.TextField socialSecurityNumberTextField;
215:        java.awt.TextField addressTextField;
216:        java.awt.TextField mothersMaidenNameTextField;
217:        java.awt.Button okButton;
218:        java.awt.Button cancelButton;
219:        java.awt.Label nameLabel;
220:        java.awt.Label socialSecurityNumberLabel;
221:        java.awt.Label addressLabel;
222:        java.awt.Label mothersMaidenNameLabel;
223:        //}}
224:
225:        class SymWindow extends java.awt.event.WindowAdapter {
226:
227:            public void windowClosing(java.awt.event.WindowEvent event)
228:                    {
229:                Object object = event.getSource();
230:                if (object == CustomerDialog.this)
231:                    Dialog1_WindowClosing(event);
232:            }
233:        }
234:
235:        void Dialog1_WindowClosing(java.awt.event.WindowEvent event) {
236:
237:            hide();
238:        }
239:
240:        class SymAction implements java.awt.event.ActionListener {
241:
242:            public void actionPerformed(java.awt.event.ActionEvent
243:                    event) {
244:
245:                Object object = event.getSource();
246:                if (object == okButton)
247:                    okButton_Action(event);
248:                else if (object == cancelButton)
249:                    cancelButton_Action(event);
250:            }
251:        }
252:
253:        void okButton_Action(java.awt.event.ActionEvent event) {
254:
255:            myOKPressed = true;
256:            setVisible(false);
257:        }
258:
259:        void cancelButton_Action(java.awt.event.ActionEvent event) {
260:
```

14

```
261:            setVisible(false);
262:        }
263:
264:        class SymText implements java.awt.event.TextListener {
265:
266:            public void textValueChanged(java.awt.event.TextEvent
267:                    event) {
268:
269:                Object object = event.getSource();
270:                if (object == nameTextField)
271:                    nameTextField_TextValueChanged(event);
272:                else if (object == socialSecurityNumberTextField)
273:                    socialSecurityNumberTextField_TextValueChanged
274:                            (event);
275:                else if (object == addressTextField)
276:                    addressTextField_TextValueChanged(event);
277:                else if (object == mothersMaidenNameTextField)
278:                    mothersMaidenNameTextField_TextValueChanged(event);
279:            }
280:        }
281:
282:        void nameTextField_TextValueChanged(java.awt.event.TextEvent
283:                event) {
284:
285:            okButton.setEnabled((nameTextField.getText().length() > 0)
286:                    && (socialSecurityNumberTextField.getText().
287:                    length() > 0) && (addressTextField.getText().
288:                    length() > 0) && (mothersMaidenNameTextField.
289:                    getText().length() > 0));
290:        }
291:
292:        void socialSecurityNumberTextField_TextValueChanged(java.awt.
293:                event.TextEvent event) {
294:
295:            okButton.setEnabled((nameTextField.getText().length() > 0)
296:                    && (socialSecurityNumberTextField.getText().
297:                    length() > 0) && (addressTextField.getText().
298:                    length() > 0) && (mothersMaidenNameTextField.
299:                    getText().length() > 0));
300:        }
301:
302:        void addressTextField_TextValueChanged(java.awt.event.TextEvent
303:                event) {
304:
305:            okButton.setEnabled((nameTextField.getText().length() > 0)
306:                    && (socialSecurityNumberTextField.getText().
307:                    length() > 0) && (addressTextField.getText().
308:                    length() > 0) && (mothersMaidenNameTextField.
309:                    getText().length() > 0));
310:        }
311:
312:        void mothersMaidenNameTextField_TextValueChanged(java.awt.
313:                event.TextEvent event) {
314:
315:            okButton.setEnabled((nameTextField.getText().length() > 0)
316:                    && (socialSecurityNumberTextField.getText().
```

14

continues

Listing 14.4. continued

```
317:                          length() > 0) && (addressTextField.getText().
318:                          length() > 0) && (mothersMaidenNameTextField.
319:                          getText().length() > 0));
320:      }
321: }
```

Now, let's inspect what is happening under the hood of `CustomerDialog.java`. When the OK button is pressed, `okButton_Action()` (lines 253-257) is called. This method hides the `CustomerDialog` and sets a flag to indicate that the dialog was closed by pressing the OK button (the `BankApplet` checks this flag to determine whether the `CustomerDialog` information should be processed). `cancelButton_Action()` (lines 259-262) behaves similarly but does not set this flag.

When the `Customer` name text field changes (in other words, the user presses a key in the field), the `nameTextField_TextValueChanged()` method (lines 282-290) is called. The method disables the OK button unless a value is entered into all the text fields (that is, the length of the text in each field is greater than zero), in which case the OK button is enabled. (The Cancel button is always enabled and, thus, can be pressed at any time.) Each text field has a method that behaves similarly: `socialSecurityNumberTextField_TextValueChanged()` (lines 292-300), `addressTextField_TextValueChanged()` (lines 302-310), and `mothersMaidenName TextField_TextValueChanged()` (lines 312-320) all duplicate this behavior.

The next component of the `BankApplet` is the `AccountDialog`, an illustration of which appears in Figure 14.6 and whose window hierarchy appears in Figure 14.7. `AccountDialog.java`, which (you guessed it) consists mostly of generated code, appears in Listing 14.5.

Figure 14.6.

`AccountDialog`
window.

Figure 14.7.

`AccountDialog`
window hierarchy.

14

Listing 14.5. `AccountDialog.java`.

```
1: // AccountDialog.java
2:
3: import java.awt.*;
4:
5: public class AccountDialog extends Dialog {
6:
7:     // Set to true if this dialog was completed by pressing OK.
8:     public boolean myOKPressed = false;
9:
10:     public AccountDialog(Frame parent, boolean modal) {
11:
12:         super(parent, modal);
13:
14:         //{{INIT_CONTROLS
15:         GridBagLayout gridBagLayout;
16:         gridBagLayout = new GridBagLayout();
17:         setLayout(gridBagLayout);
18:         setVisible(false);
19:         setSize(insets().left + insets().right + 277, insets().top
20:                 + insets().bottom + 124);
21:         setBackground(new Color(-4144944));
22:         Group1 = new CheckboxGroup();
23:         checkingRadio = new java.awt.Checkbox("Checking", Group1,
24:                 true);
25:         checkingRadio.setBounds(insets().left + 2, insets().top +
26:                 29, 82, 23);
27:         GridBagConstraints gbc;
28:         gbc = new GridBagConstraints();
29:         gbc.gridx = 0;
30:         gbc.gridy = 1;
31:         gbc.anchor = GridBagConstraints.WEST;
32:         gbc.fill = GridBagConstraints.NONE;
33:         gbc.insets = new Insets(2, 2, 2, 2);
34:         ((GridBagLayout)getLayout()).setConstraints(checkingRadio,
35:                 gbc);
36:         add(checkingRadio);
37:         savingsRadio = new java.awt.Checkbox("Savings", Group1,
38:                 false);
39:         savingsRadio.setBounds(insets().left + 2, insets().top +
40:                 56, 74, 23);
41:         gbc = new GridBagConstraints();
42:         gbc.gridx = 0;
43:         gbc.gridy = 2;
44:         gbc.anchor = GridBagConstraints.WEST;
45:         gbc.fill = GridBagConstraints.NONE;
46:         gbc.insets = new Insets(2, 2, 2, 2);
47:         ((GridBagLayout)getLayout()).setConstraints(savingsRadio,
48:                 gbc);
49:         add(savingsRadio);
50:         initialBalanceTextField = new java.awt.TextField();
51:         initialBalanceTextField.setBounds(insets().left + 122,
52:                 insets().top + 99, 86, 23);
```

14

continues

Listing 14.5. continued

```
53:        gbc = new GridBagConstraints();
54:        gbc.gridx = 2;
55:        gbc.gridy = 3;
56:        gbc.weightx = 1.0;
57:        gbc.anchor = GridBagConstraints.SOUTH;
58:        gbc.fill = GridBagConstraints.HORIZONTAL;
59:        gbc.insets = new Insets(2, 2, 2, 2);
60:        ((GridBagLayout)getLayout()).
61:                setConstraints(initialBalanceTextField, gbc);
62:        add(initialBalanceTextField);
63:        okButton = new java.awt.Button();
64:        okButton.setActionCommand("button");
65:        okButton.setLabel("OK");
66:        okButton.setBounds(insets().left + 212, insets().top + 2,
67:                63, 23);
68:        gbc = new GridBagConstraints();
69:        gbc.gridx = 3;
70:        gbc.gridy = 0;
71:        gbc.anchor = GridBagConstraints.NORTHEAST;
72:        gbc.fill = GridBagConstraints.HORIZONTAL;
73:        gbc.insets = new Insets(2, 2, 2, 2);
74:        ((GridBagLayout)getLayout()).setConstraints(okButton, gbc);
75:        add(okButton);
76:        cancelButton = new java.awt.Button();
77:        cancelButton.setActionCommand("button");
78:        cancelButton.setLabel("Cancel");
79:        cancelButton.setBounds(insets().left + 212, insets().top +
80:                29, 63, 23);
81:        gbc = new GridBagConstraints();
82:        gbc.gridx = 3;
83:        gbc.gridy = 1;
84:        gbc.anchor = GridBagConstraints.NORTHEAST;
85:        gbc.fill = GridBagConstraints.HORIZONTAL;
86:        gbc.insets = new Insets(2, 2, 2, 2);
87:        gbc.ipadx = 10;
88:        ((GridBagLayout)getLayout()).setConstraints(cancelButton,
89:                gbc);
90:        add(cancelButton);
91:        accountTypeLabel = new java.awt.Label("Account Type");
92:        accountTypeLabel.setBounds(insets().left + 2, insets().top
93:                + 2, 86, 23);
94:        gbc = new GridBagConstraints();
95:        gbc.gridx = 0;
96:        gbc.gridy = 0;
97:        gbc.anchor = GridBagConstraints.WEST;
98:        gbc.fill = GridBagConstraints.NONE;
99:        gbc.insets = new Insets(2, 2, 2, 2);
100:       ((GridBagLayout)getLayout()).
101:               setConstraints(accountTypeLabel, gbc);
102:       add(accountTypeLabel);
103:       initialBalanceLabel = new java.awt.Label("Initial Balance");
104:       initialBalanceLabel.setBounds(insets().left + 2, insets().
105:               top + 99, 91, 23);
```

14

```
106:        gbc = new GridBagConstraints();
107:        gbc.gridx = 0;
108:        gbc.gridy = 3;
109:        gbc.weighty = 1.0;
110:        gbc.anchor = GridBagConstraints.SOUTHWEST;
111:        gbc.fill = GridBagConstraints.NONE;
112:        gbc.insets = new Insets(2, 2, 2, 2);
113:        ((GridBagLayout)getLayout()).
114:                setConstraints(initialBalanceLabel, gbc);
115:        add(initialBalanceLabel);
116:        dollarLabel = new java.awt.Label("$", Label.RIGHT);
117:        dollarLabel.setBounds(insets().left + 97, insets().top +
118:                99, 21, 23);
119:        gbc = new GridBagConstraints();
120:        gbc.gridx = 1;
121:        gbc.gridy = 3;
122:        gbc.anchor = GridBagConstraints.SOUTHEAST;
123:        gbc.fill = GridBagConstraints.NONE;
124:        gbc.insets = new Insets(2, 2, 2, 2);
125:        ((GridBagLayout)getLayout()).setConstraints(dollarLabel,
126:                gbc);
127:        add(dollarLabel);
128:        setTitle("New Account Information");
129:        //}}
130:
131:        //{{REGISTER_LISTENERS
132:        SymWindow aSymWindow = new SymWindow();
133:        this.addWindowListener(aSymWindow);
134:        SymAction lSymAction = new SymAction();
135:        okButton.addActionListener(lSymAction);
136:        cancelButton.addActionListener(lSymAction);
137:        //}}
138:    }
139:
140:    public void addNotify() {
141:
142:        // Record the size of the window prior to calling parent's
143:        // addNotify.
144:        Dimension d = getSize();
145:
146:        super.addNotify();
147:
148:        if (fComponentsAdjusted)
149:            return;
150:
151:        // Adjust components according to the insets
152:        setSize(insets().left + insets().right + d.width, insets().
153:                top + insets().bottom + d.height);
154:        Component components[] = getComponents();
155:        for (int i = 0; i < components.length; i++) {
156:            Point p = components[i].getLocation();
157:            p.translate(insets().left, insets().top);
158:            components[i].setLocation(p);
159:        }
160:        fComponentsAdjusted = true;
161:    }
162:
```

continues

Listing 14.5. continued

```
163:    // Used for addNotify check.
164:    boolean fComponentsAdjusted = false;
165:
166:    public AccountDialog(Frame parent, String title, boolean modal)
167:            {
168:
169:        this(parent, modal);
170:        setTitle(title);
171:    }
172:
173:    public synchronized void show() {
174:
175:        Rectangle bounds = getParent().bounds();
176:        Rectangle abounds = bounds();
177:
178:        move(bounds.x + (bounds.width - abounds.width) / 2,
179:             bounds.y + (bounds.height - abounds.height) / 2);
180:
181:        super.show();
182:    }
183:
184:    //{{DECLARE_CONTROLS
185:    java.awt.Checkbox checkingRadio;
186:    CheckboxGroup Group1;
187:    java.awt.Checkbox savingsRadio;
188:    java.awt.TextField initialBalanceTextField;
189:    java.awt.Button okButton;
190:    java.awt.Button cancelButton;
191:    java.awt.Label accountTypeLabel;
192:    java.awt.Label initialBalanceLabel;
193:    java.awt.Label dollarLabel;
194:    //}}
195:
196:    class SymWindow extends java.awt.event.WindowAdapter {
197:
198:        public void windowClosing(java.awt.event.WindowEvent event)
199:                {
200:
201:            Object object = event.getSource();
202:            if (object == AccountDialog.this)
203:                Dialog1_WindowClosing(event);
204:        }
205:    }
206:
207:    void Dialog1_WindowClosing(java.awt.event.WindowEvent event) {
208:
209:        hide();
210:    }
211:
212:    class SymAction implements java.awt.event.ActionListener {
213:
214:        public void actionPerformed(java.awt.event.ActionEvent
215:                event) {
216:
```

14

```
217:                 Object object = event.getSource();
218:                 if (object == okButton)
219:                     okButton_Action(event);
220:                 else if (object == cancelButton)
221:                     cancelButton_Action(event);
222:             }
223:     }
224:
225:     void okButton_Action(java.awt.event.ActionEvent event) {
226:
227:         myOKPressed = true;
228:         setVisible(false);
229:     }
230:
231:     void cancelButton_Action(java.awt.event.ActionEvent event) {
232:
233:         setVisible(false);
234:     }
235: }
```

Because the `AccountDialog` is even simpler than the `CustomerDialog`, it takes no time at all to review. The `okButton_Action()` (lines 225-229) and `cancelButton_Action()` (lines 231-234) methods behave identically to their counterparts in `CustomerDialog`; all other code is generated by the GUI builder.

The final component of the `BankApplet` (or any applet, for that matter) is an HTML file containing an `<APPLET>` tag. The HTML file should be placed in the same directory as the `BankApplet.class` file that is output from the Java compiler. In the case of the `BankApplet`, this can be a very simple HTML file, as in Listing 14.6.

Listing 14.6. `BankApplet.html`.

```
 1: <HTML>
 2: <HEAD>
 3: <TITLE>BankApplet, a sample CORBA applet</TITLE>
 4: </HEAD>
 5: <BODY>
 6: <APPLET CODE="BankApplet.class" WIDTH=404 HEIGHT=327>
 7: <PARAM NAME=org.omg.CORBA.ORBClass
 8: VALUE=com.visigenic.vbroker.orb.ORB>
 9: </APPLET>
10: </BODY>
11: </HTML>
```

14

In particular, note three aspects of the `<APPLET>` tag in the `BankApplet.html` file. First, note the `CODE="BankApplet.class"` parameter in line 6. This indicates the file in which the main part of the applet resides (in other words, the class that derives from `java.awt.applet.Applet`). Next, note the `WIDTH` and `HEIGHT` parameters, also in line 6. These indicate the initial size of the applet window. Finally, notice the parameter `<PARAM NAME=org.omg.CORBA.ORBClass VALUE=com.visigenic.vbroker.orb.ORB>` in lines 7 and 8. This parameter, intended for Visigenic's VisiBroker for Java 3.0, tells the browser to use the supplied VisiBroker classes instead of the built-in classes (for browsers, such as Communicator, that have VisiBroker built in).

Running the Applet

As mentioned before, the server components used with the `BankApplet` are unchanged from those used with the Java version of the `ATMClient`. You can refer to Day 13 to review the process for starting up the `BankServer`, the `Bank`, and the `ATM`. To make things interesting, you might want to start more than one `Bank` and `ATM` so you can see how the choice boxes work when you run the `BankApplet`.

When the server components are up and running, you might be required to run other components as well, depending on the CORBA product you are using. To enable applets to connect to other hosts, for example, Visigenic's VisiBroker includes the GateKeeper, which serves as a gateway between applets and CORBA servers. If you're using VisiBroker, starting the GateKeeper is simple enough:

```
GateKeeper
```

The GateKeeper responds with output similar to the following:

```
VisiBroker Developer for Java [03.00.00.C3.05] (SEP 08 1997
16:55:51) IIOP GateKeeper started: Mon Nov 03 01:50:51 GMT+00:00
1997
Java: Version 1.1.4 from Sun Microsystems Inc.
OS:   Windows 95 version 4.0; CPU: x86
Adding search path: .
Adding search path: C:\Bin\Devel\Java\VCafe\BIN\COMPONENTS\
SYMBEANS.JAR
Adding search path: C:\Bin\Devel\Java\VCafe\JAVA\LIB
Adding search path: D:\Bin\Devel\VisiBroker\lib\vbj30.jar
Adding search path: .
Adding search path: D:\Bin\Devel\TeachYourselfCORBA\BankExample\
ch14
Adding search path: D:\Bin\Devel\TeachYourselfCORBA\BankExample\
ch14\Customer
Writing IOR to D:\Bin\Devel\TeachYourselfCORBA\BankExample\ch14\
BankApplet\gatekeeper.ior
```

The actual output depends on your `CLASSPATH` setting, but if you get something resembling the preceding, you are ready to run the `BankApplet`.

You have two options for running the `BankApplet`: using the `appletviewer` application provided with the Java Developer's Kit or using a Java-enabled Web browser such as Netscape Navigator, Netscape Communicator, Microsoft Internet Explorer, and so on. Now you'll learn how to run the applet in both environments.

14

Using `appletviewer`

As stated before, `appletviewer` is a utility that ships with Sun's Java Development Kit (JDK) and is included with Java development products. The `appletviewer`'s purpose, which can be deduced from its name, is to run applets. To run the `BankApplet` in the `appletviewer`, first ensure that the `appletviewer` exists in your PATH. (If you have previously installed the JDK or another Java development tool, chances are that your PATH is already configured properly.) Next, as always, you want to be sure that your CLASSPATH is configured correctly. Finally, change to the directory that contains `BankApplet.html`, `BankApplet.class`, and so on, and start the `appletviewer`:

```
appletviewer BankApplet.html
```

If you're using VisiBroker, you will see something similar to the following within a few seconds:

```
VisiBroker Developer for Java [03.00.00.C3.05] (SEP 08 1997
16:55:51) started Mon Nov 03 12:55:19 GMT+00:00 1997
Visigenic Software: http://www.visigenic.com/
Locator: 153.36.240.254:-1
Local Environment:
        Java: Version 1.1.4 from Sun Microsystems Inc.
        OS:   Windows 95 version 4.0; CPU: x86
Remote Environment:
        Java: Version 1.1.4 from Sun Microsystems Inc.
        OS:   Windows 95 version 4.0; CPU: x86
```

After a few more seconds, the `appletviewer` window appears. Within a few more seconds, it initializes the `BankApplet`, resulting in a display that resembles Figure 14.8.

Figure 14.8.

BankApplet *running in* `appletviewer`.

If you see a Bank name and an ATM name in the appropriate choice boxes, then so far, so good. If you don't, make sure that at least one Bank and ATM server has been started, and then restart the `appletviewer`.

Now, press the New button next to the Customer choice box. A dialog box appears, like the one in Figure 14.9. Enter some information into the dialog, as in Figure 14.10. When you've entered something in every text box, you will see the OK button enabled. When you're satisfied with what you've entered, press OK.

14

Figure 14.9.

Initial `CustomerDialog` *display.*

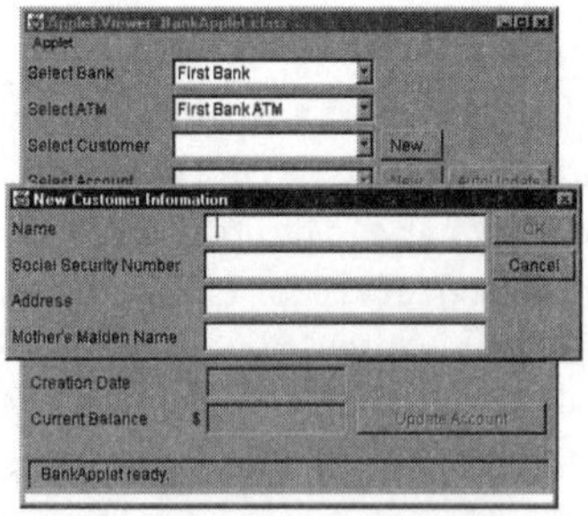

Figure 14.10.

`CustomerDialog` *display filled in.*

When you press OK in the `CustomerDialog`, you are returned to the main `BankApplet` screen, with the message `Creating new Customer...` appearing in the status display. After a moment, the status returns to `BankApplet ready` and your new `Customer`'s name appears in the `Customer` choice box.

Now, create a new `Account` for the `Customer` by pressing the New button next to the `Account` choice box. The `AccountDialog` window will appear, as shown in Figure 14.11.

Figure 14.11.

Initial `AccountDialog` *display.*

In the `AccountDialog`, leave `Checking` selected for the `Account` type. Enter an initial balance into the appropriate text field, as demonstrated in Figure 14.12. Then press OK. (The applet accepts a blank initial balance; in this case, the `Account` is given an initial balance of zero.)

14

Figure 14.12.
AccountDialog *display filled in.*

Now the main BankApplet screen reappears, displaying for a moment the message Creating new Account... in the status area. The status then returns to BankApplet ready, at which point the window displays the Account information, as shown in Figure 14.13.

Figure 14.13.
BankApplet *displaying* Account *information.*

Try a few transactions. Enter an amount into the Transactions text box and press the Deposit or Withdraw button. See what happens when you try to withdraw too much money. When you're convinced that transactions work correctly, press the AutoUpdate button. After a minute at most, you will see the Account's balance increase by 5 percent (don't you wish your own bank balance would increase so quickly?)

Feel free to put the applet through its paces. Create a number of Customers and various Accounts for them in different Banks. Switch between Customers and Accounts and watch the information on the screen update accordingly.

Using a Web Browser

You can also run the applet inside a Java-enabled Web browser such as Netscape Communicator, although setting up the applet is more involved. First, you need access to a Web server (also called an HTTP server or an HTTP daemon). You then need to place the BankApplet.html file and the .class files for the BankApplet in a directory visible to the Web server (consult the documentation for the Web server if you're unsure how to do this). Run the server components (and GateKeeper, if necessary) as you did in the previous step.

14

When all the servers are running, start your Web browser and enter the appropriate URL for the page containing the `BankApplet`. (The correct URL depends on the configuration of your Web server and the location of the files you created.) The applet might take a moment or two to start, but when it does, your browser window will resemble the one appearing in Figure 14.14.

Figure 14.14.

`BankApplet` *running in a Web browser.*

Congratulations! You have successfully deployed a Web-based CORBA application. (You should appreciate that this is a much more significant achievement than writing a cute little animated applet.)

Summary

Today, a grand finale for the sample `Bank` application, you built a Java applet to replace the `ATMClient` from Day 13 with a graphical user interface. Due to limited space, many details of developing applets in Java were not discussed today, but nevertheless, you were able to run the applet using both the `appletviewer` utility from the JDK and a Java-enabled Web browser. You now recognize the potential that comes with the capability to deploy CORBA applications—even just the end-user interface of such applications—on the Web. In many cases, the capability to run an enterprise-wide application within a Web browser demonstrates sound benefits: Java's portability enables the application to be distributed to a wide range of platforms. Also, the delivery mechanism is simplified, compared to previous methods, making it a relatively trivial matter to distribute updates to users geographically dispersed throughout an enterprise.

14

Q&A

Q **Why are the listings in this chapter, especially BankApplet.java, so much longer than in previous chapters?**

A Because the example in this chapter implements an application with a Graphical User Interface (GUI), it is understandably more complex than its simpler, console-based counterpart. Creating the various user interface components and handling the events generated by them adds a great deal of complexity to the application. Fortunately, most of the code required to implement GUI interfaces is generated by development tools.

Q **I don't have Visual Café; can I still run the sample applet from this chapter?**

A Although Visual Café was used to produce the sample applet in this chapter, you don't need it—or any other Java development tool, for that matter, other than the freely available JDK—to run the sample applet. Having Visual Café enables easier modification of the applet, but you should be able to work with virtually any Java development tool.

Workshop

The following section will help you test your comprehension of the material presented in this chapter and put what you've learned into practice. You'll find the answers to the quiz in Appendix A.

Quiz

1. Why might it be advantageous to deploy a CORBA client as a Java applet?
2. Why is it useful for browsers to include CORBA-related classes that are built in (for example, Netscape's Communicator includes Visigenic's VisiBroker for Java runtime)?
3. What is a potential disadvantage to the bundling scheme described in question 2?

Exercise

Extend the BankApplet to do even more cool stuff. You could add tabbed panels to display the Accounts belonging to a particular Customer. Or you could extend the applet to allow multiple Customers to be associated with an Account and extend the Account information correspondingly to show all the Customers associated with a given Account. (Because this is an open-ended exercise, no answer is given.)

14

WEEK

2

In Review

In the first part of the second week, you continued to enhance the sample application carried over from the first week. You then shifted gears to handle some more advanced topics such as CORBA design issues, use of the Dynamic Invocation Interface (DII), and the use of various CORBAservices and CORBAfacilities. Days 13 and 14 introduced you to the use of CORBA with the Java programming language and gave you the opportunity to develop a Java applet that implemented the client side of the application.

Developing a CORBA Application, Part 2

On Day 8 you added a simulated Automated Teller Machine (ATM) capability to the sample application, further enhancing its functionality. Day 9 introduced you to push technology, explained how the concept of push fits into CORBA, and gave you the opportunity to integrate push features in the sample application.

Advanced CORBA

Day 10 introduced you to some various design issues associated with CORBA, bringing you to an advanced level of CORBA discussion. Day 11 continued the advanced topics by introducing the Dynamic Invocation Interface (DII), a mechanism that allows clients to learn about server interfaces at runtime. Day 12 brought your attention to the various CORBAservices and CORBAfacilities, which, as you learned, include both horizontal services (which are useful to all types of applications) and vertical services (which are useful to particular industries). Day 13 demonstrated how you can use the Java programming language with CORBA, and on Day 14 you continued the Java/CORBA discussion by re-implementing the client side of the sample application as a Java applet that could be deployed in a Web browser.

All in all, this book has brought you through a wide range of topics concerning the Common Object Request Broker Architecture, from the fundamentals of the architecture, to important design considerations, to deploying CORBA applications on the World Wide Web. Even though no book can make you an expert on the subject of CORBA overnight—or even in 14 days—you achieved a level of competency with the fundamentals of distributed application development using CORBA, raised your awareness of design issues associated with CORBA, and prepared yourself for the challenge of designing and developing real-world CORBA applications. Welcome to the exciting and challenging world of developing distributed applications with CORBA!

Appendix

A

Answers to Quizzes and Exercises

Day 1: Getting Familiar with CORBA

Quiz

1. What does IIOP stand for, and what is its significance?

   IIOP (Internet Inter-ORB Protocol) is a protocol that allows ORBs from various CORBA vendors to interoperate with each other, using the TCP/IP protocols. Implementation of IIOP is a requirement for CORBA 2 compliance.

2. What is the relationship between CORBA, OMA, and OMG?

   The Object Management Group (OMG) is the organization that controls the OMA and CORBA standards. The Object Management Architecture (OMA) consists of Object Request Broker (ORB) functionality, CORBAservices, CORBAfacilities, domain interfaces, and application objects. Finally, the Common Object Request Broker Architecture (CORBA) is the standard implementation for the ORB functionality of the OMA.

3. What is a client stub?

   A client stub is a piece of code, usually generated by an IDL compiler, that allows a client application to interface to CORBA server objects. The interface presented by the client stub is exactly the same as the interface of the server, giving the client the illusion that method calls are performed locally.

4. What is an object reference? An IOR?

   An object reference is a pointer to a CORBA object. A client makes all method calls to a CORBA object through a reference to that object. An IOR, or interoperable object reference, is the CORBA/IIOP terminology for an object reference.

Day 2: Understanding the CORBA Architecture

Quiz

1. What is marshaling?

   Marshaling is the process of converting method parameters to a format that can be transmitted across the network. (Unmarshaling is simply the reverse of marshaling.)

2. What are the responsibilities of an ORB?

   An ORB locates an object implementation given an object reference, prepares a server to receive requests, and marshals and unmarshals parameters in a method call.

3. Where do server skeletons and client stubs come from?

Server skeletons and client stubs are generated by the IDL compiler.

4. Which server activation policy describes a server that is started and stopped manually?

This is the persistent server policy.

5. How does the use of IDL enhance language independence of CORBA objects?

IDL provides a language-independent mechanism for describing the interfaces of CORBA objects. The language-independent constructs of IDL can then be mapped to language-specific constructs using an IDL compiler for a particular language.

Day 3: Mastering the Interface Definition Language (IDL)

Quiz

1. Define a type (using `typedef`), called `temperatureSequence`, that is a sequence of sequences of `floats` (yes, this is legal).

The IDL definition would look like this:

```
typedef sequence<sequence<float>> temperatureSequence;
```

2. Why might a type like the one described in the preceding question be useful?

Imagine a temperature-measuring system that periodically samples the current temperature. The temperature readings gathered through a single day could potentially be stored in a `sequence<float>`. Now imagine that at the end of each day, the set of temperature data produced for that day is stored in another sequence. This sequence type would be a `sequence<sequence<float>>`, which is precisely the answer to question 1.

3. Why are exceptions useful?

Exceptions are useful for at least two reasons. First, consider a method that returns a `boolean`. If exceptions were not available, the method would have to reserve certain return values to signal error conditions. Of course, doing this eliminates one possible valid return value. In the case of a `boolean` return value, there are only two possible return values, so giving up one of them to signal an error condition is not practical. Second, when used in languages that directly support exceptions, they can greatly simplify error handling. Rather than check the return value of each method call for an error condition result, a developer can create a more generic error handling mechanism, resulting in cleaner code. Additionally, because unhandled exceptions are passed up the call stack, a hierarchy of exception handlers can be created.

4. Why is the `module` construct useful?

The `module` construct is useful because it facilitates the partitioning of a system. A well-partitioned system is easier to define and implement than a monolithic system because the divide-and-conquer approach creates independent or semi-independent components of manageable size. A monolithic design, by comparison, does little to create manageable components of the system.

5. Name some practical uses for the `octet` data type.

The `octet` data type is useful for any type of data that should not undergo any sort of translation. For instance, if a bitmapped image is sent across the network, it should arrive in exactly the same format in which it was sent. The image can be sent as an array of `octet`s, which guarantees that there is no translation from the image's source to its destination. Other types of data that can be transmitted in this way include executables, Java class files, and most multimedia files. (By contrast, all other IDL data types can undergo a format conversion when being transmitted between different hardware platforms, operating systems, and/or languages.)

6. Define an enumerated type containing the months of the year.

The type definition would look like this (though you can give it whatever name you like):

```
enum MonthsOfYear {
    January,
    February,
    March,
    April,
    May,
    June,
    July,
    August,
    September,
    October,
    November,
    December
};
```

7. Why might a nonblocking remote method call be advantageous, compared to a blocking method call?

Consider the case in which a CORBA client is an interactive application. While the client makes calls to CORBA servers, the user might want to interact with the application. If remote method calls, which might be lengthy, were to block, the responsiveness of the client application would be greatly diminished. Nonblocking method calls solve this problem by allowing the client to continue processing during a method invocation so that the client can handle user input in a timely manner. (Again, the use of multithreading in the client is almost always the best solution because `oneway` method invocations are unreliable.) Day 10, "Learning About CORBA Design Issues," explores this and other issues in greater depth.

8. Imagine a compound data type with a large number of data members. This data type will frequently be used by a client application that needs to access each of the data members. Would it be more efficient to encapsulate this data type into a `struct` or an `interface`? Why?

Given that there are a large number of data members in this data type and that the client application needs to access each of these data members, it would be more efficient to send the data to the client as a `struct`. The reason for this is that accessing each of the data members of an `interface` (recall that the implementation object is passed by reference) requires a separate method call for each member, resulting in a great deal of overhead. By contrast, a `struct` is sent by value; therefore, after the `struct` is returned to the client, the client can then access the member data with its own local copy.

9. Because an IDL method can return a value, what is the purpose of `out` and `inout` parameter types?

If a method needs to simultaneously return more than one value of more than one type, `out` and `inout` parameters can be used, in addition to (or in lieu of) the return value. This is a similar mechanism to passing parameters by reference in C++. In this way, a single method call can return more than one value.

10. Why is a oneway method unable to return any value to the caller? Can you think of a mechanism, using oneway calls, to return a result to the caller?

Because a oneway method does not block, the caller does not wait for a result. Consequently, there is no way for a oneway method call to return a result to the client. (Incidentally, exceptions cannot be raised either, for the same reason.) However, a system of oneway calls can be set up as follows: The client makes a oneway call to the server and continues its processing. The server, after it has executed the method, makes a oneway call back to the client (extra credit if you identified this as a callback) with the result information for the previous call.

Exercises

1. Consider the following classes: `Conduit`, `Faucet`, `FuseBox`, `Outlet`, `Pipe`, `WaterHeater`, `WaterPump`, and `Wire`. How would you partition these classes? What relationships, if any, are there between the partitions you have created?

Often, when partitioning a system, there is no clear answer as to which classes belong in what partitions. Many are obvious, but there are those that potentially fall into one of several partitions. In such cases, there is no right or wrong answer. Also, how a particular system uses these classes might affect the partitioning; a partitioning that makes sense for one system might not make sense for another.

Of the classes in this exercise, `Conduit`, `FuseBox`, `Outlet`, and `Wire` clearly belong in one partition (call it `Electrical`). `Faucet` and `Pipe` clearly belong in another partition (call it Plumbing). WaterHeater and WaterPump, however, could go either way. They are part of the plumbing system, to be sure, but they are also electrical devices, so they could also be considered part of the electrical system. Here there is no right or wrong answer; depending on system requirements, either partition is reasonable.

Assuming you were to place WaterHeater and WaterPump in the Plumbing partition, there would probably be a relationship between WaterHeater and Outlet (or between WaterHeater and FuseBox, if they were connected directly). A similar relationship would exist for WaterPump. Because there are few relationships between the two partitions and close relationships within each partition, you can consider this partitioning scheme a reasonable one.

2. Create an interface that describes a clock radio (which can set hours, minutes, alarm time, and so on).

There are many potential answers to this exercise, but your interface might resemble the following:

```
// Interface to a clock/radio device. This interface chooses to
// emulate the interface of many clock/radio controls, e.g. a
// "button" to set the hour, another "button" to set the minute,
// and so on.
interface ClockRadio {
    // Get the current time. The result is returned in the output
    // parameters hour, minute, and second.
    void getTime(out short hour, out short minute, out short second);
    // Advance the current hour by one; reset to zero if the hour
    // exceeds the maximum (23). This method can be used to set the
    // time. Returns the new value of the hour.
    short IncrementHour();
    // Advance the current minute by one; reset to zero if the minute
    // exceeds the maximum (59). This method can be used to set the
    // time. Returns the new value of the minute.
    short IncrementMinute();
    // Advance the alarm hour by one; reset to zero if the hour
    // exceeds the maximum (23). This method can be used to set the
    // alarm time. Returns the new value of the hour.
    short IncrementAlarmHour();
    // Advance the current alarm minute by one; reset to zero if the
    // minute exceeds the maximum (59). This method can be used to set
    // the alarm time. Returns the new value of the minute.
    short IncrementAlarmMinute();
    // Activate the alarm.
    void activateAlarm();
    // Deactivate the alarm.
    void deActivateAlarm();
};
```

Day 4: Building a CORBA Application

Quiz

1. What is the purpose of server skeletons and client stubs?

   Server skeletons provide the framework (skeleton) set of classes, which provide skeleton methods for which the developer provides implementations (either through inheritance or through delegation). Client stubs provide the clients with an interface to the server methods.

2. Why does the server need to register the implementation object with the CORBA Naming Service?

   The server needs to register with the CORBA Naming Service because, otherwise, there is no way for clients to locate the server. There are other methods of achieving visibility, such as writing a stringified object reference to a well-known and accessible location such as a disk file (assuming a networked file system), a Web server, or an FTP server. The Naming Service provides a standard, convenient method for publishing object references.

3. Why do the client and server need to catch exceptions, especially when none are raised by the IDL operations you defined?

   Recall that every remote method can potentially raise an exception and that these exceptions need to be caught and handled. Even if the IDL definition for a method does not specify any exceptions, that method can still raise a CORBA system exception (which would be raised if there were a network error, for example).

Exercises

1. It was pointed out in the StockMarket example that it would be a good idea to raise an exception in the getStockValue() method if an invalid StockSymbol was passed in. Modify StockMarket.idl so that the method can raise an InvalidStockSymbolException. (You'll also need to add a definition for this exception.)

   The resulting StockMarket.idl might look like this (you might have included additional data members in the definition for InvalidStockSymbolException):

   ```
   // StockMarket.idl

   // The StockMarket module consists of definitions useful
   // for building stock market-related applications.
   module StockMarket {

       // The InvalidStockSymbolException is raised when a
       // method is passed an invalid stock symbol.
       exception InvalidStockSymbolException { };
   ```

   continues

```
// The StockSymbol type is used for symbols (names)
// representing stocks.
typedef string StockSymbol;

// The StockServer interface is the interface for a
// server that provides stock market information.
// (See the comments on the individual methods for
// more information.)
interface StockServer {

    // getStockValue() returns the current value for
    // the given StockSymbol. If the given StockSymbol
    // is unknown, the results are undefined (this
    // would be a good place to raise an exception).
    float getStockValue(in StockSymbol symbol)
        raises (InvalidStockSymbolException);

    // getStockSymbols() returns a sequence of all
    // StockSymbols known by this StockServer.
    sequence<StockSymbol> getStockSymbols();
};
};
```

2. In the StockMarket example, an implementation was provided that used the delegation approach. Implement the StockServer to use the inheritance approach. (Extra credit: Include the exception-raising mechanism from the first exercise.)

3. The changes required are to modify the server so that it actually raises the InvalidStockSymbolException when an invalid stock symbol is encountered; similarly, the client must be modified to catch and handle this exception. For the server, here is the new implementation for the getStockValue() method (all other code remains unchanged):

```
// Return the current value for the given StockSymbol.
public float getStockValue(String symbol) throws
        InvalidStockSymbolException {

    // Try to find the given symbol.
    int stockIndex = myStockSymbols.indexOf(symbol);
    if (stockIndex != -1) {

        // Symbol found; return its value.
        return ((Float)myStockValues.elementAt(stockIndex)).
                floatValue();
    } else {

        // Symbol was not found.
        throw new InvalidStockSymbolException();
    }
}
```

The changes to the client are limited to the doSomething() method, which now catches the exception and prints a warning message:

```
// Do some cool things with the StockServer.
protected void doSomething() {
```

A

```
try {

    // Get the valid stock symbols from the StockServer.
    String[] stockSymbols = myStockServer.getStockSymbols();

    // Display the stock symbols and their values.
    for (int i = 0; i < stockSymbols.length; i++) {
        try {
            System.out.println(stockSymbols[i] + " " +
                    myStockServer.getStockValue(stockSymbols
                    [i]));
        } catch (InvalidStockSymbolException ex) {
            System.out.println("Invalid stock symbol.");
        }
    }
} catch (org.omg.CORBA.SystemException ex) {
    System.err.println("Fatal error: " + ex);
}
}
```

Day 5: Designing the System: A Crash Course in Object-Oriented Analysis and Design

Quiz

1. Identify the potential objects in the system described here: An ordering system allows customers to order products from a particular company. Each order consists of one or more line items, each of which identifies a quantity and a particular product. Each product, in turn, has an associated price.

   Possible objects in this system can be identified by picking out the nouns: *order, line item, quantity, product,* and *price.* (Further analysis might reveal that some of these—particularly *quantity* and *price*—do not work well as objects, but that depends on the application.)

2. What is UML, and what is it good for?

   The UML, or Unified Modeling Language, is used to facilitate the object-oriented analysis and design process. UML can be used to model a number of aspects of the system, from static design (such as class diagrams) to dynamic (such as use cases and scenarios).

3. For an order-processing system design, one requirement given is "must be fast." Is this a reasonable expression of this requirement, or could it be improved? If so, how?

   Because *fast* by itself is not an easily quantifiable term and thus cannot be tested readily, "must be fast" is probably not a reasonably expressed requirement. A more quantifiable requirement would be to require an average system response time of, for example, one second or less.

Exercise

Modify the system design so that a Bank consists of Branches, each of which owns some of the Customer Accounts. Draw the class diagram for the modified design.

Your modified class diagram should resemble the one shown in Figure A.1. Note that the Account creation responsibility has been moved from the Bank to the Branch, although the Bank and its constituent Branches share the capability to enumerate and close Accounts.

Figure A.1.

The modified Bank *application class diagram.*

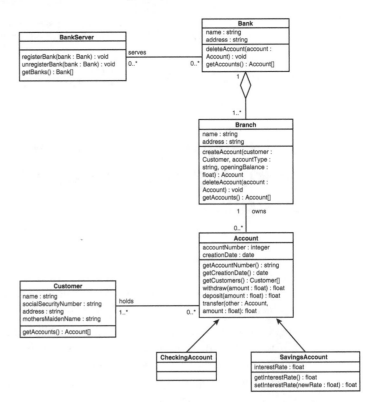

Day 6: Implementing Basic Application Capabilities

Quiz

1. It was noted earlier that _is_equivalent() is not guaranteed to return TRUE when two object references refer to the same object. Can you think of a mechanism that would more reliably determine whether two references refer to the same object? (For simplicity, assume the objects are of the same type.)

A mechanism could assign global unique identifiers (GUIDs) or universal unique identifiers (UUIDs) to objects and make the identifiers available to client applications (through an accessor method such as getGUID()). Such a mechanism could more reliably determine object identity by comparing identifiers; two objects that return the same GUID must be the same object.

2. What would happen if _release() were not called on an object that had earlier been _duplicate()d?

If _release() were not called on an object, the object would live forever; its reference count (in a reference counting implementation) would never reach zero.

3. Why does NewCustomerMain.cpp have a try ... catch (const CORBA::Exception& ex) block?

The CORBA::Exception is a generic exception that can be thrown by any remote method. Because a number of remote methods are called in NewCustomerMain.cpp, they are done so inside this try ... catch block.

Exercise

Modify the client application so that it prints the names of the Customers who are associated with the Account that was created. (The single Customer printed should be the same Customer whose information was entered on the command line.)

After line 85 of NewCustomerMain.cpp (refer to Listing 6.21), add the following code. This code gets the Account owners using the getCustomers() method, then iterates through the sequence of Customers returned by that method, printing the name of each Customer (as returned by name()).

```
// Print out list of Customers owning the Account.
cout << "  Printing list of Account owners:" << endl;
CustomerList* customers = account->getCustomers();
for (CORBA::ULong i = 0; i < customers->length(); i++) {
    cout << "    Owner " << i + 1 << ": " << ((*customers)[i])->
            name();
}
```

Day 7: Using Exceptions to Perform Error Checking

Quiz

1. What does it mean to raise (or throw) an exception?

To raise an exception means that a new exception is created and passed to the caller of the method that raised the exception. The caller can then handle the exception or pass it to its caller.

2. What does it mean to catch an exception?

To catch an exception means to handle an exception that was raised by a method that was called. Catching an exception might involve displaying an error message to the user, trying to resolve the condition that caused the exception to be raised, or doing nothing at all.

3. Why are exceptions useful?

Exceptions are useful because they provide a structured form of error handling. For example, without exceptions, a given method would have to reserve certain return results to signify an error condition; a caller of such a method would have to check for each of these special return codes. Exceptions greatly simplify the complexities that can otherwise arise from error handling mechanisms.

Exercises

1. Modify the following interface definition so that appropriate exceptions are raised in appropriate places.

```
exception InvalidNumberException { };
exception NoIncomingCallException { };
exception NotOffHookException { };

interface Telephone {

    void offHook();

    void onHook();

    void dialNumber(in string phoneNumber);

    void answerCall();
};
```

One potential solution is as follows:

```
exception InvalidNumberException { };
exception NoIncomingCallException { };
exception NotOffHookException { };

interface Telephone {

    void offHook();

    void onHook();

    void dialNumber(in string phoneNumber)
        raises (InvalidNumberException, NotOffHookException);

    void answerCall()
        raises (NoIncomingCallException);
};
```

This solution assumes that it is not valid to dial a number unless the `Telephone` is already off the hook. It might be equally reasonable for `dialNumber()` to call `offHook()` if the `Telephone` is not already off the hook.

2. Implement the interface from exercise 1, raising the appropriate exceptions under the appropriate conditions. (Most of the methods probably won't do anything, except for `dialNumber()`, which will likely check the validity of the given phone number).

The complete solution is not given here, but the implementation for the exercise 1 solution would look like this (the following is in pseudocode):

```
void dialNumber(string phoneNumber) {

    if (telephone is on hook) {
        raise NotOffHookException;
    }
    if (phone number is invalid) {
        raise InvalidNumberException;
    }

    proceed to dial the number...
}

void answerCall() {

    if (no incoming call is being placed) {
        raise NoIncomingCallException;
    }

    proceed to answer the call...
}
```

Day 8: Adding Automated Teller Machine (ATM) Capability

Quiz

What are the four steps you'll usually follow to make enhancements to a CORBA application?

The steps are to define additional requirements, modify the system design, modify the IDL definitions to reflect the new design, and, finally, implement the new functionality.

Exercise

Add an operation to the ATM interface that allows funds to be transferred between Accounts. Be sure to provide appropriate exceptions as well.

The IDL should look something like this:

```
float transfer(in ATMCard card, in Account fromAccount, in Account
        toAccount, in short pin in float amount)
        raises (AuthorizationException, InvalidAmountException,
        InsufficientFundsException);
```

Note that the implementation of this method will likely need to use the ATMCard to check the authorization for both the fromAccount and toAccount parameters. (Actually, it might be reasonable to allow transfers to any Account, but real ATM cards allow transfers only between accounts on which those cards are authorized.)

Day 9: Using Callbacks to Add Push Capability

Quiz

1. Why does the issue of thread safety become important in the sample application developed in this chapter?

   Thread safety is important because multiple threads might attempt to access the same data simultaneously. To prevent the possible corruption of data, access to such data must be made thread-safe.

2. Instead of using oneway methods to notify clients of updates, can you think of another way to efficiently send update messages to clients? (Hint: Multithreading could come in handy here.)

   Launching a new thread to send each client update messages significantly enhances the efficiency of non-oneway message delivery. This is because, rather than require a single thread to wait for each client response before delivering the next message, each thread can block while waiting for a response from its respective client.

Exercises

1. It was noted earlier in the chapter that no facility currently exists to cancel the automatic account update service. Provide an IDL method signature for such an operation. Don't forget to include appropriate exceptions, if any.

   The method signature, which would be added to the Bank interface, should resemble the following:

   ```
   void cancelUpdateService(in Account account)
           raises (InvalidAccountException);
   ```

   The InvalidAccountException would be raised if the Account does not belong to the Bank on which the operation was called. Optionally, you would either raise this exception or ignore the operation if it were called on an Account that was already subscribed to this service.

2. Implement the account update cancellation method from exercise 1.

   The complete implementation is not given here, but the following pseudocode provides the general algorithm:

```
void cancelUpdateService(Account account) {

    if (account does not belong to this Bank) {
        throw InvalidAccountException;
    }

    if (account is already subscribed to the auto update service) {
        throw InvalidAccountException;
    }

    (otherwise)
    remove the account from list of Accounts subscribed to the auto
            update service
}
```

Day 10: Learning About CORBA Design Issues

Quiz

1. What is the major issue associated with mixing client and server functionality in a single-threaded CORBA application?

   Depending on what the application is doing, mixing client and server functionality in a single-threaded application introduces the potential for deadlock to occur.

2. How can the use of reference counting in a CORBA application lead to problems?

   When an application component crashes, none of the reference counts for the objects it referenced will be decremented. Consequently, those objects might not be destroyed when they should be.

3. Which version of X11 (the X Window System) would be required to safely run multithreaded X-based applications?

   X11R6.1 or later is necessary to safely run multithreaded applications. Earlier versions don't have thread-safe libraries.

4. Why is the capability to pass objects by value sometimes useful?

   If an application component intends to perform a number of operations on an object, it is often more efficient to use a local copy of that object rather than make numerous method invocations on a remote object.

5. Why is it usually inadvisable to use the Exclusive oneway Call design pattern introduced earlier in this chapter?

   Because oneway methods are unreliable, the Exclusive oneway Call design pattern is difficult to implement for situations in which reliable message delivery is required.

Day 11: Using the Dynamic Invocation Interface (DII)

Quiz

1. Would you expect DII to be useful to most CORBA application developers? Why or why not?

   As emphasized numerous times in this chapter, DII will probably not be useful to most CORBA application developers. This is primarily because, for most applications, the interfaces are almost always known at compile time anyway. Also, DII adds a great deal of complexity that developers are well advised to avoid altogether.

2. What are the advantages of DII over static method invocation?

   DII has two advantages over static method invocation: the flexibility for a client to invoke operations on interfaces that were unknown at the time the client was compiled, and the ability to use one of several options for obtaining the return result from a remote method invocation.

3. What are the disadvantages of DII compared to static method invocation?

   The disadvantages to using DII are its complexity, its lack of static-type–checking ability, the additional overhead incurred by its call mechanism, and the overhead associated with interface discovery.

Day 12: Exploring CORBAservices and CORBAfacilities

Quiz

1. Who defines the specifications for CORBAservices and CORBAfacilities?

   The specifications for CORBAservices and CORBAfacilities are defined by the Object Management Group (OMG).

2. Who provides the implementations for CORBAservices and CORBAfacilities?

   The implementations for CORBAservices and CORBAfacilities are provided by the vendors themselves. The OMG does not provide their implementations, only their specifications.

3. What CORBAservices and/or CORBAfacilities, if any, must a vendor provide with an ORB product in order to be considered CORBA 2 compliant?

   No CORBAservices or CORBAfacilities implementations are required from a vendor for CORBA 2 compliance. Compliance is determined by a product's ORB capabilities alone.

4. Why are vertical market facilities useful?

Vertical market facilities are useful because they can enhance interoperability between applications within a particular industry. In addition, they can facilitate the sharing of data between companies within an industry.

Exercises

1. Provide an overview of how the Object Trader Service could be used to replace the BankServer in the sample Bank application.

In the sample Bank application, the BankServer component exists solely to allow other application components to locate Banks and ATMs. As it turns out, locating objects by type is precisely the capability provided by the Trader Service. Rather than locate and register with a BankServer component, Banks and ATMs could instead register with the Trader Service. These components would subsequently be available to other application components—namely, Customers—that could locate the components through the same Trader Service. Thus, the functionality of the BankServer component is effectively replaced.

2. Describe how the Event Service could be used within the Bank application. (Hint: Consider the automatic account update feature added on Day 9.) What would be the benefit of using this approach?

Currently, the automatic account update feature requires the Bank to iterate through its Accounts that are subscribed to the update service. The Bank invokes a callback method on each of the Customers who are associated with those Accounts. Using the Event Service, the Bank could become a publisher of Account balance update events to which Customers could subscribe. The benefit of this approach is that it eliminates the complexity of delivering update messages to Customers in the Bank application; the details of message delivery are shifted to the Event Service.

3. (Extra Credit) If you have any products available to you that implement one or more CORBAservices, try to integrate the functionality provided by a service of your choice with the sample Bank application. (See the section of this chapter labeled "Choosing CORBAservices" to determine which services might integrate well with the sample application.) Because of the numerous possibilities available to you, no answer is provided for this exercise.

Day 13: Developing for the Internet Using CORBA and Java

Quiz

1. What IDL construct resembles Java's package?

The Java package is very similar to the IDL module.

2. What is an advantage of Java Remote Method Invocation (RMI) over CORBA? Of CORBA over RMI?

One advantage of RMI over CORBA is that RMI allows objects to be passed by value. Some advantages of CORBA over RMI are language independence and robustness.

3. Why might a developer want to use Java to develop a CORBA application?

Java's portability makes it especially attractive for developing CORBA client applications that might be required to run on a variety of platforms.

Day 14: Web-Enabling the Bank Example with Java

Quiz

1. Why might it be advantageous to deploy a CORBA client as a Java applet?

Two potential advantages for using Java applets for CORBA clients are the Java language's portability and the applet's simplified deployment mechanism through Web browsers.

2. Why is it useful for browsers to include built-in CORBA-related classes (for example, Netscape's Communicator includes Visigenic's VisiBroker for Java runtime)?

Because the classes required for CORBA connectivity are included with the browser, they do not have to be downloaded with the applet each time the applet is downloaded, thus reducing the download time required.

3. What is a potential disadvantage to the bundling scheme described in question 2?

A possible disadvantage to this scheme is that the CORBA classes provided with the browser might become outdated, thus requiring new versions of the classes to be downloaded with the applet anyway.

Exercise

Extend the BankApplet to do even more cool stuff. For example, you might add tabbed panels to display the Accounts belonging to a particular Customer. Or, you might extend the applet to allow multiple Customers to be associated with an Account and extend the Account information correspondingly to show all the Customers associated with a given Account. (Because this is an open-ended exercise, no answer is given.)

APPENDIX

B

CORBA Tools and Utilities

This appendix provides a brief overview of some of the CORBA products available today. Although every attempt was made to make this information as up-to-date as possible, there are always products that slip between the cracks. Also, as the interest in CORBA grows, new products are announced all the time. Here, then, is a brief overview of all CORBA-related products known to the author at the time this was written.

A Look at CORBA ORB Products

The products described in this section include Object Request Brokers (ORBs) and are used to develop and deploy CORBA applications. Usually, these products don't provide full development environments but simply the ORB itself, an Interface Definition Language (IDL) compiler, and other miscellaneous tools useful for CORBA application development.

BBN's Corbus

Corbus is a CORBA 2.0-compliant ORB that is free for government and noncommercial use (subject to certain conditions, details being available on BBN's Web site). Corbus is available for Solaris, SunOS, and HP-UX.

Information on Corbus, as well as downloadable copies, is available on BBN's Web site at `http://www.bbn.com/products/dpom/corbus.htm`.

BEA Systems' ObjectBroker

BEA, perhaps most famous for its Tuxedo transaction-processing monitor, offers a CORBA ORB (which it acquired from Digital around March 1997). ObjectBroker supports 20 platforms (BEA's Web site doesn't indicate which) and provides integration with OLE on Windows platforms. BEA claims that ObjectBroker is the most mature ORB available, having first shipped in 1991 (indeed, this is an eternity in CORBA years).

Information on ObjectBroker is available on BEA's Web site at `http://www.beasys.com/products/obb/index.htm`.

Chorus Systems' CHORUS/COOL ORB

Chorus, recently acquired by Sun Microsystems (September 1997), offers a CORBA 2.0-compliant ORB in its CHORUS/COOL ORB product. CHORUS/COOL ORB is available for an impressive array of operating systems, including AIX, CHORUS realtime and embedded OS's, HP-UX, Linux, SCO OpenDesktop and OpenServer, SunOS, Solaris, Windows 95, and Windows NT.

Information on CHORUS/COOL ORB, as well as a downloadable evaluation copy, is available at Chorus's Web site at `http://www.chorus.com/Products/Cool/index.html`.

DNS Technologies' SmalltalkBroker

A rare breed, DNS Technologies' SmalltalkBroker is a CORBA 2.0-compliant ORB for Smalltalk applications. SmalltalkBroker also provides a handful of CORBAservices implementations—CORBA Naming Service, CORBA Life Cycle Service, CORBA Event Service, and CORBA Transaction Service.

Information on SmalltalkBroker is available on DNS Technologies' Web site at `http://www.dnstech.com/stbprod.htm`.

Expersoft's CORBAplus Products

Expersoft's CORBAplus family comes in a variety of flavors:

- ☐ *CORBAplus for C++*, a CORBA 2.0-compliant ORB, supports Windows 95, Windows NT, Solaris, HP-UX, and AIX. It also provides implementations for the CORBA Naming Service, the CORBA Event Service, and the CORBA Relationship Service.

- ☐ *CORBAplus Java Edition* is a 100% Pure Java ORB implementation that supports JDK 1.0.2 and JDK 1.1.

- ☐ *CORBAplus ActiveX Bridge* provides interoperability between ActiveX and CORBA objects, enabling, among other things, the development of CORBA applications using Visual Basic.

- ☐ *CORBAplus Enterprise Edition* adds asynchronous messaging capability, along with multithreaded application support, a dynamic type manager (used in conjunction with the Dynamic Invocation Interface), and URL object-addressing capability.

Information on the CORBAplus product line, along with downloadable evaluation copies, is available on Expersoft's Web site at `http://www.expersoft.com/Products/CORBAplus/corbaplus.htm`.

Hewlett-Packard's ORB Plus

ORB Plus is Hewlett-Packard's entry into the CORBA market, with support for (of course) HP-UX, Solaris, and Windows NT. In addition to being a CORBA 2.0-compliant ORB, ORB Plus provides implementations for the CORBA Life Cycle Service, the CORBA Naming Service, and the CORBA Event Service. A unique feature of ORB Plus is that it supports DCE CIOP (essentially the equivalent of IIOP for DCE), at least on HP-UX.

Hewlett-Packard has been instrumental in the development of proposals to build bridges between CORBA and Microsoft technologies, such as DCOM and ActiveX, so developers interested in spanning the two worlds will want to keep an eye on Hewlett-Packard.

More information on ORB Plus is available on Hewlett-Packard's Web site at `http://www.hp.com/gsy/orbplus.html`.

B

IBM's SOMobjects

SOMobjects, IBM's offering in the CORBA world, is available for AIX, OS/2, and Windows NT. SOMobjects provides implementations for a variety of CORBAservices, including the CORBA Event Service, the CORBA Life Cycle Service, the CORBA Persistent Object Service, the CORBA Concurrency Service, and the CORBA Transaction Service.

Information on SOMobjects, as well as a downloadable copy, is available at IBM's Web site at `http://www.software.ibm.com/ad/somobjects/`.

IONA Technologies' Orbix, OrbixWeb, and Other Products

IONA and Orbix are perhaps two of the most well-known and well-respected names in CORBA. IONA offers a number of CORBA products to serve a wide range of needs:

☐ *Orbix*, perhaps the most prolific CORBA ORB in existence, is available on a plethora of operating systems, including a wide range of UNIX systems (Solaris, HP-UX, IRIX, AIX, and Digital UNIX), Windows NT, Windows 95, OS/2, VxWorks, QNX, and MVS. Orbix supports language bindings for Smalltalk, Ada95, and C++. IONA also goes one step further with Orbix: On Windows, Orbix supports integration with OLE and ActiveX; on MVS, Orbix provides full support for COBOL, CICS, DB/2, and IMS.

☐ *OrbixWeb for Java* brings the power of Orbix to Java applets and applications. Because OrbixWeb is 100% Pure Java, it will run in any Java-enabled browser. OrbixWeb is the first ORB to support JDK 1.1, and JDK 1.0.2 is also fully supported.

☐ *Orbix Wonderwall*, a companion product to OrbixWeb, provides security in the form of an IIOP firewall (recall that IIOP, or Internet Inter-ORB Protocol, is the standard mechanism by which ORBs from different vendors can communicate).

☐ IONA also provides implementations for many of the CORBAservices specifications with such products as *OrbixEvents* (CORBA Event Service), *OrbixManager* (CORBA application monitoring and management tools), *OrbixNames* (CORBA Naming Service), *OrbixOTS* (CORBA Transaction Service), *OrbixSecurity* (CORBA Security Service), *OrbixTalk* (a multicasting implementation of the CORBA Event Service), and *OrbixTrader* (CORBA Trader Service).

IONA seems to be making itself a one-stop shop for a wide variety of CORBA solutions. Information on Orbix, OrbixWeb, and other IONA products—many of which can be downloaded as trial versions—is available from the IONA Web site at `http://www.iona.com/`.

Netscape's Navigator and Enterprise Server

Netscape licenses Visigenic Software's VisiBroker for Java (covered in greater detail later in this appendix) and includes the ORB technology in its popular Web browser, Navigator 4.0 (and, by extension, Communicator). This is a boon for intranet (and, to a lesser extent, Internet) developers because the client end (the part written in Java that runs in the browser) of a CORBA application can be made smaller (requiring less code to be downloaded to the client) because the ORB is integrated with the browser. Because VisiBroker is 100% Pure Java, such an application also works with non-Netscape browsers as well, although the VisiBroker code has to be downloaded to those browsers. (Of course, other vendors are free to include ORB technology in their browsers as well.)

Netscape also bundles Visigenic's ORB technology with Enterprise Server 3.0, bringing CORBA functionality to the server side as well.

Information on Navigator, as well as a downloadable copy, is available at Netscape's Web site at `http://www.netscape.com/`; developer information for Netscape products is available at `http://developer.netscape.com/`.

Object-Oriented Concepts' OmniBroker

OmniBroker, from Object-Oriented Concepts, is another CORBA 2.0-compliant ORB that is freely available for noncommercial use. As well as being freely available, full source code is included with OmniBroker. OmniBroker fully supports IDL mappings for C++ and Java, and, because source code is available, can theoretically work on virtually any platform. OmniBroker for C++ has been tested on IRIX, Solaris, HP-UX, AIX, Linux, Windows 95, and Windows NT; OmniBroker for Java works with Sun's JDK 1.0.2 or 1.1.3, as well as Microsoft's Visual J++ 1.1.

Information on OmniBroker, as well as a downloadable copy, is available on Object-Oriented Concepts' Web site at `http://www.ooc.com/ob.html`.

Object-Oriented Technologies' DOME

DOME is another freely available (though redistribution details are not clear) CORBA ORB supporting C++ and C. DOME is available for a wide variety of platforms, including Solaris, SunOS, AIX, HP-UX, Digital UNIX, Windows 3.1, Windows 95, Windows NT, VMS, OS/2, OS-9, pSOS, and Linux.

More information about DOME is available on Object-Oriented Technologies' Web site at `http://www.oot.co.uk/`.

Objectspace's Voyager

Voyager, although not yet CORBA-compliant (Objectspace is planning CORBA interoperability in the next release), should still be of great interest to Java developers. Just one look at the list of features will explain why: In addition to all the ORB-like features one would expect (such as remote method invocation, naming services, and so on), Voyager provides much, much more. For example, any Java class can be remote-enabled non-intrusively (even if the source code is unavailable). Voyager also supports a wide variety of messaging services, as well as mobile objects (objects can literally be moved onto any Voyager server on the network) and even autonomous agents (objects can move themselves to other Voyager servers). Voyager adds more, such as support for persistence through various databases (as well as its own simple built-in persistence mechanism) and a custom Security Manager.

And, as if all this weren't enough, Objectspace is making Voyager available free of charge. (Objectspace charges for Voyager support, although the level of support given for free is quite reasonable.) That Objectspace is giving away the use of this technology is amazing, especially considering the product's capabilities. Although Voyager is a Java-only product (and 100% Pure Java at that), when CORBA support is added, Voyager objects can interact with CORBA applications. In addition, Objectspace is planning support for DCOM interoperability as well.

Java developers owe it to themselves to check out this product; the rest of the CORBA community should stay tuned. Information on Voyager, along with the free download, is available on Objectspace's Web site at `http://www.objectspace.com/voyager/`.

The Olivetti and Oracle Research Laboratory's omniORB2

omniORB2, from the Olivetti and Oracle (an interesting combination) Research Laboratory, will be a particularly appealing product to some developers because of one outstanding feature: The product is freely available, even for commercial use. That's correct. ORL has placed omniORB2 under the GNU General Public License and GNU Library General Public License. At the time this was written, omniORB2 was not yet a complete CORBA 2.0 implementation because it lacked support for Typecodes and the any type; also, the Dynamic Invocation Interface (DII) and Dynamic Skeleton Interface (DSI) were not supported. Nevertheless, omniORB2 can prove useful for a great many of development projects.

The GNU General Public License

Details of the GNU General Public License (GPL), also known as the *copyleft*, are available from the Free Software Foundation (FSF) Web site at `http://www.fsf.org/copyleft/gpl.html`. Similarly, details of the GNU Library General Public License are available at `http://www.fsf.org/copyleft/lgpl.html`. Essentially, software distributed under these terms can be copied and distributed freely, or even modified or sold, but the source code must always be included with the product using such software. The GPL is very popular among users of free UNIX-like operating systems such as Linux or FreeBSD.

B

Information on omniORB2, along with the (freely available) distribution, is available at ORL's Web site at `http://www.orl.co.uk/omniORB/omniORB.html`.

SunSoft's NEO and Joe

Sun's CORBA product line consists of four major products:

- [ ] *Solaris NEO* is a CORBA 2.0-compliant ORB that includes implementations for the CORBA Naming Service, the CORBA Property Service, the CORBA Event Service, the CORBA Relationship Service, and the CORBA Life Cycle Service. Solaris NEO also boasts other features, such as SNMP (Simple Network Management Protocol) management capability, support for workgroups, concurrent requests, persistent object storage, and more.

- [ ] *Joe* is a CORBA ORB implemented in 100% Pure Java. Joe is bundled with Solaris NEO and is also available as a separate product.

- [ ] *NEO Connectivity for Microsoft Windows* enables Windows 95 and Windows NT, using ActiveX, OLE, and COM interfaces, to communicate with CORBA objects.

- [ ] *Solstice NEO* enables CORBA system administration, providing capabilities such as managing ORBs, displaying status of CORBA objects and processes, load balancing, and other management capabilities. Solstice NEO, which is Java-based, is bundled with Solaris NEO or available separately.

Information on NEO and Joe, along with downloadable copies of some of Sun's products, is available on Sun's Web site at `http://www.sun.com/solaris/neo/`.

Sybase's Jaguar CTS

Although the current version (1.1) of Jaguar CTS is not CORBA-compliant, Sybase is promising CORBA interoperability in version 2. In the meantime, Jaguar CTS is particularly interesting because of its wide range of support for various technologies and products. Jaguar CTS interoperates with Java, ActiveX, PowerBuilder, and C/C++. It supports connectivity through HTTP, TDS, and (in version 2) IIOP. It also supports database connectivity through JDBC, ODBC, or CTlib to databases such as (of course) Sybase, Oracle, Informix, SQL Server, or mainframe-based databases.

Information on Jaguar CTS is available on Sybase's Web site at `http://www1.sybase.com/products/jaguar/`.

TIBCO's TIB/ObjectBus

TIBCO's strong suit is messaging, and it leverages this strength with its TIB/ObjectBus product, a CORBA 2.0-compliant ORB that TIBCO claims is "the only ORB that takes advantage of both broadcast and reliable multicast communication to initiate ORB requests and distribute ORB events across an unlimited number of servers and users." In addition to supporting the CORBA Naming Service and CORBA Event Service, TIB/ObjectBus provides CORBA-compliant mechanisms for publish-subscribe and request-reply models of communication. TIB/ObjectBus supports a variety of platforms, including Solaris, HP-UX, VMS, Digital UNIX, OS/2, AIX, and Windows NT. In addition, TIBCO is planning possible support for Java, the CORBA Transaction Service, and other features.

More information on TIB/ObjectBus is available on TIBCO's Web site at `http://www.tibco.com/objctbus/tib_object_bus.html`.

Visigenic Software's VisiBroker and Other Products

Visigenic is quickly making a name for itself in the CORBA industry. The company has been successful in licensing its ORB technology to a number of high-profile vendors, including Borland, Netscape, Novell, Oracle, SGI, and Sybase. In addition to licensing its technology, Visigenic also offers the following products:

- *VisiBroker for C++* is a complete CORBA ORB for developing CORBA applications in C++. VisiBroker is available on a variety of platforms, including Solaris, HP-UX, AIX, IRIX, Digital Unix, Windows 95, and Windows NT.

- *VisiBroker for Java* is a 100% Pure Java implementation of a CORBA ORB. Visigenic has the distinction of bringing to market the first CORBA 2.0-compliant ORB written in 100% Pure Java.

- Visigenic also provides implementations for a number of CORBAservices with its *VisiBroker Naming Service* (CORBA Naming Service), *VisiBroker Event Service* (CORBA Event Service), and *TPBroker* (CORBA Transaction Service).

Visigenic has recently announced the *Distributed Application Platform Architecture* (Visigenic/ DAP), its plan for a CORBA development platform. Along with the CORBAservices presently offered, Visigenic plans to add other services, such as the CORBA Trader Service, integrated transaction capability, and asynchronous messaging capability.

Information on VisiBroker and other Visigenic products, many of which can be downloaded as trial versions, is available from Visigenic's Web site at http://www.visigenic.com/.

Xerox PARC's ILU

Strictly speaking, ILU (Inter-Language Unification) is not a CORBA 2.0-compliant ORB, although it supports IIOP along with the CORBA language mappings for C, C++, and Java. The capabilities provided by ILU are a superset of CORBA. For example, languages supported by ILU, in addition to the aforementioned C, C++, and Java, include Python, Common LISP, and Modula-3. Also, ILU includes, of all things, an implementation of HTTP (Hypertext Transport Protocol, the mechanism used by the World Wide Web).

According to the ILU Web page, one of the implementation goals is to maximize compatibility with existing open standards, and this goal is reflected in the availability list for ILU: SunOS, Solaris, HP-UX, AIX, OSF, IRIX, FreeBSD, Linux, LynxOS, SCO, Windows 3.1, Windows 95, and Windows NT. Additionally, ILU supports a number of threading and event loop models. Again, ILU is not strictly a CORBA 2.0-compliant product, but it is freely available with no restrictions (other than that a copyright notice must accompany any copies of the software).

Information on ILU, as well as a freely available downloadable copy, is available at PARC's Web site (actually their FTP site) at ftp://ftp.parc.xerox.com/pub/ilu/ilu.html.

A Look at CORBA-Aware Development Tools

This section describes development tools that are "CORBA-aware," meaning that they have at least some knowledge of CORBA application development methodology. For instance, such a tool can generate and parse IDL definitions or enable a developer to graphically create a set of IDL interfaces to define the workings of a CORBA application.

Note that a number of development products might include ORBs (as mentioned previously, Visigenic Software licenses its ORB technology to a number of other software vendors). Development products that include ORBs without providing CORBA-specific development tools are not mentioned here.

Aonix's Software through Pictures

Software through Pictures is a family of tools that supports, among other things, object-oriented analysis and design of applications. Software through Pictures supports a variety of OO methodologies, including the Unified Modeling Language (UML), Object Modeling Technique (OMT), and Booch. Software through Pictures supports graphical editing of business requirements, use cases, object models, dynamic models, functional models, object interaction diagrams, and class tables. Software through Pictures also integrates with a variety of languages and tools, such as Smalltalk, C++, Java, and IDL (making it useful as a CORBA design tool); FrameMaker and Interleaf are supported for automatic generation of documentation. Finally, Software through Pictures supports SunOS, Solaris, HP-UX, AIX, Digital UNIX, and Windows NT.

More information on the Software through Pictures family of products is available on Aonix's Web site at `http://www.aonix.com/Products/StP/stp.html`.

Black & White Software's CORBA Development Tools

Black & White Software offers a plethora of CORBA development tools:

☐ *OrbixBuilder* is a family of products that plug in to various development tools. OrbixBuilder provides graphical utilities and code generation for CORBA clients and servers and is bundled with IONA Technologies' Orbix or OrbixWeb (depending on whether a C++ or Java flavor of OrbixBuilder is chosen). In addition to supporting Black & White's own UIM/Orbix and Web/Enable, OrbixBuilder supports Symantec's Visual Café.

☐ *Object/Observer* provides diagnostic and trace mechanisms for CORBA applications, facilitating the monitoring of server activity, network traffic, and other communication details.

☐ UIM/Orbix is a graphical application builder tool geared towards the development of CORBA applications in C++. In addition, UIM/Orbix is extensible through other products offered by Black & White.

☐ *Orb/Enable* is a set of tools that simplify CORBA application development. It enables the user to create and import IDL files as well as visually browse the CORBA server interfaces available in an Interface Repository.

☐ *Web/Enable*, an add-on to UIM/Orbix, facilitates the development of CORBA applications in Java, complementing UIM/Orbix's C++ development facilities. Web/Enable also includes IONA Technologies' OrbixWeb.

☐ *Object/LM* provides access control and usage metering for CORBA applications as well as license management and a security mechanism.

More information on Black & White's CORBA development products is available on the Black & White Web site at `http://www.blackwhite.com/products/corbadev.html`.

ParcPlace's Distributed Smalltalk

Distributed Smalltalk is an interactive tool that supports the development of CORBA applications in—what else—Smalltalk. In addition to providing graphical design and development tools, Distributed Smalltalk includes a CORBA 2.0-compliant ORB and implementations for the CORBA Naming Service, the CORBA Event Service, the CORBA Transaction Service, and the CORBA Concurrency Service. Distributed Smalltalk also includes other CORBA features, such as an Interface Repository browser and the capability to generate IDL from existing Smalltalk classes. Distributed Smalltalk supports Windows 3.1, Windows 95, Windows NT, MacOS, HP-UX, AIX, Solaris, and SunOS.

More information on Distributed Smalltalk is available on ParcPlace's Web site at `http://www.parcplace.com/products/dst/info/dst.htm`.

Rational Software's Rose

Rational Rose is the most popular visual design tool on the market today. The tool supports Booch, Object Modeling Technique (OMT), and Unified Modeling Language (UML) notations and provides tools for use case analysis, class and object modeling, component modeling, and more. Rose also supports a number of languages, including Visual Basic, PowerBuilder, C++, Forté, Java, Smalltalk, and SQLWindows. In addition, Rose can be used to create logical models for relational databases, supporting Oracle7, Sybase, SQL Server, Watcom SQL, and ANSI SQL. Of particular use to CORBA application developers is Rose's capability to generate IDL from graphical object models. Rose is available on a number of platforms, including Windows 95, Windows NT, IRIX, Solaris, AIX, Digital UNIX, and HP-UX.

More information on Rose, as well as a downloadable evaluation copy, can be found on Rational's Web site at `http://www.rational.com/products/rose/index.html`.

TakeFive Software's SNiFF+

SNiFF+ is a development tool (or actually a family of tools) that supports a wide variety of languages, including C, C++, FORTRAN, Java, IDL, and others. Useful to CORBA developers is SNiFF+'s capability to generate and parse IDL files. Of course, SNiFF+ offers a variety of graphical tools, such as a class browser, a debugger, and more.

More information on the SNiFF+ family of products, along with downloadable evaluation software, can be found on TakeFive's Web site at `http://www.takefive.com/products.htm`.

TRW's Universal Network Architecture Services (UNAS)

TRW's Universal Network Architecture Services (UNAS) is a development tool combined with a CORBA ORB, supporting some beyond-CORBA features such as object monitoring and control, performance evaluation and tuning, and fault tolerance. UNAS also supports the CORBA Naming Service and SNMP (Simple Network Management Protocol) management. Also supported are the C++ and Ada languages, SunOS, Solaris, HP-UX, AIX, IRIX, Digital UNIX, OpenVMS, DEC CMW, ULTRIX, Rational Apex, Rational R1000, SCO UNIX, and Windows NT platforms.

More information on UNAS is available at TRW's Web site at `http://www.trw.com/unas/`.

APPENDIX C

What Lies Ahead?
The Future of CORBA

This book has focused largely on what you can do with CORBA today. But what about six months from now, or a year from now, or even further in the future? To plan for the systems you will build tomorrow, you want to know where CORBA is going to be at that time. This chapter looks at some proposed additions to CORBA and examines the overall direction CORBA is taking.

Looking Briefly Through the Rearview Mirror

To predict where CORBA is heading, it is helpful to know some of its history. Recall from Day 1, "Getting Familiar with CORBA," that CORBA first materialized around 1990, shortly after the Object Management Group—CORBA's controlling organization—was founded. CORBA 1.0, followed shortly by CORBA 1.1, laid the groundwork for distributed object communication. In 1994, the OMG adopted the 2.0 version of the CORBA specification, the primary goal of which was to define a standard for interoperability for ORBs produced by different vendors. (Recall that an ORB, or Object Request Broker, is the component of CORBA that facilitates communication between objects.) CORBA 2.0 was a major step towards achieving interoperability between various products, but it still lacked some capabilities. Most notable was its inability to pass objects by value (as discussed on Day 10, "Learning About CORBA Design Issues"). Simultaneously, the OMG developed specifications for additional functionality in the form of CORBAservices and CORBAfacilities.

In the Near Future: CORBA 2.1

CORBA 2.1, adopted in September 1997, made some incremental changes to the CORBA specification:

- Revisions to the interoperability specification
- Extensions to the IDL language, notably the long long (64-bit) integer types and wchar (wide character) type
- The inclusion of two standard language mappings: COBOL and Ada

None of these changes is earth-shattering, but the IDL extensions in particular bring CORBA up-to-date with respect to languages and operating systems that support 64-bit integer types and multi-byte character sets.

On the Horizon: CORBA 3.0

Coming up on the horizon is the CORBA 3.0 standard, the next major step in the evolution of CORBA. At the time of this writing, the OMG has not yet announced what capabilities and enhancements will be included in CORBA 3.0, but by taking a look at the current Requests For Proposals (RFPs) and Requests for Information (RFIs), you can make some reasonable guesses about what to expect in the next major iteration of the CORBA specification.

OMG Task Forces

A knowledge of how the OMG operates is also helpful in predicting what CORBA 3.0 might include. The OMG includes two Technology Committees (TCs) that charter various Task Forces to solve particular problems. To this end, the Task Forces issue RFPs and RFIs to find potential solutions from the industry at large.

Currently, the Domain Technology Committee and the Platform Technology Committee have chartered a number of Task Forces that have current outstanding RFPs and RFIs. This section provides a brief overview of these Requests, which will probably drive much of the content of CORBA 3.0 when it is adopted.

Task Forces of the Platform Technology Committee

The work performed by the Platform Technology Committee Task Forces is included in the CORBA specification itself at some point. For example, there are Task Forces to resolve issues of COM/CORBA interworking (recall that COM is Microsoft's Component Object Model), to create IDL mappings for various programming languages, and to propose additional features to CORBA. Currently, the Task Forces of the Platform Technology Committee include the Object Analysis and Design Task Force (OA&D TF) and the ORB/ Object Services Task Force.

Most of the descriptions here are quoted directly from the OMG Web site. Details on the various Task Forces are available at http://www.omg.org/omg00/task.htm; details on the work in progress of the Technology Committees (as well as descriptions of the RFPs and RFIs themselves) are available at http://www.omg.org/library/schedule.htm.

ORB and Object Services Platform Task Force

According to the charter of the ORB and Object Services Platform Task Force, its mission is to solicit, evaluate, and select specifications for recommendations to the Platform Technology Committee for adoption by OMG in the areas of ORB technology (which falls under the CORBA specification) or general purpose Object Services (which fall under CORBAservices). Furthermore, the charter states that such specifications should be fundamental for developing useful CORBA-based applications composed of distributed objects, should provide a universal basis for application interoperability, or support higher level facilities and frameworks.

The current RFIs and RFPs issued by the ORB and Object Services Platform Task Force include the following:

☐ *ORB and Object Services RFI 1* (Internet). An RFI on Internet-related services and interfaces, to help with the integration and inclusion of OMG and CORBA objects on the Internet. The overall goal of this RFI is to collect information from various communities to help guide the OMG's IPSIG and the OMG in the adoption of specifications that will scale the OMG Object Management Architecture to the Internet and further populate or align with Internet standards, protocols, tools, and utilities. This RFI solicits relevant information in several areas: requirements, architectures, designs, projects, products, protocols, and standards.

☐ *ORB and Object Services RFI 2* (Realtime). This Request For Information solicits input regarding the need for and availability of technology for the following: realtime operating environment suitable for supporting realtime Object Request Brokers; realtime Object Request Brokers; object services, common facilities, and extensions for realtime; and general realtime features that would apply to the above in an object technology context.

☐ *Multiple Interfaces and Composition RFP.* Multiple Interfaces RFP deals with the resolution of conflict between multiple IDL interfaces on the same object. The composition facility provides the means for objects to be composed of logically distinct services by the use of multiple interface definitions. The composition facility has been proposed as a base of many system requirements.

☐ *Messaging Service RFP (ORBOS RFP1).* An RFP soliciting proposals of services and ORB enhancements designed to manage asynchronous messages in distributed object systems, including ordering and quality of service of requests.

☐ *Objects-by-Value RFP (ORBOS RFP2).* This RFP seeks proposals for interfaces that provide for the passing of CORBA objects by value (rather than by reference) as parameters in CORBA object operations. Passing objects by value is more efficient and straightforward in many circumstances.

☐ *Java to IDL RFP (ORBOS RFP5).* This RFP solicits proposals that will enhance the CORBA Java language mapping with a Java-to-IDL mapping. A Java-to-IDL mapping will enable developers to build distributed applications directly in Java and communicate via IIOP. By generating IDL from Java code, many languages have access to these Java-written components.

☐ *DCE/CORBA Interworking RFP (ORBOS RFP6).* This RFP solicits proposals for the following: Application Level Interworking, CORBA clients interacting with DCE servers and DCE clients interacting with CORBA servers, provisioning CORBAservices and CORBAfacilities (for example, security, naming, time) with existing DCE components (for example, security services, directory services, distributed time facility).

- *Persistent State Service, Version 2.0 RFP (ORBOS RFP7).* The intent of this RFP is to solicit proposals that provide coherent and pragmatic specification for CORBA persistence. The RFP focuses on a facility to be used by the object implementer that wishes to achieve and maintain persistence. It is important to address whether and, if so, how the PSS interacts with other OMG specifications, such as the POA, the Concurrency Service, the Transaction Service, and the Objects-by-Value Service.

- *CORBA Component Model RFP (ORBOS RFP8).* This RFP solicits proposals for a distributed component model that is based on the OMA and is capable of interoperating with other emerging component technologies, particularly the JavaBeans component model.

- *CORBA Scripting Language RFP (ORBOS RFP9).* This RFP is intended to form part of a coordinated strategy to introduce a component model into the OMA. The RFP solicits proposals for a scripting language that is capable of scripting CORBA components.

- *Minimum CORBA RFP (ORBOS RFP10).* This RFP solicits proposals for the following: A reduced CORBA core specification that implements basic client/server functionality, enabling configurations of subsets of the full OMG IDL definition, and the effect on existing CORBA and Common Object Services resulting from configuring out CORBA capabilities. Minimum CORBA is intended to help build embedded systems.

- *Realtime CORBA 1.0 RFP.* This RFP's intent is to standardize realtime CORBA extensions and promote the use of the OMA in the realtime area. For example, Chorus's COOL is a commercial example of a CORBA ORB with realtime facilities, and this and other non-standard realtime CORBA variants are already being used in applications such as in-flight radar tracking software on board AWACS planes.

- *Data Interchange Facility and Mobile Agent Facility RFP.* The Data Interchange Facility is a facility supporting interoperability between objects. The key elements of the service include the data interchange interfaces, the data object type, the life cycle of data objects, and the data translation interfaces. The use of metadata is another important area. To implement mobile agents, three key features need to be supported by ORB: launching and loading of agents on what is traditionally thought of as the client side of the ORB, time asynchrony, and notifying senders and receivers of arrival of packets intended for them. The mobile agent facility proposes these changes.

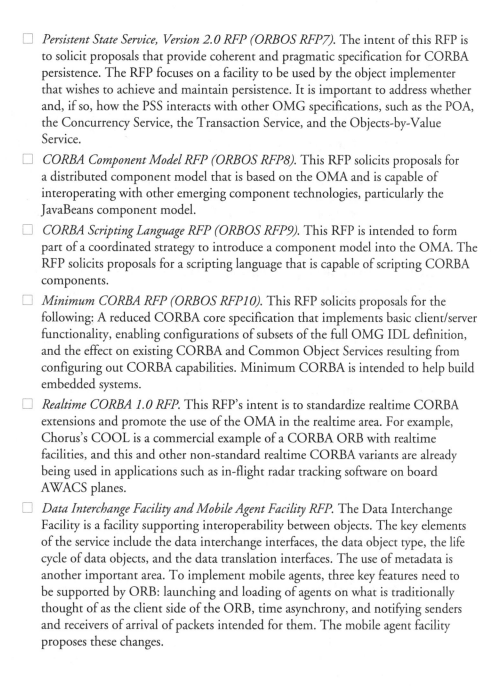

- *Input Method Manager Facility RFP.* This RFP solicits proposals for specifications for the common features of the Input Method Manager Facility that enables management of input methods for (but not limited to) multi-octet Asian characters on CORBA platforms.

- *Firewall RFP.* This RFP solicits proposals for the following: Specification of the use of IIOP in network firewalls, for the purpose of controlling limited use from the Internet or intranet of an organization's CORBA-based applications, and optionally, similar specifications with respect to any other inter-ORB protocols.

- *Printing Facility RFP.* An RFP soliciting proposals for printing facility objects. This facility handles management (scheduling, spooling, locating) of print servers and routing of print jobs. The printing facility should be able to meet a range of printing requirements from simple documents up to high volume production printing.

Analysis and Design Platform Task Force

The Object Analysis and Design Task Force's charter states that its mission is to enable developers to better understand how to develop applications using OT, thereby increasing the market; to recommend technology for adoption to enable interoperability across the life cycle of, and to enable reuse of, designs/work products developed using OA&D tools; to recommend technology for adoption of common semantics, metamodels, and abstract syntax for OA&D methodologies; to leverage existing OMG specifications; to facilitate advances in the state of the art of OA&D methodologies; and to recommend liaison with other appropriate organizations. Certainly this is a hefty responsibility to be taken on by the OMG's newest Task Force. Already this Task Force has generated two Requests for Proposals, involving a framework for analysis and design tools and a meta-object facility that would enable further interoperability between CORBA tools and applications.

The current RFPs generated by the Analysis and Design Platform Task Force include the following:

- *Analysis and Design Task Force RFP1.* This Request for Proposals focuses on creating a framework for analysis and design-tool semantic interoperability, through an Analysis and Design Facility. This facility will contain the interfaces and semantics needed to support the creation and manipulation of OA&D models that define the behavior of object applications with the Object Management Architecture. This includes a set of notations that can be used to describe these models in a consistent fashion.

  - This RFP has already been successfully completed with the adoption of OMB UML 1.0, proposed by Rational, IBM, Objectime, and other submitters. The formal spec should be published in early 1998.

Task Forces of the Domain Technology Committee

The work of the Domain Technology Committee comes to fruition in the form of CORBAfacilities, particularly in the vertical facilities such as health care, manufacturing, and telecommunications.

Currently, the Domain Technology Committee has chartered the following Task Forces:

☐ Business Object Task Force

☐ Electronic Commerce Domain Task Force

☐ Financial Domain Task Force (CORBAfinancials)

☐ Manufacturing Domain Task Force (CORBAmanufacturing)

☐ CORBAmed Task Force (Healthcare)

☐ Telecommunications Task Force (CORBAtel)

☐ Transportation Domain Task Force (CORBAtransport)

(Note that many of the Task Forces composing the Domain Technology Committee are organized around vertical domains.)

Business Object Domain Task Force

Again referring to the OMG Web site, the mission of the Business Object Task Force is to define the domain of OMG Business Objects. It will work to facilitate and promote the use of OMG-distributed object technology for business systems; commonality among vertical domain task force standards; simplicity in building, using, and deploying business objects for application developers; interoperability between independently developed business objects; the adoption and use of common business object and application component standards; and issuance of requests and evaluation of responses and proposals for adoption by the OMG specifications for objects, frameworks, services, and architectures applicable to a wide range of businesses.

Certainly the role of the Business Object Domain Task Force is an important one. Because the purpose of most distributed enterprise-level applications is to facilitate the communication between business objects, the goals of the Business Object Domain Task Force have much in common with the goals of the distributed application developer: to enable the development and deployment of robust, interoperable business objects.

The current RFPs and RFIs issued by the Business Object Domain Task Force include the following:

☐ *Common Business Object and Business Object Facility RFP.* This RFP solicits proposals for Common Business Objects, those objects representing business semantics that can be shown to be common across most businesses, and a Business Object Facility that provides the infrastructure required to support business objects operating as cooperative application components in a distributed object environment.

☐ *Workflow Management Facility RFP.* The Workflow Management Facility defines interfaces and their semantics required to manipulate and execute interoperable workflow objects and their metadata. The Workflow Management Facility will serve as a high-level integrating platform for building flexible workflow management applications incorporating objects and existing applications. This RFP solicits proposals for the Workflow Management Facility.

☐ *Common Business Objects RFI (CBO RFI).* The Common Business Object Working Group is attempting to define a reference architecture that provides a concise and effective framework within which the dependencies between individual domains can be understood and reconciled. The Working Group invites input from individuals and organizations with insights or information that could provide a basis for work in this area.

Manufacturing Domain Task Force

The Manufacturing Domain Task Force, the successor to the Manufacturing Special Interest Group, has a mission to foster the emergence of cost-effective, timely, commercially available, and interoperable manufacturing domain software components through CORBA technology; to recommend technology for adoption that enables the interoperability and modularity of CORBA-based manufacturing domain software components; to encourage the development and use of CORBA-based manufacturing domain software components, thereby increasing the object technology market; to leverage existing OMG specifications; and to recommend liaison with other appropriate organizations in support of the preceding goals.

Current RFPs and RFIs generated by the Manufacturing Domain Task Force include the following:

☐ *Manufacturing High-Level Requirements RFI (MFG RFI1).* This Request for Information seeks input on clarifying and revising the Manufacturing Object Model as well as identifying a high-level partitioning of that model and improving the list of infrastructure requirements. This partitioning will be used as the basis for a road map and future RFPs from the Task Force.

☐ *Manufacturing DTF RFI-2.* This RFI solicits input from ERP users and vendors on recommendations for the number of RFPs and subject areas to be covered by RFPs, and on ERP systems to be issued by the Manufacturing DTF. ERP includes systems referred to as Materials Requirements Planning (MRP) and Manufacturing Resource Planning (MRP-II). ERP's major relationship is to the Production Planning business process.

☐ *Product Data Management Enablers RFP (MFG RFP1).* This RFP looks to establish standard interfaces for the services provided by Product Data Management (PDM) systems. These interfaces, made available through ORBs, will provide the standard needed to support a distributed product data-management environment, as well as provide standard interfaces to differing PDM systems.

Electronic Commerce Domain Task Force

Electronic commerce is a hot area of computing right now. Fueled particularly by the explosion of the World Wide Web phenomenon, many companies are looking for ways to sell their products through electronic channels and, just as important, to protect their copyrighted works and other intellectual property. The Electronic Commerce Domain Task Force was chartered to address the issues associated with electronic commerce.

The goals of the Electronic Commerce Domain Task Force are to garner Domain Technology support and involvement in OMG; to continue reliance on domain experts and issue RFPs; to seek broad industry and domain response to RFPs (where applicable); and to work toward outlining the scope of work for the Domain Task Force, including more specifically defining content management and rights and royalties, electronic payment, and online retail (electronic commerce).

The Electronic Commerce Domain Task Force has currently issued the following RFPs and RFIs:

☐ *Electronic Payment Facility (EC RFP1).* This RFP solicits Proposals for Object Framework that support the implementation of industry-standardized electronic payment protocols in an OMA-compliant system and specifications for one or more industries' payment protocols using the Object Framework.

☐ *Negotiation Facility RFP (EC RFP2).* This RFP solicits proposals for: a business process or processes, expressed in IDL and enabling multi-participant negotiation; and an object framework supporting dynamic negotiation rule substitution, rule verification, and interfaces through which domain policy can be used to control the disclosure of information and control the decisions taken during the course of negotiation.

☐ *Electronic Healthcare Claims Facility RFP (EC RFP3).* This RFP solicits proposals for the interface of a healthcare claims facility to administer and manage standardized electronic claims exchanges using established healthcare data formats.

☐ *Asset and Content Management RFI (EC RFI1).* The technical scope of this RFI is the collection of technologies and necessary interfaces to the asset and content-management areas, such as creation and capture of digital asset and content search and access of digital asset and content, as well as distribution of digital asset and content. Responses should identify relevant standards associated with this RFI. These include de facto industry standards as well as de jour standards developed by recognized standards organizations.

☐ *Enabling Technologies and Services for EC (EC RFI2).* This RFI specifically addresses the technology necessary to facilitate interactions between consumers, providers, and interested third parties over a communication network.

Telecommunications Domain Task Force

The mission of the Telecommunications Domain Task Force is to issue RFIs and RFPs for CORBA-based technology relevant to the telecommunications industry; to evaluate RFI and RFP responses and RFCs for recommended adoption by the Domain Technology Committee; to communicate requirements from the telecommunications industry to the Architecture Board, the Platform Technology Committee, and other OMG subgroups, as appropriate; to assist and advise the Liaison Subcommittee regarding its relationship with telecommunications-related standards organizations and consortia; and to promote the use of OMG technologies as solutions to the needs of the telecommunications industry.

Currently, the Telecommunications Domain Task Force has generated the following RFPs and RFIs:

☐ *Topology RFP (Telecom RFP2).* The purpose of this RFP is to solicit proposals for a Topology Service that will manage relationship information that enables systems and application integration.

☐ *Notification Service RFP (Telecom RFP3).* This RFP solicits proposals for a service that extends the capabilities of the OMG Event Service to support filtering capability; a service that satisfies scalability demands of event-driven applications running within large, distributed, heterogeneous networks; a service that satisfies event management demands of distributed systems, network, and telecommunications management applications; and a specification of notification types and contents applicable to particular vertical domains.

☐ *CORBA/TMN Interworking RFP.* The objective of this RFP is to define a set of Interworking mappings and CORBA Telecom Domain Interfaces which enable the development of CORBA-based TMN systems that can interwork with non-CORBA-based TMN systems that export interfaces based on standard management object models such as OSI Management or Internet Management, and standard management protocols such as CMIP or SNMP; and the development of CORBA-based TMN systems in compliance with the OSI Management Reference Model or Internet Management Model, without using CMIP or SNMP.

☐ *Issues for Intelligent Networking with CORBA (Telecom RFI).* This RFI seeks information on five issues: what issues exist for providing interoperability between existing systems using the SS7 protocol suite, what issues exist for using the SS7 protocol suite as an environment-specific Inter-ORB Protocol for communications between CORBA-based implementations, what additional requirements are needed for enhancements to the existing set of CORBA specifications, what current or prospective standardization activities exist in these areas, and which CORBA objects are needed for IN-CORBA systems that encapsulate the functionality for the various IN Functional Entities.

Financial Domain Task Force

The mission of the Financial Domain Task Force, or CORBAfinancials, is to promote the use of financial services and accounting software that incorporate OMG standards; to provide an internationally recognized forum for industry focus on financial services and accounting facilities; to identify relevant standards, business architectures, research, and technologies in this area of computing; to coordinate end-user requirements in the financial services domain through a liaison with the End-User SIG; to facilitate advances in the state of the art of OA&D methodologies; to coordinate potential future specification activities with the Common Facilities Task Force, to involve all interested members of the OMG in the OMG Financial Domain Task Force; to create a CORBAfinancials architecture and road map for the financial services industry worldwide; to issue RFIs, RFPs, and RFCs for CORBA-based technology relevant to the financial services industry; to evaluate RFI and RFP responses and recommend technology adoption by the OMG's Domain Technical Committee; and to assist and advise the Liaison Subcommittee regarding its relationship with related standards organizations and consortia. (That's quite a mouthful!)

CORBAfinancials has currently generated the following RFPs and RFIs:

☐ *Currency RFP (Finance RFP1)*. The objective of this RFP is to solicit interfaces that support the definition and management of currencies. This is distinct from money that is an amount of one or more currencies. This RFP solicits proposals for currency representation, currency validation, and money algebra.

☐ *Finance/Insurance Party Management Facility RFP (Finance RFP2)*. This RFP solicits proposals for specifications for the common features of a Party Management Facility for the Financial Service Industry. These facilities are part of systems that are commonly known as Client or Customer Information Systems.

☐ *Financial DTF Insurance RFI*. Goals of this RFI are to improve the quality of customer service and reduce costs by utilizing CORBA technologies for interoperability throughout the global insurance community, and to standardize interfaces for insurance objects.

CORBAmed Domain Task Force

The CORBAmed Task Force is chartered with the following mission: to improve the quality of care and reduce costs by the use of CORBA technologies for interoperability throughout the global healthcare community; to utilize the OMG technology adoption process to standardize interfaces for healthcare objects; to communicate the requirements of the health-care industry to the Platform Technical Committee; and to assist and advise the Liaison

Subcommittee regarding the relationship with healthcare standards organizations and consortia. CORBAmed also has the following goals: to educate both the system developers and the user community in the health care industry; to issue RFIs and RFPs related to the health care industry based on CORBA technologies; and to evaluate RFI and RFP responses and RFCs for recommended adoption by the Domain Technical Committee.

Currently, CORBAmed has issued the following RFPs and RFIs:

- [ ] *Patient Identification Services RFP (CORBAmed RFP1)*. This RFP solicits proposals for specifications for the common features of a patient identification system that enables multiples of these patient identification systems to interoperate.

- [ ] *Healthcare Lexicon Service RFP (CORBAmed RFP2)*. This RFP solicits proposals for specifications of IDL interfaces for the common features of a set of lexicon query services. This RFP describes the requirement for services to support lexicons in a distributed object system conforming to OMA.

- [ ] *Clinical Observations RFI (CORBAmed RFI2)*. This RFI solicits information about requirements that will provide guidance to the CORBAmed DTF of the OMG in developing specifications for healthcare information systems dealing with patient observation data. The overall goal will be to adopt vendor-neutral common interfaces for interoperability between systems, applications, and instruments that detect, transmit, store, and display medical information dealing with observations of a particular patient's medical condition.

- [ ] *Clinical Decision Support RFI (CORBAmed RFI3)*. This RFI solicits information about requirements that will provide guidance to the CORBAmed DTF of the OMG in developing specifications for Clinical Decision Support Systems (DSS). The overall goal will be to adopt vendor-neutral common interfaces that improve the quality of care and reduce costs by utilizing CORBA technologies for interoperability between systems, applications, and instruments that detect, transmit, store, and display medical information used in Clinical DSS.

- [ ] *Lifescience RFI*. This RFI seeks information to help the Life Sciences Research Domain Special Interest Group (LSR-DSIG) make useful and efficient decisions in the life sciences research technology adoption process. As the first steps in this process, LSR-DSIG will develop an architecture description, a schedule for issuing additional RFIs and RFPs (a technology road map), and one or more RFPs soliciting OMG IDL interfaces and corresponding semantic descriptions. Therefore, this RFI requests information on architectures, interoperability, object and data models, interfaces, existing systems, standards, legal issues, and their priorities.

☐ *HL7 RFI.* This Request for Information (RFI) solicits information about requirements that will provide guidance to the CORBAmed Domain Task Force (DTF)
of the Object Management Group (OMG) in the area of CORBA-based HL7
implementation approaches. The overall goal of CORBAmed is to adopt vendor-
neutral common interfaces that may improve the quality of care and reduce costs.
CORBAmed DTF will utilize the OMG's open technology adoption process to
standardize interfaces in the healthcare arena.

Transportation Domain Task Force

It is the mission of the Transportation Domain Task Force to promote the development and
use of transportation-related systems that incorporate OMG specifications and technologies;
to identify relevant standards, business objects, components, and technologies in the field of
transportation, and to disseminate this information to the OMG; to work within the OMG
committees and task forces to ensure that the CORBA, CORBAservices, CORBAfacilities,
Business Object, and domain specifications are conducive to the needs of the transportation
industry; to recruit additional Transportation DSIG membership from corporations in the
transportation systems development community; and to establish a global forum for the free
exchange of distributed object systems development ideas amongst the various members of
the transportation community and its partners.

The Transportation Domain Task Force, one of the newest Task Forces in the OMG, has
issued the following RFI:

☐ *CORBAtransport RFI.* This RFI solicits information about requirements, projects,
and products that will provide guidance for transportation-related object system
interoperability. The overall goal will be to adopt vendor-neutral common interfaces. Responses to this RFI will be used to define one or more RFPs that will
solicit OMG IDL interfaces and other corresponding materials, such as semantic
descriptions, sequencing, and timing constraints. CORBAtransport intends to
produce specification sets in at least four major vertical domains (air, marine,
highway, and rail) and a common horizontal specification across the breadth of
the transportation domain.

What It All Means

Certainly the OMG is hard at work enhancing current specifications and creating new ones.
But what does it all mean? In particular, who stands to benefit from the products of the
various Technology Committees and Task Forces?

☐ *Everyone.* That is, all developers of CORBA applications will benefit from many of the enhancements being made to CORBA. The Platform Technology Committee Task Forces—namely, the ORB and Object Services Platform Task Force and the Analysis and Design Platform Task Force—are working on specifications that will benefit virtually all CORBA developers. Features such as a CORBA component model, the capability to pass objects by value as well as by reference, persistent CORBA objects, a scripting language for CORBA objects, and printing capability are useful to a wide variety of developers.

☐ *Developers using other technologies.* Developers using Microsoft's COM object model will benefit from enhanced interoperability between COM and CORBA objects; those using the DCE-distributed computing model will realize similar benefits. And, of course, Java will enjoy improved interoperability with CORBA, particularly with the capability to convert Java interfaces to IDL interfaces.

☐ *Users of electronic commerce.* As mentioned previously, electronic commerce has the potential to become a killer app for the Internet, and CORBA will be there. Thus, anyone wishing to take advantage of electronic commerce capability stands to benefit from the work being done by the Electronic Commerce Domain Task Force in this area.

☐ *Developers of vertical applications.* A great deal of work is being done to support a variety of vertical industry applications. The standards being developed for these markets will promote interoperability between such applications.

Again, as of the time of this writing, the OMG had not yet specified the contents, or even an availability date, of CORBA 3.0. Therefore, which of the specifications described here will be included in the next major CORBA release is anybody's guess. When these specifications do become available, however, all CORBA developers will be the winners.

Looking Beyond

The current Requests for Proposals and Requests for Information issued by the various Task Forces within the OMG give a good indication of where CORBA is heading in the near future. But what about beyond that? How will CORBA affect the development of distributed applications in the not-so-near future? And what challenges will it face? Although it is difficult to predict anything in the area of software development technology, this section addresses some of these questions.

CORBA Development in the Future

Despite its current shortcomings, CORBA is nonetheless a very powerful development tool already. It still can stand to see some improvement, however, particularly in one area: So far, nobody has ever accused CORBA of being too easy to develop with.

Face it, CORBA's awesome power, plus its unmatched cross-platform and cross-language capabilities, come at a price. Developing for CORBA means learning to develop for yet another platform, as it were. The benefits that come with learning and applying this skill are immense, but in this age of rapid application development, emphasis is often placed on the speed of deployment of an application rather than on the power and robustness of a design. If CORBA is to continue to enjoy success as a development platform, it must learn to play in this world of instant software development.

Does this mean sacrificing CORBA's power, cross-platform capability, or robustness for ease of use? Of course not, although development tools could go a long way towards making CORBA application development easier on the developer. Already, such tools are starting to appear, and initiatives such as the ORB and Object Services Platform Task Force's Java to IDL RFP suggest that additional strides will be made towards making CORBA more seamless with application development.

The *seamless* concept will eventually be the key to CORBA's success. Although the use of some CORBA services, facilities, and the like will always require some developer knowledge, the developer should be insulated as much as possible from the plumbing of a CORBA application. Details of memory management, reference counting, and perhaps of IDL itself, should be handled by the development tools themselves, invisible to most developers. (Granted, a developer should still be able to drill down to this level of detail when desired, and a good development tool will always enable this level of interaction.) Freed from having to worry about the details of implementation, the developer can concentrate more on the design of the application itself.

In short, CORBA is already at the point where some very impressive things can be done with it. Additional features will push the usefulness of CORBA even farther, but to ensure CORBA's success, development tool vendors must provide tools that make CORBA application development easier than ever. (In the meantime, publishers are happy to bring to you such books as *Teach Yourself CORBA in 14 Days*!)

Challenges Facing CORBA

Despite the power and capability of the CORBA architecture and the Object Management Architecture surrounding it, CORBA still faces a number of challenges to its success. These challenges come in the form of competing technologies, or in the very process by which CORBA and related specifications are adopted. This section will briefly describe some of the challenges facing CORBA today.

Microsoft DCOM

Not surprisingly, CORBA is not without its competition. Although CORBA has the backing of almost the entire industry, including some very big players, its universal acceptance faces at least one major obstacle. This challenge comes in the form of another distributed object model from a vendor that enjoys an extremely dominant position in the industry. The vendor, of course, is none other than Microsoft, which is heavily pushing its Distributed Component Object Model (DCOM) as a de facto standard for a distributed computing platform.

Microsoft is quite clear regarding its position on CORBA, the open standard backed by just about every other player in the industry. Perhaps this position is best summed up in the words of COM Product Manager Cornelius Willis, as reported by *InfoWorld Electric* on August 18, 1997: "Of course, we want COM3—now known as COM+—to make CORBA irrelevant." (The original article is available at *InfoWorld Electric*'s Web site at http://www.infoworld.com/cgi-bin/displayArchives.pl?970818.wsoft.htm.) Apparently, Microsoft prefers to extend its already expansive industry domination to include distributed computing standards as well, rather than support a widely accepted industry standard. To its credit, Microsoft has turned over parts of its COM, DCOM, and ActiveX technologies to The Open Group, an independent standards organization, and is partnering with Software AG to provide DCOM implementations on operating systems other than Windows. (More details are available at http://www.activex.org/ and http://www.softwareag.com/corporat/dcom/default.htm.)

Of course, Microsoft is welcome to compete in this space. If anything, competition will help to keep the OMG and CORBA product vendors on their toes, providing the best possible specifications, implementations, and interoperability they can. However, given the near ubiquity of Microsoft's operating systems—and, by extension, DCOM—backers of CORBA will be fighting an uphill battle against Microsoft's leveraging of one of its platforms to create another. However, there is hope—CORBA currently enjoys some advantages over DCOM, as outlined in an article available at the OMG Web site at http://www.omg.org/news/activex.htm. Another OMG article, a response to a report published by the UK-based analyst group Ovum, also provides some relevant information comparing CORBA and DCOM; the article is available at http://www.omg.org/news/pr97/ovumpr.htm.

Other Challenges

Of course, there are other challenges facing CORBA as well. Consider, for example, the issues involved with managing an organization with more than 750 members. Granted, not all the OMG members vote on proposals, but the associated overhead is not insignificant. One of the OMG's greatest strengths—its strong backing by the industry—might also be one of its greatest weaknesses because the resulting bureaucracy can slow the development and acceptance of new specifications. The OMG has done exceptionally well so far, especially considering its size. With competition from Microsoft's DCOM, the OMG will need to take great care to ensure that the organization doesn't collapse under its own weight, possibly taking CORBA with it.

Summary

CORBA has already come a long way. With a membership of more than 750 and still growing, the OMG has definitely achieved a position of great relevance in the marketplace. CORBA as a standard has been growing and maturing for more than seven years now—an eternity in computer time. CORBA products are available on a wide variety of platforms and operating systems from dozens of vendors. (Among the platforms supported by CORBA are AS400, HP-UX, MacOS, MS-DOS, MVS, OpenVMS, OS/2, SunOS and Solaris, Windows 3.x, Windows 95, Windows NT, and many flavors of UNIX not already mentioned.) Clearly, CORBA has grown from its humble beginnings into an established, mature platform for distributed application development.

CORBA isn't done growing; new capabilities and enhancements are being added all the time. Today you've seen some of the enhancements currently proposed, from horizontal features such as a CORBA object model, support for various languages, and support for passing objects by value, to specifications for vertical facilities such as the healthcare, telecommunications, and manufacturing industries. The OMG has big plans for CORBA, and with the backing of a plethora of vendors producing CORBA products, these plans are being realized. CORBA has already become a powerful, robust platform for the development of distributed enterprise applications and is well on its way to becoming far more useful than it already is. In the future, not only will CORBA become even more powerful and robust, but it will also become more seamlessly integrated with application development. The future certainly has some exciting things in store for CORBA and its developers.

C

INDEX

M